The Gun Digest Book Of COMBAT HANDGUNNERY

ALL NEW 4TH EDITION

By Chuck Taylor

DBI BOOKS
a division of Krause Publications, Inc.

STAFF

SENIOR STAFF EDITORS
Harold A. Murtz
Ray Ordorica

PRODUCTION MANAGER
John L. Duoba

ELECTRONIC PUBLISHING DIRECTOR
Sheldon L. Factor

ELECTRONIC PUBLISHING MANAGER
Nancy J. Mellem

ELECTRONIC PUBLISHING ASSOCIATE
Laura M. Mielzynski

GRAPHIC DESIGN
John Duoba

COVER PHOTOGRAPHY
John Hanusin

MANAGING EDITOR
Pamela J. Johnson

PUBLISHER
Charles T. Hartigan

ISBN 0-87349-186-6   Library of Congress Catalog #83-072347

TABLE OF CONTENTS

TABLE OF CONTENTS

INTRODUCTION

DURING THE LAST thirty years, the art and science of combat handgunning has grown by leaps and bounds. Spurred by continuous technical advancements and deteriorating social/political/cultural conditions, it has now reached unprecedented levels of popularity and acceptance. In a way, that's a sad commentary on the evolution of society.

Thirty years ago, the police officer was still an object of respect and admiration, homeowners could leave their houses unlocked when they made a quick trip to the store, and people could walk the streets after dark without worry.

Sadly, those days are gone and more and more citizens feel that the ultimate responsibility for self-protection rests not with society but with the individual. There simply aren't enough policemen to do it. If there were...well, do you really want to live in a police state?

The individual's right of self-protection dates back to the Magna Carta, Blackstone's Commentaries and before that. In fact, it goes all the way back to that interesting and illuminating document, the Bible. The Good Book is chock full of violence, yet nowhere in its pages does it condemn violence per se, only some of the reasons for it.

I think one of the primary reasons many people have reservations about using deadly force in their own defense is due to a misinterpretation during translation of the Commandment, "Thou Shalt Not Kill." In original texts, it actually said, "Thou Shalt Not Murder," which makes much more sense, especially considering the rest of the Bible's content. Though I read that book from cover to cover, nowhere could I find a condemnation of justifiable homicide. Quite the opposite.

The handgun is intended as a reactive, defensive arm, used by its wearer to regain control of his immediate environment. This means that the techniques and tactics inherent to its utilization must reflect cognizance and a complete understanding of this critical fact. Sadly, such is not always the case.

Many of the techniques thought to be state of the art

Chuck Taylor, through his American Small Arms Academy, teaches self-defense principles and fundamentals that are time-tested and proven.

today were developed by instructors who lack real-world experience or whose expertise is derived from a competitive background. Under the controlled conditions of the firing range, these competition-oriented techniques often appear to be simpler or faster. However, under the strain of actual combat they fail, often with deadly consequences. You will find no such material here.

Instead, you will find a no-holds-barred, truthful and all-encompassing look at what combat handgunning is really about, with no games being played, commercial interests being promoted or egos being flexed. When you finish reading this book, you'll have a clear, realistic perspective on the subject and will be able to make intelligent decisions, without myths, legends, prejudices or distortions to get in your way and maybe even get you killed.

Every day I receive telephone calls and letters from students whose lives have been saved by the techniques and tactics presented in these pages. The communications number in the hundreds over the last twenty years and are proof that, though I make no claim to having all the answers, I at least have a clear understanding of the questions that make up this diverse and sometimes confusing subject.

If I at times appear a little feisty or in vehement disagreement with some of my colleagues, so be it. I've seen too many people die because they followed the wrong advice and, as a result, made poor decisions. As one of the few full-time professionals in this business, I have a responsibility to tell it like it is, straight-out and without hesitation. Because of this approach, I can look at myself in the mirror each morning and know that I haven't got someone killed because they put their trust in me and my techniques. If I err, it is on the side of caution, of prudence, of reason.

Moreover, as one of the few writers who has repeatedly "been there and seen the elephant," I feel that the breathless commentaries we read month after month on "The Magic Bullet Of The Month" or "The Ultimate Combat Handgun" are dangerous, irresponsible and unprofessional. Life and death are too serious to be left to amateurs.

The techniques and tactics you'll see in this book were devised with the idea that human beings are going to use them in deadly earnest and under the greatest stress, and those folks might well die if they fail. Factored into their development and analysis are the elements of time, motion, geometry and the laws of physics, plus how people react and behave under stress.

The result is a combat handgunning system that, coupled with the intelligent use of tactical principles, provides the most effective yet easily learned self-defense package in existence.

These techniques have already been responsible for saving the lives of hundreds of civilians, soldiers and law enforcement personnel. They work because they were carefully conceived and tested using shooters of all skill levels, and then the results were painstakingly analyzed. Where improvements were needed, they were made. Where a technique proved to be faulty, it was replaced with one that worked. Only then were they taken "into the street." What's in these pages works—on the street, in the battlefield or in your living room at 3 a.m.

Although the information in this book has already saved many lives, it is my hope that you'll never find yourself in a situation that requires the use of deadly force with any kind of weapon. Physically, emotionally and financially, the consequences are far-reaching and often severe. Still, if such a confrontation is unavoidable, you—like the old gunfighters—must decide that "being judged by twelve beats being carried by six" and take action...or accept an ignominious death.

If we handle ourselves ethically and properly, and thus win the fight, we at least have the consolation of knowing that we had no other choice, that the actions of our attacker(s), not ours, escalated the situation to deadly force levels. The discomforts and stresses that follow, while unpleasant, are temporary. Death is not.

THE ROLE OF THE HANDGUN

ONE OF THE most difficult and confusing issues confronting anyone interested in combat handgunning is that of weapon selection, i.e., which kind of handgun is "best." Indeed, at times it seems like we're hit from all sides with opinions, theories and recommendations, many of which contradict each other to the point of obfuscating the issue entirely. For over twenty years, I've watched it happen in gunshops, on firing ranges and even at cocktail parties—someone suggests a particular kind of gun, while another vehemently discredits the suggestion, offering instead an often contradictory recommendation of their own.

Some claim the handgun is obsolete and that other weapons such as the shotgun or submachine gun outperform it by a considerable margin at all close-combat (0-100 meters) ranges. Here we have a situation where the technical capability of the weapon is given precedence over tactical, legal and social considerations. I've always felt that apples and oranges really don't compare. Nonetheless, usually due to personal prejudice or ignorance, for some, the urge remains strong to claim that one type of weapon system is superior to another, meaning that the less-effective weapon is therefore useless.

This is potentially dangerous thinking because it excludes important criteria from the issue. Let's be realistic here—it does little good to concern ourselves with shotguns or submachine guns when our tactical needs or socio-political and legal prohibitions dictate otherwise. For example, if we need a light, portable, concealable self-defense weapon, a pistol is

obviously a better choice, even if it isn't as potent or tactically flexible as the submachine gun or shotgun. And, regardless of its real or presumed efficiency, a submachine gun or sawed-off shotgun isn't a viable option if it's considered illegal in the jurisdiction in which we live.

In an effort to actually determine how the three weapon systems (pistol, shotgun and submachine gun) technically compare, I conducted a year-long scientific study and evaluation program to analyze the performance of all three systems in the eight most typical tactical situations encountered in what's called CQB—close-quarters battle. My intent wasn't to prove that one system was better than another, but to disclose the strengths and weaknesses of each system in proportion to one another. My reasoning for conducting the tests was two-fold: 1) In order to fully understand each weapon system and effectively determine how to best employ it, we simply must know its true—not theoretical—capabilities and weaknesses. 2) An all-inclusive, *scientific* study like this has never before been conducted. Thus, the myriad opinions constantly espoused as to which weapons perform best have been based upon pure theory, ignorance and even personal bias, rather than on *fact*. I was interested in discovering facts to dispel such myths, unfounded theo-ries and misconceptions, thus providing life-saving data for training and educational purposes, not to pursue the propagation of a pet theory or personal bias.

The format, administrative data and results of the study accompanying this text bear serious scrutiny. If you examine them carefully, you will see that the weapon *operator*, rather than a type of weapon system or specific kind of weapon within a given system, is the determining factor. However, as you peruse the performance charts, be careful, because a superficial or more focused analysis shows the pistol to be inferior to both the submachine gun and shotgun. Don't become trapped in the technical results and overlook the trends the statistics disclose or forget the other considerations we've discussed previously. For instance, will we be able to carry a shotgun, as on a bonafide law enforcement mission?

At one time or another, most novice combat handgunners find themselves confused about this and wish for some weapon other than a handgun. Sometimes the subject of combat handgunning seems as complicated and mysterious as voodoo or alchemy, but in reality such is not the case. In truth, once the myths, legends and other superficial or non-applicable material are stripped away, it's really quite sim-

During Taylor's extensive ASAA comparison study of pistol, shotgun and submachine gun weapon systems and individual designs within each system, the most popular types were utilized. Here Taylor ("Shooter A"), holding a Smith & Wesson M39 9mm, briefs the other four participants on the handgun portion of the test format.

ple. The novice's real problem is how to go about doing this. Here, I offer a suggestion of my own: Ignore everything you've read or heard about self-defensive handgunning until you've first defined a few things on your own.

The first question you should ask yourself concerns an issue more important than what kind of handgun is "best," and that is *mission definition*. Putting it in another way, what do you want from the weapon? What is the purpose for which you need it? This *must* be defined before consideration of other issues is appropriate. Why? Stop for a moment and think about it—everyone's lifestyle is different, meaning that their needs, therefore, are different. So, before you can intelligently pursue the matter of weapon selection, you must first answer these questions:

Will you carry the weapon daily, keep it in your automobile or store it in your home? If you intend to carry it, how will you do so? Will it be in the open or will it be concealed? Either way, *where*? In your waistband? In a holster, purse or fanny pack? If you need it for vehicular and/or home defense, where will it be placed? Will you be the only operator, or will other personnel also be involved? And what about the other potential users of the weapon? Are they trained in its safe, efficient use? In fact, are *you*? If not, do you intend to seek formal training?

See what I mean? All of these things significantly influence your choices, so you'd better consider them carefully before you rush off to the gun shop with cash in hand.

In short, define the questions before you look for answers. Otherwise, you'll quickly find yourself immersed in a sea of confusion, controversy and disappointment. And let's not forget that we're talking about *lives* here—yours and those of your loved ones. Inefficiency in this environment translates to increased personal risk, the very thing you seek to reduce by purchasing a gun in the first place. This being the case, careful analysis of mission definition and its subtopics is time well spent.

In the chapters that follow, we'll give you everything you need to know in order to make good decisions in not only weapon selection, but in literally every other facet of combat handgunning as well. As a professional weapons and tactics instructor and writer of more than twenty years' experience, and with a reputation for "telling it like it is," my job is to save lives. In order to do this, I must accomplish two things: 1) shatter the myriad myths, prejudices, unfounded theories and inaccuracies that permeate the field of combat handgunning; 2) give the reader/student a clear, reasonable perspective on this multi-faceted and, at times, abstract subject, so he can make intelligent choices that may quite literally make the difference between not only his own life and death, but those of his loved ones as well.

Incidentally, what *is* the mission of the defensive handgun? *The purpose of the combat handgun is to provide its user with the means to control or regain control of his immediate environment, as quickly and with as few shots fired as possible*. To maintain a clear perspective on the subject and truly understand the content of the chapters that follow, it is essential that you keep this fact in mind.

My entire view of the subject is—and should be—predicated upon this fundamental premise. Yet, unfortunately, we seldom hear it spoken or see it in print. Nonetheless, this is the nucleus of combat handgunning and the central axis around which all of its integral characteristics revolve; as such, we cannot afford to ignore it. For if we do, we face the very real risk of inadvertently predetermining our own destruction.

Having defined our needs, what kind of handgun is "best?" In fact, is there a "best" handgun? Quite frankly, I don't think there is such a thing. Since everyone's needs are different, simple logic dictates that what may work magnificently for one person might very well be completely unsatisfactory for another. Still, having said this, there is an old gunfighter's axiom that universally applies: "Use the most powerful gun that you can conceal, yet shoot quickly and accurately."

This quaint bit of advice from the survivors of a bygone era says much in only a few words and bears serious consideration. For some, it means a larger, more powerful caliber and/or a bigger, heavier gun. Perhaps due to lesser physical capability or the need for concealment, a smaller, lighter gun is a necessity for others. As we will see later on, handgun power is an abstract, complex and often controversial issue. However, a careful examination of our needs provides the criteria by which to decide what's best for each of us.

Must our defensive handgun be new or can it be an older model? There have been literally thousands of gun designs produced over the last hundred years. Some are better than others, and these have survived the decades that have passed since they first appeared. Many feel that the quality and workmanship of older guns is superior to those produced more recently. Conversely, some claim that because of their age, they may be worn to the point of being less than reliable and should therefore be avoided. In reality, the truth is somewhere in between.

It's my opinion that as long as the weapon is of an efficient, serviceable design, and parts are obtainable, there is no reason to exclude it from consideration because of its age. However, a thorough checkup of such guns by a competent gunsmith should be completed before it is carried into the field. The rule of thumb should thus be that the gun was "used, but not abused."

In the early chapters, we'll take a look at the various types of handguns, the single-action and double-action revolver and self-loader, the "semi-double action" (Glock), snubbies, and the so-called pocket pistol. We'll also examine the strengths and weaknesses of each and how they compare to one another. Read these chapters carefully, for they contain information critical to your first decision as a combat handgunner—selecting which type of handgun is best for you.

EVALUATING HANDGUN EFFECTIVENESS

CHUCK TAYLOR AND four other shooters gathered representative handguns, shotguns and submachine guns, and shot them in controlled tests against the clock in the eight most-common close-quarters-battle (100 meters and under) shooting scenarios. This was the first-ever scientific test of how these weapon systems compare against each other in this type of shooting. All weapons were used as correctly as possible. The submachine gun, for example, was never fired fully auto at ranges over 15 meters; the shotgun used #1 buckshot at 25 meters and under, but slugs past 25 meters.

In all cases, the shooting began on an electronic signal and the clock stopped automatically when the last target struck the ground. The "problem" was not considered solved until then.

Because of the greater mass of lead in its load, the shotgun would slam the close-range steel targets to the ground faster than the other types of guns could drop them. This fact gives the shotgun a mechanical advantage in these tests—though not necessarily one when it comes to a real-life encounter.

During the study, two hits were required from both the pistol and SMG, in keeping with proper tactics on single targets. Here Shooter A has presented his weapon from a concealed holster and hit his target solidly twice. This procedure was executed five times at each range specified in Test 1.

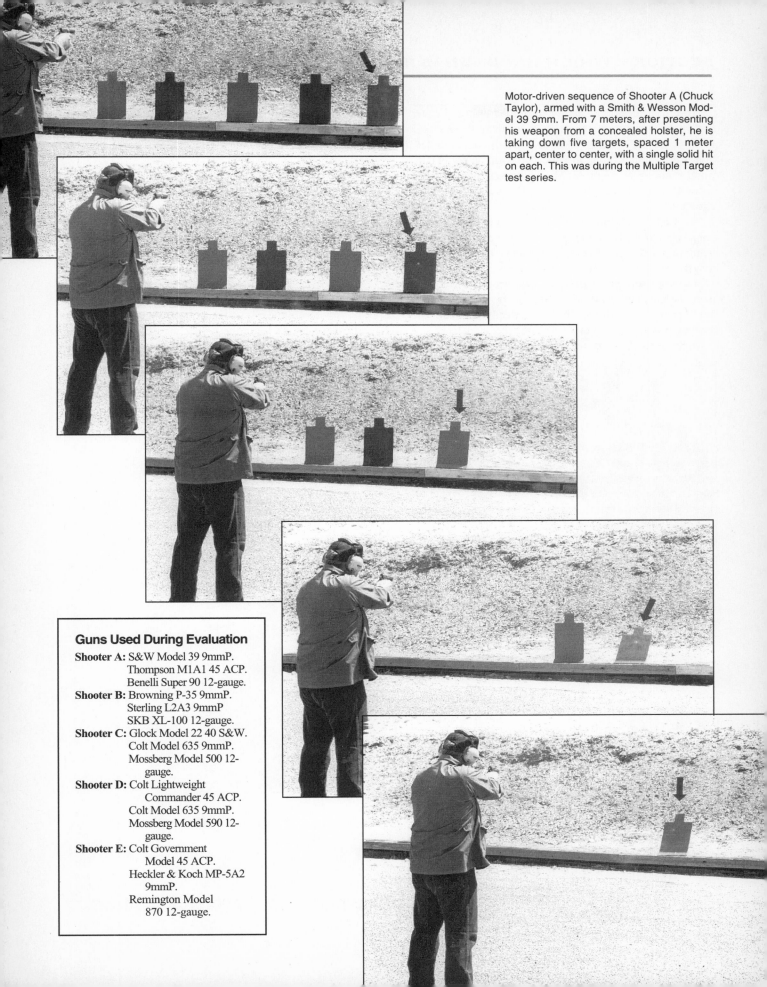

Motor-driven sequence of Shooter A (Chuck Taylor), armed with a Smith & Wesson Model 39 9mm. From 7 meters, after presenting his weapon from a concealed holster, he is taking down five targets, spaced 1 meter apart, center to center, with a single solid hit on each. This was during the Multiple Target test series.

Guns Used During Evaluation

Shooter A: S&W Model 39 9mmP.
Thompson M1A1 45 ACP.
Benelli Super 90 12-gauge.
Shooter B: Browning P-35 9mmP.
Sterling L2A3 9mmP
SKB XL-100 12-gauge.
Shooter C: Glock Model 22 40 S&W.
Colt Model 635 9mmP.
Mossberg Model 500 12-gauge.
Shooter D: Colt Lightweight Commander 45 ACP.
Colt Model 635 9mmP.
Mossberg Model 590 12-gauge.
Shooter E: Colt Government Model 45 ACP.
Heckler & Koch MP-5A2 9mmP.
Remington Model 870 12-gauge.

Test 1

Test 1 required the shooter to draw from the holster and make two hits on the target, a metal silhouette 7 meters away. The time to knock it down was recorded, and if the shooter failed to knock it down, he could continue shooting as required. Misses were penalized three seconds. The test was repeated five times to give an average time.

As a continuation of this test, the target distance was lengthened to 10, 15 and 25 meters, with the same shooting being required. The times to knock down all targets at all ranges were averaged into one number, given in Chart 1.

The same series of targets was then fired using the submachine gun, and again with the shotgun, these weapons being presented from the Rhodesian Ready position. The shotgun was required to shoot only one shot in all tests.

In the charted results, the shooters are A, B, C, D and E.

Their times with each weapon are given in Chart 1. Note that each recorded number—for example, the 2.2 seconds for Shooter A using a handgun—represents the average of firing forty shots; two per target, repeated five times over four ranges.

We see that the shotgun times were the fastest for all five shooters in this test. However, that is not the major point. Note instead that the handgun times are *not far behind* those of the other two types of weapon at these relatively close ranges, even working from the holster. You're probably more likely to have a handgun than a submachine gun or shotgun under your jacket or in your purse.

Test 2

Test 2 had similar shooting requirements as Test One, but at longer ranges. Here the targets are at 50, 75, and 100 meters. Again the 3-second penalty applies, and it can be

Chart 1: Elapsed Time						
			Shooter			
	A	B	C	D	E	Average
Test 1						
Handgun	2.2	2.8	2.5	2.2	2.2	2.4
Submachine gun	1.7	1.9	1.7	1.9	2.0	1.8
Shotgun	1.5	1.6	1.4	1.6	1.6	1.5
Test 2						
Handgun	7.7	7.4	15.2	14.8	8.0	10.6
Submachine gun	5.3	6.7	3.2	6.2	4.8	5.2
Shotgun	6.2	6.6	4.6	5.4	15.9	7.7
Test 3						
Handgun	7.6	11.5	7.2	8.7	7.2	8.4
Submachine gun	3.3	4.8	4.3	5.4	3.6	4.3
Shotgun	3.7	3.6	3.4	5.9	4.7	4.3
Test 4						
Handgun	18.9	28.7	25.1	42.1	33.8	29.7
Submachine gun	6.3	13.3	6.8	11.2	15.4	10.6
Shotgun	7.7	10.0	11.5	14.2	9.8	10.6
Test 5						
Handgun	10.5	18.4	23.3	14.1	14.7	16.2
Submachine gun	8.0	15.8	13.6	8.2	6.7	10.5
Shotgun	17.6	14.4	26.6	11.2	17.0	17.4
Test 6						
Handgun	1.9	2.1	2.1	2.4	2.1	2.1
Submachine gun	1.7	1.7	1.7	2.6	2.0	1.9
Shotgun	1.9	2.1	2.1	2.4	2.0	2.1
Test 7						
Handgun	2.2	2.3	1.9	2.1	2.4	2.2
Submachine gun	1.9	2.6	2.4	2.3	2.4	2.3
Shotgun	1.7	1.9	2.3	1.4	2.0	1.9
Test 8						
Handgun	1.9	2.8	2.4	3.8	2.5	2.7
Submachine gun	1.8	1.9	1.9	2.3	4.4	2.4
Shotgun	1.9	2.8	2.4	3.8	2.5	2.7
Overall averages						
Handgun						74.3
Submachine gun						39.0
Shotgun						48.1

Elapsed Time: Time in seconds required to neutralize all targets. Begins with start signal and ends when last target strikes the ground.

seen from the times for data that this probably came into play for Shooters C and D. It's harder to hit with a handgun at longer range; but then, the need to shoot in self-defense at 50 or 100 meters is nowhere near as common as it is close-up. For the three other shooters, the handgun times are not very far behind those for the submachine gun and shotgun.

Taylor noted that it was hard—but not impossible—to hit the 100-meter target twice before it hit the ground.

Test 3

Test 3 involves multiple targets. The handgun is held in the ready position. On command, the shooter engages five targets at a range of 7 meters, ideally firing only one shot on each. Again, the clock stops when the last target hits the ground. He repeats the test five times to give good averages. He then shoots at five targets at 10, then 15, and finally 25 meters. Then he repeats all of these shooting tests with his submachine gun, then again with his shotgun. His times for each gun at all four ranges are averaged, and the results are presented in Chart 1. This time there was no penalty for misses. Note that shooter B apparently had problems stopping the clock with his handgun, a 9mm. We assume he had to hit his distant target several times to drop it.

Test 4

Test 4 is identical to 3, but at longer ranges, 50, 75 and 100 meters.

Analysis of the trends indicates that increased range has a devastating effect on performance. The average handgun time for all five shooters to hit five targets at 50 to 100 meters is half a minute.

Test 5

Test 5 constitutes multiple targets (five) at unknown ranges, from 7 to 50 meters. The *pistolero* has his handgun

Chart 2: Points Per Second						
	Shooter					
	A	B	C	D	E	Average
Test 1						
Handgun	4.6	3.6	3.9	4.5	4.5	4.2
Submachine gun	6.0	5.3	5.8	5.4	5.1	5.5
Shotgun	6.7	6.2	6.9	6.2	6.3	6.5
Test 2						
Handgun	1.3	1.3	0.7	0.7	1.3	1.0
Submachine gun	1.9	1.5	3.2	1.6	2.1	2.0
Shotgun	1.6	1.5	2.2	1.9	0.6	1.6
Test 3						
Handgun	6.6	4.3	6.9	5.8	6.9	6.1
Submachine gun	15.4	10.4	11.7	9.3	13.8	12.1
Shotgun	13.6	13.8	14.5	8.5	10.6	12.2
Test 4						
Handgun	2.6	1.7	2.0	1.2	1.5	1.8
Submachine gun	8.0	3.8	7.3	4.5	3.2	5.4
Shotgun	6.5	5.0	4.3	3.5	5.1	4.9
Test 5						
Handgun	4.8	2.7	2.1	3.5	3.4	3.3
Submachine gun	6.3	3.2	3.7	6.1	7.5	5.3
Shotgun	2.8	3.5	1.9	4.5	2.9	3.1
Test 6						
Handgun	5.3	4.7	4.9	4.1	4.9	4.8
Submachine gun	5.9	6.0	6.0	3.8	5.1	5.4
Shotgun	5.3	4.8	4.8	4.2	5.0	4.8
Test 7						
Handgun	4.5	4.4	5.3	4.9	4.1	4.6
Submachine gun	5.3	3.9	4.1	4.3	4.2	4.4
Shotgun	6.0	5.2	4.4	6.9	5.0	5.5
Test 8						
Handgun	5.3	3.6	4.2	2.7	4.0	3.9
Submachine gun	5.7	5.3	5.3	4.3	2.3	4.6
Shotgun	5.3	3.6	4.2	2.7	4.0	3.9
Overall Average Points/Time						
Handgun						29.9
Submachine gun						44.7
Shotgun						42.5

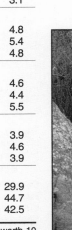

Points per second: Total points accumulated during the elapsed time period. Each silhouette is worth 10 points. Thus, the possible score is divided by the elapsed time.

holstered when the bell rings. He then has to knock each of the five targets down. He repeats this test twice for a representive average. The test is then repeated with the submachine gun and then with the shotgun.

Note that in the case of Shooter A, his slowest time was with the shotgun. In fact, in all but two cases the shotgun times were the slowest. There was perhaps a tactical reason for this. The shotgun would have been loaded initially with buckshot, which worked well for closer shots. However, when or if it failed to drop the 50-meter target, the shooter had to load a slug, taking additional time. Three out of five shooters shot faster with the handgun than with the shotgun. The submachine gun made an excellent showing here.

Test 6

In Test 6 the targets were partially obscured, leaning to right and left from cover, with 40 percent of the target

obscured. The handgun was held at the ready position, as were the other weapons. On command, the shooter had to fire two shots at the partially hidden target. This test was repeated to give averages. Targets were at 7, 10, 15 and 25 meters, but only one target was engaged at a time, and each must be knocked down to conclude the drill.

For top-level shooters, these were still pretty big targets, but not easy ones. As might be expected at close range, the times for all weapons for all shooters were very similar. For four shooters, the absolute fastest time was with the submachine gun, but *not by much*.

Test 7

Test 7 was at the same short ranges as Test Six, but the target was much smaller, roughly head size with a bit of the shoulder thrown in. The handgun was presented from Ready. The results indicate little difference in overall aver-

Chart 3: Points Per Round						
	Shooter					
	A	B	C	D	E	Average
Test 1						
Handgun	5.0	4.7	4.4	5.0	4.9	4.8
Submachine gun	5.0	4.9	4.8	5.0	4.9	4.9
Shotgun	10.0	10.0	10.0	10.0	10.0	10.0
Test 2						
Handgun	3.9	4.4	1.2	3.3	3.6	3.3
Submachine gun	4.7	2.9	3.9	4.2	5.0	4.1
Shotgun	9.4	7.9	8.3	9.4	6.3	8.2
Test 3						
Handgun	7.4	7.1	6.9	6.7	7.7	7.2
Submachine gun	8.7	8.3	8.0	7.1	9.5	8.3
Shotgun	10.0	10.0	10.0	10.0	10.0	10.0
Test 4						
Handgun	6.5	5.0	5.8	5.8	5.2	5.6
Submachine gun	9.4	7.9	8.3	7.1	7.9	8.1
Shotgun	9.4	6.5	8.8	8.8	9.4	8.6
Test 5						
Handgun	7.7	6.7	3.0	7.1	5.3	6.0
Submachine gun	8.3	5.3	3.6	9.1	9.1	7.1
Shotgun	5.9	8.3	5.9	8.3	6.3	6.9
Test 6						
Handgun	5.0	4.9	4.6	4.6	5.0	4.8
Submachine gun	5.0	4.9	4.4	4.3	5.0	4.7
Shotgun	10.0	10.0	8.4	10.0	10.0	9.7
Test 7						
Handgun	8.9	10.0	10.0	8.9	8.0	9.2
Submachine gun	10.0	8.9	8.0	8.9	8.0	8.8
Shotgun	10.0	8.9	6.7	10.0	8.0	8.7
Test 8						
Handgun	9.2	7.5	8.0	5.5	9.2	7.9
Submachine gun	9.2	10.0	8.6	9.2	9.2	9.3
Shotgun	8.0	6.3	6.7	6.7	10.0	7.5
Overall Average Points/Shot						
Handgun						48.7
Submachine gun						55.3
Shotgun						69.7

Points per round expended: Total points accumulated per shot fired in the drill.

age handgun or shotgun times, but a slight slowdown in submachine gun times. Hits took about 2 seconds.

Test 8

Test 8 was a hostage situation fired at 7, 10, and 15 meters. You engaged only one target and had to knock it down. If you hit the good guy you lost three seconds. The bad-guy target, with only two-thirds of the head exposed, was smaller than in Test Seven.

In this final test, the times were only about half a second slower than in Test Seven, and all shooters averaged under 3 seconds.

As matters of interest, Shooters A, B, and C were three of the world's only five certified ASAA Four-Weapon Combat Masters, meaning these guys can *really shoot* just about anything. (Shooter A is author Taylor.)

Shooters D and E were Distinguished graduates of ASAA's three levels of Defensive Handgun courses (Basic, Intermediate and Advanced). They had taken ASAA's Basic course in the use of the shotgun, but had no

previous training with submachine guns. The high level of their performances ought to be of interest to law enforcement and SWAT trainers.

Chart 1 presented here shows the average times of each shooter with all three guns, for all tests.

Chart 2 shows the points per second accumulated, with each silhouette worth 10 points. This is another way of presenting and seeing the data other than simply against the clock. Note that the overall averages indicate that the submachine gun and shotgun don't have such high percentage ratings "better than the handgun" in this comparison, compared with the overall time averages in Chart 1.

Chart 3, the points per round expended, is perhaps most significant, because it indicates the effectiveness of each shot. This gives insight into the amount of shooting needed with each type of weapon to solve the problem, and therefore tells something of the efficiency of each. Remember, you are responsible for the effects of your misses. Lo, the handgun is not very far behind the other two types of weapon, when viewed in this light.

An old gunfighter's axiom says, "Use the most powerful gun we can conceal and shoot quickly and accurately." This is good advice, provided it isn't taken to extremes. Careful consideration of our needs provides us with the perspective needed to make intelligent choices here.

REVOLVER OR SELF-LOADER?

FOR MORE THAN a century, the revolver—first in single-, then double-action form—has served the American law enforcement officer and civilian alike, and served him well. So well, in fact, that it became regarded as the generic policeman's weapon, synonymous with his badge and blue uniform. Yet, even as far back as thirty-five years ago, there were indications of discontent with the trusty "wheelgun" among a great many police personnel.

Although the DA revolver itself and its use had been refined to unprecedented levels, some still weren't satisfied. The revolver lacked "firepower," they said. Its five or six shots just weren't enough, and it took too long to reload. It was too fragile under extreme field conditions, they claimed, citing as proof the worldwide shift among military organizations to the self-loader after World War II.

Moreover, it didn't really conceal very well when plainclothes duties demanded compactness. Its cylinder didn't fit or stay tucked into waistbands, and chafed many a hipbone on long stakeouts.

And so it went, with most police administrators, traditionalists to a man, giving only cursory attention to the ravings of what they affectionately—and sometimes not so affectionately—considered to be their department's lunatic fringe, "macho" types who actually liked guns and enjoyed getting "down and dirty" with the bad guys out there.

For the nearly three decades preceding 1988, in spite of the perceptible groundswell of discord with the cherished revolver, there was no change in the status quo—it remained "king of the hill." The self-loaders that were in actual use were generally of the backup-gun variety—small caliber, diminutively configured hideaway pieces worn under belt buckles or in ankle holsters. Only the highly innovative departments actually carried autos for general service functions.

As well, civilians interested in self-defense generally followed the example set by the police. Civilian training personnel and street cops alike happily shot their revolvers on the PPC course as prescribed, and administrators continued to jot down their scores for the record. Everything was just fine.

Or was it? Out in Southern California, there were a few firearms journalists and trainers who didn't think so. These were guys who weren't committed to, or satisfied with, the status quo. This was because out on the street some curious—and dangerous—trends were beginning to emerge. The bad guys were getting better and were beginning to get

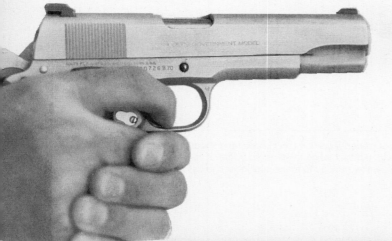

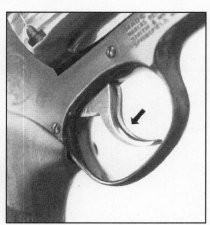

The revolver has a tradition as a law enforcement arm spanning over a century. In fact, until just a few years ago, it was as much a symbol of the police officer as his badge and blue uniform.

those who carried them demonstrated an awesome degree of skill, the result of long-term evaluations of and improvements upon existing techniques.

Moreover, improvements based on established, pragmatic needs began to surface. Intelligent, effective ways to fight—really *fight*—with a handgun began to emerge. A few more departments began to listen and learn, and the cops began winning, a definite exception to the norm begun in the chaotic Sixties.

Things stayed pretty much this way until the mid-1970s, when the second generation of self-loader disciples like myself appeared. We learned from the pioneers—Weaver, Carl and Cooper—and took up their cause, building on their techniques. As more and more data on gunfights became available, we analyzed, theorized upon, abandoned, created and further refined more revolutionary techniques to provide the self-defense shooter with the tools needed to stay alive. We of the new breed further championed the auto-pistol and, through our own disciples, gave it the widespread recognition it now enjoys.

With its radical increase in popularity, the auto has also received a large-scale face-lifting, with an unprecedented number of types now on the market in great volume. Names such as SIG, Beretta, Glock and Ruger have joined domestic giants like Colt and Smith & Wesson in the marketplace, and the array of self-loaders adorning the display cases of every gunshop in the U.S. has become mind-boggling.

The self-loader has quite literally taken the gun world by storm, with both large and small law enforcement departments switching over on a daily basis. With even the FBI authorizing the 10mm and 45 ACP, the most constructive change in self-defense handgun policy in nearly forty years is now in full swing. The FBI has a momentous effect on the

serious. They had better weapons than before, and they used them with an ever-increasing amount of skill. Worst of all, they no longer were deterred from committing crimes by the mere presence of the police.

These California-based shooters felt that something had to be done. In their view, the police profession had become enmeshed in the net of complacency, thus failing to perceive the need for a new look at weapons and methods of using them.

Guys like Eldon Carl, Jack Weaver and Jeff Cooper began the crusade. Here and there, a few more departments began to issue previously unheard-of pistols to their officers—weapons like the Colt M1911 45, Browning P-35 9mm and S&W M39. Of equal importance was the fact that

The heart of the DA revolver is its DA trigger pull. This must be mastered before any degree of skill with the weapon can be achieved, and it demands practice, dedication and self-discipline.

While more difficult to operate under stress due to its long DA trigger pull, the revolver can be utilized quite effectively. Compared to a SA auto like the Colt M1911 45 ACP or Browning P-35 9mm, the typical DA revolver is about 25 percent more difficult to operate. However, compared to a DA auto, it is only about 15 percent tougher to use.

law-enforcement community as a whole, for it looks up to the FBI and tends to religiously follow its lead. Within a few years, I expect virtually all police agencies to be armed with some form of auto, with a great many being of the larger-caliber variety.

As one of the self-loader's leading advocates, especially in a big bore configuration, I am naturally heartened. It's been a long road all these years, but the superior performance of the modern auto—in truth, also the result of superior training concepts—is saving lives. That's what the crusade has always been about, as far as I'm concerned.

But is the auto really superior to the old wheelgun? Is it really more robust and reliable? Is it really faster, more accurate, more concealable, simpler and more efficient? Provided that proper training is part of the equation, *yes*. The modern service auto is certainly simpler than any revolver, not as difficult to maintain, at least as accurate, capable of

holding a greater number of rounds, and generally easier to shoot well under stress. However, in the typical environment in which it is carried and utilized by cops and self-defense-minded civilians on a daily basis, it is not more reliable than the DA revolver.

To test the reliability of a variety of handguns under harsh conditions. I recently conducted some extreme cold weather testing in Alaska, where temperatures reached -40 degrees Fahrenheit. The test format required the shooter to leave the weapon and ammo outdoors for one hour to allow it to cool to outside temperature, after it had been cleaned and lubricated for arctic conditions. Once this was accomplished, the tester loaded the gun, fired it rapidly until empty, reloaded it and dropped it into the snow, leaving it untouched for fifteen minutes. He then retrieved it and repeated the process, following the format until the weapon failed entirely or the 750-round test program was completed.

The superior ease of use of the auto makes it more tactically flexible, allowing the shooter to accomplish more tasks more efficiently with less work. This is its major asset.

The DA test revolver was a 3½-inch-barrelled Smith & Wesson M27 357 Magnum, which sailed right through the entire program without a single stoppage. Of the self-loaders tested with this same procedure, only the Colt M1911, Browning P-35 and Glock M17 equaled its performance. The SIG P226, Beretta M92, and Smith & Wesson M39 included in the tests all experiencing varying numbers of malfunctions and failures.

The idea that autos are more reliable is true only in the military environment, where field conditions demand that the weapon withstand inescapable abuse sometimes bordering on the incredible. Realistically, no law enforcement or civilian self-defense handgun is subjected to this kind of torture. Thus, for all practical intents and purposes, the revolver is, in this category, equal.

On the other hand, autos are easier to use well under stress, providing the shooter is properly trained (something needed with the revolver, too); much flatter or thinner and therefore easier to conceal; and able to hold more ammunition. However, gunfight statistical data for the last twenty-five years indicates that fewer than three shots are fired in the typical encounter, thus relegating this last characteristic to being more of an academic, rather than a practical, advantage.

Also, the fact that an auto is easier to reload either quickly or tactically is more theoretical than practical, since those same data also show that one doesn't normally have the time to use that extra ammo. Nonetheless, that it is available is admittedly a comfort to many, based upon the thesis, "It's better to have and not need, than the other way around!"

Exceptions to the norm do occur, after all.

So, after nearly fifty years of evolution, the self-loader—in large measure assisted by the huge boost in efficiency it received from modern training methods—has finally defeated the revolver's long tradition and has come of age.

The self-loader, though not much faster to the first shot than a DA revolver, is simpler to master, easier to conceal, and easier to use well under stress.

(Below) The flatness of the self-loader makes it easier to conceal than a revolver.

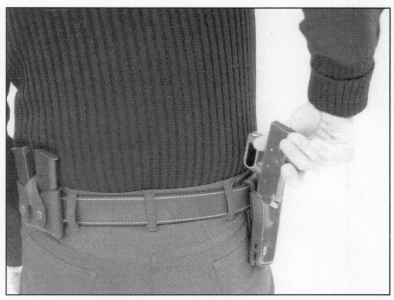

The detachable magazine of the auto also makes weapon handling, such as reloading, considerably easier than with a revolver and is a more compact spare ammo container than a speedloader.

IS SINGLE ACTION RIGHT FOR YOU?

DATING BACK 165 years to 1831, the single-action revolver boasts the title of being the first repeating—and thus serious—defensive handgun. Before that, from both a technological and tactical standpoint, the single shot weapons considered to be state of the art at the time provided their owners with little advantage.

Why? Because the one-shot-and-reload concept meant that once the shot was fired, the shooter was forced to either reload while the conflict was still in progress (a time-consuming and difficult process under stress) or abandon the handgun entirely and instead utilize some other weapon, such as a saber, knife or club, to handle any further action. The repeating handgun, in the form of the Colt Paterson, made this often fatal and always dicey chore unnecessary, and made obsolete not only the single shot handgun, but all forms of edged and blunt weapons as well.

Although it was mechanically fragile and not particularly powerful, the Paterson demonstrated that a handgun capable of repeat shots without reloading was in fact possible and subsequently became the research platform from which more reliable and effective handguns evolved. Among these were the guns that made history—the Colt Walker; 1st, 2nd and 3rd Model Dragoons; 1851 Navy; Remington 1858 Army; Colt 1860 Army; and, finally the most famous, the Colt 1873 Single Action Army, which became known commercially as the Peacemaker.

The Peacemaker became a symbol of the American West, seeing immense proliferation on both sides of the law well into the 20th century. In fact, it was *so* popular that even the advent of more efficient weapons, such as the double-action revolver and self-loading pistol (1890-1910), failed to cause its immediate replacement. The old six-gun, as it was often called, continued in service until it simply wore out and was then replaced by a more modern design. Even today, it lives on and serves with distinction as a recreational firearm used for hunting and plinking, its most notable examples made by Colt, Ruger and several European importers.

However, from a *tactical* standpoint, *the SA revolver is dangerously obsolete.* It requires the hammer to be manually cocked for each shot, making it ponderously slow for the

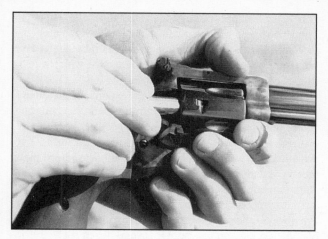

The most serious criticism of the single-action revolver is that its long hammer fall makes accurate shooting at high speed difficult. SA revolvers also require that expended cases must be ejected and then reloaded one chamber at a time, making them too slow for serious combat use.

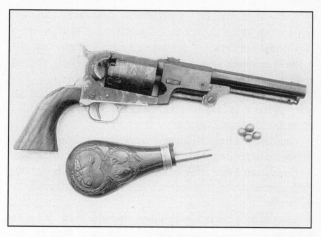

One of the most famous pre-Civil War SA revolvers is the 44-caliber Colt 3rd Model Dragoon. It saw much action during the American Civil War and on the frontier as well.

repeat shots typically required in handgun encounters. Because spent cartridges must be extracted and replaced one at a time, the gun cannot be quickly reloaded. In addition, its grip design causes a pronounced upward bounce in recoil which, although it absorbs recoil energy, makes it virtually uncontrollable and therefore unsatisfactory in comparison to more modern designs.

Another concern about single-action revolvers involves safety. Virtually since its inception, the SA six-shooter was considered safe only when carried with five chambers loaded and the hammer down on the sixth, which is left empty. Were the hammer to be left down on a loaded chamber, a sudden impact on the hammer spur could cause the weapon to inadvertently fire. With the increase in civil liability that began in the 1970s, and the lawsuits that resulted, Ruger changed the design of their popular Blackhawk series to prevent this from happening. However, Colt and the various European replica makers have retained the original 1873 design and care should be taken with them. For casual carry, load them as outlined above and *only load a full six rounds for exceptional circumstances,* say, for example, a bear encounter.

For these reasons, the SA revolver should not be our first choice for self-defense missions. In its day, the SA revolver was the cutting edge of weapon technology. However, that day is long past, and that fact must be recognized. Virtually every other design available since 1910 (the SA self-loader, double-action revolver and self-loader) is far more efficient, relegating the venerable SA "wheelgun" to its proper place as a revered and cherished piece of American history.

So, hunt with it, plink with it and have fun with it. But don't make it your first choice for self-defense. If, in an extreme emergency, you find one lying on the floor, then by all means, scoop it up and go for it. Under such circum-

stances, one uses whatever one must to survive. But from a comparative standpoint, against more modern weapons it hasn't a chance.

The single-action semi-auto appeared right at the turn of the century and was, until the advent of the double-action (DA) auto in 1929, the only form of self-operating pistol available. Easily identified by its "cocked and locked" appearance when carried ready for imminent action, its most prolific and popular examples include the legendary Colt M1911 45 ACP and graceful Browning P-35 9mm.

As applied to the self-loading concept, the term single action means that the weapon is manually loaded and cocked via the motion of the slide during firing, and the hammer then remains in the full-cock position. There is normally some form of thumb-operated manual safety that can then be engaged; hence, the descriptive term, cocked and locked. While not in any way unsafe, the appearance of a SA auto in Condition One, the technical terminology for cocked and locked, is disturbing to many people and has resulted in the erroneous notion that the piece is somehow unsafe because it is carried cocked.

Such is patently untrue. Although the sear, rather than the hammer itself, is blocked by the thumb safety, some feel that a metallurgical failure of the hammer could allow the pistol to fire. However, it should be noted that almost all of the battle and assault rifles of recent history utilize this same concept and, like the SA auto, have for the last fifty-plus years shown virtually no propensity for such failures.

Nonetheless, many law enforcement agencies, ever fearful of the ominous image projected by a Condition One self-loader, and ignorant of their excellent and long-standing safety record, have opted instead for the DA self-loader carried with the hammer down.

It would perhaps be a good idea to mention here that *all* self-loaders utilize these classic Conditions of Readiness:

Condition One, as described earlier, means that the weapon is loaded (e.g. a cartridge in the chamber), cocked and has a fully loaded magazine in place as well.

Condition Two, on the other hand, means that while the weapon has a loaded round chambered and a fully loaded magazine in place, the hammer is down.

Condition Three entails the hammer being down on an empty chamber, but with a fully loaded magazine in the gun.

Condition Four means that the weapon is empty with the hammer down, but with a loaded magazine carried on the person.

Condition Five is identical to Condition Four, but with the magazine placed at some other location than on the weapon-carrier himself.

The term "auto," while it applies to both SA and DA designs, actually means that the pistol automatically fires one shot and then reloads itself with each pull of the trigger, *not that it is capable of fully automatic fire.* Of late, due to political rhetoric and continual use of the term by the news media, considerable confusion as to its meaning has been generated. So much, in fact, that many (particularly image-conscious law enforcement agencies) now refer to the weapon as a "semi-auto," or "self-loader" to avoid being misunderstood by the public.

The SA auto has been in worldwide use, with great success, since the appearance of the Colt Model 1911 45 ACP. The Browning P-35 (also called the Hi-Power) 9mm surfaced in 1935. Both weapons have seen worldwide use ever since and have become the standard against which all so-called "combat" handguns are judged.

Upon investigation, it has been my experience that claims of unsafeness generally result from two sources: 1) unsafe and/or improper weapon handling by people who, for various reasons, do not wish to admit their error; and 2) an unserviceable weapon, that is, a gun with operational parts broken or damaged. Of these, the former is by far the more common, but due to concerns about civil liability, particularly if someone is injured by the unintentional discharge that always follows, few can afford to admit their error. They blame it on the gun instead. Of several dozen such suits in which I was retained as an expert witness, only one involved an actual mechanical failure of the weapon itself. The rest were proven to be operator error.

Is the SA self-loader too complicated for the average self-defense shooter? Does it require special training to master, as some suggest? The answer to both questions is *no.* In my twenty-plus years as a weapons and tactics instructor/consultant, I have seen fewer accidental discharges with SA autos than with any other design. Moreover, because it is easier to shoot well, especially under stress, performance levels with it tend to be substantially higher. On the other hand, the SA auto is *not* for everyone. The novice is often

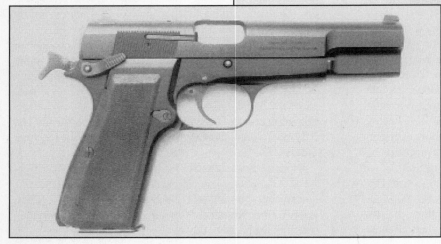

(Below) Many feel that the Condition One (cocked and locked) carry of the SA self-loader is unsafe. While patently untrue, this concern has greatly contributed to the recent upsurge in popularity of the double-action auto, especially in police work.

(Above) The 7.63mm "Broomhandle" Mauser is one of the earliest and most famous SA self-loaders. Then-Lieutenant Winston Churchill used one at the famous Last Cavalry Charge at Omdurman, Africa, shortly after the turn of the century.

intimidated by the cocked-and-locked concept. Thus, it is most typically selected by the more experienced shooter, who better understands it.

As far as training is concerned, the SA auto requires nothing extraordinary, but I suggest that anyone who wishes to master it (or any other kind of weapon, for that matter) should invest in some formal training, such as we offer at Front Sight Firearms Training Institute. Such training not only shatters the myths and misconceptions about all forms of weapon design, but provides the student with a clear perspective and all the fundamental skills needed to use it safely and efficiently in a high-stress environment. As such, it will save him much aggravation, money, energy, time and perhaps even grief, while giving him maximum efficiency in return.

There are those who claim the SA auto is functionally unreliable and requires extensive gunsmithing before it can be trusted. There are also those who claim it is inaccurate. In truth, neither claim is valid. Simple logic tells us that since the SA auto was the first self-loading design to appear (almost a full century ago), were its design malfunction-prone, it would have shown up long ago. The opposite has been the case. Its extreme reliability under the widest variety of environmental conditions tells us all we need to know.

This is not to say that the SA—or any other auto—cannot benefit from minor polishing and chamber mouth polishing,

particularly if the shooter intends to use bullets of non-typical shapes. But in general, the SA self-loader will feed and function quite reliably with most types of ammunition.

It is also interesting to note that virtually all the accuracy records at Camp Perry were set by SA autos, mostly in the form of the Colt M1911 45 ACP. But the simple fact is that accuracy should be considered from a somewhat different standpoint. For combat shooting, we must balance the elements of accuracy and speed. If the handgun is capable of placing all its shots in a man's chest at 50 meters, it's more accurate than it can be shot under stress. Any serviceable handgun possesses more inherent accuracy than that. Therefore, the claim that SA autos are inaccurate is pure bunk. In fact, I have personally investigated several dozen such claims and found that the *real* problem was that the *shooter*, not the weapon, was inaccurate. So, we must consider the source of the claim carefully before we accept it as fact.

The SA auto is the easiest self-loader to shoot well under stress, requires no special training, and is functionally reliable. Moreover, it is highly accurate and enjoys the reputation of being the standard against which all other systems are judged. Still, *it's not for everyone.* Those who find its cocked-and-locked visual image disconcerting, or cannot bring themselves to trust the mechanical concepts upon which it is based, should consider some other design.

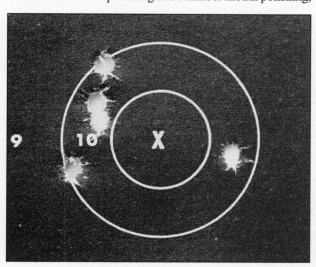

Some claim the SA self-loader is inaccurate. Here is a five-shot group shot offhand by the author from 25 meters with a Colt M1911 45 ACP. Judge for yourself. Virtually all of the handgun accuracy records at Camp Perry are held by this pistol.

The most famous SA self-loader of them all—the Colt M1911 45 ACP. After over eighty years of worldwide service, this pistol still ranks near the top of the list as a fighting handgun and has become the standard of performance against which all others are judged.

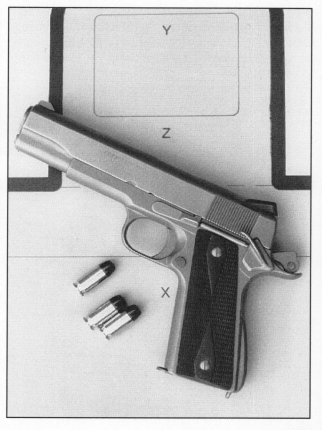

IS DOUBLE ACTION RIGHT FOR YOU?

THE DOUBLE-ACTION (DA) revolver actually appeared in usable form during the American Civil War, but due to the extreme and rapid fouling caused by the blackpowder propellants of the day, it didn't reach full maturity until the 1890s. This metamorphosis was due specifically to the invention of smokeless powder and saw not only the appearance of a number of DA revolver designs, but the SA self-loader as well.

Critics point out that it is more fragile and therefore less mechanically reliable than any type of self-loader, and that, due to the virtual impossibility of perfectly aligning each chamber with the barrel, it's less accurate. Let's stop for just a moment, take a deep breath, and look at history. If the DA revolver were worthless or even seriously deficient in either of these areas, it could not have survived all these years, much less become as popular as it is. From a pure logic standpoint, yes, it is more complex and thus more fragile than a self-loader, but let's not lose our sense of proportion.

Usually, functional reliability is considered on the basis of military requirements, which, to say the least, subject any weapon to considerably more abuse than would any police officer or civilian. Of necessity, the military battlefield is the most demanding and requires the toughest weapon designs possible, and this is why the self-loader now dominates the

Some claimed weaknesses of the DA revolver are 1) that it's mechanically fragile (top left), e.g., its crane—and resulting cylinder alignment with the barrel—is easily damaged; 2) its ejector rod (bottom left) is easily bent or unscrews from the ejector, thus placing the gun out of action; and 3) its locking mechanism (below) is fragile and cannot withstand serious field use.

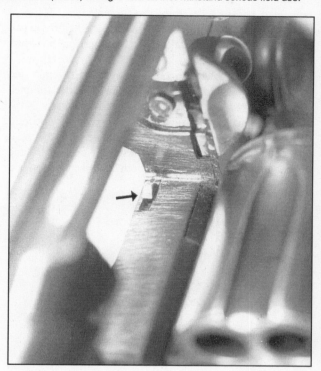

field. However, history shows us that the DA revolver was used by quite a few military organizations as late as World War II, and even for a decade or so thereafter. If it wasn't capable of at least satisfactory functioning, this could not have happened.

Neither you nor I will subject our DA revolver to such rigorous conditions, using it instead in a more "civilized" environment. And used within that environment, it works quite well, certainly well enough to bet our lives on, as many police officers have been doing for more than ninety years. As a matter of fact, it may surprise you to discover that the DA "wheelie" is tougher than most people think. It sure surprised me!

Here's an example. I took an S&W M27 357 Magnum to Alaska and tested it at -40 degrees Fahrenheit, firing six shots as rapidly as I could, then quickly reloading it and dropping it in the snow, where it remained for fifteen minutes. It was then recovered, aimed at a target and, guess what—it worked perfectly for my entire 750-round test. *No stoppages of any kind!* In total, it was reloaded and dropped in the snow 125 times, but continued to function normally. Is that reliable enough for you? It is for me.

As well, I have repeatedly fired six-shot 100-meter groups from the rollover prone position with Colt Python 357 and Smith & Wesson M29 44 Magnum revolvers that measured under 4 inches. So, obviously, any DA revolver in

The most-often-heard criticism of the double-action revolver is that, because it only holds five or six shots, it lacks "firepower." A second-often-stated concern is that, because its cylinder is unlocked and out of battery while it is being reloaded, it cannot be fired in an emergency and is therefore obsolete. In truth, combat handgun encounters rarely require more than three or four shots and are generally over in 3 seconds or less. Thus, both concerns are more academic than practical.

decent condition is capable of more accuracy than any shooter can produce, especially under deadly stress.

Some also claim that the DA revolver is difficult to shoot, but this, too, must be kept in context. To help understand the issue, here are some definitions and commentary. The term "double action" connotes that the weapon can be fired in two ways: 1) by manually cocking the hammer for each shot, e.g., the weapon is used in the SA mode; 2) by merely pressing the trigger which, in turn, both cocks the gun and revolves the cylinder from chamber to chamber for each shot. Of the two, the second (now known popularly as the "DA mode") is the fastest and simplest, particularly for combat shooting. However, from the standpoint of trigger control, it is also the most demanding. Necessarily, the trigger-pull poundage needed to both cock the weapon and

revolve the cylinder is quite heavy, making weapon control considerably more difficult. Because of this, the DA revolver is about 25 percent more difficult to shoot well under stress than a SA self-loader or Glock.

Often, the heavier pull causes the novice to yank or mash the trigger. Yanking means to press the trigger rearward using correct methodology, but too quickly, ruining sight alignment and sight picture, and pulling the muzzle radically to the right and occasionally upward as well. Mashing is contracting all the fingers of the firing hand to discharge the gun, rather than pressing with only the trigger finger, resulting in a downward and sometimes left or right diving of the muzzle, and the total destruction of sight picture and alignment.

On the other hand, the DA revolver is simple and straightforward in concept, and is thus popular with both

For many years, the mainstay of the police officer was the Smith & Wesson M28 Highway Patrolman 357 Magnum. Big, tough and potent, this weapon and its more fancy brother, the M27, are the guns that made the 357's reputation.

The graceful Colt Diamondback 38 Special is the Rolls Royce of 38s—with a pricetag to match! However, you get what you pay for. It handles and shoots beautifully, and is now a much sought-after item.

Two famous 357 Magnums—the Colt Python (top) and Smith & Wesson M27.

(Below) Some claim that because of the revolver's multiple chambers and elaborate timing system, it is capable of producing no more than mediocre accuracy. This is untrue. Here is a 100-meter, five-shot group shot by Taylor from the rollover prone position with the S&W M27 357 Magnum.

novice combat shooters and, in its more powerful examples, hunters as well. Its cylinder swings out for quick, easy inspection to determine if the weapon is loaded or not. The fact that it does not feed cartridges from a detachable magazine allows considerable flexibility in the selection of bullet shapes and styles.

From the time it first appeared until around 1990—about ninety years—the DA revolver was both the cherished friend and very symbol of the American police officer. In the past five years, concerns about its lack of "firepower" began to surface, and as a result, its popularity has faded somewhat. Like most criticisms of any system, this one, too, is taken out of context.

Year after year, statistical data on police handgun encounters substantiates that the vast majority of such fights

not only occur at very close ranges and therefore take place quickly, but that an average two or three shots total are fired. Since every DA revolver of which I am aware holds at least five shots, it would seem that this new passion for "firepower" is somewhat misplaced.

These same statistics show a shockingly low 17 to 18 percent average hits which, in spite of the trend towards self-loaders and large-capacity magazines, have remained fairly constant. This means that although the police are shooting more (because they now have guns that possess a larger ammunition capacity), they're not hitting more. This shows clearly that the low hit percentages stem from faulty shooting under stress, which is a training failure, not a lack of ammunition capacity. After all, in a gunfight *you can't miss fast enough to matter*, right? And you can't win the fight by

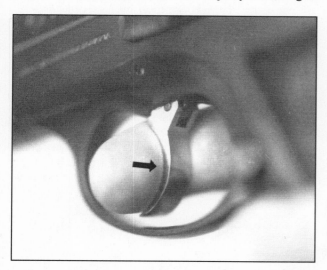

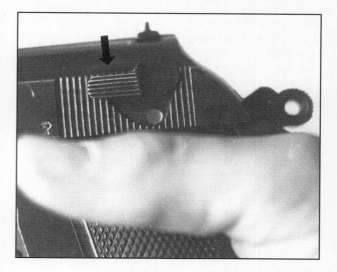

(Above and below) The most legitimate criticism of the DA self-loader is that, due to the fact that it shifts from DA to SA after the first shot, the trigger position changes radically, making accurate shooting at high speed a tough proposition. This is true, but often overstated.

(Above and below) Another weakness of the DA self-loader is the hammer-drop safety. Poorly placed for quick operation and occasionally allowing an accidental discharge, it is the nucleus of the claim that DA autos are unsafe. To solve this problem, most modern versions have a firing-pin block system that is deactivated by pulling the trigger.

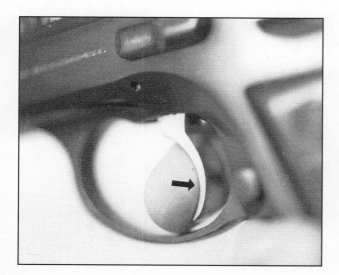

missing, either! It should also be understood that, due to its longer, heavier trigger pull, the DA revolver is about 25 percent harder to shoot well under stress than a SA auto. However, this can be overcome with proper training and a little extra practice time.

It may be true that the DA revolver is experiencing a slump in popularity due to the widespread law enforcement shift to large-capacity self-loaders. However, officer performance in actual gunfights hasn't been any better than with the DA revolvers they previously used. This uncomfortable fact proves conclusively that 1) ammunition capacity is no substitute for marksmanship, and 2) the problem of poor hit percentages has nothing to do with the DA revolver or its five- or six-round ammunition capacity.

In my opinion, this is why the venerable DA revolver continues in service with not only a great many law-enforcement personnel, but with civilians as well. It is a good basic weapon system, especially for the semi-trained or those who need a self-defense weapon for limited tactical requirements.

So enjoy that Smith & Wesson Model 10, 12, 13, 15, 19, 24, 25, 27, 28, 36, 38, 49, 57, 58 or 60. Enjoy that beautiful Colt Python, Agent, Detective Special, Diamondback or Cobra. While not nearly as efficient as the SA self-loader, they're valid weapons with a long, glorious history of life-saving performance and are *entirely* worthy of your confidence.

The double-action self-loader appeared toward the end of the 1920s and was immediately accepted as an alternative to the cocked-and-locked SA auto. Like the DA revolver, it utilizes a dual system of operation and is usually carried loaded with the hammer down on a loaded chamber and a loaded magazine in place (Condition Two). However, unlike the revolver, only the first shot is trigger-cocked. Subsequent shots are discharged from the single-action mode, as the weapon cycles, reloads and recocks itself.

This makes trigger control more difficult and, for most shooters, necessitates a shift of the trigger finger from one position to another. Obviously, this is more time-consuming, increases the shooter's sense of urgency and makes the weapon noticeably more difficult to shoot well under stress. The problem is sufficiently urgent that some experts advocate simply firing the first shot into the air or ground, just to get the gun into the SA mode. However, I feel that this is not a viable option, due to both tactical and legal concerns.

Tactically, one or two seconds and a round of ammunition are wasted by this process, time that in a deadly encounter you simply don't have. So, I recommend simply squeezing your way through that long, heavy, often gritty DA pull; using extra concentration on sight picture, sight alignment and trigger control; and getting that all-important first hit, even if it does take longer. Yes, it's a compromise, but there simply is no better alternative.

Legally, from both a criminal and civil liability standpoint, the responsibility for "blowing off" that first round by firing it into the air or ground rests with the shooter. In other words,

The controversial Beretta M92 9mm. Perhaps due to curious circumstances surrounding its adoption by the U.S. Army in the middle 1980s, it is continuously attacked by critics as being highly susceptible to dirt and grit. Actually, although much of the action is exposed to the elements, it performed satisfactorily during Operation Desert Storm and has achieved some degree of popularity with police departments, particularly in the Southeastern U.S.

Perhaps the most efficient DA autos now available—the SIG P225 (right) and P226, both in 9mm. The P226 is used by U.S. Navy SEAL teams, while the P225 is the favorite of German police.

what goes up must also come down, and if it hits something it shouldn't, you're responsible. Need I say more?

One effort to alleviate the problem is the DA-only self-loader. Unfortunately, while eliminating one of the weapon's two operational systems theoretically simplifies things, leaving only the DA mode makes acceptable performance under deadly stress even more difficult. For this reason, such weapons should, if at all possible, be avoided.

Another attempt to cure the difficulties of the DA auto is to make it capable of either DA or SA function, such as seen with the Czech CZ-75 series. However, it must be realized that incorporating two systems into one does complicate the gun, making it less reliable. Moreover, the thumb safety on such guns is placed too high for fast, convenient manipulation except by those with exceptionally long thumbs. I feel that it is better to choose one or the other and avoid this kind of solution, for it may create more problems than it solves.

Some of the more popular examples of the DA auto include the Walther PP/PPK (of James Bond fame), Walther P-38, Beretta M92, the Smith & Wesson M39 and M59 series (which includes virtually every S&W self-loader made in the last forty years), and the SIG P series (the P220, 225, 226, 229, 230, etc.).

Why is the DA auto popular if it's harder to shoot? Good question, but one which entails more political than technical concerns. Essentially, police chiefs—who, of necessity, are image-conscious—are disconcerted by the image of the cocked-and-locked (Condition One) SA auto. They opt instead for the DA auto because it projects a softer image to the public. In addition, many people are still under the erroneous impression that the Condition One SA self-loader is somehow unsafe, while the Condition Two (hammer down) DA auto is not.

So much for the claim that DA autos, like their SA counterparts, are inaccurate! Here is a 50-meter group shot offhand with the SIG P226 9mm, using NATO 124-grain ball ammunition.

Firearms writer Jeff Cooper once jokingly labeled the DA auto as, "an ingenious solution to a non-existent problem," meaning that its concept is based upon misimpressions of and assumptions about the SA auto that, as discussed above, have long since been proven false.

Still, those impressions remain. As long as they do, the shift toward the DA auto will continue. However, from an efficiency standpoint, it can never produce the speed and accuracy combination easily achieved with the SA auto. Thus, as Cooper also put it, "While with it [the DA auto] you can perform some interesting rendition of 'Chopsticks,' with other designs you can have Beethoven! When your life's on the line, which do you want?" A point well taken, don't you think?

I have successfully completed the extremely difficult American Small Arms Academy (ASAA) Handgun Combat Master Qualification Course with eight different handguns: 1) Colt Government Model 45 ACP; 2) Colt Lightweight Commander 45 ACP; 3) Smith & Wesson M10 38 Special; 4) Browning P35 9mm; 5) Glock M17 9mm; 6) Glock M22 40 S&W; 7) CZ-75 9mm; and 8) Smith & Wesson M39 9mm. The course has 400 possible points and requires a minimum of 90 percent (360 points) to pass. Of the weapons listed above, I shot my lowest score with the DA M39. In fact, I made the pass/fail cutoff by a mere one point (90.3 percent), whereas with the other seven handguns (which utilized the SA auto and DA revolver concepts), my performance never fell below 95 percent. Why? That first double-action shot, that's why! Under time-pressure, it's tough to concentrate on squeezing through that long pull for the first shot and then, as the piece reverts to SA and the trigger changes position for subsequent shots, play "catch up" to meet the time limits.

Is the DA auto easier to train with? No, it is not. By virtue of its complexity, it requires more from the shooter than any other kind of system, while giving back less in return. As such, it presents a greater psychological obstacle for the student to overcome.

Is the DA self-loader safer? No, it is not. In fact, in my twenty-plus-year career as a firearms trainer and consultant, I have seen more accidental discharges with DA autos than with SA self-loader designs, because it forces its operator to perform more physical procedure with it. Not surprisingly, the novice often becomes confused to the point where safety is negatively affected.

Am I saying that the DA auto is worthless? Not at all. However, I am saying that *the concept upon which it is based limits your performance*. In other words, with proper training, you quickly reach a point where your skill level exceeds the capabilities of the weapon. It is without question the most difficult handgun design to master and is selected in preference to other weapon designs almost exclusively for political rather than technical or tactical reasons. As such, it is not the best choice for anyone who wishes to elevate his shooting skills to the highest point possible.

SA VS. DA SELF-LOADERS

FOR THE LAST few years we have seen an ever-increasing number of double-action (DA) self-loaders flood the market, some of good quality and some not. An astonishing stream of promotion has accompanied the flood, extolling the DA auto as being the solution to "contemporary combat handgunning problems."

Excuse me—contemporary combat handgunning problems? What differentiates so-called contemporary problems from "traditional" problems?

The basis for this claim to superiority appears to center on the issue of liability, rather than any real tactical or mechanical superiority. However, while I certainly don't discount that liability is a fact of modern life, its influence on the tactical aspects of life and death handgun encounters should not be allowed to reach disproportionate levels.

Some even go so far as to have us believe that protection against liability is more important than survival, e.g., the it's-better-to-be-killed-than-sued syndrome, or that you're more likely to be jailed or lose a civil suit if your pistol utilizes the single-action (SA) rather than DA concept.

Whoa now; just a minute, partner—slow down a mite.

By law, the determination as to what justifies the use of deadly force is based upon a comparison of events versus the written law, not what modifications were made on the weapon used or the mechanical concept it utilizes. Thus, if the weapon was legal and the reasons for its use were legitimate, everything else is irrelevant. Therefore, from a criminal liability standpoint—going to jail—there is no basis whatsoever for concern about whether the self-loader you use to save your life is SA or DA.

It is only in the event of a civil suit following the use of deadly force that attempts to prejudice you with a jury by using weapon type, trigger pull or modifications you made to your gun might occur. Moreover, the potential for such travesties is highly regionalized, with the northeastern part of the U.S. being at the top of the list, and is by no means a nationwide trend.

Think about this—a police investigation in your favor is pretty potent medicine in a subsequent civil suit, isn't it? So, perhaps too many are, in essence, putting the cart before the horse.

The "horse" we're talking about is self-defense efficiency—i.e., accuracy, power and speed—not lawyers. Like it or not, it is an irrefutable fact that with operators of equal skill, *the DA or "semi-DA" auto will always lose to the SA auto.* Why? The SA is faster and simpler to use under stress.

The old saw that cocked-and-locked (Condition One) SA autos are unsafe is just so much bunk, as is the notion that they require more training than a DA auto or revolver. As a professional trainer of more than two decades, I can in good conscience advise that this myth is quite easy to dispel. Just give me ten minutes with you on the range.

Yep, that's all it takes—*ten minutes.*

As a matter of fact, many people shoot better with a DA revolver than with a DA auto, due to the shift of the weapon from DA to SA after the first shot, necessitating a change in trigger finger position and a serious alteration of the shooter's thought processes.

With the exception of the Glock, which is claimed to be a "semi-DA" (which also makes it a semi-*SA*, by the way; it's just unpopular right now to call it such—liability, you know!), the DA-only concept as an attempt to rectify the DA-to-SA problem only makes it worse.

It does, however, offer a commercially viable option for advertising purposes, even if, from a human engineering and tactical standpoint, it's a step backward. As Jeff Cooper used to say, "It's an ingenious solution to a non-existent problem." Let's not forget that the nominal daddy of the SA auto, John Browning, originally designed it to be carried cocked and *unlocked*. His ideas eventually crystallized into the leg-

Taylor makes a good argument for the single-action auto as the better tool for winning the fight. This is the Colt M1911 45 ACP, the most famous combat handgun of the 20th century—and an SA auto.

endary Colt Model 1911 45, and again into the Browning Model 1935 9mm Hi-Power.

The inclusion of a grip safety and, eventually, a thumb safety was due to the U.S. Army's understandable concern over their troops' lack of safe pistol-handling ability, not the reliability or safety of the weapon's operational mechanism. In keeping with the fact that accidental discharges occur because people press the trigger when they shouldn't—not because they drop the cocked and unlocked gun—Browning abandoned the grip safety altogether when designing the P-35, with no ill effects whatsoever.

For in excess of six decades, these two pistols have amassed a battle record *galaxies* beyond that of any that have come along since. This could not possibly have happened if, as the primary representations of the classic SA auto, they were inherently unsafe, inaccurate or unreliable.

What matters to those who bet their lives on a handgun is that, because it's simpler in concept and easier to use, the SA auto is faster to the first shot than any DA and at least equal to a semi-DA like the Glock. This translates to higher hit probabilities under stress. Put in plain terms, it means that you can place accurate hits more quickly, particularly when presenting the weapon from a holster, than with any other design.

In contrast, as any cop who really knows about guns will admit, with a DA auto you can either: 1) throw away the first shot—the DA one—to quickly get the gun into SA mode, or 2) slow way down and grind your way through that awful DA trigger pull to accurately place your first shot.

All of this while the other guy is filling the air around your head with bullets.

Option number 1 wastes time you obviously do not have, thereby increasing your tactical liability. It also increases your criminal and civil liability because you're responsible for every shot you fire, no matter where it goes. Option number 2 also takes too long, thereby increasing your tactical liability by giving your opponent more time to neutralize you first.

Personally, I'd rather win the fight first and worry about being sued later. Wouldn't you? As the old gunfighter said, "I'd rather be judged by twelve than carried by six."

Most DA autos exhibit another problem, too. Their slide-mounted safety/hammer-drop/decock lever is poorly placed and is useless under stress if used as a safety. This results in most operators carrying the gun with it in the Off position. Talk about liability! Yet we rarely hear about this design flaw and the dangers it poses.

No one complains about the Glock safety either, even though it only blocks the trigger. Instead, they keep telling us that cocked-and-locked SA autos, in which the sear is blocked by the thumb safety, are somehow unsafe and therefore a liability hazard.

Whether this is deliberate disinformation or simple misinformation due to ignorance, the result is the same: The facts don't back up the claims. In fact, they contradict them. This is why there are more accidents with DA autos than with any other action type. Safer? Nope.

Let's not forget that the mission of the handgun is to provide its wearer with a reactive, defensive weapon with which he can regain control of his immediate environment when someone else attempts to take control away from him. The obvious priority, therefore, is to bring the piece into action quickly and neutralize the attacker with a minimum of shots fired and in the shortest possible period of time. By virtue of its superior speed and ease of operation, the SA auto offers the best means by which to accomplish this life-saving task.

The mission hasn't changed in over a hundred years, although many people seem to have forgotten this fact. Therefore, there is, in the tactical sense, no difference between contemporary and traditional combat handgunning problems.

What *has* changed, however, is that vicarious liability lawsuits have become something of a pastime in certain parts of the country. The gun manufacturers realize this and, like you and I, have no wish to become involved in such goings on if they can avoid it. Like everyone else, they're in business to make money, so why *not* promote the DA-is-safer idea for profit while protecting yourself at the same time? How can this be accomplished if you don't claim superiority? It's simple marketing; nothing more, nothing less. As far as I'm concerned, this is the *real* basis for the widespread promotion of the DA auto, even if no one wants to admit it.

The tactical mission of the handgun remains unchanged. Therefore, the means by which to best accomplish that mission—accuracy, power and speed—also remain unchanged. It is crystal clear that the SA auto, with its superior speed and ease of use under stress, is superior.

This is why the SA auto is anything but dead and the reason why I will continue to carry my cocked-and-locked Colt 45 or Browning P-35 and advocate them to others. First and foremost, *I want to win the fight.*

Then, and only then, will I concern myself with something that, by comparison to being killed, can only be regarded as being of secondary importance.

PICKING A POCKET PISTOL

OF ALL THE handguns used for self-defense, none is more underrated, derided or misunderstood than the pocket pistol. Because of its small size and low power, most experts dismiss it with a shrug, saying that it has no place in the world of combat handgunning.

I disagree. Among the earliest type of defensive handgun to appear, the pocket pistol has a history dating back more than 200 years and has enjoyed ever-increasing worldwide popularity and proliferation. Were it useless, as some would have us believe, this could not have taken place. As we have seen several times already, it's merely a matter of perspective.

Yes, the pocket pistol is small, making it the easiest kind of handgun to carry and conceal, a real advantage to many people. Everyone is different physically and socially, meaning that no one is built the same or lives the same lifestyle. In short, what is expected from the weapon, from person to person, is different. Unfortunately, too many writers and instructors give the impression that nothing smaller than a 9mm or 38 Special service handgun will suffice.

Nothing could be further from the truth. The most potent defensive handgun does us little good if, due to social requirements or lifestyle, its size and weight preclude us from carrying it. A 5-foot, 2-inch, 105-pound woman carrying a purse simply cannot reasonably conceal or conveniently carry a Colt M1911 45 ACP or some other form of service handgun because it's simply too large and heavy. Instead, she will opt for something smaller, something that she can carry with reasonable comfort and concealability. Most often, that "something" is a pocket pistol which, let's face it, beats nothing hands down when trouble comes calling.

The biggest so-called negative characteristic of the typical pocket pistol—sights that are too small to be seen quickly at high speed (or no sights at all)—isn't really much of a handicap when we consider the mission the weapon is intended to fulfill. Almost always, the weapon is utilized at ranges just outside arm's reach or even closer, thus it doesn't have to be capable of taking a man down at a range of 50 meters, as does the service handgun. A more realistic scenario for it would be a nurse, flat on her back in a darkened parking lot, fighting off a would-be rapist on top of her.

In the Ian Fleming novel *Goldfinger*, the villain showed

The pocket pistol, whether a revolver or self-loader, is typically small, light and not very potent. It is a highly specialized form of combat handgun demanding special attention.

(Below) The AMT Back Up 380 ACP has no sights of any kind. This should give us a clue as to the circumstances for which such weapons are intended—very close, very fast and very desperate!

James Bond his preferred handgun, a Colt Pocket 25 ACP auto, stating, "I always shoot for the right eye, and I never miss!" While clearly a bit of bravado, his statement tells us the pocket pistol's true purpose—up close and personal shooting. Under such conditions, its small or non-existent sights would pose no handicap.

No, the typical pocket pistol isn't very powerful, being chambered for the 22 rimfire, 25 ACP, 32 ACP or 380 ACP. However, again, let's remember the circumstances under which it is intended to be used. Our nurse stuffing her pocket pistol into the face or eyes of a rapist and pulling the trigger until the gun runs dry doesn't need all that much power to solve the problem. If you don't believe it *would* solve her problem, you'd better think again. Even small-caliber bullets that enter the cranial and/or ocular cavities cause nearly instant death or, at the very least, great discomfort, disorientation and loss of muscle coordination.

So, though the pocket pistol controversy rages endlessly, these guns continue to be purchased, carried and used by millions of people throughout the world, demonstrating irrefutably that, no matter what anyone says to the contrary, they do have a place. To gain a clear perspective, just look at it this way: Which would you rather have if attacked by a knife-wielding felon, a pocket-pistol or nothing? See what I mean?

Fortunately, in recent years, three handguns small enough to qualify as pocket pistols, yet with good sights and with service-pistol power, have appeared: the lightweight Colt Officer's Model in 45 ACP and two "micro-Glocks," the Model 26 9mm and Model 27 in 40 S&W. Nearly as small as a Walther PP or PPK, they possess the two most important characteristics of the full-size, duty-type handgun—high visibility sights and very good stopping power—thus making them highly desirable. Up until they appeared, the best we could hope for in lieu of a true pocket pistol was a small-

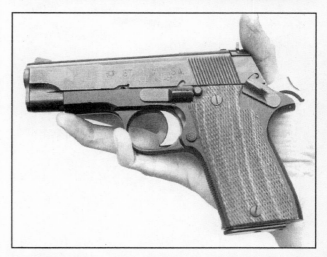

Although not true pocket pistols, the highly compact Star PD (above) and Colt Officer's Model 45 ACP subcompacts are nearly as small as a true pocket gun and much more powerful. They deserve serious consideration for such duty.

frame 38 Special such as the S&W Model 36 Chiefs Special or LadySmith Model 49 Bodyguard, Colt Detective Special or Cobra.

The reason pocket pistols suffer such constant criticism is that when they're evaluated, service-pistol rather than pocket-pistol criteria are usually used as the standards of judgment. As a result, the pocket model fares poorly because it cannot fulfill those requirements. Viewed from the proper perspective, all this means is that apples and oranges don't compare, not that pocket pistols are useless. As opposed to the service handgun, the little guns are intended for a tactically limited rather than general-purpose function—extreme close range and last-ditch emergencies, no more, no less.

If your lifestyle has social prohibitions to carrying a full-size, full-power duty-type handgun, or your physical build prevents you from efficiently handling one, then the pocket pistol offers an alternative to using your hands. In contrast to the many years it takes to learn the game of unarmed combat, you can learn to effectively use that pocket pistol in just a few days.

For this reason, I feel that these guns form a valid weapon system and, if used within their limitations, an effective one. Just be certain to first clearly define your needs.

Nearly as small as a true pocket pistol, the new Glock M26 (9mm)/M27 (40 S&W) offers virtually everything one could want from a fighting handgun, but in a *very* small package. This weapon is considerably more desirable than any true pocket pistol or 38 Special snubbie.

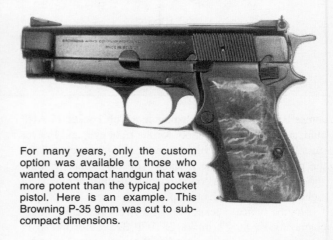

For many years, only the custom option was available to those who wanted a compact handgun that was more potent than the typical pocket pistol. Here is an example. This Browning P-35 9mm was cut to sub-compact dimensions.

This Colt Pocket 25 ACP has rudimentary sights, simply a groove running longitudinally down the top of the slide. For the ranges intended, they work.

The most potent of typical pocket pistols has been the venerable 38 Special "snubbie," but this is changing. At top is the Colt Cobra; bottom is the Smith & Wesson Model 36 Chiefs Special.

UNDERSTANDING THE SEMI-DOUBLE ACTION

FIRST APPEARING IN 1989, the Glock utilizes what has become known as a "semi-double-action" design, meaning that it is half-cocked when loaded. The first half of its trigger pull completes the cocking process, then the second half allows the gun to fire in the usual manner. A number of designs are similar, but for simplicity we'll confine our comments in this chapter to the Glock. This means that the clas-

sic Readiness Conditions apply, but in a slightly different form; e.g., since the weapon isn't fully cocked, there is technically no Condition One (cocked and locked) or Condition Two (loaded chamber, hammer down). Instead a sort of "Condition One-and-a-Half" is appropriate, however, Conditions Of Readiness Three, Four and Five legitimately apply.

First appearing in the late 1980s, the Glock "semi-DA" self-loader has taken the combat handgunning world by storm. Simple, accurate, yet highly reliable, it is perhaps the best fighting handgun in the world today, and it's available in several different configurations and calibers. At top is the M17 (9mm)/M22 (40 S&W), with the compact M19 (9mm)/M23 (40 S&W) below.

The Glock and its various clones, such as the Smith & Wesson Sigma series, make great use of polycarbonates for their frames and a number of working parts, thus allowing lighter weight, but without loss of structural integrity. The Glock, being essentially a military handgun, is finished with a super-tough matte Teflon-based substance that resists both the elements and holster wear very well.

In fact, the gun was the subject of considerable media attention in 1989-90, when several anti-gun political figures claimed that because of its polycarbonate construction it would pass through airport metal detectors unnoticed. This was, of course, untrue, since the slide, barrel and many of the internal parts are steel, and anyone who travels by air knows about the high degree of sensitivity of airport metal detectors. (I set them off with just a few small pieces of shrapnel I still carry from my military days.) In truth, the Glock is no more detection-proof than any other gun.

Nonetheless, had the law enforcement industry not gone to bat for the Glock, it would never have been approved for importation into the U.S., since it's a military weapon and thus subject to the restrictions imposed upon such hardware by the U.S. government. As far as I'm concerned, it's a good thing that they did, for the Glock is truly an excellent handgun, needing only minor modifications as it comes from the box to achieve its maximum potential.

Shortly after it first appeared, the Glock suffered consid-

erable criticism of its safety mechanism, because it merely blocks the trigger. This criticism was largely due to a number of spectacular accidental discharges by members of a large northeastern police department to whom it had just been issued. Actually, the real problem was poor training due to budget constraints, for the problem had existed with that particular department long before they began using Glocks. Placing the trigger finger in the trigger guard and contacting the trigger, thus unknowingly deactivating the safety of the Glock, had also caused a great many accidents with the Smith & Wesson Model 10 DA revolvers previously used by that department. This is, naturally, embarrassing and potentially dangerous, so no one guilty of the error wanted to admit their mistake. They blamed the gun instead.

The result of this well-publicized series of accidents sensitized Glock to the point where they felt compelled to counteract the negative publicity by embarking upon a large-scale publicity campaign of their own in which they described its concept of operation as a "Safe-Action" design, a term they still use today.

Was this just hype? No. There is nothing unsafe about the Glock pistol. The trigger-block safety is as effective as any other kind of safety, but by virtue of its inherent simplicity, it demands that the shooter be cognizant of where he is placing his trigger finger. This is a function of training, not mechanical design. In the interest of keeping a proper perspective, I

Another unique feature of the Glock is the rectangular, rather than circular, firing pin. At left is a 40 S&W cartridge fired in a Glock; at right, one fired in a Browning P-35.

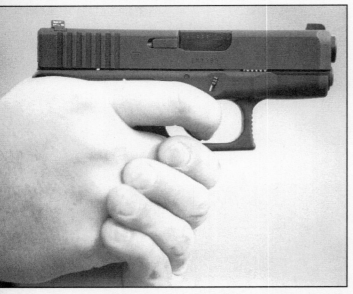

In the summer of 1995, Glock introduced the subcompact M26 (9mm)/M27 (40 S&W). These, too, have become highly sought-after sidearms and have added a new dimension to the world of pocket pistols.

The Glock's safety is a simple trigger block, actuated by pressing the trigger. Critics claim this to be unsafe, but an examination of accidents supposedly caused by this feature shows the operator and his training—or lack of it—to be the real culprit, not the gun.

must point out that the problem of putting the trigger finger inside the trigger guard and touching the trigger has caused many negligent discharges with all the other weapon designs, too. Again, training—or, in this case, a lack of it—was the real culprit here.

The Glock is perhaps the only truly revolutionary pistol design to surface since the first two decades of this century and reflects great engineering skill. It's simple, easy to disassemble and maintain, accurate and rugged almost beyond belief. In fact, I've been trying to wear one out for over five years without success. So far, my Model 17 9mm has ingested more than 125,000 rounds of full-power ammunition and is still going strong.

During the course of the test, the gun has been presented from a holster over 500,000 times, speed and tactical reloaded in excess of 100,000 times, and carried all over the world in virtually every natural environment possible. Yet, it has continued to function without so much as a hiccup. In my experience, no other handgun—even the legendary Colt M1911 45 ACP—can approach, much less duplicate or exceed, this performance.

From the box, the Glock is edge-free and ready to go, needing only replacement of its plastic sights, which wear too quickly when the gun is carried in a holster, to achieve full potential. In contrast to any other handgun, it thus requires far less modification to reach maximum efficiency.

However, for best results I recommend that you get one with the normal 5$\frac{1}{2}$-pound trigger, rather then the whopping 8-pound "New York" trigger, which is impossible to control at high speeds.

Some suggest that the Glock magazine is deficient because it often fails to fall clear of the weapon when the magazine release is actuated. I submit, however, that over-attention to the speed-loading concept, rather than any fault of the magazine or gun, is the basis for the complaint. Glock magazines hold from nine to as many as nineteen shots, depending upon caliber and whether or not the original or newer "politically correct" magazines are used. Realistically viewed, any of them hold more than enough ammunition to win a handgun encounter. So *who cares* if they don't always fall clear.

I've conducted more than 4000 handgun fight case studies and found only a dozen or so in which quick reloading was ever attempted. *In no case* did it materially affect the outcome of the fight. Why? Because the shooter was missing his targets and unnecessarily ran his pistol dry. Therefore, the real problem was poor marksmanship, not quick reloading capability. Without exception, in every case I evaluated, the shooter continued to miss his targets after he reloaded and, in the process, lost the fight.

Other critics claim the Glock is inaccurate, but such is not at all the case. My tests show it to be fully as accurate as any other handgun. Moreover, it is far less ammunition-sensitive

(Above and below) Another Glock innovation was the use of plastic sights, first in an adjustable version, then in fixed form. While the rear sights demonstrate adequate longevity, the plastic front blades wear down and are easily damaged, one of the few weaknesses of the Glock system.

Glock pistols in 40 S&W are rapidly gaining popularity in law enforcement circles because they offer an excellent combination of stopping power, accuracy, mechanical reliability and operational simplicity. Taylor feels that the 40 S&W Glock M22 ranks with the legendary Colt M1911 45 ACP as a top combat handgun.

than any other self-loader and feeds virtually any bullet shape without difficulty. Again, when I've investigated claims of inaccuracy, I found without exception that the real problem was that the shooter was at fault, not the gun. Again, we must consider the source of the complaint carefully before accepting it as fact.

Yet another, if somewhat bizarre, criticism is that Glocks are ugly. To this I can only respond that beauty is in the eye of the beholder. Self-defense weapons are tools, not *objet d'art* or toys. As such, aesthetic beauty is totally irrelevant and, in fact, may even be detrimental. Why? Because due to concerns about marring its aesthetic beauty you often won't carry it the way you should, making it much less effective as

From January, 1989 to July, 1996, Taylor attempted to wear out a Glock M17 9mm, firing over 125,000 rounds of full-power ammunition through it in all kinds of weather. The result? The gun is still going strong, though showing slight finish wear.

a life-saving instrument. As well, if environmental conditions are severe, for this same reason you may not carry it at all, leaving you completely unable to defend yourself.

In the case of the Glock, the term "beauty" must be defined from a functional standpoint, as a tool. Yes, there is not much we can do to make a Glock pretty, especially in comparison to the graceful lines of the Colt M1911 or Browning P-35. But let's not forget that the Glock will outlast them and function in a far wider spectrum of adverse environmental conditions than any other handgun in the world, meaning that viewed from the proper perspective it is beautiful indeed. Besides, its lack of aesthetic beauty is actually a boon. Because of it, we don't develop undue concerns for it and will carry it both when and how we should for maximum efficiency.

Excluding the long-slide target versions, Glocks are available in three sizes. The full-size versions are the M17 9mm, M20 10mm, M21 45 ACP and M22 40 S&W. Then there are the compacts: the M19 9mm, M23 40 S&W and M28 45 ACP. And, finally, the subcompacts: the M26 9mm and M27 40 S&W. This means that there is a Glock for virtually every tactical need.

Within both the law enforcement and civilian communities, the Glock has gained a huge measure of popularity because it is a viable alternative to both the SA and DA auto, without loss of efficiency in the process. In other words, it is "politically correct," but still highly efficient. It is one of the easiest handguns to shoot well under stress; simple to operate, disassemble and clean, accurate, rugged, and highly reliable. It is also the cleanest shooting self-loader I have ever seen, making the chore of weapon maintenance much easier.

The plain facts indicate the Glock is quite safe and easy to shoot, and it needs little to achieve its maximum potential. It's also tough, accurate and utterly dependable. In my opinion, this *is the best combat pistol in the world today* and well worth your consideration.

Glock Accuracy Test (25 Meters)

Glock Model	Load	Bullet (wt. grs./type)	Powder (wt. grs./type)	Group (ins.)
17 9mm Para.	Factory NATO	124/Ball	—	1.25
17 9mm Para.	Federal Hydra-Shok	124/JSP	—	.69
17 9mm Para.	W-W Black Talon	147/JHP	—	.86
17 9mm Para.	Federal Hydra-Shok	147/JHP	—	2.00
17 9mm Para.	W-W L.E.O.*	147/JHP	—	2.00
22 40 S&W	Handload	175/LSWC	4.8/Unique	1.75
22 40 S&W	W-W	180/FMJ	—	1.48
22 40 S&W	W-W Black Talon	180/JHP	—	1.25
22 40 S&W	Handload	190/LSWC	4.8/Unique	1.56
23 40 S&W	Handload	175/LSWC	4.8/Unique	2.05
23 40 S&W	W-W	180/FMJ	4.8/Unique	2.05
23 40 S&W	W-W Black Talon	180/JHP	—	1.69
23 40 S&W	Handload	190/LSWC	4.8/Unique	2.25

All groups fired from Ransom Rest.
*Law Enforcement Only

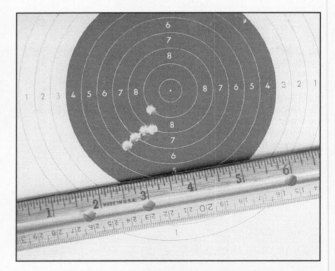

Some claim that the Glock isn't accurate, which is bunk. Here is a five-shot group with the Glock M17 9mm offhand from 25 meters.

COLD WEATHER & GUN RELIABILITY

OVER THE YEARS, many claims have been made about the mechanical reliability of various handguns. Many such claims originate from manufacturers who, understandably, want you to buy their product. Other opinions on this subject are endlessly cussed and discussed at the local gun shop.

In such places, a wide spectrum of customers from all walks of life and with an equally diverse firearms background espouse their views on many subjects. But I note that the topic of which handgun is the most reliable seems to come up more often than other subjects.

As the discussions progress from action types (revolver versus self-loader) to design types (DA or SA auto) to specific examples of each design (Beretta M92 vs. Glock M17, etc.), the discussions become more specific and, at times, heated.

And yet, although those involved in the discussions extoll the virtues of their particular choice, only rarely do they quote definitive data—that is, information derived from real-world, non-partisan sources.

Most information on firearms originates from promotional literature produced by manufacturers, which means that it may or may not be legitimate. We've all seen manufacturer's claims that are so fanciful that they can't possibly be taken seriously.

So, what sources are worth believing?

Good question—and one which had troubled me for years. Specifically, I wanted hard data on cold weather performance, lubricants, etc., but found little such information available that was not manufacturer-generated.

So, I went to Alaska with a suitcase full of handguns and various lubricants to find out for myself what got the job done in cold weather. With the assistance of resident American Small Arms Academy instructor Steve Myer, I was able to determine just that.

The test guns were either new or in mint condition and represented what I think to be a cross-section of typical designs encountered today:

Glock Model 17 9mm Parabellum
Browning P-35 9mm Parabellum
SIG P226 9mm Parabellum
S&W Model 39-2 9mm Parabellum
Beretta Model 92F 9mm Parabellum
Colt Model 1911 45 ACP
S&W Model 27 357 Magnum

I included the M27 Smith 357 as a control gun to examine the oft-made claims that revolvers are not as reliable as, or more reliable than, self-loaders. Not much real data on this can be found; so, I reasoned, why not create some?

First, to determine which gun design performed best, the question of lubricant performance had to be answered. The generality of modern lubes (Break-Free, Triflow, Rem-Oil, etc.) were all examined in a three-day test. In the -40 degree Fahrenheit temperatures in which the tests were conducted, it was found that a light coat of Rem-Oil performed the best.

Thus, the results that follow represent a best-case situation (i.e., results with other lubricants were less satisfactory than with Rem-Oil). Due to its Teflon composition and low viscosity, Rem-Oil has little density to congeal at low temperatures or trap powder fouling, both of which contribute to sluggish mechanical operation.

The gun test procedure was as follows:

A. All weapons were detail-stripped, cleaned thoroughly, and lightly lubricated with Rem-Oil as appropriate to each.

B. For each gun, 750 rounds of test ammunition (military-issue 124-grain 9mm Parabellum, 230-grain 45 ACP ball and standard factory 158-grain 357 Magnum) was inspected and allocated.

C. Each gun was loaded to specified capacity (full magazine or cylinder), rapidly fired until empty, quickly reloaded and then placed in the snow for fifteen minutes. It was my desire to test the guns realistically; thus, I did not freeze them in blocks of ice, etc., because doing so proves nothing.

D. The procedure was repeated until a malfunction was experienced and/or the 750 rounds were successfully expended.

E. The type and cause of each stoppage was noted, the weapon cleared, and the test procedure reinstituted until the gun either malfunctioned again or completed the test.

Please understand that I have no prejudice toward any particular weapon type or specific design. My motive here was simply to obtain data that could be of use in saving lives. All the guns used represent the high points of the technologies that produced them, and the test environment is one of the most difficult in existence. No one involved in the tests, myself included, had any idea what the results would be. Here is what I found:

S&W Model 39 9mm Parabellum

Type One malfunctions (failure to fire) occurred as follows:

Rd. #21 (5th shot, 3rd magazine)
Rd. #33 (1st shot, 5th magazine)
Rd. #38 (6th shot, 5th magazine)

Rd. #65 (1st shot, 9th magazine)
Rd. #89 (1st shot, 12th magazine)
Rd. #95 (7th shot, 12th magazine)
Rd. #129 (1st shot, 17th magazine)
Rd. #177 (1st shot, 23rd magazine)
Rd. #185 (1st shot, 24th magazine)
Rd. #186 (2nd shot, 24th magazine)
Rd. #193 (1st shot, 25th magazine)
Rd. #194 (2nd shot, 25th magazine)
Rd. #231 (7th shot, 29th magazine)

Comments: Full failure to function occurred on the 231st shot. The gun failed to complete the test program. All thirteen cartridges that failed to fire were loaded into the Beretta M92F and successfully fired.

Beretta Model 92F 9mm Parabellum

1. Type One malfunctions (failure to fire):
Rd. #2 (2nd shot, 1st magazine)
Rd. #3 (3rd shot, 1st magazine)
Rd. #222 (12th shot, 15th magazine)
Rd. #227 (2nd shot, 16th magazine)
2. Type Two stoppages (failure to eject):
Rd. #245 (5th shot, 17th magazine)
Comments: The gun successfully completed the 750-round test program.

The biggest surprise of Taylor's arctic tests was the flawless performance of the S&W Model 27 357 Magnum DA revolver, shown here being recovered from the snow during the tests.

SIG P226 9mm Parabellum

1. Type One stoppages (failure to fire):
  Rd. #88 (13th shot, 6th magazine)
  Rd. #89 (14th shot, 6th magazine)
  Rd. #90 (15th shot, 6th magazine)

Note: This malfunction was cleared each time, yet the gun still failed to fire. After the third stoppage, the weapon began to function again. Ice forming in the trigger linkage inside the frame was suspected, but we could not visually locate any evidence of this. The gun was reassembled and testing continued.

Comments: The gun successfully finished the 750-round test.

Glock Model 17 9mm Parabellum, Browning P-35 9mm Parabellum, Colt Model 1911 45 ACP, S&W Model 27 357 Magnum

Comments: No malfunctions of any kind were experienced. All successfully completed the test program.

Interesting, but what did we really learn? Careful analysis yields these conclusions:

I. Type One stoppages (failures to fire) are by far the predominant type in cold-weather operations. Why? Because springs lose much of their power at such low temperatures.

II. Ammunition propellant combustion at sub-zero temperatures is less than optimum, causing lower projectile velocities and breech pressures, and increased fouling from unburned powder.

The solution? A careful combination of strong striker/hammer and firing-pin springs, and a recoil spring that is not too heavy, will do much to either eliminate the problem entirely or reduce it to manageable levels.

III. From a design standpoint, new is not necessarily better. Of the four guns that completed the test without mal-

functioning, three—the Smith Model 27, the Colt M1911 and the Browning P-35, were all designed more than fifty years ago. The Glock M17 was the only weapon of modern design that successfully completed the test without stoppages.

The wild card was the Smith & Wesson Model 27. Many old-timers claim that, properly lubricated (read that as being lightly lubricated with a proper lubricant for the weather conditions), the DA revolver is as reliable as a self-loader. While the "wheelie" cannot withstand the field abuse an autoloader can tolerate and remain functional, our tests showed it can, without a doubt, be successfully prepared and utilized effectively in extreme cold weather environments.

IV. A Teflon-based, low-viscosity lubricant provides the reliable functioning we seek in sub-zero environments. For use above zero degrees, most conventional lubes will perform as claimed, but for sub-zero work, Rem-Oil is exceptionally efficient.

V. Some designs shoot considerably cleaner than others. Post-test examination of the four successful competitors showed the Glock 17 to be the cleanest. The other three—the Colt 1911, Browning P-35 and S&W Model 27—exhibited substantially more fouling. This fact was clearly obvious and was immediately commented upon by all personnel present.

The test provided the information I sought, and in some cases, the data it yielded surprised everyone involved. However, again I ask the reader to remember that it was conducted solely for the purpose of gathering information, not as an endorsement or condemnation of any particular handgun or design.

However, it also showed something that didn't surprise me at all—it graphically demonstrated that proper weapon selection and preparation can easily make the difference between life and death.

STOPPING POWER

FOR AT LEAST three decades, arguments have raged as to which handgun cartridges provide the best performance against human adversaries. In fact, even the methods by which they are evaluated have become controversial, causing no small amount of confusion among the less well informed and those charged with the responsibility of making departmental decisions on the subject. Speaking frankly, this has often placed law enforcement officers and defense-minded civilians in the position of being not only inadequately armed, but grossly outgunned by the criminal underculture.

Stopping-Power Math

It is tempting to use simple mathematics to rate cartridges; after all, this is how the manufacturers themselves rate them. Easily derived since the coming of the pocket calculator, kinetic energy (KE) was for a long time accepted as being a legitimate measurement of stopping power. Kinetic energy is computed by squaring bullet velocity (V), multiplying it by projectile weight (W) and then dividing by 450,240 to obtain the total in foot-pounds (ft-lbs). The higher the kinetic energy figure, the more efficient the cartridge is considered to be.

Four popular self-defense rounds (from left): 9mm Parabellum, 40 S&W, 10mm Auto, 45 ACP. Newcomers to the world of combat handgunning, the 40 Smith & Wesson and 10mm Auto cartridges now fill the void between the 357 Magnum and 45 ACP. Of the two, the 40 S&W has seen widespread acceptance and rapid proliferation, while, because of its lack of controllability with full-power loads, the 10mm is clearly on the way out.

$$KE = \frac{WV^2}{450,240}$$

But even way back, there were a few who doubted KE's veracity, particularly those who had actually seen handgun action. Among these was General Julian Hatcher, who noted that, more often than not, actual handgun-fight results contradicted KE-based predictions. As a result, when the Army commissioned Springfield Armory commandant Gen. John T. Thompson (of Thompson SMG fame) and Medical Corps surgeon Col. Louis LaGarde to conduct studies into the matter, Hatcher took a hard look at the results.

The resulting "Thompson-LaGarde Report," as it became known, was immediately accepted and for more than seven decades was the most respected study of the subject. Even today, eighty-five years later and in spite of our modern technology, many still consider it to be the most accurate and scientific study of its kind yet made.

The Thompson-LaGarde tests were unique because they utilized human cadavers and live cattle. These were surgically shot and, via autopsy, immediately examined to determine the physiological results. Today, socio-political considerations preclude this method, in spite of the existence of modern electronic analytical equipment.

After evaluating the tests, Hatcher revised his views on subject incapacitation and included momentum, cross-sectional area, and a form factor derived from projectile shape and composition. Appearing in the early 1920s, his now-famous "Hatcher's Formula of Relative Stopping Power"

$$H = \frac{MAF}{2}$$

mathematically appears thus:
where H = Hatcher's relative stopping power number; M = momentum; A = bullet cross-sectional area in square inches; and F = Hatcher's form factor, given below.

$$H = \frac{WAVF}{450,240}$$

This expression can be stated as:
where W = bullet weight in grains and V = muzzle velocity in fps.

$$H = \frac{Wd^2VF}{573,263}$$

will also give the same number if you'd rather not compute the area of the bullet.

Hatcher's form factor F is as follows:

Hatcher Form Factors	
——Bullet type——	F
FMJRN: Full metal jacket round-nose	900
LRN: Lead round-nose	1000
LFP: Lead flat point	1050
LSWC: Lead semi-wadcutter	1250
LWC: Lead wadcutter	1250

Being highly limited and therefore very specialized, all typical pocket pistols, such as this Walther PPK, utilize cartridges that exhibit very poor stopping power.

While somewhat complex and favoring the larger calibers, Hatcher's formula has long been accepted as being the closest "educated guess," as he himself put it, of why some cartridges incapacitate human targets more quickly than others. KE, on the other hand, leans heavily toward the higher velocity, smaller calibers like the 9mm Parabellum, 38 Special and 357 Magnum.

In the mid-1970s, handgun aficionado Jeff Cooper simplified Hatcher's formula into a more easily computed formula. His "Cooper Short Form" retains many of the essential concepts of Hatcher's work, but uses rounded-off values for bullet weight and velocity.

$$C = \frac{WVA}{1000}$$

A score of 20 or higher is "passing."

While without question on the right track, Cooper's for-

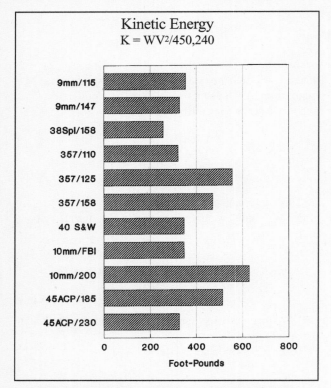

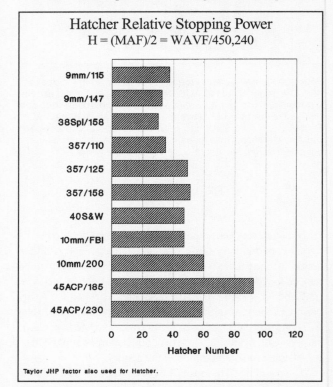

Taylor JHP factor also used for Hatcher.

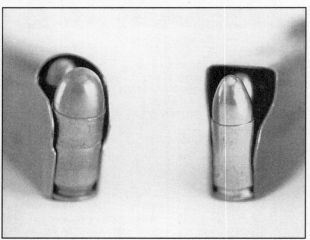

One of the longest-standing controversies in firearms history is the 45 ACP versus 9mm debate. It's been raging since the first decade of this century and continues as this is written. Which is "best," the large-caliber, heavy, slow-moving bullet of the 45 or the lighter, smaller, higher-velocity 9mm Parabellum?

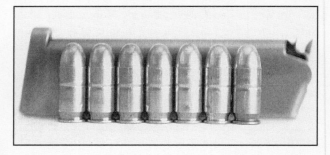

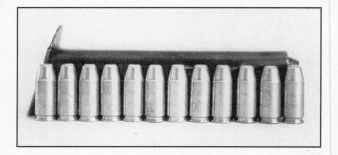

mula has two critical weaknesses. First, rounding off values reduces the formula's accuracy. Second, the formula does not include any form factor for different bullet shapes or composition.

In 1980 I expanded Cooper's basic concept by incorporating the critical form factor, which I call Y. I also use the exact bullet weight and velocity, thus providing a more accurate computation. Furthermore, I felt that jacketed hollowpoint (JHP) and jacketed softpoint (JSP) bullets also

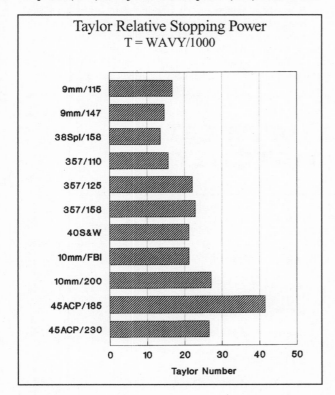

Taylor Relative Stopping Power
T = WAVY/1000

require consideration. Thus, I assigned them a form factor rating of 1.25 if their velocity exceeds 1088 fps, the speed of sound at sea level and the generally accepted velocity at which bullet expansion begins. Below 1088 fps, bullet expansion rarely occurs, earning a Y factor of 1.00, the same as a lead round-nose projectile. For that and other shapes I divide Hatcher's form factor by 1000.

My formula for Taylor Relative Stopping Power is

$$T = \frac{WAVY}{1000}$$

As with Cooper's formula, a score of 20 is passing.

Using my TRSP formula, a typical 38 Special load computes thus:

$$T = \frac{158 \times 0.1 \times 875 \times 1.0}{1000} = 13.8$$

The RII Blunder

In 1975 the National Institute of Justice, on behalf of the Law Enforcement Assistance Administration, published its famous—or infamous, depending upon how you view it— "Relative Incapacitation Index" (RII), sending copies of its summary report to every police department in the nation. Based upon the idea that the volume of the "maximum temporary cavity" was the prime factor in target incapacitation, the RII contradicted both the laws of nature and common logic. Yet, because it was government sponsored, it received for more than a decade what can only be called blind acceptance by many law enforcement agencies and most gun writers.

From the moment it first appeared, I vigorously opposed

Stopping Power is complicated by myriad different kinds of projectile weights, configurations and descriptive terminologies. To illustrate, here is a small cross-section in 9mm Parabellum (from left): S&W 90-grain RNJSP; Remington 117-grain JHP; Winchester 117-grain Silvertip JHP; S&W 124-grain JHP; Speer 127-grain JSP and JHP; 124-grain NATO Ball; Hornady 124-grain JTC; and KTW Teflon-coated AP. Critics of the 9mm claim that while it's easy to shoot well under stress, it demonstrates only marginal stopping power.

Perhaps the most famous combat handgun cartridge of all time is the 45 ACP (from left): Federal 187-grain JHP; Remington 187-grain JHP; Winchester Silvertip 187-grain JHP; Federal 187-grain Target (wadcutter); handloaded 200-grain Hensley & Gibbs #68 SWC; handloaded 227-grain RNL, Winchester 230-grain FMJ; Hornady 230-grain JTC; and Norma 230-grain JHP.

the RII as being not only invalid but actually dangerous, and I challenged it at every opportunity. In the August 1979 issue of *Soldier Of Fortune*, in an article entitled, "Handgun Stopping Power Revisited," I wrote:

> Many individuals have attempted more testing [than Hatcher's] by using gelatin blocks, modeling clay and even water to test bullet impact reaction. The key here is that none of these tests uses live organisms, and therefore their results are only academic measures of how various cartridges compare with each other in that medium.
>
> I have always been suspicious of such tests because of this fact. They cannot be considered relevant in the stopping-power issue since their conclusions are based on results obtained from testing with irrelevant mediums. Normally, the recommendations from such testing do not conform,

even remotely, with results that are actually observed in real gunfights. Obviously, something is drastically wrong, and I, for one, choose to believe in what actually happens when people shoot each other on the street or battlefield, rather than some test conducted out of context.

The most recent, and notorious, of such tests were conducted by the Law Enforcement Assistance Administration of the U.S. Justice Department. The testing medium was composed of gelatin blocks, with high-speed X-ray photography of bullet passage and resultant temporary wound cavity. The results were based on the assumption that: 1) hollowpoint bullets that expand in gelatin also expand in human bodies; 2) the temporary wound cavity created at the instant of bullet passage causes incapacitation; and 3) human vulnerabilities are the same from person to person.

First, it is a well-documented fact that HP and SP bullets do not reliably expand in humans. Anyone who doubts this

SIMILARITIES BETWEEN TAYLOR AND HATCHER

THE CLEVER READER will notice the similarity of Hatcher's formula to Taylor's. It can be shown that they differ only by a constant, as follows:

$$H = \frac{WAVF}{450,240} \quad \text{and} \quad T = \frac{WAVY}{1000}$$

$$\frac{H}{T} = \frac{\dfrac{WAVF}{450,240}}{\dfrac{WAVY}{1000}} \quad \text{or} \quad \frac{WAVF}{WAVY} \times \frac{1000}{450,240}$$

Cancelling the WAVs and reducing the fraction, we get:

$$\frac{H}{T} = \frac{\dfrac{F}{Y}}{450.24}$$

We know that Hatcher's F = 1000 times Taylor's Y, or F = 1000Y. Plugging this into the above, we get:

$$\frac{H}{T} = \frac{\dfrac{1000Y}{Y}}{450.24}$$

The Ys cancel and we arrive at H/T = 1000/450.24, or H/T = 2.22

This tells us that if we know either of the values, Taylor's or Hatcher's, we can easily find the other.

Chuck Taylor added the form factor for bullet types that were not invented at Hatcher's time and hedges his bet by

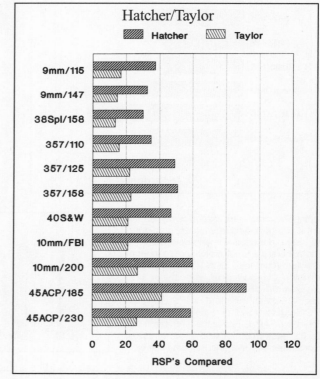

giving a velocity above which the bullet may expand, resulting in 25-percent better stopping power than otherwise. Taylor's values are a bit easier to calculate and comprehend, hence their popularity over Hatcher's.

is free to examine the approximately 100 bullets I have in my possession that have passed through living organisms, including humans. The discomforting fact of the matter is that such bullets, while immensely salable and nice to look at, only expand about 50 percent of the time.

The second fallacy of the LEAA "tests" is the assumption that the temporary wound cavity created at the instant of bullet passage through the target is critical to incapacitation. In reality, that cavity collapses within milliseconds of bullet exit, leaving the real cause of incapacitation—the permanent wound cavity, i.e., the real amount of damage done to the tissue during bullet passage. This is why the big-bore cartridges are superior: They punch bigger holes.

Not quite two years later, in *The .45 Auto Handbook* (Harris Publications, New York City, May 1981), I again stated my opposition. In the chapter titled, "Stopping Power: An In-Depth Review," I stated:

> As far as the temporary wound cavity is concerned, I categorically disagree. The human body paste is amazingly flexible, and that temporary cavity collapses within milliseconds of the bullet's passing, leaving what I feel is a more important and relevant measure of its effect: the permanent wound cavity. It is here that the extent of tissue/nerve damage can be assessed more definitively.
>
> It is ridiculous to assume that a "computer man" can produce results commensurate with reality when there are so many uncontrollable variables ignored by the LEAA. What is proven, however, is that when one feeds garbage into a computer—one gets garbage out of a computer. No more, no less.

I took RII to task a third time in my book, *The Complete Book of Combat Handgunning* (Paladin Press, Boulder, Colorado, April 1982). In Chapter Six, "Handgun Stopping Power: The Name of the Game," I wrote:

Here's a selection of loads for the famous 38 Special, long-standing friend of the American lawman from 1902 until about 1990, when it was generally phased out due to concerns about its marginal stopping power and the limited ammunition capacity of revolvers chambered for it (from left): Glaser Safety Slug; Winchester 110-grain JHP; Winchester 125-grain JHP; Winchester 158-grain SWCHP (semi-wadcutter hollowpoint); Remington 158-grain SWCHP; and Federal Nyclad 158-grain SWCHP.

To say the least, the results were interesting, and the so-called preliminary report was circulated to every law enforcement agency in the U.S. The "findings" disclosed in the preliminary report failed totally to correspond to reality.

The subsequent full report contradicted the preliminary report substantially. However, it was not widely circulated, for some reason. In an effort to explain the horrendous difference between reality and the results of the preliminary report, at least one firearms expert of considerable reputation advised me that he knew for a fact that the entire program was an attempt to justify the small caliber for law enforcement use, and that members of the test staff had actually admitted this in private.

Whether or not this is true, it is safe to say that many of the assumptions made by the LEAA test group were arbitrary and, to say the least, invalid. Therefore, it is certainly no surprise that when these assumptions were programmed into the computer in conjunction with the other data, the results were less than accurate.

RII Exposed

During the following decade, an ever-growing number of ballisticians and forensic pathologists agreed, the most noteworthy of whom was Dr. Martin Fackler, former head of the prestigious U.S. Army wound ballistics laboratory. In the much-publicized 1987 FBI-sponsored "Wound Ballistics Workshop," Dr. Fackler minced no words:

> Much responsibility must lie with the National Institute of Justice for whom the seriously flawed Relative Incapacitation Index studies were done. The studies ranked bullets solely according to the temporary cavity produced in ordnance gelatin. They assumed that incapacitation of the human target by a given bullet is directly proportional to temporary cavity size. No physiologic mechanism was even postulated for this supposed effect—much less proved. Temporary cavity for a given bullet can be

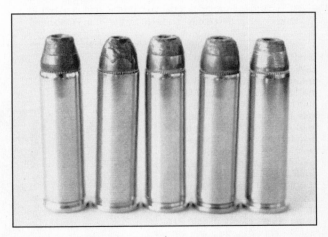

The much "cussed and discussed" 357 Magnum is perhaps the most misunderstood handgun cartridge in existence (from left): ancient Super-Vel 110-grain JHP; Remington 125-grain JHP; Federal 127-grain JHP; Speer 140-grain JHP; and Federal 158-grain JHP.

increased very simply by decreasing bullet weight and increasing velocity. The 9mm 115-grain Silvertip bullet which penetrates only 21.1cm (in ballistic gelatin) is an example of the new generation of lighter-weight/higher-velocity bullets that have been produced as a result of this unfortunate but influential study.

The critical consideration is that the bullet produce its permanent tissue disruption to sufficient depths to ensure major vessel disruption from any angle. Of the bullets that attain this goal, common sense would indicate that the largest one would be the most effective, since it would put a larger hole in heart or vessels.

For fifteen years, I was attacked by a number of writers because I continually pointed out that recorded history, simple mathematics and common logic disputed RII-based "proof" of the 9mm Parabellum's equality to the 45 ACP. But now I no longer had to stand alone. I had an ally—Dr. Fackler, whose scientific and medical conclusions mirrored my own, which were based upon real-world field experience.

It didn't stop there. Dr. Carrol Peters, University of Tennessee Space Institute, also stated:

For commonly used handgun loads, temporary cavity formation plays a negligible role in tissue damage. Therefore, the widely publicized RII methodology, which relates incapacitation only to the size and shape of the temporary cavity, is incorrect and should be abandoned.

A handgun/load combination should not be selected solely on the basis of soft-tissue performance. Other factors which should be considered include: 1) capability of penetrating "hard" materials and textile body armor, 2) the controllability of the load in the handgun selected, and 3) the occasional need for adequate terminal-ballistic performance at ranges exceeding a few meters.

With the best of the currently available bullets, the 45 ACP cartridge provides a damage profile that is closer to optimum than the profile produced by the 9mm Parabellum cartridge. For similar impact kinetic energies, a similar bullet [to that of the 45 ACP] will cause more tissue damage than is caused by a smaller and lighter bullet. Consequently, I recommend that the 45 ACP be at least an optional pistol.

The avalanche began. Yet another preeminent scientist, Dr. O'Brien C. Smith of the University of Tennessee Medical Center, then publicly stated:

Caliber is the basic bullet dimension which produces injury at any given wound depth (a function of mass, velocity and shape). If a 45 and 9mm expand to the same diameter at the same rate and reach the same depth, they will produce identical injury. If they do not expand, the 45 produces more injury at the same depth than does the 9mm.

Hollowpoint bullets are good in concept, but no bullet should be selected if it depends upon or requires bullet expansion. Frequent failures to expand will be encountered due to abdominal shots, intermediate targets with closure of the tip, cocoons forming from lofted fiber insulation in clothing, etc.

RII Rejected

Following the 1985 "Dade County Massacre," in which two FBI agents were killed and five more seriously injured by a felon already shot through the heart with a 115-grain 9mm Silvertip JHP, requests for authorization to use the 45 ACP were repeatedly received at FBI headquarters. The Bureau immediately responded by initiating a series of handgun stopping power tests of their own, which subsequently *contradicted the RII*. As a result, the 45 ACP 230-grain "hardball" and Remington 185-grain JHP loads were quickly approved. Simultaneously, because it provided slightly better penetration, a special reduced 10mm (180-grain JHP at 933 fps) load was also approved.

There was much banter about the then-new 10mm cartridge, and, inevitably, claims about its equality or superior-

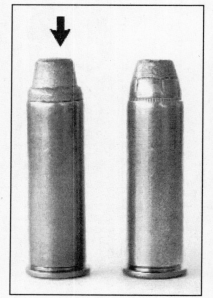

A classic case of mistaken identity is the 41 Magnum. Initially intended as a law enforcement replacement for the 38 Special and 357 Magnum back in 1964, it was available in both standard (called "mid-range" at the time) and magnum loadings. However, most police departments mistakenly obtained the hot 225-grain JHP load (right), rather than the mid-range 210-grain SWC load intended for self-defense (arrow). Finding it to be painfully uncontrollable in fast DA shooting, they quickly abandoned it, triggering an immediate slide in the cartridge's popularity. Today, the 41 Magnum has all but disappeared as a self-defense cartridge, which is unfortunate because it exhibits excellent stopping power.

The 44 Special is a highly accurate cartridge with mild recoil that offers good stopping power (from left): Glaser Safety Slug; 247-grain Keith SWC handload; 250-grain JTC; and factory 246-grain round-nose lead.

ity to the 45 ACP quickly surfaced. The original 10mm load propelled a 200-grain JTC bullet at a sizzling 1200 fps, producing 30,000 psi breech pressure, which was far in excess of that which a typical self-loader was designed to tolerate. Not only did the load abuse the weapon, but muzzle flip and felt recoil were so excessive as to make the load unmanageable. Hence came the FBI's decision to use the reduced load.

In *Combat Handguns* (Harris Publications, New York City, December 1988), in an article entitled, "A Hard Look at the Colt Delta Elite 10mm," I concluded: "For combat purposes, the 10mm has not yet reached maturity. At present it is excessively penetrative and generates too much recoil and muzzle flip for defensive use."

Also included in that article was my recommendation that loads in the 900 fps bracket would provide the degree of weapon control necessary for satisfactory defensive use. Shortly thereafter, Federal commercially introduced their highly publicized "FBI Load," consisting of a 180-grain JHP at 933 fps. The load was a success and continues to be offered as this is written.

The reduced 10mm load, while quite accurate and comfortable to shoot, fails to equal the 45 ACP in any service

Originally intended to be used in the Model 1917 Colt and Smith & Wesson revolvers, the 45 Auto Rim duplicates the performance of the rimless 45 ACP, but with a rimmed cartridge for normal loading and extraction. The rimless 45 ACP requires half- or full-moon clips to work best (above). For those who prefer a big-bore DA revolver, it's an excellent choice. The 230-grain RNL factory load (left) is compared to the author's favorite self-defense hand-load, the 250-grain Keith SWC and a stout load of Unique.

loading, a point many shooters have failed to realize. The FBI's ranking of the 10mm ahead of the 45 was based upon the Norma 200-grain JTC at 1200 fps, not the load they subsequently adopted. Nonetheless, that the Bureau's own tests discredited the RII was a milestone in handgun history, as was its decision to authorize larger calibers.

By 1991 Dr. Fackler had successfully achieved another important goal, the correlation between bullet performance in living tissue and ballistic gelatin. This gave us the means by which to realistically evaluate said performance using an artificial medium. To his further credit, Fackler adamantly included in his findings that the corollary does not take into consideration bones or clothing, or intermediate objects such as automobile bodywork, wood, body armor, etc.

For this reason, in 1992 I programmed my computer to provide an overall evaluation of some typical service handgun loads, factoring in these percentages of the following criteria:

Performance Factors

Item	Relative importance overall
Kinetic Energy	20%
Taylor Relative Stopping Power	30%
Muzzle Flash & Recoil	30%
Penetration, Body Armor	10%
Penetration, Automobile Glass & Bodywork	10%
Total	**100%**

Factored Performance Ratings

Cartridge	Rating
9mm Parabellum	
1. Glaser Safety Slug	82.21
2. Com Ball, 115 gr.	87.41
3. Rem JHP, 115 gr.	105.67 *
4. W-W Silvertip JHP, 115 gr.	100.66 *
5. Mil Ball, 124 gr.	96.63
6. U.S. Gov't JHP +P+, 147 gr.	104.28 *
38 Special	
1. Glaser Safety Slug	101.70 *
2. US "Treasury Load" JHP +P+, 110 gr.	99.21
3. W-W JHP +P, 125 gr.	82.46
4. US Gov't M-41 Ball, 130 gr.	72.11
5. Federal LSWCHP +P, 158 gr.	117.41 *
357 Magnum	
1. Glaser Safety Slug	128.80
2. W-W JHP, 110 gr.	121.45
3. Federal JHP, 125 gr.	131.05 *
4. Rem JHP, 158 gr.	141.20 *
5. Federal LSWC, 158 gr.	150.55 *
45 ACP	
1. W-W Silvertip JHP, 185 gr.	143.72
2. Rem JHP, 185 gr.	148.72
3. Speer Lawman JHP, 200 gr.	161.70 *
4. Mil Ball, 230 gr.	153.55 *

* Top performers.

Defensive Cartridge Stopping Power Ratings
Table 1: 9mm Parabellum

| Maker | —Bullet— | | Velocity | Kinetic Energy | —Hatcher— RSP Expand? | | —Taylor— RSP Expand? | |
	Wgt. grs.	Type	(fps)	(ft-lbs)	Yes	No	Yes	No
Glaser	79	SS	1455	371	31.6	25.3	14.2	11.4
Hirtenberger	100	JSP	1381	424	38.1	30.4	17.1	13.7
CCI	100	JSP	1254	349	34.5	27.6	15.5	12.4
W-W	115	FMJ	1069	292	-	24.3	-	10.9
Chicom	115	FMJ	1143	334	-	26.0	-	11.9
R-P	115	JHP	1176	353	37.2	29.7	16.7	13.4
Cor-Bon	115	JHP+P	1333	454	42.1	33.7	19.0	15.2
Federal	115	JHP	1142	335	36.1	28.9	163	13.0
W-W	115	JHP	1175	353	37.1	29.7	16.7	13.4*
Mullins	115	JHP+P+	1443	532	45.6	36.5	20.5	16.4
CCI	115	JHP	1174	352	37.1	29.7	16.7	13.7
Federal	123	FMJ	1048	300	-	25.5	-	11.5
NATO	124	Ball	1146	362	-	28.1	-	12.7
Federal H/S	124	JHP	1109	339	37.8	30.2	17.0	13.6
Federal H/S	147	JHP	1000	326	40.4	32.3	18.2	14.6
W-W(LEO)	147	JHP	979	313	39.6	31.6	17.8	14.2
W-WB/T	147	JHP	988	319	39.9	31.9	18.0	14.4
Cor-Bon	147	JHP	1001	327	40.5	32.4	18.2	14.6*

Table 2: 38 Special

| Maker | —Bullet— | | Velocity | Kinetic Energy | —Hatcher— RSP Expand? | | —Taylor— RSP Expand? | |
	Wgt. grs.	Type	(fps)	(ft-lbs)	Yes	No	Yes	No
Glaser	80	SS	1512	406	33.6	26.9	15.4	12.3
W-W LEO	110	JHP+P+	1129	311	34.5	27.6	15.8	13.4
Cor-Bon	110	JHP+P	1289	406	39.4	31.5	17.7	14.2
R-P	125	JHP+P	847	199	29.4	23.5	13.5	10.8
W-W	125	JHP+P	861	206	29.9	23.9	13.7	11.0
W-W	130	Ball	709	145	-	18.4	-	8.5
W-W New	130	Ball	983	279	-	25.6	-	11.5
Cor-Bon	147	JHP+P	989	319	40.4	32.3	18.5	14.8
R-P	158	LSWCHP+P	833	244	36.6	36.6	16.5	16.5
Federal	158	LSWCHP+P	874	268	38.4	38.4	17.3	17.3
W-W	158	LSWCHP+P	875	269	39.2	39.2	17.6	17.6
R-P	158	RNL	855	257	-	30.0	-	13.5*
WCC-60 USAF	158	Ball	775	211	-	24.9	-	11.2

Table 3: 357 Magnum

| Maker | —Bullet— | | Velocity | Kinetic Energy | —Hatcher— RSP Expand? | | —Taylor— RSP Expand? | |
	Wgt. grs.	Type	(fps)	(ft-lbs)	Yes	No	Yes	No
Glaser Safety Slug	80	SS	1563	434	34.7	27.8	15.9	12.8
W-W	110	JHP	1146	321	35.0	28.0	16.1	12.6*
Cor-Bon	115	JHP	1344	461	42.9	34.3	19.3	15.5
Cor-Bon	125	JHP	1423	562	49.4	39.5	22.3	17.8
W-W	125	JHP	1411	553	49.0	39.2	22.1	17.7
Federal	125	JHP	1421	561	49.3	39.3	22.2	17.8
R-P	125	JHP	1414	555	49.1	39.3	22.1	17.7*
Speer	140	JHP	1321	543	51.4	41.1	23.1	18.5
W-W	158	LSWC	1267	563	-	55.6	-	25.0
Federal	158	JHP	1158	471	50.8	40.7	22.9	18.3*
R-P	158	JHP	1134	451	49.8	39.8	22.4	17.9

Table 4: 40 S&W

Maker	—Bullet— Wgt. grs.	Type	Velocity (fps)	Kinetic Energy (ft-lbs)	—Hatcher— RSP Expand? Yes	No	—Taylor— RSP Expand? Yes	No
Cor-Bon	150	JHP+P	1327	587	69.6	55.7	31.4	25.1
R-P	155	JHP	1012	353	54.9	43.9	24.7	19.8
CCI	155	JHP	1023	360	55.5	44.4	25.0	20.0
Cor-Bon	180	JHP+P	1034	427	65.1	52.1	29.3	23.5
W-W	180	JHP	956	365	60.2	48.2	27.1	21.7
CCI	180	JHP	941	354	59.3	47.4	26.7	21.3
Federal H/S	180	JHP	930	346	58.7	46.9	26.4	21.1
W-W	180	B/T JHP	933	348	58.8	47.0	26.5	21.2
W-W	180	SXT JHP	936	350	58.9	47.2	26.5	21.3
R-P	180	JHP	932	347	58.7	47.0	26.4	21.2*

Table 5: 10mm Auto

Maker	—Bullet— Wgt. grs.	Type	Velocity (fps)	Kinetic Energy (ft-lbs)	—Hatcher— RSP Expand? Yes	No	—Taylor— RSP Expand? Yes	No
Cor-Bon	135	JHP+P	1442	623	68.1	54.5	30.7	24.6
Federal	155	JHP+P	1322	602	71.7	57.4	32.3	25.8
W-W S/T	175	JHP+P	1190	550	72.9	58.3	32.8	26.2
Federal	180	JHP	933	348	58.8	47.0	26.5	21.2
W-W	180	JHP	924	341	58.2	46.6	26.2	21.0
R-P	180	JHP	932	347	58.7	47.0	26.4	21.1*
R-P	200	FMJ+P	1189	628	-	60.0	-	27.0*
Norma	200	JTC+P	1216	657	-	71.6	-	32.3

Table 6: 45 ACP

Maker	—Bullet— Wgt. grs.	Type	Velocity (fps)	Kinetic Energy (ft-lbs)	—Hatcher— RSP Expand? Yes	No	—Taylor— RSP Expand? Yes	No
Cor-Bon	185	JHP+P	1133	528	92.5	74.0	40.9	33.3
W-W S/T	185	JHP	876	315	71.6	57.2	32.2	25.8
Federal	185	JHP	901	334	73.6	58.9	33.1	25.5
R-P	185	JHP	914	343	74.7	59.7	33.6	26.9
R-P	185	JHP+P	1118	514	91.3	73.1	41.1	32.9*
CCI	200	JHP	1010	453	89.2	71.3	40.1	32.2
Cor-Bon	200	JHP+P	1034	475	91.3	73.0	41.1	32.9
Cor-Bon	230	JHP+P	943	454	95.8	76.6	43.1	34.5
Federal H/S	230	JHP	840	360	85.3	68.2	38.4	30.7
R-P	230	FMJ	797	324	-	58.5	-	26.4
W-W	230	FMJ	800	327	-	58.7	-	26.5
Federal	230	FMJ	801	328	-	58.8	-	26.5
WCC-'62	230	Military Ball	799	326	-	58.7	-	26.4*

A minimum Hatcher score of 50 is considered satisfactory, as is a minimum Taylor score of 20.
* indicates this load was used in the accompanying bar-charts.
Abbreviations: S/T=Silvertip; H/S=Hydra-Shok; LEO=Law Enforcement Only; JHP=jacketed hollowpoint; JSP=jacketed softpoint; Ball=FMJ=full metal jacket; W-W=Winchester-Western; B/T=Black Talon; LSWCHP=lead semi-wadcutter hollowpoint; WC=wadcutter; SS=Safety Slug +P=Loaded to higher than industry specifications; +P+=Loaded to *considerably* higher than industry specifications, and thus not recommended for sustained use, as it will shorten weapon service life.
Test Guns: 9mm=Glock M17 (4.5-inch bbl.)
38 Special=S&W Model 10 (4-inch bbl.)
357 Magnum=Colt Python (4-inch bbl.)
40 S&W=Glock M22 (4.5-inch bbl.)
10mm Auto=Colt Delta (5-inch bbl.)
45 ACP=Colt Government Model (5-inch bbl.)

The listing shows how these cartridges rank on an aggregate basis. By using this format, no one thesis is dominant, thus eliminating prejudice. Some interesting and enlightening data is obtained, regardless of caliber preferences.

More Theories

Later in 1992, yet another "study" emerged, this time in a book concerning handgun stopping power. Authored by two gun writers, the book espoused some interesting "revelations," among which was the repeated claim that the authors' favorite load, the 357/125 JHP, was a better manstopper than the proven 45 ACP/230 ball.

The conclusions of this book were supposedly based upon a review of several hundred police shootings, the actual sources of which were never disclosed. I, for one, wonder about this because, due to civil liability concerns, law enforcement agencies are loath to disclose such information to their own firearms-training personnel, much less to the general public. Many people have therefore questioned the credibility—and even the existence—of the source material itself.

Moreover, even a casual perusal of the book shows that its real focus is 1) to lend credence to the pet theories of its authors, the 357 Magnum/45 ACP business discussed above being one example, and 2) to discredit the concept of the one-shot stop, which the authors call a "myth." This issue was addressed and discarded more than a decade before the book appeared. This goal has been a long-time, vehement and well-publicized pet project of both writers, who have also written many magazine articles devoted to that end.

While several hundred shootings were supposedly analyzed, there was never any discussion of where the victims were actually hit. Thus, no corollary to anything was ever established. The controversy of the one-shot stop has for more than six decades centered on a comparison of the various calibers/loads with hits in the thoracic (chest) cavity. Yet, there was no comparison of one caliber/load to another within that category.

To my knowledge, no one has ever seriously claimed that a superficial or abdominal hit with a 45 was more effective than a thoracic hit with a 357, 9mm or anything else. Therefore, the book's conclusions are out of context and, by implication, meaningless. If anything, all that is proven is that its authors fail to understand the issues integral to the subject about which they write.

The latest study (1993) of handgun stopping power is the so-called "Strasbourg Tests," in which a sizeable number of live goats were shot and the results collated, analyzed and subsequently published. Immediately, a number of pathologists pointed out that goats aren't people and that results from a study using them, unless linked to some kind of corollary or computer model, are meaningless.

They have a point. It's true that, while goats might approximate average human weight and general organic geography, people exhibit a number of characteristics that goats—or any other non-human animal—do not. Among these are a highly variable day-to-day emotional state, pronounced differences in physical build (muscle bulk and tone, bone structure, etc.), and a unique nervous system.

All of these things greatly influence stopping power and must be addressed. However, on the other hand, shooting live animals beats simply shooting inert substances like clay, phone books and water jugs, and then making sweeping conclusions based upon the results obtained in those media alone.

Final Choices

So, there you have it, seventy-five years of stopping power controversy. My conclusions? What do I prefer? Well, its never been a secret that I'm a proponent of the big-bore (40/10mm minimum) in general, and the 45 ACP in particular. But, as you consider this, remember that my preference is based upon a detailed historic review, considerable personal experience and, now, properly collated scientific data as well.

Nonetheless, you must reach your own conclusions. However, don't forget that you may weppll be betting your life on them, a sobering fact that should at all times be kept in mind.

In general, I recommend that you use the most potent handgun/load that *you can effectively use*. A miss or poorly placed hit with a 45 cannot possibly be as effective as a solid thoracic hit with something smaller.

Hollowpoints, if they expand, enhance performance and reduce overpenetration concerns, but they must be given realistic consideration. They are not capable of causing night-to-day improvements in performance.

Remember that only the hits count. Get some competent formal training in how to use that weapon/cartridge/load. There is much more to the subject of defensive pistolcraft than just guns and ammunition. Tactical, criminal and civil liability demand that you do this or you're courting disaster, no matter what your weapon and ammunition choices.

If you give these considerations proper emphasis, you can't go too far wrong.

CONTROLLABILITY: FLASH, BLAST AND RECOIL

IF YOU WERE to ask the average self-defense handgunner, "What do you think is the most important element in combat handgunning?", what do you think his answer would be? Some would reply that accuracy is the keystone of successful shooting; others that stopping power is the most critical factor. Still another might claim that without penetration, nothing happens, while someone else will say that it all starts with functional reliability. Yet another might respond that weapon controllability should take precedence.

As is perhaps obvious, all of these elements are important, critical, in fact, to successful self-defense shooting. However, no one element is all-encompassing—they're all part of an overall package in which each shares nearly equal importance, and they must all be present to achieve maximum efficiency.

Stopping power was dealt with previously, so let's consider those issues that remain—accuracy, penetration, functional reliability and weapon controllability. How much

accuracy do we need for self-defense? Well, many writers, IPSC competitors, and the gunsmiths who cater to them claim that nearly every handgun needs extensive modification and so-called "accurizing" to produce best results.

I disagree. The vast majority (more than 90 percent) of handgun encounters take place at close range, 7 to 10 *feet* (not yards or meters) being the norm. Therefore, considering that accurizing also reduces the tolerances critical to reliable functioning, I honestly don't feel that it's necessary. In fact, I doubt seriously if there is a shooter whose ability exceeds the accuracy capability of their handgun as it comes from the box. At typical combat handgunning ranges, hitting a man in the chest (the average dimensions of which are approximately 11 inches wide by 13 inches high) doesn't require National Match accuracy. Even at 50 meters, virtually all service handguns are sufficiently accurate to hit a target that size. . . but is the shooter? Statistically, the answer is no, which is one reason engagement ranges tend to be so short.

Even when small or partially obscured targets at close range are involved, the real problem isn't related to the weapon's inherent accuracy. It's getting the shooter to focus on what I call the Three Secrets of Successful Shooting: sight alignment, sight picture and trigger control. And make no mistake, when you're terrified to the point of being in fear for your life, this task becomes *quite* difficult, far more so than most people realize.

How do we overcome this problem? Training, that's how. And I don't mean just going to the nearby dump and potting at tin cans or taking a few lessons from a local police instructor. I mean *serious, organized, formal* training, such as is provided at Front Sight Firearms Training Institute, or American Small Arms Academy. Such training utilizes programs and instructional techniques that expose you to all the elements—accuracy, speed, power, urgency—required to successfully survive a deadly encounter, and does so in a professional, no-nonsense way that you cannot expect from a local amateur. As well, in the event that you must actually use the skills they've taught you, a certificate received from such an institution provides increased protection from the hazards of civil liability.

Be careful here—there is more to being a professional self-defense shooting instructor than simply taking money for services rendered. True professionalism requires decades of skill-building, research, a dedicated attitude and, perhaps most important of all, real-world experience. Few local instructors can satisfy these criteria. Many amateur instructors want you to think they're pros, but the real professionals can be counted on the fingers of your hands with a few fingers left over.

Even when extensively modified with a muzzlebrake, such as this Keeper System, the 44 Mag is totally uncontrollable with full-power ammo. As a result, it must be either loaded down or 44 Special ammo used instead.

So, while accuracy is an important element, it isn't the only or most important element. Look at it like this—from a *tactical* liability standpoint, if you miss, you fail to solve the problem and, because you've now demonstrated your intentions, might even make it worse. If you miss, you waste time. If you miss, you waste ammunition. From a *civil* liability standpoint, if you miss and your shots strike someone downrange, guess who's liable? *You*, that's who!

Yes, accuracy is important, but *it comes more from the shooter than from his weapon.* Unfortunately, most people fail to realize this and spend most of their money on unnecessary weapon modifications instead of proper training. Then, when the chips are down, they fail and often die wondering what went wrong. Don't make that same mistake.

Next, how much penetration do we need? Easy—just enough for our bullet(s) to reach the target's vital organs.

Virtually all 38 Special loads are quite controllable since they demonstrate little felt recoil and minimal muzzle rise during firing.

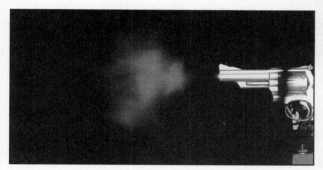

Typical 158-grain RNL produces little muzzle flash. However, this load has a reputation of being a poor manstopper and should be avoided if possible.

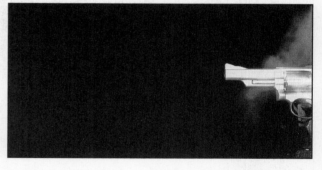

The fast-burning powder used for this low-velocity 148-grain Target WC shows no muzzle flash, but slight flash at cylinder gap.

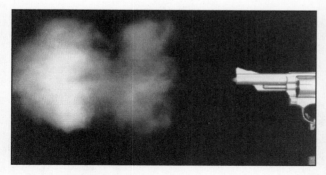

In the Winchester 110-grain +P JHP, the slower burning powders used to achieve higher velocities also produce more substantial flash.

While still controllable in rapid DA shooting, muzzle flash is very pronounced in the Law Enforcement Only (L.E.O.) 110-grain +P+ JHP, even to the point of reducing the shooter's low-light vision.

Past that point, penetration becomes a liability. If your bullets completely penetrate the target and strike a non-involved person downrange, again, you are responsible—though in court a good case on your behalf can be made as long as you did, in fact, hit your target first.

High-velocity (1000-1500 fps) bullets normally demonstrate excessive penetration, thus increasing this hazard. Cartridges that have shown special propensity for overpenetration include the 9mm Parabellum, 357 Magnum, 10mm Auto, 41 Magnum and 44 Magnum, so be very careful in your choice of ammunition.

The functional reliability of your weapon is one of the first issues you should consider. No matter how accurate it might be, the gun won't do you much good if it doesn't go "Bang!" when you want it to, every time. Yet, most new gun owners simply assume that the handgun they just purchased will work, so they load it up and, without testing it in any way, put it in the nightstand or begin carrying it.

Don't think that because you've had a gunsmith modify your handgun, you're exempt from the testing requirement. I knew a young police officer who saved for many months to have his Colt Python duty gun tuned up by a famous gunsmith who had once been a champion PPC shooter. He sent off the gun, then waited several weeks for its return.

The big day came—his gun arrived! After examining it briefly, he tried the trigger a few times, noting its smoothness. He then loaded it, put it back in the holster and again

began carrying it on duty. Two weeks later, at a local combat shooting match, he came to the 7-yard line, assumed his shooting stance and, when the whistle blew, drew the piece and pulled the trigger six times. . . with absolutely no effect whatsoever. Click-click-click-click-click-click!

It seems that the gunsmith who had performed the tune-up had set up the officer's gun to function with an extremely light trigger pull, which would only fire primers of a certain manufacture, a fact that he had neglected to relate to

Even in a heavy-frame gun, the 357 exhibits severe recoil and is considered uncontrollable for fast combat shooting missions.

A quick two-shot burst is generally accepted as being the best solution to a single-assailant attack (above). However, even with a super-tuned large-frame revolver like this 4-inch barreled Colt Python (right), this is impossible with any 357 load because of muzzle blast and recoil. Note that shooter here has missed with his second shot, greatly reducing his chances of incapacitating the attacker. In comparison, this is relatively easy with the 9mm, 38 Special, 40 S&W, 44 Special, 45 ACP and 45 Colt. The shooter above is using a Smith & Wesson M39 9mm. Compare the recoil shown in these two photos to see what the author means.

(Left) Four-inch-barreled revolvers typically used for self-defense produce considerably lower muzzle velocities than six-inchers, increasing muzzle flash and recoil, but reduced bullet performance. Here are two of the all-time great 357s—the Colt Python (top) and the first 357 ever made, the Smith & Wesson Model 27.

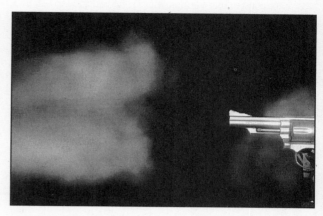

Regardless of bullet weight or style, all 357 loads demonstrate huge muzzle flash, making them less than desirable for the low-light shooting typical of self-defense encounters. Here is Remington's 158-grain JHP from a 4-inch-barreled S&W Model 66 stainless.

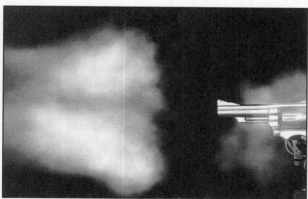

The Winchester 110-grain JHP produces moderate muzzle flash at the muzzle and cylinder. This is detrimental to safety in dark self-defense situations.

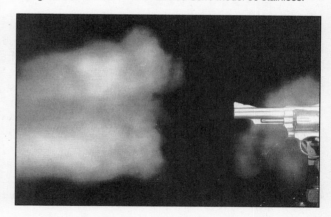

While the Winchester 125-grain JHP shows the least flash of any 125-grain offering, it still shows pronounced flash at both muzzle and cylinder gap.

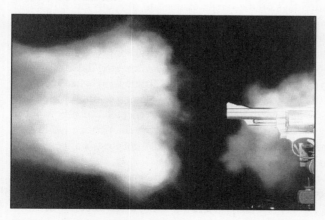

An intense fireball is produced from both muzzle and cylinder gap with the Remington 125-grain JHP. Flash of this magnitude all but destroys night vision.

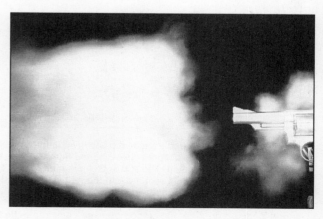

Here is the brightest flash of all the 357 Magnums—the Federal 125-grain JHP.

his young customer. When ammunition utilizing a primer of any other manufacture was used, the gun lacked the power to drive the firing pin home with enough force to fire.

It doesn't take much imagination to figure out what would have happened to that young officer if he had tried to use that gun to save his life. Happily, the event occurred in a harmless environment and graphically made the point that he should have tested the weapon extensively before carrying it.

Weapon controllability entails two factors—recoil and muzzleblast. In general, most people think that the more powerful the cartridge, the more pronounced its recoil, muzzleblast and flash, but such is only true of recoil. Some very heavy-recoiling handguns have almost no flash, because the powder is burned in the barrel, not in the air. With light bullets these guns have less recoil, but severe blast—they're very loud. Newton's Third Law of Motion dictates that for every action, there is an equal and opposite reaction. Therefore, the hotter the load, the lighter the gun and the heavier the bullet used in it, the heavier the recoil will be.

Muzzlebrakes offer some relief, but work more efficiently with cartridges that generate higher pressures. The best countermeasures against recoil are to choose your gun, caliber and ammunition carefully, then use the most stable shooting stance possible. I prefer the Weaver, because it incorporates the entire upper torso as part of the stance, reducing recoil and muzzle flip by 40 to 60 percent without using exceptional muscle power. The Isosceles stance utilizes only the arms to control recoil, and by virtue of its rigidity and the fact that the weapon's mass is above the hands, it actually causes upward flip when the weapon fires,

THE RANSOM REST—ULTIMATE CONTROL FOR ACCURACY TESTING

FOR MANY YEARS, Chuck Ransom, himself an avid and highly competent competitive shooter, manufactured the Ransom Rest, a beautifully crafted, brilliantly conceived device intended to allow consistent handgun accuracy testing. Ah, you say, but I'm a good shot. Why do I need such a device? Well, for one thing, like it or not, few of us are so good that we can outperform the Ransom Rest. (I actually did manage to do that—once. That was on the best day I ever had in my entire shooting career, and I have not done as well since!)

Then there's the problem of day-to-day changes in our

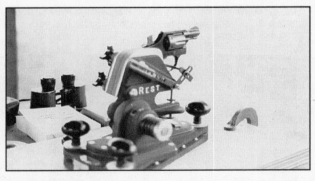

The Ransom Rest is probably the best piece of equipment available for testing handgun accuracy because the human element is almost entirely eliminated. The rest is first mounted to a solid shooting bench. The gun is secured into the rest with precisely fitted clamping pads, then aligned with the target. The gun is fired by a lever to the trigger, and the recoil is arrested by a spring-loaded drag. The gun is then pressed back into battery for succeeding shots.

eyes and general physical and psychological condition. These elements are just not consistent enough to depend upon if we're truly attempting to determine what guns and ammunition are the most accurate. In short, we just can't perform that well on demand, consistently, day after day. That's why you need a Ransom Rest. If offers consistent weapon behavior from shot to shot and is not susceptible to variances in the human condition.

How does it work? Simply stated, you mount it to a hefty piece of plywood, clamp it down on something rigid, and mount the handgun being tested in the appropriate set of grip inserts, which are then placed and secured in the rest. Load up, bingo, you're in business.

As a professional, I often find myself required to spend entire days on the range, evaluating weapons and ammo. This is, to say the least, a highly fatiguing process and one that is not conducive to consistent performance. Yet from shot to shot, hour after hour, the Ransom Rest keeps on shooting them exactly the same way, making those bullets go exactly where the gun is aimed. There is no better way to really tell how well our gun(s) and ammo perform.

Expensive? Well, it's true that no piece of precision equipment is cheap, but viewed from the perspective that one gets what one pays for, the Ransom Rest is a bargain. For the price of an out-of-the-box Colt 45, you can buy it, several sets of grip inserts and a mounting board. I highly recommend the Ransom Rest to any serious student of the handgun. Personally, I can't afford not to have one. If you're a serious self-defense handgunner, neither can you.

Based on a heavy frame, Smith & Wesson's M25-5 45 Colt is a fine self-defense revolver. Accurate and potent yet controllable, it is a good choice for someone who prefers a big-bore wheelgun over the self-loader.

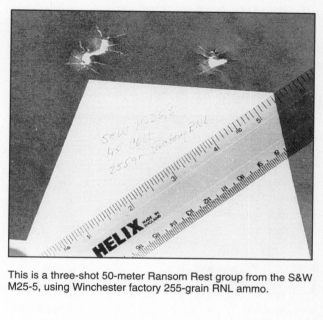

This is a three-shot 50-meter Ransom Rest group from the S&W M25-5, using Winchester factory 255-grain RNL ammo.

Controllability Exercises, Average Time Comparisons

Drill	Time (sec)		
	357 Mag/125-grain JHP	45 ACP/230-grain Ball	Time Diff.
1. Standard Exercise (2-shots, from holster)			
3 meters	1.44	1.07	.37
7 meters	1.88	1.43	.45
10 meters	2.07	1.67	.40
15 meters	2.34	1.83	.51
25 meters	2.89	2.24	.65
2. Close Range Emergency (2-shots, from holster)			
1-meter Stepback	1.51	.89	.67
1-meter Speedrock	1.34	.99	.35
3. 7-meter Singles (2-shots, from holster)	1.46	.99	.47
4. Standard Exercise (From Ready)			
3 meters	1.03	.68	.35
7 meters	1.18	.77	.41
10 meters	1.44	1.12	.32
15 meters	1.79	1.43	.36
25 meters	2.21	1.76	.45
5. Two Targets from 7 meters* (From holster, 1 shot on each)	2.57	2.03	.54
6. Small targets at Close Range (Head shot only, from Ready)			
3 meters	1.22	.91	.31
5 meters	1.34	1.04	.30
7 meters	1.47	1.19	.28

*=shot on 25-lb. 18x30 inch knockdown steel silhouettes—times were from start signal to when 2nd silhouette struck the ground. All other stages were shot on "Taylor Police Combat" silhouettes—times began with start signal and ended with second shot, but *center hits were required for all shots.*

Test Guns: 1. Super-tuned Colt Python with 4-inch barrel by Richard Aldis, Precision Enterprises, Prescott, AZ.
2. Duty-tuned Colt Government Model by Richard Aldis, Precision Enterprises, Prescott, AZ.
Ammo: 1. 357 Magnum—Winchester 125-grain JHP.
2. 45 ACP—WCC-62 230-grain FMJ ball.
Holsters: 1. 4-inch Colt Python—G. Wm. Davis #3570 Police Duty.
2. Colt GM 45—G. Wm. Davis T-Omega.

increasing recovery times and fatigue. Therefore, it greatly limits the shooter. This makes little difference if only fundamental skills are sought. However, if the shooter wishes to elevate his skills to his highest potential, the Isosceles will quickly become an obstacle, whereas the Weaver will not. Moreover, the Weaver better lends itself to flashlight

techniques, multiple target engagements, shooting on the move and other functions where weapon control is the critical factor.

Muzzle flash is influenced by 1) the burning rate of the propellant powder used in the cartridge; and 2) the length of the barrel in which it must burn. This is why cartridges like

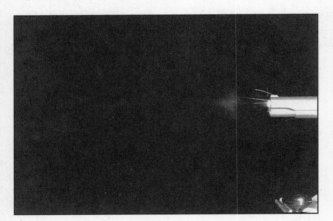

Intrinsically one of the most accurate handgun cartridges ever invented, the 45 ACP owns virtually all of the accuracy records at Camp Perry, Ohio. Here is a three-shot 50-meter Ransom Rest group fired from an *unaltered first-production-run (made in 1912)* M1911 with 230-grain military ball ammo. Group size is less than 1 1/2 inches.

Many erroneously believe that because it has such a reputation as manstopper, the 45 ACP is tough to control. However, such is entirely untrue. Here is a Colt M1911 at the moment of discharge, showing very little muzzle rise.

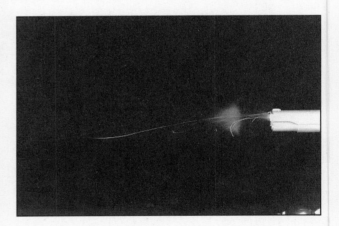

Muzzle flash with almost any 45 ACP 230-grain FMJ is virtually non-existent, as shown by these photos (clockwise from top left) of military ball, Remington, Winchester and Federal versions.

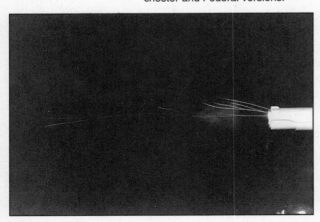

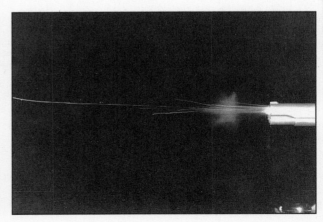

the 9mm or 38 Special can produce muzzle flash reaching astounding levels, even though they're hardly considered to be powerhouse cartridges.

Pronounced muzzle flash might look good in the movies,

but it can be quite detrimental to your low-light vision. A quick perusal of the latest FBI Uniform Crime Report will confirm the fact that most anti-personnel shootings occur between sunset and sunrise, meaning that you are by far

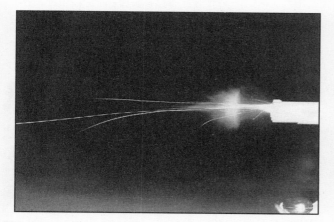

A comparison of 45 ACP loads in the M1911. The Glaser Safety Slug gives a small flash with a few sparks, not much more.

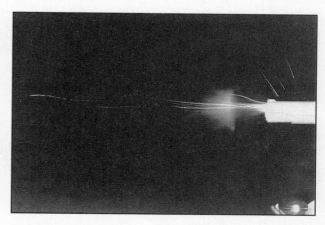

This 1960s-vintage Super-Vel 190-grain JHP shows minimal flash, but produces a whopping 1020 fps.

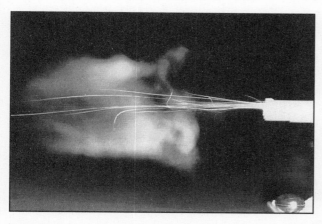

Hotter loads using lighter bullets to achieve higher velocities also increase muzzleblast as with the Winchester 185-grain Silvertip JHP.

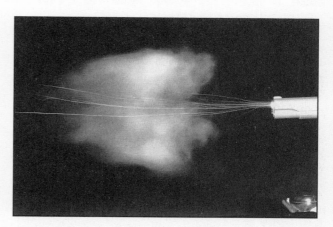

The Federal 230-grain Hydra-Shok JHP shows substantial flash, but is highly accurate.

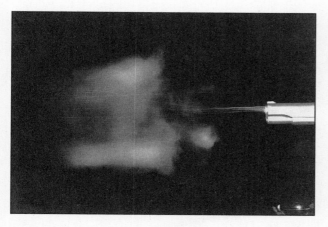

While higher velocities increase the chance for JHP expansion, they also produce a higher-intensity flash like the Speer 230-grain Gold Dot JHP.

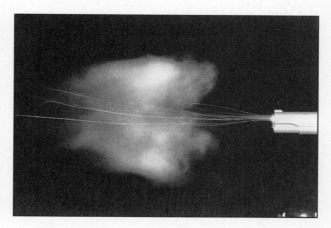

The brightest flash of any 45 ACP the author has tested—the Remington 185-grain +P JHP. Though it produces over 1100 fps from a typical pistol, recoil and muzzleblast are severe.

Full-power 10mm loads produce severe recoil and substantial muzzle flash and blast, much like the 357 Magnum, making it uncontrollable for fast shooting missions. Noting this, the FBI ordered it loaded down, resulting in what became known as the FBI load. This was a 180-grain JHP at 933 fps. Appearing two years later, the 40 S&W duplicates these specs from a smaller, more efficient case, making the 10mm obsolete.

more likely to use your defensive handgun during the hours of darkness. If your ammunition produces a muzzle flash bright enough to dazzle or momentarily blind you, you're asking for trouble, regardless of how accurate it is or how good a manstopper it might be.

There can be no question that law enforcement officers and military personnel frequently engage opponents in dim light and sometimes even in full darkness. Year after year, the FBI Uniform Crime Report confirms that the majority of handgun fights take place in dim light. The reason is simple enough—darkness provides good concealment. So much so, in fact, that in the military environment, virtually all movement of personnel and supplies takes place during the hours of darkness. With modern surveillance and detection devices, plus indirect-fire weapons capable of pinpoint accuracy, daylight action is regarded as suicidal.

Controllability Exercises, Overall Time Averages

| Test # | ——Elapsed Time—— | |
	357 Mag. 125-gr.	40 S&W 180-gr.
1	3.02	**2.05**
2	9.33	**7.56**
3	9.44	**7.56**
4	26.42	**18.69**
5	13.34	**9.33**
6	3.35	**1.76**
7	3.12	**2.01**
8	2.66	**1.84**
Total	70.68	**50.80**
Percent Better		39

Weapons presented from holster. Timed electronically beginning with start signal and ending when last target strikes the ground. Glock Model 22 40 S&W was used from M-D Labs' Taylor Thunderbolt holster, while 4-inch Colt Python was presented from Gordon Wm. Davis #3570. Winchester ammunition was used in both calibers.
Glock M22 had 3½-pound connector and Trijicon tritium sights but no other modifications. Colt Python was super-tuned, Metalife-finished and fitted with Pachmayr Gripper combat stocks.
Best times in each test are boldfaced.

The armies of the world have solved the problems of muzzle flash with their assault rifles and machine guns. By including flash suppressors as standard equipment on them, the sometimes embarrassing tactical liability of muzzle flash is virtually eliminated. Yet virtually nothing has been done within the law enforcement community to address the problem. The handgun has been totally ignored.

Military ammunition incorporates a flash-retardant chemical coating in its propellant powder, which commercial ammo, because of the additional expense, does not. If you don't believe this, shoot some military 45 ACP 230-grain ball at night and you'll see that it produces almost no flash.

The problem of flash is further aggravated when a revolver is involved, since all wheelguns utilize a revolving cylinder behind a single fixed barrel. The only way this arrangement can work is by allowing a certain amount of clearance between the cylinder face and rear end of the barrel. This allows the escape of varying amounts of burning propellant gas, which expands rapidly upon contact with the cooler, oxygen-laden air outside. The result? *Flash!*

However, revolver flash characteristics are a bit more complex than that. Analysis shows that, while the amount of cylinder gap is one factor, the burning rate of the powder, too, is influential. Normally, the slower-burning powders produce less cylinder flash, but a large muzzle flash. Conversely, the fast-burners demonstrate intense cylinder flash, but little muzzle flash.

Can we alleviate the problem? Yes, but only to a certain degree. By carefully selecting our ammunition, we can do much to reduce flash, at least to tolerable levels.

In the photos here, you will see some examples. Look at them carefully, then consider them in relation to the other factors we've already discussed in this book. Then you'll be in a better position to evaluate your choice of weaponry.

VELOCITY AND BULLET EXPANSION

THERE EXISTS CONSIDERABLE lack of perspective these days about bullet performance, the effects of velocity upon that performance, how bullets behave when they hit human targets, and just how much barrel length affects muzzle velocity. Strange as it may seem in our much-vaunted "Age Of Information," most gun enthusiasts and even many experts labor under some potentially dangerous illusions about what to expect when the sights are aligned with a target and the trigger is pressed.

I say potentially, because if the gun is being used for self-defense and it fails to accomplish its mission, a very high price indeed may be paid. Yet, surprisingly, although the deadly serious nature of the subject and its ramifications should be readily apparent, the bombardment of commercial hype, superficial or misdirected studies, and just plain paraphrasing of theory—even to the extent of ignoring history—continues unabated.

Why this has come to pass is anyone's guess, and like everyone else, I have my own suspicions. However, since this issue lies outside the scope of this text, suffice it to say that the problem of theory versus reality remains unsolved and we'll leave it at that.

Handgun performance against humans is rarely spectacular. Movie images of men doing backflips or being blown through walls when shot by the likes of Dirty Harry are pure illusion. Simply stated, handguns just aren't very powerful; certainly not powerful enough to physically knock a man from his feet. Aside from that minute portion of energy absorbed by the gun itself when it fires, the shooter absorbs the rest. Newton's Third Law of Motion—for every action, there is an equal and opposite reaction—dictates that if the gun were in fact potent enough to knock a man down by shooting him with it, it would also knock the shooter down in the process.

Since this obviously doesn't happen, we can't allow the cinema representation to take precedence over the truth. Why does it look that way in the movies? Action, my friend, action. That's what sells movies. What is often misinterpreted as visible knockdown is just muscle or nerve reaction to the shock of being struck and wounded. The direction toward which the "shootee" falls depends entirely upon where his weight and balance are at the time.

This notwithstanding, most people still believe that hollowpoint bullets *always* expand and unequivocally demonstrate night-versus-day performance over other types. Some, like the American Civil Liberties Union (ACLU) even believe this to the point where they file lawsuits against those who use hollowpoint ammunition on the grounds that it is so deadly that "the police don't have the right to act as judge, jury and executioner!"

Whether or not a hollowpoint or softpoint bullet expands depends upon three basic elements. First, the design of the bullet—is it really frangible enough to deform, or is it designed more with the idea of being commercially attractive to prospective buyers? I think that, for the most part, the latter is closer to the truth, because as exotic as most of these bullets appear, more often than not they fail to demonstrate the expansion for which they are supposedly designed.

Second, we must consider the velocity at which the bullet is propelled. This is further categorized into two additional, but poorly understood, truths: 1) the speeds at which bullets exit from real-world guns, rather than laboratory test barrels, are considerably less than published; 2) barrel length radically affects velocity, particularly in handguns.

For example, a certain commercial 110-grain JHP 357 Magnum is advertised at over 1500 fps, but when fired from a typical 4-inch-barreled revolver, it produces only 1146 fps—354 fps, nearly 26 percent, less than claimed.

From a 6-inch revolver, this same load produces 1275 fps—still 225 fps, nearly 20 percent less than its published velocity.

With the 38 Special, the situation is even more distorted. Law enforcement's current favorite, the 125-grain JHP "+P" is advertised at 1370 fps, but when fired from a 4-inch revolver it actually produces only 847 fps. That's 523 fps or 38 percent lower than claimed.

Considering the almost universal observation that with conventional JHP/JSPs around 1088 fps (the speed of sound at sea level) is required before one can expect reliable upset, this paints a grim picture indeed, especially since the selection of that particular load is supposed to ameliorate the stopping-power deficiency of the infamous 38 Special 158-grain RNL it replaced.

Another solution to the 38/158 failures was the so-called Treasury Load, a special law-enforcement-only (LEO) 110-grain JHP "+P+" touted to produce over 1300 fps from a 4-

inch barrel. Yet, it actually produces only 1129 fps, a full 171 fps less than claimed.

The third—and almost completely ignored—element is what kind of mass and resistance the bullet encounters during its passage through the target. This is why there are so many horror stories about failures to expand, even at velocities of 1400 fps or more. With no resistance, there's often no bullet reaction other than penetration and exit.

Recently, a large Western county reexamined nearly sixty police shootings that took place within their jurisdiction over the last three decades. Slightly more than half occurred with the 38/125-grain JHP; the rest with its predecessor, the 38/158 RNL. They found that the results were *virtually identical.*

Why? Because to trade bullet weight for a relatively small increase in velocity gains you nothing more than increased muzzle flash. Bullet penetration to vital organs is the most essential element of stopping power; then comes

One method of obtaining better bullet performance was the semi-wadcutter (SWC), which appeared in the 1920s. Featuring a long, tapered nose to enhance penetration and a sharp, full-caliber cutting shoulder to create a larger permanent wound channel, it offers a viable alternative to the hollowpoint, especially in smaller caliber, lower-velocity cartridges.

Even before the turn of the 20th century, the hollowpoint concept was well-known. However, it wasn't until around 1960 that serious attempts at designing a truly effective JHP bullet began. From then to 1993, few hollowpoints could be depended upon to reliably expand at typical handgun velocities, but were regarded as state of the art anyway.

(Above) Beginning back in the days of the cap 'n' ball revolver up until well after the turn of the 20th century, the lead conical, or what we now call a round-nose bullet, was considered the norm. However, although accurate in many calibers, it performed poorly as a manstopper, merely punching through its human target with little tissue/nerve damage and leaving a small permanent wound channel.

The Federal Hydra-Shok JHP utilizes a post centered in the hollowpoint cavity to force water-laden tissue radially outward, thus causing upset. A valid theory, it has not proven to be as effective as hoped against humans.

the size of the hole it punches in them. Penetration is a function of sectional density and velocity. Sectional density is a function of bullet cross-sectional area and weight. To lighten the weight thus reduces the chance of reliable penetration to vitals unless the velocity at which the bullet is traveling is *drastically* increased, which it is not with the 9mm Parabellum, 38 Special, 357 Magnum, 40 S&W, etc. Net result: no real improvement.

It is for this reason that I generally prefer a heavier, larger-caliber bullet at moderate velocity, occasionally enhanced by a semi-wadcutter bullet to cut a full-caliber permanent wound channel. We need only enough velocity to allow penetration to vitals; anything more just increases the chance of the bullet exiting, with a commensurate increase in our liability hazard. The big bullet isn't dependent upon expansion to punch a big hole in vital organs. It's already big in the first place.

In addition, if you consider the increased muzzleblast

and recoil control problems of "+P+" 38 Specials, 9mms and 357 Magnums, you can readily see why they're less efficient in self-defense missions. If the current vogue of claiming that the 357/125-grain JHP is the greatest thing since sliced bread were true, I'd use a 44 Magnum instead—because you don't get something for nothing, and if stopping power equaled overpenetration and muzzleblast, there is nothing one can do with a 357 that can't be better done with a 44.

A number of highly credible ballisticians, such as Col. Martin Fackler, have repeatedly stated pretty much the same thing, but in more scientific terms, even going so far as to decry the Glaser concept because of its ultra-light specialized bullet and decreased penetration. I'm not sure I agree with Col. Fackler on the subject of Glasers, but it is nice to hear scientific confirmation of what I've been saying and writing for the last twenty years.

So, remember that bullet performance is not nearly as

Because they work in a more diverse environment, law enforcement officers need ammunition that will perform against not only unprotected targets in the open, but clad in heavy clothing or behind light cover as well. Light cover includes windshield and Thermopane residential glass, sheet-metal bodywork and interior construction materials, such as sheetrock. Thus, they require a bullet that does not expand right away. Of these, the Speer Gold Dot JHP is by far the best.

predictable or controllable as many would have you believe. This is why I prefer historic analysis to laboratory simulations using artificial media. Perhaps the reason Col. Fackler's observations tend to coincide more closely with historic observation than those of some of his colleagues is because he also shoots hogs and then compares bullet performance on them with that obtained in ballistic gelatin, thus creating a corollary. No one else has bothered to do this since the Thompson-LaGarde tests of 1908.

Of late, we've seen a new rash of "revelations" on bullet performance obtained from irrelevant artificial media like wet phone books, clay, water jugs, limited personal experience and, even more disconcerting, pure assumption. This trend is becoming epidemic in proportion and is inundating the pages of the gun press to an extent never before seen, muddling a subject that is already very abstract and thus difficult to understand.

Perhaps it makes no difference to the casual reader, but it *does* matter to those who carry a gun for self-defense. Handgun performance—e.g., stopping power—is the very heart of self-defense shooting and should not be obfuscated by hype, theory or personal bias. As I've said many times, life and death are serious business—too serious to be left to amateurs, because the stakes are simply too high to regard the subject in any other way.

A harsh statement? Perhaps, but the sheer quantity of theory that won't even withstand an intellectual analysis, much less a life-threatening field-test, is alarming.

For example, several writers recently criticized Jeff Cooper's thesis that, depending upon the load, the 45 ACP is

Currently, many feel that the 125-grain JHP is the most effective 357 load now available. However, it, too, needs a longer barrel to achieve velocities sufficient to allow reliable bullet expansion. A speed-loader full of them looks good, but they may not work like you want them to unless you pack a long-barreled gun.

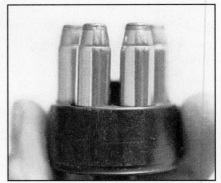

Although more potent than the 38 Special from which it came, the 357 Magnum also suffers from the lack of bullet velocities, from typical barrel lengths, high enough to expect reliable upset. This problem is further aggravated by the increase in recoil and muzzle-blast with its hotter loads. The bullets show near-ideal expansion (left) and two cases of marginal performance.

85-92 percent effective, claiming somewhat smugly that such is untrue and giving their own lesser percentages as "proof." Significantly, I noted that none of these individuals gave the source of their data, but I can tell you this—I've known Jeff Cooper for over twenty years, and while it's no secret that we disagree on many things, we share total agreement on this particular subject.

Jeff was once a professor of history and views all issues from that standpoint. This being so, from his review of historic and technical data covering over a hundred years, and his own experience, he opines that, with a thoracic cavity hit, the 45 gets the job done "nineteen times out of twenty or perhaps a little bit more."

Why the huge disparity between writers? Using totally different—and, I might add, irrelevant—criteria and technical definitions (the disclosure of which somehow got lost along the way), these particular writers undertook a far less comprehensive examination, concluding that the 45 was only about 65 percent effective. The problem has since been

magnified in that several other writers have begun paraphrasing their conclusions, thus further confusing the issue.

My point here is that, although the writers in question seem to have missed it, Jeff never claimed the 45 was infallible. Being an avid student of history myself, with a pretty fair amount of background, expertise and experience in combat weaponcraft, I see readily how he reached the conclusions he has. Moreover, his opinion is shared by people with impeccable credentials, people like General Julian Hatcher, Elmer Keith and Townsend Whelen, not to mention thousands of combat veterans and police officers.

Now, we have to be careful when compiling percentages. Were I to base my opinions on a narrow examination such as a review of the shooting files of my local sheriff's department and my own personal experience, I could quite legitimately claim that the 45 ACP 230-grain FMJ is 100 percent effective. Why? Because in all of that agency's shootings for the last fifteen years, it *succeeded*. Moreover, in the five handgun fights in which I used a 45 ACP, I won all five with

Typical 38 Special revolvers, such as the 3-inch S&W Model 10 or 2-inch Colt Cobra, simply cannot produce sufficient velocities to expect reliable JHP expansion without weapon-abusive high pressure being reached. This is why so-called +P+ 38 Special ammo is limited to law enforcement use only and not available for civilian sale.

Chart 1: Chronographed Velocities From 2-Inch-Barrel 38 Special Revolvers						
	Bullet		Velocity (fps)			
Maker	Wgt. Grs.	Type	S&W M49	Colt Det. Spl.	S&W M12	S&W M15
W-W LEO	110	JHP +P+	1053	1026	1068	1052
Super Vel	110	JHP	1040	1013	1118	1048
W-W Silvertip	110	JHP	800	808	824	755
R-P	125	JHP +P	847	820	873	820
W-W	125	JHP +P	835	844	875	844
RA-64 USAF M41	130	Ball	722	725	788	747
Federal	148	Wadcutter	626	643	653	634
R-P	158	RNL	693	682	728	703
W-W	158	LSWCHP +P	793	800	833	805
R-P	158	LSWCHP +P	827	832	839	830
Federal	158	LSWCHP +P	784	796	824	817
Federal "Nyclad"	158	SWCHP +P	841	870	890	865
CCI	158	JHP +P	777	797	824	781

a single shot each, using—you guessed it—230-grain ball ammo. My opponents collapsed so quickly upon being hit that I didn't even have the chance to fire a quick second shot. Five center hits, five one-shot stops.

On the other hand, the only two failures to stop I've had were with 124-grain 9mm Parabellum ball and a 158-grain 357 JHP. Therefore, were I to take the limited view, I could say that both are totally ineffective. But we all know that to do that would be complete rubbish and an insult to your

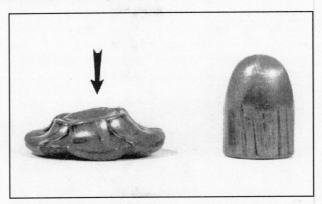

Those who discredit the light-bullet, high-velocity JHP approach usually prefer the opposite—a large, heavy bullet traveling at slower velocities. The premise here is that the big bullet creates a large permanent wound channel without being dependent upon expansion and thus does not need hand-numbing, flash-producing heavy loads to work. This S&W revolver chambers the 44 Special.

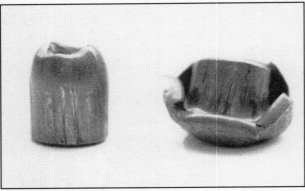

Here is typical 45 ACP JHP performance. The 200-grain JHP bullet at the right was shot into an artificial medium, while the one at the left was recovered from a criminal shot in the chest during the commission of a felony. A big difference—and one that bears close attention. This is why proponents of the big-bore discredit expansion as a viable tool, claiming that, with conventional JHP designs, expansion is too erratic to depend upon.

Sometimes strange things happen when bullets hit people, rather than artificial test media. This 230-grain FMJ (left) was found lodged fully expanded against the inside of the victim's left shoulder blade. The bullet at the right was shot into water-based clay.

Even the super-hot 44 Magnum occasionally experiences bullet failures. The bullet at right (arrow) was recovered unexpanded from the ground after passing through a human chest cavity. The victim's only reaction was to loudly complain that he'd been shot and ask several of his associates to call an ambulance. He then walked to the curb 20 feet from where he'd been hit, sat down, and waited for help to arrive.

This 1960s-vintage Super Vel 45 ACP 190-grain JHP was recovered from the car seat behind a seated felon shot in the chest. After passing through the windshield and the felon himself, it shows only marginal upset, even though it left the muzzle at 1020 fps.

intelligence. Yet, stop and think about it, exactly this is being done by several gun magazine writers, more often than the average reader realizes.

Many feel that nothing of value can be obtained by shooting artificial media, and I can understand their frustration. After all, if you want to find out what happens in gunfights, you've got to shoot *people*, right? And people differ from each other—physically, emotionally and intellectually—to the point where the uncontrollable variables prevent any detailed conclusions. Since we can't hook up a thousand or so people to electrocardiographs and electroencephalographs and then shoot them to see how they respond, we have only history, experience and artificial media to depend upon.

But let's not kid ourselves, either. The performance of a given number of bullets in any artificial medium can only be a valid comparison of how those bullets compare in that medium. There is not a shred of proof that any artificial medium is a valid substitute for a human being, nor that bullet performance in that medium is the same as in a human body. In fact, history shows us the opposite, and this is why so many comparisons seem to fly in the face of logic, physics and common sense.

Take a look at the photography of recovered bullets included with this text and you'll see what I mean. No, I'm not trying to convince you that frangible bullets never expand, only that their behavior in humans depends entirely on the velocities at which they travel and what they encounter during passage. I hope that you'll see that there is just no such thing as a free lunch.

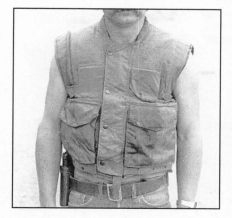
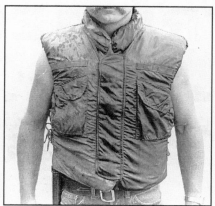

Handgun performance against body armor, too, is highly variable and requires careful research to understand. Here are the two predominant types of military body armor—the U.S. Marine Corps ceramic and U.S. Army woven type. These are intended to stop small fragmentation particles, not actual bullets, and are thus ineffective against pistol fire.

Concealable soft armor, such as this Second Chance Model Y, will stop bullets from virtually all cartridges normally used for anti-personnel missions. Some bruising results, but the alternative—serious injury or death—makes it an attractive proposition, especially for uniformed police personnel.

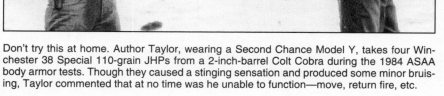

Don't try this at home. Author Taylor, wearing a Second Chance Model Y, takes four Winchester 38 Special 110-grain JHPs from a 2-inch-barrel Colt Cobra during the 1984 ASAA body armor tests. Though they caused a stinging sensation and produced some minor bruising, Taylor commented that at no time was he unable to function—move, return fire, etc.

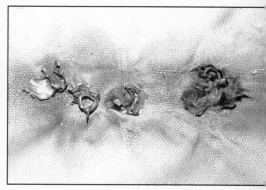

Later examination showed that the bullets penetrated only four layers, lodging in the fifth, of a total of eighteen layers.

TECHNICAL SPECS FOR POPULAR CARTRIDGES

(All dimensions in inches)

380 ACP (9MM KURZ, 9MM CORTO)

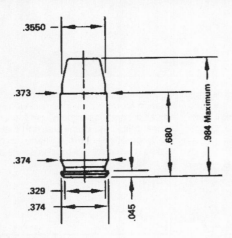

Bullet diameter: .355
Available bullet weights (grs.): 80, 88, 95
Bullet configurations available: Ball, LRN, JHP.
Nominal velocity with 95-grain bullet: 900 fps.
Typical handguns in which used:
    Walther PP, PPK and PPK/s
    Mauser HSc
    Beretta M1934
    Astra Constable
    AMT Back Up
    Beretta M70S
    Bernardelli M80
    Star Super SM
    Sterling M400

9MM PARABELLUM (9X19, 9MM LUGER)

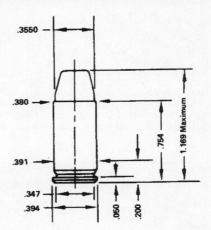

Bullet diameter: .355
Available bullet weights (grs.): 80, 88, 90, 100, 108, 115, 124
Bullet configurations available: Ball, AP, TC, LRN, JSP, JHP, SWC.
Nominal velocity with 124-grain Ball bullet: 900-1020 fps.
Typical handguns in which used:
    Luger P-08
    Walther P-38
    Browning P-35 (Hi-Power)
    Radom M35
    Broomhandle Mauser
    Heckler & Koch P-7 & VP-70
    SIG P225, P226, P228
    Glock M17, M19, M26

Beretta M92 series
S&W M908, M3913LS, M6946, M3913, M3953, M6904, M5903, M5946, MSW9F, MSW9C, M909, M3959
Brno CZ-75

38 SUPER AUTOMATIC

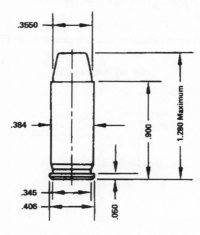

Bullet diameter: .355/9mm
Available bullet weights (grs.): All 9mm types, plus 130-grain Ball.
Bullet configurations available: Same as 9mm Parabellum.
Nominal velocity with 130-grain Ball bullet: 1170 fps.
Typical handguns in which used:
    Colt Government Model
    Star
    Llama
    Astra

38 SPECIAL

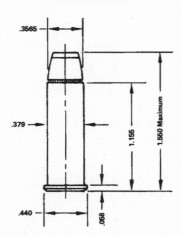

Bullet diameter: .357

Available bullet weights (grs.): 90, 100, 110, 125, 140, 146, 148, 150, 158, 160, 200
Bullet configurations available: Ball, LRN, SWC, JSP, JHP, JFP, WC.
Nominal velocity with 158-grain LRN bullet: 840 fps.
Typical handguns in which used:
    Colt Detective Special
    Colt Cobra
    Colt Diamondback
    Smith & Wesson M10, M12, M14, M15, M36, M49, M60, M67, etc.
    Dan Wesson
    Charter Arms Undercover
    Ruger Security Six
    Ruger Speed Six

357 MAGNUM

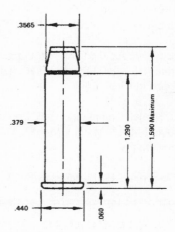

Bullet diameter: .357
Available bullet weights (grs.): Same as 38 Special.
Bullet configurations available: Same as 38 Special.
Nominal velocity with 158-grain bullet: 8³/₈" bbl. = 1370 fps, 6" bbl. = 1260 fps, 5" bbl. = 1130 fps, 4" bbl. = 1020 fps, 3¹/₂" bbl. = 970 fps, 2¹/₂" bbl. = 920 fps.
Typical handguns in which used:
    Colt Python
    Colt Trooper
    Colt Lawman
    Smith & Wesson M19, M13, M27, M28, M65, M66, etc.
    Ruger Security Six
    Dan Wesson

40 SMITH & WESSON (40 S&W)

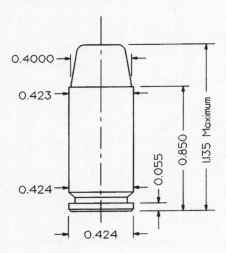

Bullet diameter: .400
Available bullet weights (grs.): 135, 155, 170, 175, 190, 200
Bullet configurations available: JHP, JTC, LRN, LSWC, LFP.
Nominal velocity with standard bullet: 150-grain JHP = 1327 fps, 155-grain JHP = 1023 fps, 180-grain JHP = 933 fps
Typical handguns in which used:
  Glock M22, M23, M27
  Colt Gov't. Model, Commander, LW Commander
  S&W M4006, M4013, M4043, M4053, MSF40F, MSW40C, M410
  SIG P229
  Beretta M96 series, M98FS series, M8040

10MM AUTO

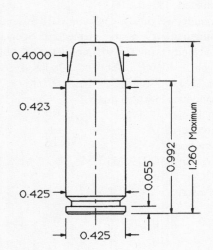

Bullet diameter: .400
Available bullet weights (grs.): Same as 40 S&W.

Bullet configurations available: Same as 40 S&W.
Nominal velocity with standard bullet: 135-grain JHP = 1442 fps, 155-grain JHP = 1322 fps, 175-grain JHP = 1190 fps, 180-grain JHP = 933 fps, 200-grain JHP = 1216 fps
Typical handguns in which used:
  Bren Ten
  Colt Delta Elite series
  Glock M20
  S&W M1006 series

41 MAGNUM

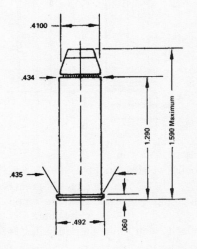

Bullet diameter: .410
Available bullet weights (grs.): 210, 225
Bullet configurations available: SWC, JSP, JHP.
Nominal velocity with 225-grain JSP bullet: 1370 fps.
Typical handguns in which used:
  Smith & Wesson M57, M58

44 SPECIAL

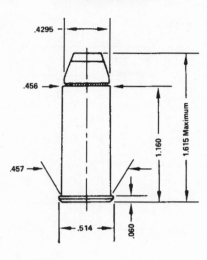

Bullet diameter: .429
Available bullet weights (grs.): 180, 200, 215, 225, 240,
                                 246, 250, 265
Bullet configurations available: LRN, SWC, JHP, JSP, JFP.
Nominal velocity with 246-grain LRN bullet: 750 fps.
Typical handguns in which used:
    Smith & Wesson M24, M624
    Charter Arms Bulldog

44 MAGNUM

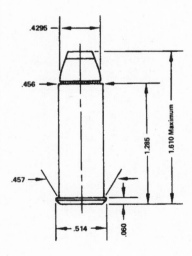

Bullet diameter: .429
Available bullet weights (grs.): Same as 44 Special.
Bullet configurations available: Same as 44 Special.
Nominal velocity with 240-grain JSP bullet: 1410 fps
                                 (8³/₈″ barrel).

Typical handguns in which used:
    Colt Anaconda
    Smith & Wesson M29, M629

High Standard Crusader
Ruger Redhawk

45 ACP (45 AUTO)

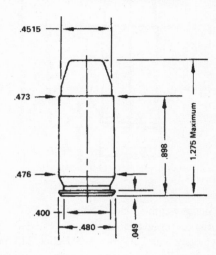

Bullet diameter: .451
Available bullet weights (grs.): 190, 200, 215, 230
Bullet configurations available: LRN, Ball, JSP, JHP,
                                 JFP, SWC.
Nominal velocity with 230-grain Ball bullet: 820 fps.
Typical handguns in which used:
    H&K USP
    Colt Government, Commander, Officer's ACP
    Star PD & Model P
    Semmerling
    Detonics
    Safari Arms Enforcer
    Smith & Wesson M25-2, M625-2, M1917
    Colt M1917
    Glock M21

45 AUTO RIM

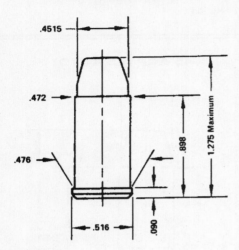

.4515
.472
.476
.898
1.275 Maximum
.516
.090

Bullet diameter: .451
Available bullet weights (grs.): Same as 45 ACP.
Bullet configurations available: Same as 45 ACP.
Nominal velocity with 230-grain Ball bullet: 825 fps.
Typical handguns in which used:
    Colt M1917
    Smith & Wesson M1917, M25-2, M625-2

45 COLT

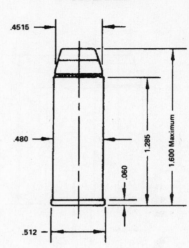

.4515
.480
.060
1.285
1.600 Maximum
.512

Bullet diameter: .451, .454
Available bullet weights (grs.): 240, 250, 255
Bullet Configurations Avaliable: SWC, JSP, JHP, LRN.
Nominal velocity with 250-grain LRN bullet: 870 fps.
Typical handguns in which used:
    Smith & Wesson M25-5 series

SECTION **II**

FILLING THE GAP BETWEEN 9MM AND 45 ACP

DOES THE CONTROVERSY between the 45 and the 9mm leave no self-defense alternatives? Of course not. The gap between those two is large enough that there is plenty of room for a cartridge that gives midway performance, one that works perhaps not as well as the 45, but better than the 9. There have been several attempts to fill the gap. Some have failed; some made the grade.

The first attempt came in the form of a hot-loaded 38 Special intended for large-frame Smith & Wesson revolvers, which Smith called the 38-44. Although this round saw favor in police circles, it wasn't the final solution by a long shot.

The next attempt was the 357 Magnum with its longer case and higher-pressure loading, a round which launched the magnum age in 1935. Prior to the inception of the 357, the most powerful handgun cartridge was the 45 Colt; there are those who say it is a better cartridge than any 357, even today.

However, the 357 was popular enough until the relatively recent swing in police circles to the use of semi-automatic handguns. This led to the need for departments and individuals to make the tough choice between the two cartridges in most common circulation, the 9mm and the 45 ACP. The parameters of this situation led cartridge designers and wildcatters to again take a long hard look at the performance gap between the two old standbys.

What follows is a bit of the history, successes and failures of the 357; next something of the factors that led to the rise and decline of the 10mm and the 41 Action Express, two designed to fill that gap; then the rise to success of the 40 S&W, a cartridge that is so obviously a good design and a good compromise that it seems like it ought to have appeared long ago.

The 357 Magnum

Since 1935 when the 357 Magnum first appeared and launched us into the magnum era, there have been myriad handguns chambered for it. The result of a Keith/Sharpe/Wesson project to upgrade the 38 Special, the longer-cased 357 subsequently evolved, thus eliminating the problem of someone unwittingly chambering the super-hot but dimensionally identical 38-44 high-velocity load in a light-framed 38 and "buying the farm."

Pressures with the 357 were—and remain—high, up to a full 35,000 psi, with velocities to match. And, perhaps not surprisingly, recoil, flash and concussion levels, too, are sufficient to send the unprepared scurrying away with a grimace and their hands held tightly over their ears.

Original velocities in the 1500 fps range from a long barrel and excellent penetration gave rise to the claim that the 357 was the world's most powerful handgun, an honor it held until the appearance of the mighty 44 Magnum in 1956. Naturally, the 357's high-powered performance required that Smith & Wesson build a special gun to handle it, and on April 8, 1935, the first Three-Fifty-Seven, as it was then called, was presented to FBI Chief J. Edgar Hoover. Based upon S&W's highly successful S-frame (later the N-frame) series, the new behemoth was finely checkered on both its topstrap and barrel rib, offered with no fewer than seven different front/rear sight combinations, and featured barrel lengths of from $3\frac{1}{2}$ to a full $8\frac{3}{4}$ inches (later reduced to $8\frac{3}{8}$ inches to conform with, of all things, NRA competition rules).

Sales of the new gun quickly outstripped S&W's capacity to produce it, a condition that persisted until the onset of World War II when, along with most of their other handguns, it was temporarily discontinued to allow S&W to give their full attention to government contracts. Total pre-war production of the Three-Fifty-Seven was 6642 guns, and

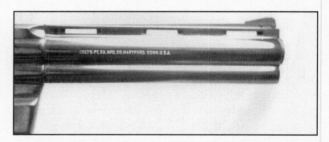

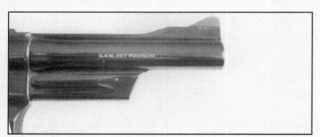

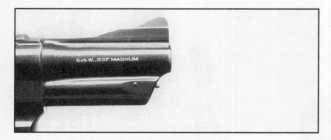

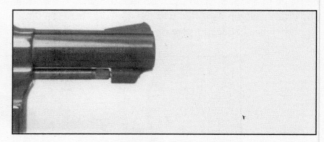

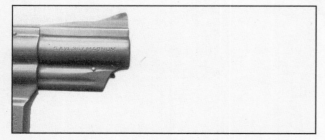

The 357 Magnum is at its best from at least a 6-inch barrel. However, due to the clumsiness of a longer-barreled gun in fast weapon presentations from the holster, the typical length used for self-defense is much less, usually $2\frac{1}{2}$ to 4 inches, cutting muzzle velocities critical to bullet expansion down to unsatisfactory levels. Since the 357 first appeared in 1935, its barrel length has been continuously reduced to make it more portable. Beginning with the original $8\frac{3}{8}$-inch tube, we've seen it cut back to 6, 5, 4, $3\frac{1}{2}$, 3, and even $2\frac{1}{2}$ inches. Once barrel lengths fall below 6 inches, the 357 loses its magic.

when production was resumed in 1948, barrel lengths of 3½, 5, 6½ and 8⅜ inches were standardized.

Sales continued to be strong, with 6322 guns sold by June 1952, and in 1957 when S&W assigned numbers to their guns, the Three-Fifty-Seven became the Model 27, a designation it held until it was discontinued in 1995. Throughout the next three decades, S&W made continuous improvements on the M27, and by September 1975, it was offered with a target hammer, target trigger, checkered Goncalo Alves target stocks and a mahogany presentation case. However, several years ago, the mahogany case was abandoned, and the 3½-, 5- and 6½-inch barrels were replaced with lengths of 4, 6 and 8⅜ inches.

In the summer of 1954, then-S&W president Carl Hellstrom asked handgun expert Bill Jordan what features he felt the ideal police revolver should entail. Jordan replied that is should be a "carry often, shoot seldom," medium-frame gun with a heavy 4-inch barrel, an extractor shroud similar to that found on the large-frame Three-Fifty-Seven, and, of course, chambered for the 357 Magnum cartridge.

Testing immediately began at Smith & Wesson to create such a gun, and on November 15, 1955, the K-frame Model 19 Combat Magnum appeared. In the first six months of its existence, more than 5000 Model 19s were produced, demonstrating popularity that continues to this day. Light, fast and accurate, the 19, like its bigger brother the 27, now holds a place of honor as the quintessential medium-frame 357.

Not to be outdone, Colt then entered the burgeoning 357 marketplace with the Trooper in 1954 and the improved Trooper Mark III in 1969. However, in 1955 Colt stunned the firearms industry by introducing what many feel to be the finest 357 ever made—the Python. Graceful, superbly accurate and heavy enough to handle the 357 Magnum cartridge in any form, it challenges the S&W Model 27 for top honors.

Without question, the 357 was here to stay, and the rest of the gun industry quickly followed suit. By 1978, DA 357s

The hottest, most popular 357 load at present is the 125-grain JHP. Rated at 1400 fps from a 4-inch barrel, it still must strike substantial mass before upset is guaranteed. The bullet at left was recovered from the floor of the room next door after passing completely through the chest of a felon and the sheetrock wall behind him. The felon was shot by police at point-blank range. The bullet at right was from the same box of cartridges, but fired into ballistic gelatin. Hmm...!

from Ruger, Taurus, Charter Arms and a host of others could also be found in gunshop display cases.

So much for the history. What about the 357 Magnum itself? What is it, really, and what can we expect from it and the revolvers chambered for it in a self-defense situation? And perhaps most important of all, can we improve on the gun/cartridge combination in any significant way?

The answer is, of course, yes. We can enhance the weapon's performance with careful selection of front/rear sight combination. We can remove sharp edges wherever we find them, to prevent abrasion of skin and clothing; give it a proper trigger, better-shaped hammer and good stocks; and carefully select the barrel length. Ammunition selection, too, is critical, because weapon control is a very real problem with any 357. Consider all of these issues carefully, because they're extremely important to get the best performance out of your gun, regardless of what specific type of 357 you have.

The 357 Magnum is steeped in legend, meaning that determining its true capabilities and limitations is often difficult. It's a potent cartridge, but one which, as a manstopper, is much misunderstood. This means that obtaining the proper balance of weapon acquisition, control and stopping power can be an elusive goal. Nonetheless, if that goal is achieved, you will have done everything possible to obtain maximum performance when trouble comes calling.

The 10mm Auto

Although briefly seen just after the turn of the century, the 10mm made its first modern appearance in the early 1960s. Known then as the 10mm G&A and used in a modified Browning P-35, it represented a successful attempt to create a compact gun/cartridge combination offering superior performance to the 9mm Parabellum. Although the 10mm G&A was all it was cracked up to be, virtually no commercial interest in it was generated, and it slowly faded into obscurity.

The concept lay dormant until 1979 when Jeff Cooper and I (then the operations manager of Cooper's now-defunct American Pistol Institute) consulted in detail upon the feasibility of its resurrection, utilizing either the P-35 or the then-new Brno CZ-75. From the outset, the theory of the 10mm as an alternative to the 9mm Parabellum was attractive; so attractive, in fact, that we literally dissected my rare-at-the-time CZ-75 in our efforts to determine its potential for use with a 10mm cartridge.

Thus, my involvement in the early stages of the project gives me a unique perspective from which to speak. I left API in September 1980, just after Cooper began discussing our 10mm idea with possible producers Dornaus and Dixon. Shortly thereafter, the program to build what was to become the Bren Ten, as Cooper called it, began in earnest. Seeing fruition in early 1984, the Bren Ten created a brief flurry of publicity, but, plagued with problems, it simply went away.

I noted at the time that the critical principles of the concept upon which Cooper and I had initially agreed had been changed. First, our 10mm cartridge propelled a 200-grain bullet at about 900 fps, thereby allowing good weapon control (remember, this was supposed to be a combat gun and cartridge), without excessive muzzleblast or penetration.

Yet, the 10mm cartridge used in the Bren Ten was considerably longer, and produced much higher velocities and breech pressures. This new 10mm, with its Norma-produced ammunition, was—and remains—hotter than the proverbial depot stove, blasting out a 200-grain JTC bullet at 1200 fps instead of the 900 fps initially specified. It's so hot, in fact, that, in my initial evaluation of the Bren Ten and its 10mm cartridge, I labeled it the 41 Magnum of auto-pistols!

The story circulated that pressures were in excess of 35,000 psi, but subsequent testing showed about 5000 psi less. However, flattened and/or cratered primers, cases expanded to the point where chambering reamer marks were clearly imprinted into them, wildly erratic velocity spreads and high-speed case ejection confirmed my concerns that the 10mm's operating pressure was still way too high.

Second, with a good deal of fanfare, Dornaus and Dixon proclaimed the Bren Ten to be the successor to the venerable Colt M1911 45 ACP instead of being an *alternative to the 9mm Parabellum*, an act which virtually sealed the doom of both the Bren Ten and 10mm cartridge.

Third, during the transition from theory into reality, the Bren Ten itself somehow became excessively large for the

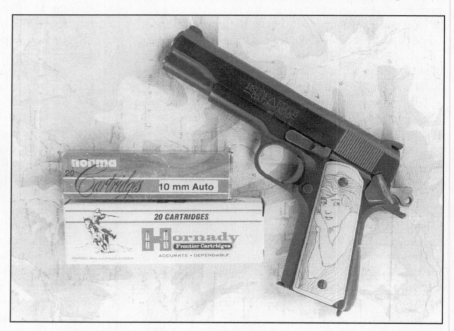

The Colt Delta Elite 10mm Auto is based on the Browning-designed, Colt-produced M1911 design. It was the second commercially available pistol chambered for the ultra-hot 10mm Auto cartridge, but the most successful.

10mm Auto chamber pressures are high—around 30,000 psi. In Taylor's opinion, this is way too hot and is abusive of both gun and shooter. These fired primers all show signs of excess pressure, a recurring symptom of the 10mm in virtually all full-power loadings.

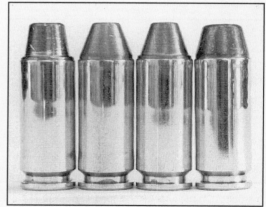

Handloaders have a fair number of 10mm cast bullet weights and styles from which to choose (from left): cast 175-grain SWC; 190-grain truncated cone; 190-grain SWC; and 200-grain flatpoint. Commercial jacketed bullets are also available in weights from 135 to 200 grains, mostly in JHP configuration.

size of the cartridge it utilized (larger than even the Colt M1911 it purported to replace), with a commensurate loss of balance and pointability. The idea had been to keep the weapon compact, hence the selection of the Browning P-35 or CZ-75 in the first place. However, in retrospect, it's probable that the increase in size was forced by the increase in power of the new magnumized 10mm cartridge.

Fourth, the absence of a reliable magazine for the Bren Ten when it was finally offered commercially astonished everyone, thoroughly annoyed many and, to some observers, indicated the lack of a proper research and development program within the project in general. This, of course, further undermined its commercial appeal and contributed substantially to its eventual demise.

As the Bren Ten drifted into obscurity, Colt, in what can only be described as a marketing coup of the first magnitude (and a classic case of poetic justice, since their bread-and-butter gun was the M1911—the very weapon the Bren Ten was supposed to replace), seized upon the 10mm concept and adapted it to the M1911 design. Shortly thereafter, in mid-1986, the Delta Elite series appeared and continues in production to this day.

By the end of the 1980s, Smith & Wesson had also introduced several 10mm pistols, receiving considerable publicity for their M1006 when the FBI granted permission for their agents to carry it, using a lower-powered 10mm load. By 1995, several additional versions of it had appeared. Glock, too, offers a 10mm auto, the M20; but, like the other 10mm autos, it has achieved virtually no popularity.

The gun upon which the Colt Delta Elite is based, the M1911, is possibly the most legendary handgun in history. The secret of its longevity lies not only in the superb performance of the 45 ACP cartridge against humans, but also in the fact that the M1911 was designed expressly to utilize a low-pressure cartridge. This means that less wear and tear are exerted upon the mechanism, allowing longer weapon service life.

Paradoxically, we now see it chambered for a cartridge that in every full-powered commercial example exhibits multiple indications of high, even excessive, pressures. How long can the weapon withstand such pressures before becoming unserviceable? Sources inside the industry claim that, utilizing any of the full-powered ammunition currently available, most of the handguns chambered for it will last no longer than several thousand rounds.

Here's the kicker—if we use the down-loaded FBI 10mm load (180-grain JHP at 933 fps), we discover that, while it outperforms the 9mm Parabellum, *it does nothing that the 45 ACP doesn't do better*!

So, when all of these negative factors are taken into consideration, the 10mm's slide into oblivion is understandable. With full-powered ammo, it is uncontrollable, exhibits excessive muzzleflash/blast and demonstrates massive overpenetration. Operating pressure remains high, in the 30,000 psi bracket, reducing gun service life and negatively affecting accuracy.

The 10mm is an interesting example of what happens when weapon and ammunition designers lose sight of their goals. The original 10mm cartridge and the compact pistol intended to utilize it offered a viable compromise of stopping power, accuracy and weapon control, all critically important factors to the self-defense shooter. However, once the project got off the track, it evolved into something like a 41 Magnum, but used in a self-loader, demonstrating all of the liabilities of each, but without any of the assets. By the end of 1994, the FBI had realized this, having experienced severe problems with the M1006, and was forced to remove them from service.

What did they replace it with? They went back to the 9mm Parabellum and 45 ACP. Surprised? Don't be, for both cartridges and all of the handguns chambered for them are well proven. But I'll make a prediction here— within a few years, they'll standardize the 40 S&W because it duplicates the performance of the FBI 10mm load from a shorter, more efficient case and, in the process, produces less gun-abusing pressure.

The 41 Action Express

Back in the Dark Ages when I was a staff member of *Soldier Of Fortune* magazine, I wrote an article appearing in the October 1979 issue entitled, "The Czech CZ-75 Pistol: 9mm Bohemian Rhapsody." It began thus:

> Sooner or later, someone had to do it. My only regret is that the 'someone' had to be a Communist [*the Cold War was still in full bloom, remember?*]. I mean, frankly, it is somewhat embarrassing for me to admit that the best conventionally designed pistol in the world was designed and is being marketed by the Czechs.
>
> It feels the best in my hand of any pistol I have ever used, and although I'm not about to run out and retire my Colt 45 ACP and replace it with a CZ-75, I would say that the 'Czech 75,' as it has become known, would be a most interesting development in a big caliber; say, 10mm.

That article, the first on the CZ-75 published in the U.S., goes on to state that the gun featured excellent high-visibility fixed sights, a well-placed thumb safety, a properly designed magazine release button, a beveled magazine well, an excellent finish, a correctly shaped tang, a reliable magazine, a smooth, polished trigger and a well-located slide-release.

My wish for a CZ in a larger caliber was granted sooner than I had expected, first in the form of the unsuccessful Bren Ten and, in mid-1987, in the 41 Action Express FIE TZ-75 Ultra and KBI-imported Jericho M941.

Sadly, the development of the 41 AE cartridge was not without major problems. Guns and ammo manufactured prior to mid-1989 exhibited several disconcerting characteristics, indicating that, like the Bren Ten 10mm auto, they weren't quite ready for "prime time." So, in April 1989 I conducted a test to fully evaluate the 41 AE, but to my dismay encountered a complex web of accuracy/weapon functioning problems that seemed to defy belief.

The only way I could isolate and identify the problems was to start at "ground zero." First, I laboriously detail-stripped both guns and micrometer-measured the parts, bores and chambers of each one, carefully comparing them with factory specifications. I found everything in perfect order.

Puzzled, I then took my search to the ammunition, gathering yet more data. Finally, I watched slow-motion video tapes of the two guns actually being fired, this allowing me to place my information in its proper perspective.

Something was *very* wrong. Disheartened, I sent a copy of my analysis to FIE, who quickly forwarded it to Tanfoglio Manufacturing, the Italian builder of the guns, and to Israel Military Industries, the ammo manufacturer. Happily, and to my considerable surprise, my report was taken quite seriously by both organizations and the problems mentioned therein were immediately rectified.

However, for the 41 AE *cartridge*, it was too late—the damage had been done.

The guns, both based on the popular CZ-75 design, would survive, but the 41 AE itself was doomed. What was wrong? Plenty, but first some background.

Sporting a rebated case head identical in diameter to the 9mm Parabellum, the IMI-produced 41 AE punched out a 200-grain JTC bullet at 900 fps or a 170-grain JHP at a sizzling 1072 fps. Intended as a big-bore alternative to both the 9mm and ill-fated 10mm, it was based on some of the clearest thinking on defensive handgun cartridges shown to that date.

Unfortunately, the diameter of the bullet used in the pre-1989 200-grain JTC load measures from .405 to .408 instead of the specified .410, resulting in less than acceptable accuracy. Moreover, case wall thickness was excessive, measuring .012-inch thick instead of the .0065 required for a .410-inch bullet to be seated without increasing the outside diameter of the case to the point where it wouldn't chamber properly. All cases used for 200-grain loads manufactured

Tanfoglio-made CZ-75-type pistol (top) in 41 Action Express, shown for size comparison to Colt M1911 45 ACP. Unfortunately, though the workmanship on the weapon was flawless, problems with incorrect case/bullet dimensions prevented reliable functioning or acceptable accuracy.

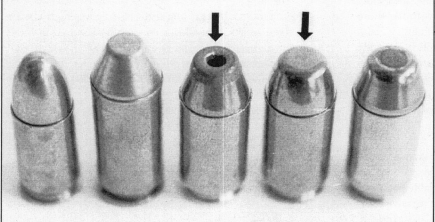

Factory 41 AE loads with a sampling of other service cartridges (from left): 9mm 124-grain NATO Ball; Norma 10mm Auto 200-grain JTC; IMI-manufactured 170-grain JHP; IMI 200-grain JTC; and handloaded 200-grain FMJ. The Norma 200-grain was the first loading available, but experienced serious problems, thus giving the cartridge a bad reputation before its difficulties could be rectified. The later IMI load functioned and shot very well, but came nearly a year too late. The appearance of the 40 S&W cartridge at the same time meant the 41 AE was doomed.

before mid-1989 measure .432 at the case mouth instead of .421 as they should, resulting in what can only be described as a press fit in the chamber—because the specified chamber diameter at that point is only .425!

Not only does this mismatch cause stoppages, but it also creates a first-magnitude handloading headache as well. Insertion of a .410-inch bullet into a case with faulty dimensions results in a too-big outside mouth diameter of .4335 when it should be only .421, making it all but impossible to chamber the cartridge.

Oddly enough, there was no problem with the 170-grain JHP load. Case wall thickness was .0065 as it should have been, thus allowing the use of a .410 bullet as specified. Accuracy with this load was excellent, with Ransom Rest five-shot groups hovering in the 3-inch range.

When I reported the preceding to IMI, I expected little or no corrective action. However, the problem was promptly investigated, confirmed and cured as quickly as possible. Unfortunately, the corrective process and subsequent manufacture of properly dimensioned ammo required nearly a year, during which time the now well-established and highly popular 40 S&W appeared. But it didn't end there. To complicate things even further, large quantities of dimensionally incorrect 200-grain ammo continued to be sold commercially. Thus, unaware that there were now two different kinds of 41 AE ammo on the market, many Ultra and M941 owners ended up with the short end of the stick, thus giving the cartridge its poor reputation and ultimately causing its demise.

This is unfortunate, because the idea upon which it was based is entirely sound. And, who knows. If the 40 S&W had not appeared for another six months, the 41 AE would probably have survived and perhaps even prospered.

40 Smith & Wesson

Appearing in mid-1989, the 40 Smith & Wesson cartridge fulfills the role for which the ill-fated 10mm Auto was intended—to be an alternative to the 9mm Parabellum, while retaining a standard-size handgun. However, its true niche has been obfuscated by some writers, who confuse the issue by recommending it as an alternative to the 45 ACP.

This is unfortunate, because it is in no way the 45's equal. Nonetheless, it does provide about 40 percent better stopping power than the 9mm with only a slight increase in felt recoil, thus making it easy to shoot well under stress.

Please don't misunderstand—this is not to infer that the 40 S&W isn't a good cartridge, *because it is*. In fact, it in every way satisfies the goals of its designers and is without question a viable compromise between the 9mm Parabellum and 45 ACP. Having been involved in an earlier attempt at creating such a compromise (the ill-fated 10mm Bren Ten project), I found the 40 S&W's 1989 emergence most refreshing. It mirrors the specifications I had earlier envi-

sioned for the original 10mm and provides a good balance of stopping power and controllability.

Still, it has experienced some growing pains in that many gunsmiths felt it to be intrinsically inaccurate, especially in its earlier commercial loadings. I do *not* share this opinion, having found via extensive Ransom Rest testing that it's as accurate as any other cartridge.

Thus, I can only suggest that this leaves questionable workmanship as the problem's only other possible source. I mean no offense to anyone, but let's face it—if the *ammunition* isn't at fault, there is simply nowhere else to look. Frankly, over the course of my twenty-plus years as a weapons and tactics consultant/instructor/writer, I have seen dozens of instances in which gunsmiths who specialize in accurizing often conveniently ignore the possibility of accuracy problems originating in their own work. To provide a complete perspective, I'd also like to point out another fact. When one of their "accurized" guns chambered for a cartridge with a proven reputation for accuracy doesn't shoot well, they make the same claim.

For the last five years, I've been evaluating the 40 S&W's capabilities, not only by shooting a number of big game animals with it, but also by analyzing dozens of law enforcement shootings in which it was used. My conclusion is that, like other cartridges in the 40/41-caliber category, it has a narrow "efficiency zone," the range of bullet weights that seem to give good overall performance.

Though I've been in seven handgun fights, I have not personally used the 40 against humans. I have, however, successfully used it on white-tailed and Axis deer, mountain lion and wild sheep, and find that, like most service-handgun cartridges, it's at its best at ranges under 30 meters.

Provided the angle of bullet entry doesn't exceed 15

Since it first appeared in 1989, the 40 S&W (at left) has taken the combat shooting world by storm. Intended as an alternative to the 9mm Parabellum, it duplicates the performance of the vaunted 10mm Auto FBI load (180-grain JHP at 930 fps) from a shorter, more efficient case. In the six years since, it has evolved into one of the best self-defense cartridges available and is now loaded with bullet weights from 135 to 200 grains, including JHP, JTC and JSP configurations.

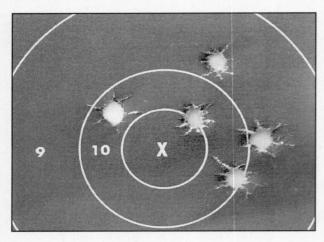

Some claim that the 40 S&W is inherently inaccurate, but Taylor begs to differ. Here is a five-shot 50-meter Ransom Rest group shot from a Glock M22 using Speer Gold Dot 180-grain JHPs. Judge for yourself.

Beaten to the punch by Glock, Smith & Wesson subsequently began offering guns chambered for their cartridge in a number of configurations. Here is the Model 4006 (bottom left) shown with another first-rate combat pistol, the Colt Government Model, also available in 40 S&W.

degrees to the right or left of perpendicular to the target, most 40 S&W JHP designs expand on animals and people 60 to 70 percent of the time, mirroring the performance of other service cartridges. When angle of entry exceeds 15 degrees, expansion is noticeably less evident, with a corresponding reduction in stopping power. Bullets recovered from animals shot at ranges over 30 meters (I tried it twice on 125-pound deer at 50 meters, using Speer Gold Dot 180-grain JHPs from a Glock M22) exhibit *some* expansion, but markedly less than experienced at closer ranges.

When heavy clothing or fur is encountered, cocooning (the packing of material into the hollow cavity of the bullet, thus preventing it from expanding) often occurs, usually resulting in less immediate effect on the target, but causing complete penetration. On a recent hunt for wild *Madero* ram (a tough, wide-horned animal in the 150-pound range, with a 3-inch thick coat of wool during the winter months) with my Glock M22 40 S&W, I personally experienced this phenomenon.

The first handgun to appear in 40 S&W was the Glock M22 (top), followed by the compact M23. Light, fast, tough as nails and simple to maintain, these pistols have seen widespread popularity, especially in the law enforcement community, where they offer a viable alternative to the classic DA auto.

Unable to stalk closer than 50 meters because the ram had seen me and was preparing to flee, I assumed a kneeling position and shot him as he stood broadside, head to the left, but turned facing me. The shot was perfect—the thunk of bullet impact clearly heard. Hit behind his left shoulder, he flinched, then started to run, but halted after two steps, obviously badly hurt. He remained on his feet, still broadside.

Disconcerted, I again took careful aim behind his shoulder and fired again with similar results, except that after a ten-second delay, he collapsed, death occurring shortly thereafter. Curiously, upon reaching him, I saw two 6-inch long spirals of wool protruding from the right side of his chest, marking the locations of bullet exit.

A later examination of his thoracic cavity showed that, although both shots had struck where aimed and exited within 4 inches of each other, the entrance and exit holes were the same diameter, indicating that neither bullet had expanded. My curiosity aroused, I returned to the field, located both spots where the ram had been hit and attempted to recover the bullets. After a short search, I found them both on the ground about fifteen meters downrange of where the ram had been standing. They were unexpanded, and the hollow cavities were packed with wool.

Due to its moderate recoil and efficient case size, the 40

Comparison of Typical Service Loads

Cartridge	—Bullet— Wgt. Grs./Type	MV (fps)	HRSP	TRSP	KE
9mm Para.	115/FMJ	1068	24	11	291
9mm Para.	115/JHP	1176	37	17	353
9mm Para.	147/JHP	942	31	14	290
357 Mag.	110/JHP	1090	33	15	290
357 Mag.	125/JHP	1416	49	22	557
357 Mag.	158/JHP	1070	47	21	402
40 S&W	155/JHP	1000	43	20	344
40 S&W	170/SWC*	970	58	26	355
40 S&W	180/JHP	933	47	21	348
10mm	175/JHP	1221	75	34	579
10mm	180/JHP	942	48	21	355
10mm	200/JTC	1226	69	31	668
44 Spl.	225/JHP	887	64	29	393
44 Spl.	246/RNL	781	62	28	333
45 ACP	185/JHP	970	64	29	387
45 ACP	230/FMJ	800	59	26	327

Chronograph: Oehler Model 35P; **Elevation:** 5800 ft ASL; **Temperature:** 70° F; **Humidity:** 37%.
HRSP: Hatcher Relative Stopping Power.
TRSP: Taylor Relative Stopping Power.
KE: Kinetic energy in foot-pounds.
*Select handload, author's favorite.
Hardcast 170-grain SWC/4.8 grains Hercules Unique.
Test Guns: 9mm = SIG P226; 357 Mag = Colt Python 4-inch barrel; 40 Auto = Glock M22; 10mm Auto = Colt Delta Elite; 44 Special = S&W M24 4-inch barrel; 45 ACP = Colt M1911A1.

S&W saw immediate acceptance and has proliferated quickly. Virtually all of the major gun manufacturers produce pistols chambered for it, and factory ammunition is now available in a wide variety of bullet weights and styles. However, a few recently manufactured light-bullet loads exhibit symptoms of the "magnumizing" such as we saw a few years ago with the 10mm, producing high pressure and excessive recoil. Obviously, since they abuse both weapon and operator, these should be avoided.

Curiously, although Smith & Wesson created the 40 S&W cartridge, Glock beat them to the punch by almost a year in marketing a pistol chambered for it. This gave their M22, compact M23 and subcompact M27 a head start no other manufacturer has been able to catch, especially within the law enforcement industry. Nonetheless, as this is written, Smith & Wesson, SIG, Beretta and Ruger also now offer pistols chambered for the 40 S&W.

All the major ammunition makers, too, have jumped on the bandwagon, seeing a bright future for the 40, and produce myriad loads for it, in a wide variety of bullet weights and styles from 135 to a full 200 grains.

Regardless of bullet configuration, I feel that the 200-grainers should be avoided because their weight prevents them from achieving decent velocities without increasing recoil to uncomfortable levels. On the other hand, although they don't kick much, I've found the super-light 135-grain JHP to have too little bearing surface for acceptable accuracy, a bright muzzleflash and poor penetration. The 155-grain JHP is in the 1000 fps range, exhibits moderate—and certainly controllable—recoil, little muzzle flash, good accuracy, but only marginal penetration.

This leaves the 180-grain JHP as being the best general-purpose performer, providing little or no flash, low recoil, excellent accuracy and deep but not usually excessive penetration. The Winchester Black Talon, Speer Gold Dot, Hornady XTP and Federal Hydra-Shok 180-grainers are, in my opinion, the best choices.

Because the 10mm Auto and 41 Action Express failed to satisfy the need for a medium-power service cartridge, the 40 S&W is a classic case of a well-conceived cartridge being in the right place at the right time. Based on its timely appearance and easily understood concept, its commercial appeal is therefore irresistible, and well-made pistols chambered for it are appearing on an ever-increasing basis.

Due to the fact that it's a reasonable compromise between the 9mm Parabellum and 45 ACP, as both a law-enforcement and civilian self-defense cartridge the 40 has a great future. Without question, it's one of the best-balanced combat cartridges in the world today, providing reasonable stopping power, excellent accuracy, controllable recoil and, with wise ammunition selection, low muzzle flash. It's been a long time coming, and it traveled a path strewn with pitfalls; but yes, the 40 S&W is not only here to stay, but will probably see eventual military adoption as well.

PROPER INSTRUCTION IS VITAL

FOR MANY YEARS, a good many people, yours truly included, have offered what is called "combat" or "practical" handgun instruction to the public. The approaches taken by the various instructors within the profession differ considerably, often radically, giving rise to a good deal of controversy. Often, the difference is so extreme that the student can't help but wonder: 1) Why the disparity? 2) Who *really* knows what they're talking about? and 3) Whose instruction is the most useful?

Although it cannot initially be obvious to the novice, many "combat" handgunning instructors are actually *competitive* shooters rather than real-world types. Thus, their entire philosophy centers around the competitive approach. They can't be blamed for this, because their exposure to—and therefore their perspective on—the subject occurred over a period of years and was the result of the various competitions they've attended. Still, virtually everything about even so-called "practical" (really a synonym for "combat")

A humanoid-shaped target is essential for effective combat training. However, when used in competition, the use of non-realistic courses of fire, handguns, ammo and other equipment negates its effectiveness.

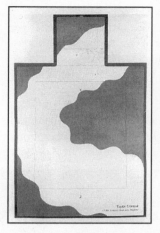 

Taylor feels that most commercial targets do not accurately reflect the need to balance accuracy and speed, thus making them less effective as training tools. The vast majority are too large and feature irrelevant scoring methodology. However, the Taylor Advanced Combat target (above left) is designed to demand the most realistic balance of accuracy and speed from the shooter without loss of administrative convenience. This target is much smaller than any other silhouettes used. Also, graphic targets lend additional realism to shooting-house and outdoor reaction-range simulators. However, they are expensive and thus require discretion in their use.

competition reflects a lack of knowledge of what the combat handgun is about and the nature of the environment in which its used. This being the case, it should not be surprising that the techniques, tactics, scoring methods and even the preferred targets fail to address the issues so critical to surviving a real gunfight. Not knowing this, many students are disappointed or even angry when they discover their instructor's true background, and the situation is often aggravated by the time and money spent to enroll in that instructor's program. I know that I expect to get what I pay for and can certainly sympathize with those who have experienced this annoying problem.

Many observers of "practical" competition comment that there is little about it that is truly practical. In fact, the more astute among them go so far as to make the observation that what they see in such events is suicidal if attempted in an actual gunfight. I agree, but why does this situation exist? Simple. Competition is considered to be its own end, rather than a means to achieve a higher goal.

If not carefully controlled to keep it on the track, any form of competition quickly deviates from its original path, quickly evolving into something bearing little resemblance to what it once was. This is what happened to "combat" competition. In the interest of finding better ways to do things, better techniques, tactics, etc., the concept of unrestricted competition became the norm. Given human nature, this led to its participants fudging from the original concept by using sub-power ammunition for better weapon control, bizarre holsters for a faster presentation, guns that look like they came from a Hollywood set, and tactically irrelevant courses of fire. For this reason, I discourage the competitive

approach, except as a carefully controlled stress simulator, because I recognize the dangers involved. Also, since defensive survival, rather than recreational shooting, is my specialty, I must make a clear distinction between the two.

Being among the few writers/instructors of combat weaponcraft who have actually "been there and seen the elephant," I have some strong feelings about life and death. I feel that confusion about competition's true focus might well cost someone his life. Simply stated, we need to know the difference between the two and must understand that they represent endeavors that are diametrically opposed to one another.

Still, "practical" competition has been in full swing now for over two decades and has promoted a number of potentially deadly (to ourselves) concepts we should know about. Among these concepts: 1) The use of highly specialized—

even bizarre—guns, holsters, ammunition and ancillary equipment to gain an edge. 2) Always firing two shots per target, regardless of the number of targets involved. This is a *guaranteed* ticket to getting killed if multiple assailants are encountered. While the quick two-shot response is indeed the best solution to a *single* assailant attack, firing two shots per target in a multiple assailant scenario takes far too long, giving at least one of your attackers plenty of time to kill you. A far better response is to hit each assailant once, bring the weapon back down to Ready, assess the effect of your

hits and, if any of the assailants continue to present a deadly threat to you, reengage, but on a failure-to-stop basis, shooting them in the head rather than again in the chest. If the initial trauma of being shot failed to neutralize them, subsequent shots to the chest will have little or no incapacitating effect because the nervous system has shut itself down in protective reflex.

A few others: 3) Excess physical movement, specifically the so-called "assault courses" that have no tactical value, especially when handguns are involved. Movement to

(Right and below) Steel targets react to being hit with a distinct "whop" of bullet impact and often fall as well. In addition to being quick and easy to reset, they last indefinitely and more than justify the expense of their initial manufacture. However, care should be taken to ensure that silhouettes, rather than simple disks or squares, are used to properly indoctrinate students to the idea of shooting at humans. Unlike so-called "practical" competition, self-defense is no game!

Full mastery of the fundamentals via "standard exercises" must be achieved before the student should attempt solving tactical problems. Here, under Taylor's supervision, students of an American Small Arms Academy Basic Defensive Handgun Course engage single targets from the holster under time pressure. This particular drill requires the student to present his weapon and fire two shots into the chest area of the target in 1.5 seconds. Does that sound too fast to believe? With proper training, this can be achieved in less than two hours on the range.

stimulate metabolic stress should be completed *before* the shooter begins to shoot, not as part of the shooting course of fire itself. 4) Overemphasis on speed reloading including the unnecessary abandonment of magazines and ammunition.

This is why both my instructional endeavors and writing reflect the approach they do: When the chips are down, it's *fundamental skill* that will save your life, not fancy guns, holsters, foot-racing, clever tactics or ambidextrous weapon-handling procedures. To teach weak-hand weapon presentation and shooting in a basic course is a waste of time because the student isn't ready for it. He has his hands full learning *fundamentals* that are the bases from which all subsequent skill-building will evolve. If he doesn't have complete mastery of the fundamentals, all the fancy guns, equipment and techniques in the world won't save him when his life is on the line.

In reviewing thousands of shooting case-studies, I found that in no instance did weak-hand presentation or shooting make any real difference. Thus, to provide the student with

Though often neglected, close-range emergency reaction techniques are also an important part of any competently administered training program. Here, Taylor demonstrates the Speed Rock.

Chuck Taylor's Defensive Handgun Practice Drills

Stage	Par Time (Sec)			
	Basic	Intermediate	Advanced	Master
1. Standard Exercises: Perform once each; single target; two shots each; from holster.				
a. 1 meter Speed Rock	—	1.5	1.2	1.0
b. 1 meter Stepback	—	1.5	1.2	1.0
c. 3 meters	1.5	1.3	1.2	1.0
d. 7 meters	1.7	1.6	1.5	1.3
e. 10 meters	2.5	2.3	2.0	1.8
f. 15 meters	3.0	2.7	2.5	2.3
g. 25 meters	—	3.5	3.0	2.8
h. 50 meters	—	—	7.0	6.0
Total shots for Stage 1:	8	14	16	16
Possible score:	40	70	80	80
2. Multiple Targets: 5 meters; targets 1 meter apart, center-to-center; one shot on each; perform each once; from holster.				
a. two targets	2.0	1.7	1.5	1.2
b. three targets	—	2.0	1.8	1.5
c. four targets	—	2.5	2.0	1.8
d. five targets	—	—	2.3	2.0
e. six targets	—	—	2.6	2.3
Total shots for Stage 2:	2	9	20	20
Possible score:	10	45	100	100
3. Single Shots: 7 meters; single target; perform six times; from holster.				
Presentation Drill	—	1.5	1.2	1.0
Total shots for Stage 3:	—	6	6	6
Possible score:	—	30	30	30
4. Responses Right, Left and Rear: 7 meters; single target; two shots each; perform each once; from holster.				
a. Response Right	—	1.5	1.2	1.0
b. Response Left	—	1.5	1.2	1.0
c. Response Rear	—	—	1.5	1.2
Total shots for Stage 4:	—	4	6	6
Possible score:	—	20	30	30
5. Small Targets At Close Range: headshot only; one shot only; perform each three times; from ready.				
a. 3 meters	2.0	1.2	1.0	.8
b. 5 meters	2.5	1.5	1.2	1.0
c. 7 meters	2.7	1.8	1.5	1.2
Total shots for Stage 5:	9	9	9	9
Possible score:	45	45	45	45
Total shots for entire drill:	19	42	57	57
Possible score:	95	210	285	285
6. Malfunction Clearing:				
a. Position One (empty chamber)	2.0	1.5	1.2	1.0
b. Position Two (stovepipe)	2.0	1.5	1.2	1.0
c. Position Three (feedway)	6.0	5.0	4.0	3.5
7. Speed Loads				
auto:	2.0	1.7	1.5	1.2
revolver:	7.0	6.0	5.0	4.0
8. Tactical Loads				
auto:	6.0	5.0	4.0	3.5
revolver:	7.0	6.0	5.0	4.0

For maximum learning efficiency, all range instruction must include a detailed discussion and demonstration of whatever technique is being taught at the time. Here, Taylor first discusses the step-by-step process of weapon presentation from the holster (below), then demonstrates what the procedure should look like. After this, he analyzes the student's performance and suggests improvements.

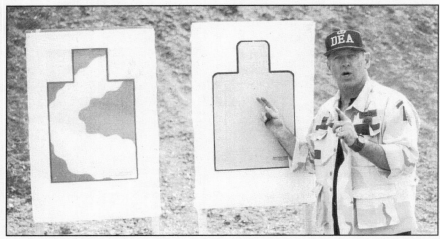

The best response to a single-assailant attack is to place two quick hits in the attacker's chest. However, speed and accuracy in balance provide the best means of success. At left, Taylor demonstrates what too much accuracy looks like, placing two shots nearly on top of one another from 5 meters in 1.2 seconds. Then he shows what a *proper* balance of speed and accuracy looks like—two hits 6 inches apart in under 1 second. Since both are well centered in the chest of the target, which would you bet your life on?

the highest degree of relevant skill and understanding, weak-hand work should be restricted to higher skill-level courses where it belongs.

One writer even created a scoring system that requires the shooter to amass a predetermined point score before he can consider his target neutralized. If he sees that his score is less than required, he then reengages, shooting the target again in the chest, until his point total is sufficient. Sounds great because it forces the student to look at his target after shooting to see what has happened, right?

Wrong! Only rarely can you see bullet holes in a human being. If your initial hits failed to incapacitate him, you should be going for the head. Only a hit in the cranial (brain) or ocular (eye) cavities can guarantee a "stop" under such circumstances.

This is a good example of "the firing-range mind-set"—

Multiple targets require a single hit on each as quickly as possible, followed by the weapon being returned to the Ready position and the shooter assessing the effect of his shots on the targets. If the competition-oriented tactic of hitting each target twice is used, it gives your opponents too much time to get you.

One of Taylor's toughest multiple-target drills is the Nutcracker. It consists of presenting the weapon from a holster and firing one shot on each target—engaging the first two targets in 1.2 seconds, then three in 1.5 seconds and, finally, four in 1.8 seconds. Up until the last five years, this feat was considered to be impossible. Yet, ASAA and Front Sight Master-level shooters routinely accomplish this feat. It's all a matter of training and proper technique.

the creation of tactics and techniques that work only under controlled conditions and reflect a lack of understanding of the true issues. A handgun fight does *not* take place under such conditions. In a real gunfight, you must look for only one thing—*target reaction*. Did he collapse or not? Is he down, but still functioning? Is he still a deadly threat? Does he have friends? These are of far more importance than trying to determine whether or not your *point total* is satisfactory.

This is why I often find myself at odds with some of my colleagues—sometimes on a friendly basis, sometimes not. But, doggone it, life-and-death encounters are serious business, demanding a pragmatic, conservative approach. Fancy methodology is dangerous, as is theory that cannot withstand a logical analysis, much less an actual field test, with people literally betting their lives on the outcome.

The sole reason for self-defense training is to save lives, whatever it takes, regardless of who invented what techniques. Only a clear perspective of the nature of a handgun encounter, the handgun itself, its capabilities and limitations, and mastery of its fundamental skills can accomplish this task.

Today, more than ever before, we have at our fingertips the most advanced level of weapon skill in history. Science has given us the technology to compile data on shootings of all kinds, in all environments. Without question, all of these things are important, for without them analysis is impossible. On the other hand, technical data must be handled with care to ensure that it isn't misinterpreted.

For example, science gave us the ability to determine kinetic energy. Few aviation or space accomplishments could have taken place without it, but it has also been used, usually in error, to determine the efficiency of small arms. We have seen vast amounts of space in various publications occupied by such data. Unfortunately, it often misleads the inexperienced reader.

How can simple kinetic energy be taken as a definitive measurement of handgun stopping power? What about the other aspects of the issue, like target composition, nervous system sensitivity, degree of assailant determination, water content, muscle bulk/tone, bone structure and even clothing? Obviously, all of these things exert significant influence on stopping power, but because they can't be simulated, should we ignore them in preference to simple arithmetic?

What about bullet penetration through a human target? How much energy is transferred if the bullet exits and continues downrange? Then there is the matter of how much time the bullet spends passing through its target. None of these things can be computed with any degree of accuracy because of the wildly varying circumstances involved.

This is why experience is so important. It tempers consideration of raw data to prevent jumping to potentially dangerous

(Above) Man-against-man competition adds urgency, but the course of fire must be kept tactically relevant to prevent a loss of perspective, and make sure that gamesmanship doesn't overshadow proper real-world solutions.

"Shooting house" simulators are also valuable training tools, but require that the instructors truly understand tactical principles. Sadly, most set up scenarios that are either unsurvivable or tactically irrelevant instead of those which teach the student that he can win if he uses intelligent tactics.

conclusions. It has been said that knowledge is like lumber—it shouldn't be used until seasoned. In the field of combat handgunning, if knowledge is used prematurely, people die as a result. Another axiom of importance: The scientist's job is to *explain* reality, not *create* it. Amusing, yes, but also true.

The next time you see someone touting a particular gun or cartridge because it spectacularly blows up a quart can of tomato juice, watch out, because he doesn't know what he's talking about. Since when is shooting tomato juice indicative of what happens when you shoot a person? Or clay, Duxseal, Jello, water jugs or wet telephone books?

When you hear otherwise, you're hearing assumptions based on a lack of experience.

If you listen, you could pay for it with your life.

There is more to combat weaponcraft than just shooting. It involves tactics, mental conditioning, the selection and modification of weapons and other equipment, stopping power, law, the psychology of self-defense and shooting aftermath, and technique. Experience teaches us that, past the point where fundamentals are mastered, it's the seemingly little things that count. It's easy to read gun magazines, of course, but remember that many writers simply paraphrase things written by someone else who is also paraphrasing from another source—which doesn't make it true. It's experience that allows us to separate the wheat from the chaff. Use your head when considering self-defense issues and be conservative in your decisions. Keep things simple,

"Jungle lane" outdoor simulators are fun and relatively convenient to set up, but also need careful attention paid to realistic scenarios. Here, one of Taylor's students has just walked past a "bad guy" silhouette without detecting it, thus getting himself "killed." The instructor will now stop the student, point out his error, discuss how it could have been avoided and resume the problem.

Realistic outdoor simulator scenarios include targets at odd angles. Here, a student (below) engages a partial silhouette placed in a tree (above). Naturally, care is taken to ensure that a safe backstop is present wherever targets are placed along the path.

For maximum realism, Taylor has his instructors "kill" the student via discharging his weapon into the ground if he fails to detect a target in time. However, this practice is only used during higher skill-level instruction, not in basic classes.

logical and get your training from someone who knows their stuff. The life you save will probably be your own.

Aimed Versus Instinctive Shooting

Although neither aimed nor so-called "instinctive" shooting is new, the matter of which is best continually surfaces. In fact, each decade seems heralded with a new wave of revelations on the matter, whether represented by some new and improved aimed-fire shooting stance or yet another version of the "instinctive" theory. Yet in spite of all the rhetoric, nothing really new has appeared, nor has instinctive (or "point") shooting ever actually been proven superior.

Frankly, the sheer longevity of the controversy about the two concepts astonishes me. Why? Professional curiosity, I guess. Neither one is new or especially difficult to understand, and can therefore be logically analyzed and competently discussed with ease.

First, we must dispel any confusion about the definitions of the two terms. "Aimed" means that the shooter is using his sights to align the bore of the weapon with his line of sight to the target. "Instinctive," or "point," shooting means that the shooter is looking at his target, rather than at his front sight, and relying upon his natural pointing ability to align the bore of the gun with its target.

Both concepts have their advocates, with some even recommending both as the best means by which to cover all the tactical possibilities. However, probably to no one's surprise, aimed fire has by far the most proponents, among them most of the well-known experts in the weapons/tactics profession. This is possibly because the capabilities of aimed fire are well known, documented in detail, and the easiest to understand. After all, don't most guns come from the factory with sights? There *must* be a reason!

In addition, it is irrefutable that if you correctly execute the fundamentals of sight picture, sight alignment and trigger control you'll hit your target. This means that good results can be had with a minimum of practice time and effort. Instinctive shooting, however, is undeniably more abstract and complex, and as a result, achieving any degree of proficiency with it demands a substantial amount of practice.

Briefly, here are the high points of the controversy. Aimed-fire advocates criticize instinctive shooting and claim it to be inferior because: 1) There really is no such thing as instinctive shooting in the first place; e.g., you're not born with a handgun in your hand and cannot, therefore, be born with an inherent ability to shoot. They say that shooting is a learned skill and that the whole idea of instinctive shooting is invalid.

They then continue by saying that "instinctive" shooting: 2) is excessively complex for human thought processes, particularly under stress; 3) exhibits no better performance than aimed-fire methods; 4) takes far too long to learn; 5) takes too long to develop skill to the point where you can reliably bet your life on it with any reasonable degree of success; 6) requires too much time to execute under the conditions present in the typical handgun encounter; 7) is critically dependent upon pre-known absolutes, such as the target being at known ranges, heights, sizes and angles, none of which actually exists in a real gunfight; 8) is incapable of handling a wide enough variety of tactical situations, such as targets at odd angles, small targets, hostage situations, etc.; 9) is unsatisfactory when targets not directly in front of the shooter must be engaged, or when they're on a higher or lower plane than encountered on the training range, where the initial skill is developed and conditioned responses built.

On the other side of the coin, instinctive shooters claim that it: 1) really isn't too complex and difficult to use under

Use of short, fast, but relevant tactical situations adds excitement and fun to training. Here, shooters must get up from a table or exit from a bed to engage targets.

stress; 2) is faster than aimed-fire techniques and that this is the primary reason instinctive shooting was developed in the first place; 3) doesn't take that long to master; 4) does work under stress (firing range demonstrations prove it); and 5) has a long history of success, dating back as far as the times of the Old West.

Obviously, somebody is wrong...*but who*?

Let's take each point one at a time. First, is the instinctive concept valid? Well, as of the last time I checked, we aren't born with a gun in our hands. Thus we cannot possibly have an "instinct" for shooting. It is my belief, though, that its advocates actually mean something else—that we are born with the instinct to point our fingers at things. Taken from this perspective, their claim is true. However, it cannot be successfully argued that shooting isn't a learned skill because it is, a fact that can easily be proven on demand. And the icing on the cake is the fact that pointing a finger and pointing a handgun aren't the same—not even close.

Next, let's deal with complexity. Here, the claims of the aimed-fire school of thought are maybe too strict. Complex?

That's not the right word. "Abstract" is more like it. Simple logic dictates that abstract concepts are more difficult to grasp than finite ones, and I think this is really what the aimed-fire crowd is trying to say.

Do instinctive techniques take too long to learn and require more effort than aimed-fire methods? Do they requires longer training periods to become good enough to bet your life on them under stress? Are they really faster than aimed-fire? Are the results they produce any better?

My experience has been that they do take a long time to master, far too long to bother with when we consider how much more efficient and tactically versatile one can become using aimed-fire techniques. Time and time again, I have seen instinctive shooters who are supposed to be good defeated by basic-level aimed-fire shooters. This tells me all I need to know. How about you?

Why does it take longer? Because you have no mechanical assistance (sights) upon which to depend. Instead you've got to develop a feeling for alignment of the bore with the target, which, obviously, is a highly refined process, requiring a long, long time to complete. Yet, the easily grasped

Physical movement to stimulate metabolic stress is useful, but should be kept to short distances to avoid situations where the shooter's running speed equals or exceeds his shooting ability in importance. Here is an example of the proper use of physical movement during training. The student must engage a target, then move a short distance to another shooting station, engage a second target, then continue moving forward. He should increase his shooting speed as the target gets closer and closer.

idea of sights allows a high degree of proficiency in perhaps one-fifth the time spent training, maybe even less.

Instinctive shooting may well be faster than aimed fire, but not if getting hits is your goal. Getting hits under the widest possible variety of tactical and environmental circumstances is the whole point of combat shooting. Any review of gunfights, including those of the Old West, discloses that aimed, not pointed, shots struck their intended target far more often, bringing the fight to a successful conclusion more quickly, and with fewer shots fired and less risk to bystanders. Nothing has changed—this requirement remains the same today.

If we include partially obscured targets, hostage situations, targets at odd angles, targets higher or lower or to one side or another of the shooter that force him to turn to respond, the idea of instinctive shooting quickly falls by the wayside. Demonstrations on firing ranges mean little here because a range is controlled, whereas gunfights are not. The record shows that instinctive shooting fails miserably when attempted in the real world. Would you want to be a hostage facing someone trying to take out your captor using instinctive methods? Or would you prefer aimed fire?

Those who recommend using both are hedging their bets. The two are diametrically opposed philosophically and cannot be accomplished with equal skill. Thus, if you implant conflicting subconscious programs in your mind, don't be surprised if, in an actual conflict, confusion in the decision-making process occurs. The subsequent sorting out of which concept to employ under the conditions present takes time that you simply don't have in a handgun encounter, when bullets are flying around your ears.

(Above) At higher skill levels, non-typical situations should be introduced. Here, a student engages a nearly hidden "felon" behind two "hostages." Not much to shoot at, eh? This exercise is intended to demonstrate to students what they can and cannot reasonably expect to accomplish under these conditions.

Dealing with the unexpected should also be a part of any advanced training. Here an unarmed student must approach a water-filled human dummy armed with an unfamiliar pistol, turn him over, get his weapon, figure out how to make it function, and then engage several attackers downrange. This kind of training shows the student that he must think about one thing at a time and never forget his shooting fundamentals.

Logic and documented history show instinctive shooting to be more of a stunt than a useful, effective concept. Sure, you can get by with it at very close range, but you can perform just as quickly and with a higher degree of certainty of getting good hits using aimed fire. Don't believe it? Come to any Front Sight Firearms Training Institute course and I'll prove it to you—or, more correctly, you'll prove it to yourself.

With virtually any modern technique, aimed fire is far more accurate, just as fast at close range and faster at longer ranges. It's also more tactically flexible, easier to learn, and can be developed to a higher skill level in a shorter time with less ammo expended.

To be fair, the idea of instinctive shooting came about due to concerns about the slow speed and lack of weapon control with techniques that existed many decades ago. Those techniques are long gone, replaced by methods producing results so superior that they sometimes require a demonstration to be believed. This being the case, I strongly recommend aimed fire in preference to instinctive shooting.

Shooting from vehicles should be reserved for advanced-level training, after the student has a full grasp of all fundamental shooting and weapon-handling drills.

Some of Taylor's students go through the Lost Weapon Recovery drill. Taught at the intermediate level and above, this particular drill is challenging and physically fatiguing, illustrating to students the negative effect of high stress on performance.

LOADING, UNLOADING, GRIP AND STANCE

WHILE MANY FEEL it to be mundane, the act of checking a weapon to see if it's loaded or not is an important part of any shooter's repertoire of skills. So are loading and unloading procedures. In fact, more accidental discharges occur during this phase of weapon handling than with any other.

Many instructors assume that students already know how these functions are accomplished. This is a dangerous assumption, especially considering current trends in vicarious liability. So, the first part of the firing-range portion of my Basic Defensive Handgun Course deals with these subjects. When I initially instituted formal training in these functions nearly fifteen years ago, I was concerned that I might be insulting my students' intelligence. However, I found that not only did they need the instruction, they also felt more secure about themselves and the other students once they had received it.

Grip and trigger finger position, too, are often left up to the student. However, I found that it just wasn't realistic to assume they had such knowledge. One must learn to walk before he can run, so I incorporated Loading and Unloading into the first block of instruction after Condition Checking with excellent results.

The photos here explain how to load, unload and grip handguns properly and safely. The main points are to *always* assume the gun is loaded, keep the gun pointed in a safe direction, and keep *all* your fingers away from the trigger.

Shooting Stances

Stances, especially the Weaver and Isosceles, are continually controversial, although in my adult lifetime this particular controversy has come, gone, resurfaced, gone away and again appeared several times. In the paragraphs that follow, I'll give you the reasons why I feel the Weaver to be the better of the two.

If you want to pursue skill elevation to your highest possible potential, I say this to you flat out—*you'll shoot Weaver*. Comments from various writers who claim otherwise indicate that they simply have no perspective of how fast and accurately you can shoot using it, or how tactically flexible it is. This is not a lightly stated matter as far as I am concerned. I have demonstrated the truth of my premise a hundred times or more. There is nothing wrong with the Isosceles, but if you want to reach the higher levels of efficiency, you will quickly find that it greatly limits you and will eventually become a serious obstacle. In other words, your skill eventually will transcend the capabilities of the Isosceles stance.

With the recent surge in popularity of the 38 Super cartridge in IPSC competition and the melding of PPC and IPSC disciplines a la the Bianchi Cup, there has emerged a rebirth of the Isosceles stance. The explanation for this is complex and controversial, meaning that whoever you ask about it determines the answer as much as the actual technical aspects of the issue do.

As a former world-class IPSC competitor myself and a member of the famous 1978-79 U.S. team, I believe that the evolution of IPSC competition itself has influenced the trend immensely. IPSC has, over the last decade or so, become highly specialized and departed entirely from its original theme of simulating combat situations. Instead, like PPC and National Match competition, it has become a discipline unto

CONDITION CHECK

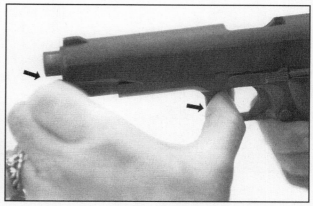

To see if a DA revolver is loaded, simply depress the cylinder release latch with your firing thumb and, using the two middle fingers of your supporting hand, press the cylinder out of battery, exposing chambered cartridges to view. Be sure to keep the muzzle pointed in a safe direction at all times.

(Above) The practice of "pinching" the SA auto open slightly to see if a cartridge is chambered is frowned upon by some. However, if correctly executed, it is perfectly safe. Proper procedure entails placing the tip of the weak-hand index finger on the slide beneath the muzzle and the tip of the thumb just inside the front of the trigger guard. Then, simply pinch, thus opening the slide slightly and exposing any chambered cartridge (below).

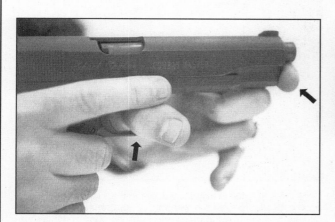

(Left) The incorrect—and unsafe—method of pinching the weapon open for inspection involves using the first knuckles of both the weak-hand index finger and thumb as shown here. If the index finger slips away from the front of the slide, the weapon lunges forward, allowing the knuckle of the thumb to press the trigger, firing the gun. This is the procedure that gave the pinch method a bad name.

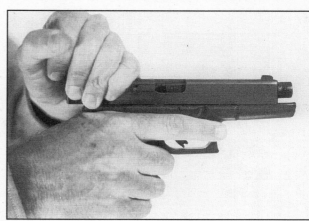

If your self-loader has a full-length recoil spring guide rod, you cannot pinch it open anyway. If this is the case, or if you simply feel awkward about using the pinch, then just grasp the slide as shown and pull back slightly, exposing any chambered cartridge therein.

LOADING

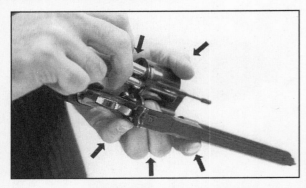

To load the DA revolver, simply grasp the cartridges two at a time and insert them into the cylinder. Then, close it and turn the cylinder until it locks into place. Failure to do this may result in a Type One stoppage, the only one for which there is a clearance drill with a revolver. Just pull the trigger again!

itself, so much so in fact that many now refer to it as "the PPC of auto-pistols."

As is seen with virtually all competitive endeavors, particularly those without the protection of basic conceptual rules, an overriding concern with competition as an end in itself, rather than as a means to an end (in this case, combat training), quickly begins to dominate. Therefore, it isn't surprising that a change in direction took place, manifesting itself in the choice of weapons, equipment, ammo, etc.

In this case, we have seen the shift from basic "street-legal" handguns to highly refined, match-tuned 38 Super pistols, replete with muzzlebrakes, counterweights and extended slides. Ammunition, too, has been tailored to the game rather than to the realities of what it takes to win a gunfight; and leather gear, perhaps more than anything else, bears an all-too-familiar resemblance to that same PPC equipment so ridiculed by IPSC competitors only a few years ago.

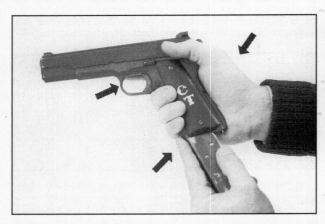

Insert a fully loaded magazine as shown here, rolling it into the magazine well from rear to front. A firing grip is maintained at all times for maximum control. Note also that the trigger finger is kept outside the trigger guard, preventing inadvertent firing.

Once the magazine is fully seated, grasp the slide overhand and cycle it briskly to load the weapon. Then press the magazine release and remove the magazine from the gun, which is then holstered.

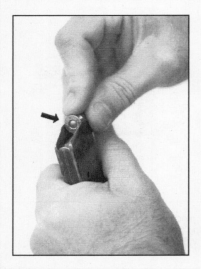

"Top off" the magazine thus...

...and reinsert it into the holstered gun. Be sure to press it into the magazine well until you hear the "click" of it locking into place.

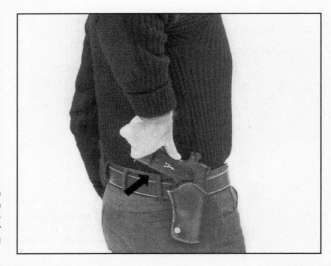

UNLOADING

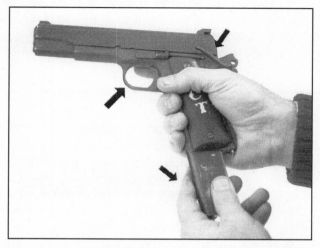

Keeping the gun in a firing grip for maximum control, depress the magazine release button and allow the magazine to drop free, catching it with the weak hand.

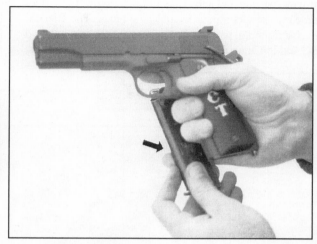

Then place it high between the ring and little fingers of the firing hand...

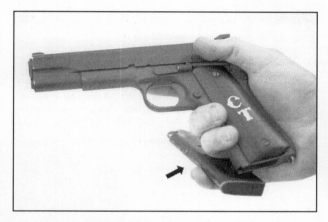

... so wet or dry, light or dark, hot or cold, scared or calm, you know that you removed the magazine before doing anything else.

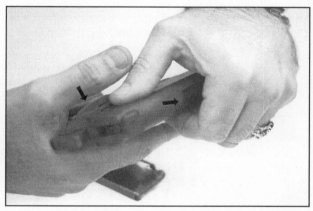

(Above) Then, being certain that the muzzle is pointed in a safe direction, cup your weak hand over the ejection port area of the slide as shown here and cycle the slide rearward. Be certain to use your fingertips to allow sufficient clearance for the chambered round to clear when it ejects (below). Then double-check the magazine well and chamber to be certain the piece is empty.

To unload a revolver, swing out the cylinder, elevate the muzzle and stroke the ejector rod. Then check to ensure that all cartridges have been ejected.

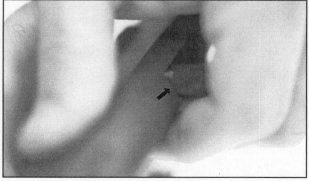

No, I'm not indicting IPSC, although, like many of the original IPSC "old hands," I'm disappointed by what some feel to be the prostitution of its original concept. The point is that with the loss and subsequent redirection of basic doctrine came new competitors and new ideas. The Bianchi Cup, for example, was the first successful attempt to blend IPSC and PPC into a single universal shooting game. Thus,

it shouldn't be a surprise that once the crossover was made, PPC-oriented philosophies would surface. The change in choices of guns, ammunition and equipment is merely a reflection of this. Since the Isosceles is dominant in PPC competition and always has been, it follows that it, too, should be seen in current IPSC competition.

While the Isosceles has unquestionably served PPC

FIRING GRIP

This is the correct grip for a DA revolver. The gun is placed in the firing hand so the bore is as straight as possible in relation to the forearm. The thumb is kept high but clear of the cylinder release lock, and the trigger finger is placed on the trigger to the first joint. The supporting hand is then wrapped around the firing fingers as shown.

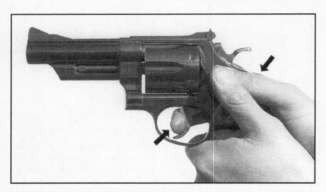

(Left) Proper trigger finger placement for a DA revolver is with the finger touching the trigger at the first joint. This gives good leverage for fast DA work without loss of control.

This is the wrong way to grasp the DA revolver. The hand should be snugly against the "hump" for best comfort and recoil control, not slack as shown here.

shooters for several decades, the kinds of firearms used in conjunction with it bear examination. For example, typical bull-barreled PPC revolvers exhibit at best only a rudimentary resemblance to the kind of guns encountered in the real world. The same can be said of the ammunition used, 38 Special wadcutters normally loaded with a paltry 2.7 grains of Bullseye.

With such guns and ammo, recoil and muzzle flip are hardly factors to consider. Thus, the Isosceles performs quite adequately. A similar situation now exists in IPSC competition. Contestants who shoot Isosceles typically use muzzle-braked, counter-weighted 38 Supers, producing essentially the same recoil characteristics as a bull-barreled PPC gun with lightly loaded ammo.

The correct grip for the self-loader. The weapon is placed straight in the firing hand with the finger placed on the trigger only to a point where the spot between the fingertip and first joint contacts the trigger. The firing thumb is kept high and the supporting hand thumb kept clear of the magazine release button and slide lock.

(Right) Taylor recommends placement of the finger like this for the DA auto. The finger contacts the trigger just forward of the joint, allowing good control for that first DA shot and subsequent SA shots that follow.

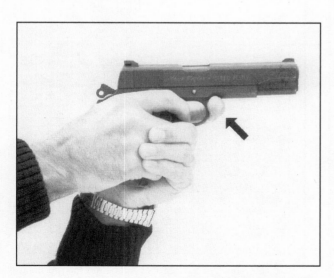

(Facing page and above) The "finger forward" grip fits best with the DA revolver. However, it reduces control with the self-loader because it places the hands too high in relation to the axis of the bore of the weapon. Thus, upon recoil, the gun slips upward, often with the forward finger completely losing contact with the front of the trigger guard. This isn't a problem with the DA revolver due to its shape.

The best two-hand grip for the self-loader is with all the fingers kept beneath the trigger guard, giving much better leverage against recoil.

From a technical standpoint, the Isosceles is fully as fast as the Weaver, right to the point where the first shot is fired. And if the weapon used produces a low recoil impulse, that stance will continue to work satisfactorily for subsequent shots—unless the shooter is required to move, turn or pivot. When this occurs, its rigidity and poor balance become a burden, requiring the shooter to work much harder to obtain results than if he were shooting Weaver. Sure, it can be done, but why work harder for no corresponding gain in efficiency?

If, in addition to this, we add multiple targets and/or more powerful weapons like the 40 S&W, 10mm, 44 Special, 45 ACP or 45 Colt, all of which produce more recoil and muzzle flip than a squib-loaded 38 Super, the Isosceles begins to show some serious flaws.

Consider this: When both arms are locked rigidly and thrust straight out in front of the shooter, there is very little leverage on the gun to prevent its recoiling upward. When we invoke the universally accepted tactical rule of always shooting a single attacker twice, this translates into increased recovery time between shots. Remember that the speed with which both shots must be placed in order to beat your attacker's nervous system to protective shutdown is of critical importance. Incapacitation, not lethality, is the overriding factor in gunfights.

On the plus side, because of its fundamental simplicity, the Isosceles stance is easy to understand and infinitely better than any one-handed method. The Weaver stance admittedly requires more mental effort by the student in the early stages of instruction. My colleague Massad Ayoob has stated often that he teaches the Isosceles in preference to the Weaver for this reason and because he also feels that it's impossible to convert an Isosceles shooter to Weaver, finding that under stress he reverts.

I understand these reasons, but in a twenty-plus-year-long instructional career, I have experienced no such problem. As a matter of fact, although I can't say it's been universal, I have had excellent success in assisting students wishing to make the change within a two-day seminar.

Because of its superior geometric configuration and the resultant better utilization of the laws of physics, the Weaver provides better control, especially of the more potent weapons, and requires much less energy expenditure. This translates into better performance with less effort, both of which are obvious advantages when one is quite literally betting one's life on the outcome.

As a professional instructor, I have found that, in assuming the Weaver, students often turn too far into the strong side, sometimes as much as a full 90 degrees. This is a serious error in that it redirects the gun's recoil force and the muscle strength of the stance from the requisite bone-to-bone contact and stability of the shoulder joint to the tendon located behind it. The problem is aggravated further if the shooter has a large upper torso; the shooting arm is obstruct-

STANCES

Old-time shooters thought that it took too long to bring the weapon to eye level and shoot, so they generally fired from waist level instead. In truth, so-called "hip shooting" produces such poor accuracy that it should be used only at very close range, if at all. Taylor advocates it only in close-range emergency situations where the assailant is inside arm's reach and you don't have room to step back from him as you present your weapon.

Over the years, unsatisfactory results with "hip shooting" (above) caused the weapon to be brought a little higher and thrust forward to resist recoil. A later version of this is the so-called FBI Crouch (top right and right), used from the 1930s until about 1990. Note the hand held across the heart to protect against incoming fire—a nice theory, but in reality a useless gesture.

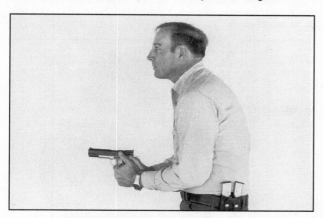

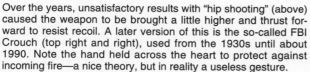

(Above and below) By the 1960s, concerns about the lack of weapon control using one hand caused the appearance of the two-hand method shown here. While providing better recoil resistance, it still failed to bring the weapon close to the shooter's line of sight, thus producing poor first-shot accuracy.

(Above) By the late 1960s, virtually all below-eye-level stances had proven to be unsatisfactory. This was due to the rediscovery that accuracy was best when the gun was aimed. Here is the Isosceles stance, where the gun is held in both hands and thrust forward with both arms locked. A far superior stance to anything that preceded it, it still falls short of the Weaver in recoil resistance and overall tactical flexibility.

ed by the strong side pectoral muscle, resulting in unnecessary strain and fatigue. Actually, the shooter rarely needs to turn into the strong side more than 30 to 35 degrees to place the weak-side shoulder sufficiently far forward to allow the arm to drop into a comfortable supporting position. The weak arm must be well below horizontal to provide proper resistance to recoil.

Another common error is in not placing the feet, hips and shoulders all facing in the same direction, causing a twisting effect, usually at the waist. This results in no gain in efficiency, while requiring excessive amounts of energy to be expended, and results in more fatigue.

Last, the Weaver is consistently more effective than the Isosceles when presenting the weapon from the holster because, even though performed at high speed, its movements take place within the natural arcs of motion of both arms, particularly at the point where the two hands intersect. Maximum efficiency can only be achieved if the complete firing grip is established well before the gun gets to eye level. This happens with the Weaver, and all the shooter needs to do is raise the gun and shoot. With the Isosceles, the grip can't be easily completed before the gun gets to eye level, and by then it's too late to be trying to get control of the weapon.

With only minor exceptions, the Isosceles is at its best with a heavy gun, firing ammo that generates a low recoil impulse. When utilized with a weapon producing a higher impulse, the Isoceles stance produces excess muzzle flip and

WEAVER STANCE

TWO-HAND SHOOTING

(Above) The modern "Weaver" stance actually surfaced in the late 1920s, as shown here in J. Henry FitzGerald's 1930 book, *Shooting*. This photo appears in Chapter 50 of that book.

(Below) In the Weaver stance, the shooter is turned about 30 degrees into his strong side, allowing his weak-side shoulder to be sufficiently forward to permit the weak arm to comfortably drop into position. Mild isometric pressure is applied to seat the shooting arm into its shoulder socket, thus bringing the entire upper torso into the stance. The Isosceles uses only the arms to achieve weapon control and is less effective.

longer recovery times. In addition, its rigidity and lack of balance under field conditions require the expenditure of more energy with no corresponding return in efficiency.

Conversely, the Weaver is not nearly so difficult to learn as some would have you believe and produces superior control, balance and flexibility, thus providing maximum performance with minimal energy expended regardless of the weapon used. For these reasons, it remains the state of the art in handgun technique and will likely be so for decades to come.

It is generally accepted that the Weaver was created by California lawman Jack Weaver back in the 1960s. Indeed, for the last two decades, Jeff Cooper and others have extolled its superiority to the exclusion of all other techniques.

However, take a look at the accompanying photograph, taken from a book published in 1930 titled *Shooting*, by J. Henry FitzGerald. The fellow in the photo is demonstrating a letter-perfect "Weaver"—a full thirty-five years before Jack Weaver rose to prominence.

I don't know why the stance was forgotten or ignored, which logic dictates it must have been, but I do know this: Without prejudicing Mr. Weaver, it appears that what we now call the "Weaver" stance had its origin a long time before any of us was born. This being the case, think of how many lives could have been saved during the thirty-five-year interval between FitzGerald's book and the accepted 1960-ish date when Weaver repioneered the stance. Who knows, maybe Jack Weaver read the book and gave the stance a try. Once you familiarize yourself with it, you'll never go back to Isosceles.

If using the Weaver, be certain to keep your firing arm extended, at least to the point where the elbow isn't excessively bent as shown at left. This results in a loss of rigidity and recoil control. The supporting arm is held down, not at or just below horizontal, for best leverage without exceptional muscle contraction.

This student is engaging multiple targets using the Weaver stance. Even though he is using a Lightweight Commander 45, weapon control is excellent. Note the lack of muzzle rise as the first shot is discharged.

PRESENTATION FROM READY AND HOLSTER

GENERALLY OVERLOOKED by the novice, weapon presentation is at least as critical to effective self-defense shooting as actually using the gun itself. Even in many formal instructional programs, the student is expected to somehow be able to bring his weapon into action quickly and safely, and then hit the target.

Weapon presentation is a carefully researched technique all its own, providing the shooter with a tremendously important tool for reaching his maximum skill potential. Virtually anyone can learn to shoot well, but when pitted against someone who properly presents his weapon, you have little chance, even if you're technically a better shot. That's how important presentation is.

The execution of all weapon-handling procedures should be done emphasizing correct step-by-step motions with smoothness, thus guaranteeing the development of both speed and consistency. However, it is common for beginning-level students to concentrate instead upon speed, forgetting that function follows form, and utilize violent muscle action to achieve it.

When this occurs, the result is quite negative and, occasionally, even unsafe. Presentation speeds are actually slower since erroneous methods entail more, not less, movement, therefore taking longer, and the shooter is forced to play catch-up, sacrificing attention to correct shooting fundamentals in order to do so. Naturally, his shooting deteriorates when this concept is used and will, if not detected and corrected, become a serious psychological obstacle.

Virtually all weapon-handling skills can be developed to a high level through dry practice. One need only ensure that he is performing the various procedures correctly, lest he unwittingly program his subconscious to respond with erroneous techniques when the stimulus to perform is received. If this happens, it can be tough to correct, but can be avoided entirely by careful attention to the basics. Hone your skills, using a conscientious dry- and live-practice program that includes weapon presentation as a major part of its curriculum.

Detailed step-by-step photo essays of the best ways to perform weapon presentations follow. Study them carefully, remember to KISS (Keep It Simple, Stupid) and practice them until virtually every repetition is executed smoothly and correctly. When you can truthfully say that you're doing so, you've achieved a major breakthrough in your training. In order to ensure that you're adhering to this concept, ask yourself this question at the conclusion of each repetition: Would I be willing to bet my life on what I just did?

In fact, then—and only then—should you attempt them in live-fire drills.

Moreover, I think you'll then notice something else—you've become fast without really thinking about it or sacrificing critically needed marksmanship fundamentals. This is the goal of all serious combat handgunners and one well worth your undivided attention.

PRESENTATION FROM READY

The correct Ready position, using the Isosceles stance. The weapon is held approximately 40 degrees below horizontal, allowing complete target visibility. Shooter attention is directed at the target; the trigger finger is *outside* the trigger guard; the manual safety, if any, is On, but with the firing thumb positioned for immediate deactivation. The safety is clicked Off and the trigger finger is placed inside the trigger guard as the weapon is brought upward from Ready to Point. Once target engagement is completed, the shooter should then bring the weapon back down to Ready, removing his trigger finger from the trigger guard area as the weapon is lowered. With the weapon held at Ready, the shooter then assesses the effect of his shots to determine if reengagement of primary or additional targets is needed. If the target is neutralized, he then checks to the left and right to see if additional targets are present. If none are detected, he can then relax, reengage the safety, holster, etc.

This is the correct Ready position (left) and Point position (right) with the Weaver stance. Regardless of the handgun used, it is critical that the trigger finger is kept *outside* the trigger guard whenever the weapon is not actually pointed at a target and being fired. The purpose of the Ready position is to allow all legal and tactical decisions to be made before actual weapon presentation begins. Once the decision to fire is made, the shooter then should concentrate only on marksmanship fundamentals.

STRONG-SIDE PRESENTATION FROM HOLSTER USING WEAVER STANCE

(Left and above) When the shooter decides to present his weapon, his firing hand obtains a solid firing grip on the holstered weapon, deactivating any holster security device in the process. The firing wrist is then locked. The supporting arm pivots at the elbow, placing the hand in a loose open-palm configuration no more than 10 inches in front of the abdomen. The trigger finger is kept outside of the trigger guard and any manual safety is left On, although the firing thumb is placed on top of it to allow later deactivation.

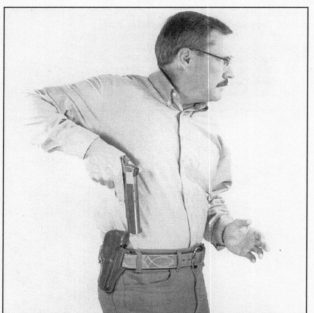

The weapon is withdrawn from the holster (left) to a point where the muzzle clears, but *no higher*. The trigger finger remains straight, outside the trigger guard; the safety, if any, is still On. The shooter's attention remains on the target. By simply dropping the elbow of the firing arm, the weapon is brought clear of the body to a point about halfway between the top of the holster and the intercept hand (right). The manual safety, if any, is now clicked Off, but the trigger finger remains outside of the trigger guard because the weapon is not yet under full control. Remember how fast this procedure is executed—the entire presentation takes under a second! If one is concerned about shooting himself in the left hand because of an inability to keep the finger off the trigger under stress, the left hand can be placed against the belt buckle at the start of the sequence.

STRONG-SIDE PRESENTATION FROM HOLSTER USING ISOCELES STANCE

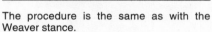

The procedure is the same as with the Weaver stance.

As the gun continues forward and upward, the supporting hand intercepts and obtains a proper grip across the firing hand as shown. This is essentially the Ready position (left). Mild isometric tension is applied to seat the hands, arms and shoulders into a solid stance. Notice that the trigger finger is still outside the trigger guard. The shooter then simply brings the weapon to Point (right), placing his trigger finger inside the trigger guard as the weapon rises. As it reaches eye level, shooter attention is brought from the target to the front sight, shooting fundamentals are executed and the target is engaged. If a single target is involved, quickly hit him twice, but if multiple targets are present, hit each one once. Either way, once your shooting is completed, bring the weapon back down to Ready, removing your trigger finger from inside the guard as the gun is lowered. Then, assess the effects of your shots and check to the right and left to see if there are additional targets. If not, then put the safety On and put the gun back into the holster.

CROSS-DRAW PRESENTATION FROM HOLSTER USING ISOCELES STANCE

This procedure is nearly the same as with the strong-side method. However, once the weapon is withdrawn from the holster, it is pivoted, muzzle down, under the intercept hand, then actual interception occurs, the two hands meet and the procedure is completed. The muzzle never crosses or points at the weak hand or arm.

STRONG-SIDE PRESENTATION FROM CON-CEALED HOLSTER USING WEAVER STANCE

The procedure is essentially the same as has already been shown for strong-side, open carry. However, to clear the concealing jacket from the weapon, a sharp sweeping motion is made against it with the ring and little fingers of the firing hand. The fingers are held about 90 degrees perpendicular to the hand itself, as shown.

WEAK-SIDE PRESENTATION FROM CONCEALED HOLSTER USING WEAVER STANCE

Although a shoulder holster is used here, the procedure is essentially the same as with a cross-draw. To clear the concealing jacket from the weapon, the weak hand grasps it firmly and pulls it aside until the weapon clears.

PRESENTATION FROM ANKLE HOLSTER

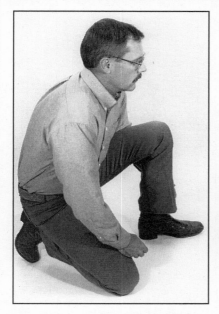

The shooter drops into a kneeling position as shown.

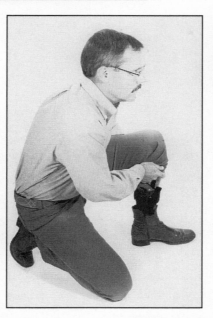

Once down in a proper kneeling position, he lifts his trouser cuff to gain access to the holstered weapon.

He then releases the security device, in this case a thumb-break, obtaining a solid firing grip in the process. Note the cuff is still held clear to avoid entanglement with the weapon.

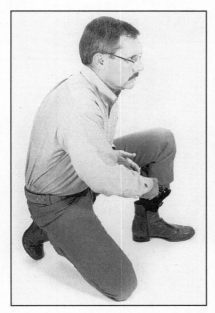

He then withdraws the gun, releases his trouser cuff and brings his supporting hand toward the weapon as it rises.

The hands intercept and a Weaver Ready is assumed. The trigger finger, as always, is kept clear of the trigger guard until the weapon is rising from Ready to Point.

In assuming the Point, this shooter has elected to use a solid Kneeling position for extra support and improved accuracy. Ankle holsters are generally used for backup guns and so are only utilized during extreme emergencies.

PRESENTATION FROM GUN PURSE (GALCO) USING WEAVER STANCE

With the supporting hand, the shooter firmly grasps the purse strap. With her shooting hand, she unzips the gun compartment. She then obtains a solid grip on the weapon holstered within.

...With a rolling motion, she withdraws it from its compartment, keeping the muzzle pointed downward.

She then releases the strap of the purse and obtains a two-hand grip at the Ready position, keeping her trigger finger outside the trigger guard of her weapon.

PRESENTATION FROM FANNY PACK (GALCO) USING WEAVER STANCE

The shooter's weak hand grasps the zipper tab and pulls it down and outward. The firing hand begins to move toward the weapon holstered inside.

As the compartment is exposed, the firing hand obtains a solid grip on the weapon, which is then withdrawn, taking care to prevent the muzzle from crossing the weak hand or arm.

The weapon is intercepted by the supporting hand, and isometric pressure is applied.

If a manual safety is involved, it is released as the weapon rises to Point.

The gun is then raised to the Point position.

PRESENTATION FROM CONCEALED SPECIALIZED FEMALE HOLSTER USING WEAVER STANCE

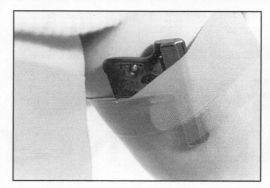

The idea that a firearm, no matter how small, can be effectively and securely concealed in the top of the nylons is pure Hollywood. In reality, it would either fall down into the stocking, thus being readily detectable, or fall out of the stocking entirely, thus not being available when needed or embarrassingly disclosing the presence of a concealed weapon.

There are, however, specialized holsters for women to effectively, securely and safely conceal a small handgun—for example, the Galco garter rig shown here. To use it, the shooter simply lifts the hem of her skirt, releases the security strap and obtains a firing grip on the gun.

She withdraws it, obtaining a two-hand grip in the process.

She then presents it to Point and fires.

CLEARING WEAPON MALFUNCTIONS

IN SOME CIRCLES it's popular to criticize the self-loader as being inferior to the revolver because of its dependency upon a separate magazine. While this observation is academically true, in reality its magnitude is considerably less serious than some critics would have us believe. This is because virtually all common self-loader stoppages are easily cleared in one to four seconds. In fact, the likelihood of experiencing them in the first place is quite small and getting smaller, as ammo quality continues to improve. Conversely, the ease of operation and use of the autoloader more than balances the fact that it occasionally malfunctions. So, let us objectively examine the possible causes.

First, the magazine. In my experience, about 75 percent of auto-pistol stoppages are caused by a damaged, poor-quality or defective magazine. True, in this age of rampant inflation, the dollar isn't worth what it once was, but to me, the too-common practice of buying cheap magazines for use in a self-defense weapon seems oddly paradoxical. After all, how much is your life worth?

Damaged magazines, however, are a more complex problem. Bent followers, weak springs, cracked or deformed feed lips, dents in the magazine body and inside/outside corrosion are all open invitations to trouble.

Still, all of these maladies are detectable. All that is required is an occasional inspection on your part, followed by discarding any magazines that are suspect. A small thing, sure, but when did you last check yours?

Defective ammunition is remedied more easily than you might think, too. A quick visual inspection of each "duty" round will eliminate the occasional defective cartridge that somehow makes it through the manufacturer's quality control process. Of these, the most common is a bulged case mouth which, if not detected, will cause a serious malfunction during your pistol's extraction/ejection cycle. Such inspection also discloses burred rims, high primers, and cracked or corroded cases. Ammo showing any of these symptoms should be immediately discarded.

Care, too, should be taken in the selection of bullet shape and composition. Remember that the self-loader was originally a military design, thus it was intended to use ball (FMJRN) ammo, not semi-wadcutters, softpoints or JHPs. Jacketed bullets are harder than lead bullets and demonstrate more reliable feeding. Polishing and/or slightly reshaping the feed ramp and chamber mouth of your pistol also improves feeding, but remember that it still may not feed as well as it would with "hardball."

With the issues now identified, let's discuss the actual clearance procedures. The first typical stoppage, known as a Type One, is a failure to fire. It has a number of causes. It could be from a dud primer, no flash hole in the primer pocket, a broken firing pin or—the cause of eight out of ten malfunctions of this type—a magazine not fully seated into the weapon during the loading process.

Bear in mind that in a pistol fight, there is no time to diagnose the exact cause of the problem, but you can, if trained, quickly recognize its *symptoms* and take immediate corrective action. A Type One stoppage is characterized by the hammer/striker falling when the trigger is pressed, but without effect other than a "click." Nine times out of ten, a "T-1" can be cleared by simply tapping the magazine floorplate briskly with the heel of your supporting hand and then cycling the action while simultaneously rolling the weapon to the right, placing it in a horizontal attitude.

If this fails to make the gun functional, quick repetition of the drill may do the trick. If it doesn't, I recommend that you quickly retrograde out of the area, because your firing pin is probably broken. Remember also that the slide must be fully retracted to ensure proper ejection of the chambered round and correct feeding of the top cartridge in the magazine. If you don't fully retract it, you will only recock the piece, leaving an empty chamber, thus re-creating the problem.

Keep the weapon at eye level to avoid wasting time by allowing it to sink downward as you clear it, requiring you to then raise it back up into firing position. By actual stopwatch timing, letting it sink wastes from .6 to a full second, much too long when bullets are whistling past your ears.

The second typical stoppage is the failure to eject, called the Type Two. This is the classic "stovepipe." It is usually caused by subpowered ammunition, a broken extractor, a defective magazine or a combination of the three. While somewhat intimidating in appearance, a "T-2" is usually cleared quickly and easily by executing the same procedure used for clearing a Type One.

Years ago, I recommended grasping the slide overhand, forward of the ejection port, with the leading edge of the index finger touching the protruding case, then "wiping" the slide to the rear, knocking the case clear and recocking/reloading the gun. However, about seven years ago I modified the old "tap-rack" method of clearing a T-1 to handle a T-2 as well, the idea being to accomplish as much as possible with the fewest movements possible.

CLEARING TYPE ONE AND TYPE TWO STOPPAGES

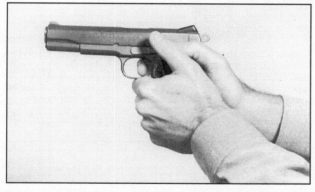

To clear a Type One (failure to fire) or Type Two (failure to eject) stoppage, you first identify the symptom. If the weapon functions, apparently normally, but fails to fire (this usually means "click!"), you've had a Type One.

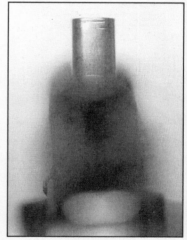

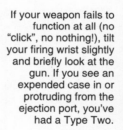

If your weapon fails to function at all (no "click", no nothing!), tilt your firing wrist slightly and briefly look at the gun. If you see an expended case in or protruding from the ejection port, you've had a Type Two.

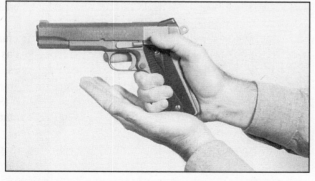

With the heel of your weak hand, briskly tap the magazine floorplate to ensure that it's fully seated. Improperly seated magazines are by far the most common cause of Type One malfunctions.

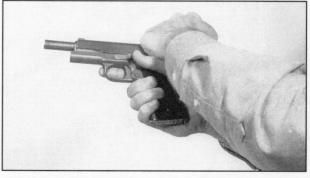

Then, without obstructing the ejection port, grasp the slide as shown and briskly cycle it once, while rolling the weapon over on its right side until it reaches horizontal. If the problem is a dud cartridge, it will be extracted, ejected and replaced with a fresh round from the magazine. If it was a stovepipe, it'll fall out of its own accord or be tossed out by the rolling motion of the gun.

I did this for two reasons:

First, large quantities of DA autos began to appear, featuring slide-mounted ambidextrous "hammer-drop" levers. I quickly found that wiping the weak hand rearward along the top of the slide often caused it to strike the lever, activating it and dropping the hammer. Just what we need, right?

Second, the KISS principle is better satisfied if a single drill can be used to accomplish multiple functions. In addition, a single procedure is quicker, more simple to learn and easier to perform under stress.

The third and by far most complex malfunction is the Type Three, the feedway stoppage, which is characterized

CLEARING TYPE THREE STOPPAGES

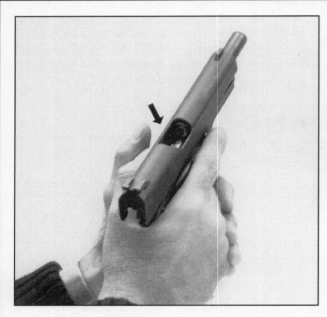

To clear a Type Three stoppage, a feedway malfunction, first identify the symptoms: your gun won't function when the trigger is pressed (no click, nothing) and the slide well is rearward of being in battery. To determine if you have a Type Three stoppage or you're simply out of ammo with the slide locked open, quickly bend your firing wrist, turn the weapon slightly upward and look into the ejection port. If you see brass in the feedway, you have a Type Three.

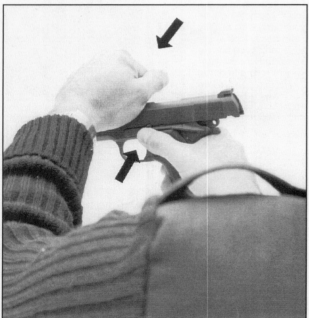

By manipulating the slide lock/release, lock the slide open.

Because of a partial feed of the top round, the magazine will usually not fall free and must be forcibly removed. With the little finger of the weak hand, stroke out the magazine and abandon it.

by a failure to extract/eject the spent round in the chamber, with resulting interference by the cartridge being fed from the magazine. The symptom for a "T-3" is that the slide is noticeably rearward of being in full battery. This is easily detected when the weapon won't fire—no click, nothing. Just "crack" your firing wrist, letting the gun tilt slightly upward, and look. If you see brass in the feedway, it's a T-3. A quick glance will confirm that either you're out of ammo (with the slide subsequently locked open) or have experienced a T-3.

To clear, you lock the slide open by manipulating the slide lock/release lever. Then, operate the magazine release

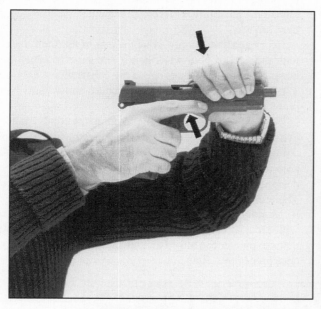

Grasping the slide with the weak hand, briskly cycle the slide two or three times to clear the feedway. Be sure not to obstruct the ejection port.

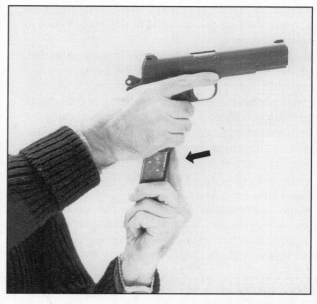

Obtain and insert a fresh magazine, rolling it into the magazine well from rear to front.

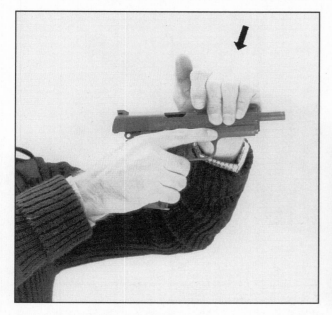

Quickly cycle the slide once to reload.

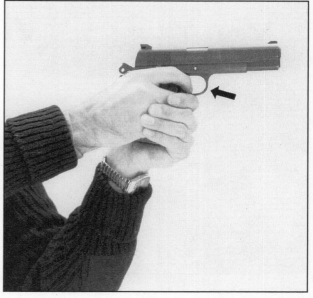

The weapon is now cleared, reloaded and ready for subsequent action.

button and "stroke" out the magazine with the little finger of your weak hand. Often, the top round in the magazine is partially fed, thus preventing the magazine from falling clear. It is necessary to lock the slide open before attempting to abandon the magazine in order to relieve recoil-spring tension on the cartridges caught in the feedway. With your weak hand, grasp the slide overhand, but without obstructing the ejection port. Then, cycle it briskly two or three times. This ensures that the feedway is cleared. Next, obtain a fresh magazine and insert it into the gun. Make certain that it is fully seated or you'll unwittingly create a Type One stoppage. Grasp the slide overhand and briskly cycle it once to reload the weapon.

If shooting is required once you're back in action, remember to really concentrate on the fundamentals—sight picture, sight alignment and trigger control. The normal tendency after clearing a malfunction is to fire without concentrating, with poor results. This occurs because the subconscious mind begins to sound a warning about all the time you've lost clearing the stoppage and urges you to hurry up.

The time for clearing a T-1 or T-2 is 1 second or less. A T-3 takes from 3.5 to 5 seconds.

Work hard to perfect your stoppage clearing skills by dry-practicing with inert (dummy) ammunition until you can make the times stated above. My own feeling is that they cannot be practiced too much. Naturally, the length of time required to attain efficiency varies from person to person, but if you dry-practice about thirty minutes per day for a week or so, you'll have no problem performing the drills within the prescribed times.

Another type of malfunction is the Type Four, failure of the slide to go into battery. A "T-4" is caused by an excessively tight muzzle bushing or by oversize ammo. Generally, when the former is the cause, a collet (finger) bushing is the culprit, but solid match bushings can also be the cause. Thus, if you have either one of these, I suggest you discard it. Functional reliability is more important than academic accuracy, anyway.

To clear a T-4, simply strike the rear of the slide sharply with the heel of your weak hand. The slide will then pop home. If an oversize cartridge is the cause, then a vigorous T-1 (tap-rack/flip) clearance procedure should solve the problem.

None of these procedures demands extraordinary intelligence or dexterity. However, like everything else worth doing, they require practice. Self-loading pistols are as reliable as a machine can possibly be; but because they're designed, built and used by humans, they aren't perfect. Therefore, occasional stoppages occur.

Murphy's Law dictates that if you have a malfunction, it will occur at the worst possible time, so no serious self-defense shooter can afford to ignore the importance of clearance procedures. Remember—egos are not bullet-proof!

CLEARING TYPE FOUR STOPPAGES

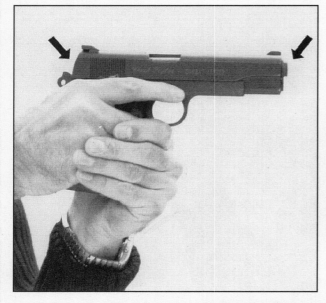

For a Type Four failure, where the slide does not go fully forward into battery, the first symptom is that the gun refuses to operate (no click, nothing). Again, identify the stoppage. Look at it briefly. If the slide is slightly out of battery, you have a Type Four stoppage.

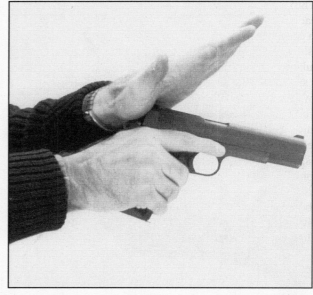

With the heel of your weak hand, briskly strike the rear of the slide, driving it home. The gun is now ready to fire. If this doesn't succeed, then apply vigorous Type One clearance procedures.

SPEED AND TACTICAL RELOADING

ALTHOUGH THE CONCEPT of speed loading the auto is well known, few are aware that it had its origin in the competitive, rather than tactical, arena. Yep, it's true, the speed reload was actually invented by well-known IPSC shooter Ray Chapman back in the late 1960s. In fact, according to Jeff Cooper, who conducted most of the early competitions in Big Bear, California, it was Ray's "masterpiece," the creation that gave him the coveted title of Combat Master.

Through such competition, the speed reload's popularity spread to the point where it has become a "required skill" in such endeavors, somewhat to the chagrin of those who prefer slower-to-reload revolvers. Why it has enjoyed such popularity is interesting to ponder, my own thesis being that it is spectacular to watch and therefore memorable. Who knows?

Tactically speaking, the speed reload is not the universal solution that it is often purported to be. However, it does have a place in the serious combat shooter's repertoire of skills, since the one legitimate reason to execute it—the situation escalating beyond the shooter's best efforts to control it—is possible, though not very probable. Therefore, it cannot be ignored. However, by the same token, it should not receive undue emphasis.

How much training time should we spend practicing it? Only 10 to 15 percent, no more. Why not more? In reviewing more than 4000 shooting case-studies over a twenty-year period, I was astonished to find that in less than a dozen instances was a speed reload involved, and in those, it made virtually no difference as to the outcome of the fight. Therefore, to spend many hours practicing it would be a waste of time. Imagine how good a shot you could

become if, instead, you spent that time learning to hit targets. Nonetheless, if kept in its proper perspective, the speed reload is a valid, if minor, tool.

For more than three decades, it has been accepted as the universal solution for all stress-reloading problems, particularly in the realm of competition shooting. Yet, although I was at one time a world-class IPSC competitor, I became disenchanted with the speed reload way back in 1979. It was—and is—simply too inflexible to be the wonder it was cracked up to be.

For example, the idea of firing two or three shots, then summarily ejecting the remaining ammo and speed reloading disconcerts me. Nor am I comfortable with the arbitrary, but nonetheless total, abandonment of only partly expended magazines.

Don't forget that the handgun is, first and foremost, a reactive, defensive arm. Therefore, its basic load of ammunition is very small in relation to that carried with offensive weapons such as rifles, submachine guns and shotguns. In short, you don't carry much ammo with a handgun, so the idea of unnecessarily throwing away perfectly good ammunition and/or magazines strikes me as being inefficient and, at worst, potentially fatal.

After all, just because you've fired your handgun doesn't guarantee that the fight is over—only that it has begun. From a tactical standpoint, in those seconds following your initial shots, the possibilities are many and varied. Your opponent may be down, but not out; he may also have friends you haven't yet met...*but will within the next few seconds!* In short, virtually anything could happen, which means that you must retain sufficient ammunition to deal

SPEED RELOAD WITH SELF-LOADER

(Left and right) Keeping the weapon at eye level, release your weak hand from the weapon and seek your spare magazine in its belt-mounted carrier. Simultaneously, flip the pistol in your firing hand to allow your thumb to reach the magazine release button. This should occur as your weak hand strikes the spare magazine in its carrier. Reestablish a firing grip as quickly as possible after you release the expended magazine. If the magazine sticks, then it will be stroked out with the little finger of the weak hand as it reaches the magazine well of the gun with the fresh magazine. Note also the proper way to grasp the magazine, with the index finger along the forward portion of the magazine.

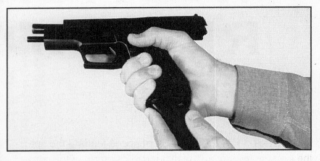

Then, carefully insert the fresh magazine into the well, rolling it in from rear to front.

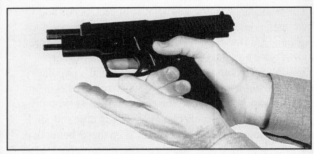

Briskly withdraw the spare magazine and bring it rapidly, but smoothly, to a point just short of the magazine well.

With the heel of the weak hand palm, sharply ram the magazine home, fully seating it.

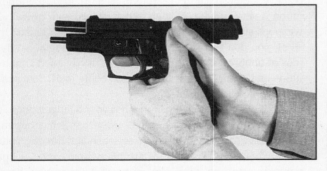

As the magazine seats, roll the weak hand upward, back into its proper support position, and release the slide with the thumb, allowing it to slam home as it loads the first round from the new magazine into the chamber.

The weapon is now reloaded and capable of being fired.

with any additional situations should they occur. If you're low on or out of ammo, you're dead.

Don't misunderstand: If the fight is still in progress when you realize that you need to reload, by all means, execute a speed reload. That's what it's for. But let's also keep in mind that most individual handgun encounters entail no more than a few rounds from each participant, thus leaving the shooter with a partially loaded weapon, held at the Ready, while he evaluates the effect of his shots. The FBI Uniform Crime Report statistical average on shots fired in police handgun fights has remained under three rounds for more than two decades. To me, this indicates a legitimate trend.

SPEED RELOAD WITH REVOLVER

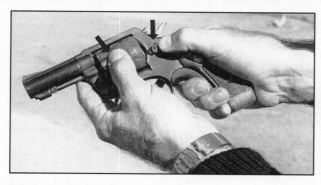

Keeping the weapon at eye level, release your weak hand from its supporting position on the gun, placing its two middle fingers on the right side of the cylinder. The index and little fingers are placed against the right side of the frame. Simultaneously, press the cylinder release latch with the strong-side thumb.

With the two middle fingers of the weak hand, press the cylinder out of battery, placing your weak-hand thumb on the ejector rod.

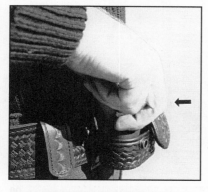

Release your firing hand from the weapon and allow it to move to the speed-loader carrier (which should be mounted on the strong side of your belt, forward of the holster area).

As your hand strikes the carrier and begins to unsnap it, your weak-hand thumb briskly presses the ejector rod downward, then abruptly releases it, allowing the spent cases to be ejected clear of the weapon. Note the muzzle is kept pointed upward.

Obtain a good grip on the speed-loader, withdraw it from the carrier and bring it to the weapon, which is being brought from shoulder to solar plexus level, muzzle downward. Index the speed-loader, release the cartridges into the cylinder, then abandon the speed-loader for later recovery.

With your firing hand, reestablish a grip. With your weak hand, close the cylinder and rotate it until it locks. Then, as the weapon is brought back to eye level, return the weak hand to its proper support position. The gun is now reloaded and ready to fire, if required.

In the vast majority of situations, after the initial encounter there is a lull in the action, which allows time to seek cover or concealment, and to perform a *tactical*—rather than speed—reload. What's the difference? The speed reload involves the rapid abandonment of unexpended ammunition/magazines from the weapon, regardless of the situation. The tactical reload requires the replacement of only expended ammo, with no loss of magazines. Neither process takes more than a few seconds, so unless there is an emergency situation still in progress—thus making the speed reload the correct choice—why not use the tactical reload to ensure that you have enough ammo to deal with any unforeseen situations that might arise within the next few seconds?

Like anything else, the tactical reload can be accomplished in several ways, but some work better than others. To me, the method that takes the least amount of time in relation to its effectiveness is preferable. Back in 1982 when I invented the tactical reload, I kept this premise in mind. The result was the procedure shown in the accompanying photo sequences. In arriving at this particular process, I tested shooters of all skill levels, constantly examining the results. After exposing them to a wide variety of circumstances, I finalized the procedure.

TACTICAL RELOAD WITH SELF-LOADER

(Left) The tactical reload is executed while the weapon is held at the Ready position. The procedure starts and ends with it at that location. Do *not* raise it upward as if you were performing a speed reload!

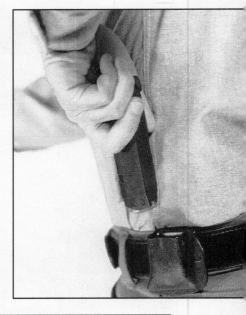

(Right) Release your weak hand from the weapon, seek your fresh magazine in its belt-mounted carrier and withdraw it.

Then bring it briskly toward the butt of the gun.

As the magazine approaches the butt of the gun, swing your weak-hand index finger away from the front of the magazine to a point around the side of it, allowing the fingertips of it and your thumb to grasp the partially expended magazine as it is released from the weapon.

Occasionally, a student or correspondent asks why I don't utilize the between-the-fingers, old-magazine-out, new-magazine-in concept promoted by some of my colleagues. The answer is simple. I once did, but in the real world, it doesn't work nearly as well. In the early stages of evaluating possible methods of performing the tactical reload, I discovered that, when using this method under stress and/or negative environmental conditions, a high percentage of the test personnel: 1) inadvertently dropped one or both magazines; 2) erroneously reinserted the partially expended magazine they had just removed from the gun; 3) because of the lack of dexterity caused by having two magazines in the hand at one time,

failed to seat the fresh magazine completely, causing a Type One stoppage (failure to fire).

In addition, it *requires the shooter to look at his hands* while performing it instead of maintaining his attention on the target area. So, in keeping with the KISS (Keep It Simple, Stupid!) principle, I modified the procedure to its present form, which does not require the shooter to look at his hand and can therefore be performed quite well in darkness or light, rain or shine, cold or hot, *calm or frightened*.

Here is the real kicker—the error percentages immediately dropped to insignificance! The other method shows a lack of thinking it through in a real-world environment and

As the magazine comes clear of the weapon, grasp it and place it *high* (to avoid obstructing the magazine well) between the little and ring fingers of the firing hand.

Roll the fresh magazine into the well from rear to front.

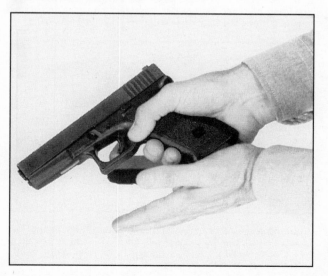

(Left) Briskly slam it home with the heel of the weak hand.

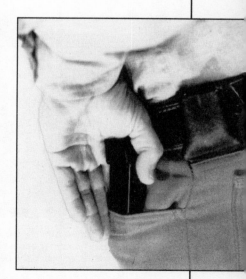

(Right) Then take the partially spent magazine and place it in your pocket.

TACTICAL RELOAD WITH REVOLVER

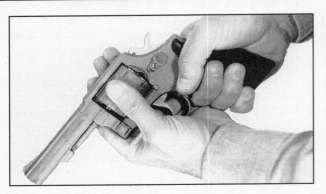

With the gun held at the Ready by the firing hand, release your weak hand from it, pressing your two middle fingers against the right side of the cylinder.

is a classic case of what I call the firing-range mind-set, which can get you killed in a hurry when the bullets fly.

The speed reload is intended to be used when the need to reload occurs during an actual exchange of fire. The tactical reload is designed to allow the shooter to bring his weapon back to full ammunition capacity during the first lull in the action. The speed reload starts and ends with the weapon pointed downrange, while the tactical reload is performed entirely with the weapon held at the Ready.

Difficult? Not at all. In fact, excellent results can be had with less than an hour of practice, provided the instruction is properly administered. Like most motor skills, the tactical reload requires neither exceptional intelligence nor dexterity, and can be mastered by any normal person. For over a decade now, it has proven to be the best solution to a truly universal handgun problem—how to bring your weapon back to full ammo capacity quickly and efficiently once it has been fired.

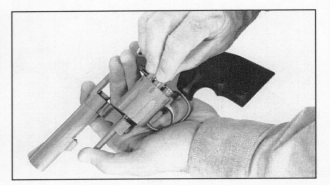

Locate the fired cartridge cases and place the index and middle fingers of the firing hand on them. With your weak-hand thumb, press the ejector rod upward about 1/2-inch. Once this is done, place the tips of your firing hand index and middle fingers on the cartridge rims and release the ejector rod. The two expended cases will remain under your finger tips while the loaded rounds drop freely back into the cylinder. Withdraw the cases and abandon them. Keep the weapon well controlled in the weak hand.

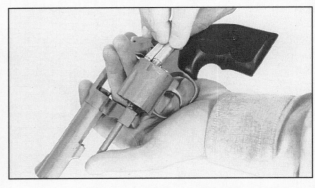

Then, with your firing thumb, operate the cylinder release latch. With the two middle fingers of your weak hand, press the cylinder out of battery, in the process placing your thumb on the ejector rod as shown.

With your firing hand, obtain two fresh cartridges from their belt-mounted carrier. The carrier should be mounted forward of the speed-loader carrier, nearer to the belt buckle.

Index and insert the cartridges into the cylinder. Then, as with the speed reload, close the cylinder with the weak hand and rotate it until it locks, while regaining a firing grip with the strong hand. Keep the weapon at the Ready.

WEAK-HAND HOLSTER PRESENTATION

FEW DEFENSIVE HANDGUNNING topics cause as much confusion as weak-hand presentation and shooting. Many police training programs abhor it; PPC competition requires it. But, in truth, does it *really* have a place?

I think it does, if only at the more advanced levels. However, I do not feel that it should receive major emphasis. The weak-hand presentation is one of those things any accomplished handgunner should know. However, he should also understand that, as with speed loading, the odds are overwhelmingly against his ever having to perform it in an actual gunfight. So, in keeping with the KISS principle and that ultimate rule of combat—Murphy's Law—weak-hand gun handling deserves a place in any serious training program.

Why? However improbable it may be, it is still possible that somehow you might find your strong-side arm occupied, perhaps holding on to something to prevent loss of balance, etc. Who knows? Remember, the mission of the handgun is to defend against the unexpected attack. In other words, control of your immediate environment has been taken from you forcibly and without warning. The handgun allows you to get it back. Therefore, any skills involved, or even potentially involved, must be considered.

The biggest problem in executing a weak-hand presentation is the initial acquisition of the butt of the gun by the weak hand. Some advocate bringing the weak hand across the front of the torso and grasping the weapon in a sort of reverse cross-draw, then withdrawing it in a rolling motion across the body while simultaneously attempting to obtain a firing grip. This method, while legitimate in the sense that it provides one way to deal with the problem, scares me silly. I don't want that muzzle rolling across my torso!

Another problem with this technique is manipulating the safety if an SA auto is involved. The rolling technique doesn't give the operator much opportunity to safely and efficiently manipulate it from On to Off. In addition, if the matter of weak-hand clumsiness under stress is considered, you should have no problem understanding my concern.

Instead, I prefer to: 1) reach behind my back, solidly grasping the butt of the gun; 2) briskly withdraw the gun with the muzzle pointing away from my body; 3) sharply bring it around to the weak side (the index finger of the weak hand is placed on top of the thumb safety of the SA auto), and then after it clears my body, disengage the safety; 4) as the gun continues upward and forward, obtain a solid firing grip; 5) as it reaches eye level, place my trigger finger inside the trigger guard and on the trigger, position my weak-side cheek against the weak-side shoulder for stability, obtain sight picture and sight alignment, and execute careful trigger control.

Many ask about speed. How can such a maneuver be performed quickly? Unfortunately, unless the shooter is extraordinarily ambidextrous—I have never seen anyone who truly is—anything done with the weak hand will always be much slower. However, inasmuch as I have been unable to find more than a mere handful of examples where anyone has actually used a weak-hand technique in a gun battle, I would say that the issue is not of major importance.

Thus, the original thesis stated at the beginning of this chapter is confirmed. We should know how to perform weak-hand functions because we can't guarantee that we'll never need them. But because the likelihood of ever doing so is both statistically and historically remote, they should not be disproportionately emphasized.

WEAK-HAND PRESENTATION FROM HOLSTER

Because it is more controlled and therefore safer, Taylor recommends this method of weak-hand presentation: Reach behind your back, bending your knees slightly, and solidly grasp the butt of the pistol.

Briskly withdraw it from the holster. Note that the muzzle remains in a downward attitude and is kept pointed away from the body.

(Above and below) As the weapon is brought around to the weak side and continues forward, the weak-hand index finger disengages the safety as shown.

The firing grip is then completed, and as the weapon reaches eye level, the trigger finger enters the trigger guard and contacts the trigger itself. Sight picture, sight alignment and careful trigger control are then executed to fire.

This is the front view of the correct weak-hand shooting stance and technique. Note that the weak-side cheek is tucked into the shoulder for stability.

PRONE AND KNEELING FIELD POSITIONS

WHILE SHOOTING KNOWLEDGE and skill levels have increased radically in the last decade, a curious phenomenon has occurred. Almost all technique development has centered on shooting while standing upright, the idea of using field-shooting positions being almost completely ignored. This may have happened because most combat takes place at close range and is fast, often denying us the time needed to assume such a position.

Yet exceptions to the norm do occur, and with ever more frequent regularity. This means that the ability to utilize field-shooting positions is not only a valuable asset to have on hand "just in case," but could, if the current trend continues, even become a required basic skill.

It's my opinion that the reason most shooters fail to recognize the value of field positions is because they think it takes too long to get into position. Actually, this assumption is false, provided the technique used is a fair compromise between speed and shooting stability. Many times, I have seen shooters perform below their capabilities because they didn't understand that field positions can be quickly executed, even under high-stress conditions.

Medium- to long-range handgun problems, while not yet the norm, do happen and demand more precision than speed. Thus, we can afford to spend two to four seconds obtaining a solid platform from which to shoot. If the terrain and vegetation allows, the Rollover Prone position is the best choice. Review the accompanying photography and you can readily see why. When correctly assumed, all body tension except

that in the hands is relaxed, thereby reducing fatigue and enhancing the shooter's concentration span. In addition, the rolling of the torso onto the strong side (hence the term "rollover") eliminates the throbbing movement of the weapon caused by heartbeat and lung activity.

For those with back injuries, or if the terrain and vegetation do not allow you to go prone, another option is Kneeling position. While not as stable as Prone, it has the sterling virtue of being achievable in under two seconds, while still providing good support. Kneeling is also a good choice in some close-range situations because it allows the shooter to take advantage of available cover or to change his angle of fire upward to minimize danger to bystanders in high-population-density areas. For the lawman or bodyguard, it offers a tremendous increase in accuracy while reducing the danger to innocents. It also works well in hostage situations and has been adopted by an increasing number of police departments.

Both of these fine field positions can be assumed very quickly and can even be accomplished as the shooter completes a Response Left, Right or Rear. Neither position is especially hard to learn, although they require a bit of practice to master. On the other hand, they're tactically versatile and quite adaptable to accommodate any differences in shooter physique. This ability, along with the fact that they greatly improve accuracy, makes them well worth learning and a valuable skill in the serious self-defense shooter's repertoire.

ROLLOVER PRONE POSITION

(Left) The Rollover Prone is the most stable shooting position available, since it actually uses the ground itself as a rest. It can be assumed in 4 seconds or less and is especially useful at ranges from 50 meters or farther. It has two disadvantages: 1) it takes longer to assume than kneeling; and 2) it takes longer to get out of, as well. As the shooter's arms execute Step One of the weapon presentation from holster, he flexes both knees slightly, pivots on the ball of his strong-side foot and turns into his strong side about 30 degrees.

(Above) He drops to both knees, placing his weak hand in front of him to break his forward fall.

He pitches forward onto his weak hand, finishing the weapon presentation as he does. Care should be taken to pitch forward in the direction established earlier and *not* toward the target.

He thrusts his firing arm downrange and places it on the ground, rolling up on his strong side as he does.

KNEELING POSITION

The Kneeling position is an excellent choice for medium-to-long-range situations or where the shooter has the option of using cover or concealment. Taylor uses this position out to 50 meters, and even farther when terrain or vegetation prohibits the use of the Rollover Prone position. Using his hands, the shooter goes to step one of the Presentation From Holster, while pivoting on the ball of his strong-side foot and, with his weak-side foot, stepping across to "two o'clock."

He then merely sits down on his strong-side heel and places the strong-side knee on the ground a comfortable distance apart from his weak-side foot, completing the weapon presentation as he does. The elbow goes onto or just past the knee. The correct Kneeling position can be checked by looking at the weak arm—it should be nearly vertical, as shown here. If not, you didn't step across far enough.

This shooter has the ball of his supporting elbow *above* his weak-side knee and has misplaced his strong-side knee as well. This virtually destroys the stability of the position. He ought to be sitting on his right foot.

He then places the front of his weak-side ankle against the back of his strong-side knee to maintain the rolled-up position. He also places his supporting hand on the weapon with the heel of the palm square on the ground. Now the safety is disengaged and the trigger finger is positioned inside the guard for shooting.

In this closeup of the correct Rollover Prone, note that the heel of the supporting hand is square on the ground, providing an extremely stable shooting rest. Author Taylor has shot several six-shot 4-inch groups from this position at 100 meters with a S&W M29 44 Magnum.

RESPONSES TO THE LEFT, RIGHT AND REAR

WHILE THE FBI Uniform Crime Report and other law-enforcement studies identify a great many tactical trends, they fail to address the matter of the direction from which the attack came, e.g., the direction the intended victim was facing when the fight began. Training is thus conducted primarily with the shooter facing his target. This is not in and of itself a bad thing and is quite logical. However, all too often, little or no emphasis is subsequently given to meeting deadly threats that come from other directions.

This is a serious deficiency and one that warranted an in-depth examination. I spent five years (1989 to 1993) reviewing every police shooting I could get my hands on, discovering that my suspicions were correct—fully 50 percent of handgun altercations begin with the intended victim facing some direction other than towards his assailant.

This means that emphasis should be placed on weapon presentation techniques that allow the shooter to smoothly turn to face the threat. In 1994, I implemented a research and development program by which I could find the best ways to accomplish this task.

Various techniques to turn this way or that have existed for many years, but most of them were created for the controlled conditions of the firing range and not for the street or battlefield. For example, the usual Response Left procedure was to step rearward a shoulder's width with the weak-side foot, while the firing hand sought the weapon, etc. This means that if the shooter is walking, he cannot execute the movement unless he first stops, then steps to the rear—from

a tactical perspective, a totally impractical requirement. Yet most of my colleagues are still teaching it.

Another example was the commonly taught Response Rear, in which the shooter stepped across and to the rear with his weak-side foot while beginning his presentation from holster and then performed a sort of reverse military "about face" toward the target. Again, the move cannot be executed while moving forward, nor does it take into consideration that the technique must be capable of execution on inclined surfaces as well as on the flat plane of the pistol range. When performed under such conditions, it is so unbalanced that it proved to be worthless. Sadly, this one, too, is still being taught at most instructional facilities.

The accompanying photo essays are the results of hundreds of hours of research before I "went to the street" with the techniques they illustrate. Perhaps not surprisingly, considering the methodology used in their creation, all three work very well, both on the range and in the real world, and by far exceed the performance of their predecessors.

Now, after over two years of testing, I've standardized them in my training programs, thus far with excellent results. I call them, simply, Responses Left, Right and Rear. They allow the shooter to quickly and consistently respond to threats from virtually any direction without significant time or energy expenditure, or disproportionate training being needed to master them. On this basis, I offer them to you here.

RESPONSE LEFT

For Response Left, as the shooting arm moves to step one of Weapon Presentation From Holster while using the Weaver stance, the shooter takes a shoulder's-width step *forward* with his right foot, placing his weight on the foot with which the step is taken. If he utilizes the Isosceles, he will step forward on a line directly in front of his weak-side foot. Although your head will probably be turned, looking at the threat, do not turn your body toward the target at this time.

He pivots into his stance on the balls of both feet, completing the presentation as his heels strike the ground, stopping the pivot. Here, the shooter is using the Weaver stance.

Then, he completes the presentation and engages the target.

RESPONSE RIGHT

To respond to threats from your right, you should imagine a line protruding in the direction you're originally facing from your right foot. If you are using the Isosceles, you will take a shoulder's-width step forward with the left foot, placing it directly on this line, as your hands assume step one of the Weapon Presentation From Holster.

However, if you are utilizing the Weaver stance, you will step across that line about 10 inches. As you step, your hands assume step one of the Weapon Presentation From Holster. Don't forget to place your body weight on the left foot, with which the step is taken.

Like you did in the Response Left, pivot on the balls of both feet into your stance facing the target, finishing your weapon presentation as your heels strike the ground, stopping the pivot, and engage the target.

RESPONSE REAR

A Response Rear is executed when you receive warning of a deadly threat behind you. This is a unique situation in that, unless you have visually detected the threat via some kind of reflective object to your front, your warning might be a vocal outcry like, "Look out...behind you!" So, remember that you must identify the threat as being deadly before you're justified in using deadly force in your own defense. You may stop your weapon presentation at the Ready position while you do so.

If the shooter uses the Weaver stance, he takes a shoulder's-width step *forward* and diagonally across at about "ten o'clock." If he utilizes the Isosceles, he must step directly across at about "nine o'clock." With either technique, the shooter places his weight on the foot with which he takes the step and assumes step one of the Weapon Presentation From Holster with his hands.

He then pivots toward the target on the balls of both feet.

Stopping in his preferred stance, he finishes his weapon presentation and engages the target.

SHOOTING IN LOW-LIGHT CONDITIONS

OVER THE LAST few decades, much has been written about various combat shooting techniques. Fully as much *controversy* has persisted for equally as long. However, after a good many years in this business, I've concluded that an individual's opinion on anything depends entirely on his perspective on the subject.

So it is with low-light shooting. There are certainly a

number of viable techniques in existence and, not surprisingly, some that are not so viable. Due to my daily professional participation in virtually all facets of combat weaponcraft, I've observed the generality of these with interest, but paid particular attention to their performance when facing the acid test—high-stress employment.

Though virtually all modern low-light shooting tech-

For low-light situations where there is enough ambient light to detect and identify the target, the superior muscle-memory and control of the Weaver stance is the best combination. The Isosceles stance does not have these attributes and, because of its geometry and rigidity, actually promotes muzzle flip.

Although it works adequately in normal light for shooters not seeking their highest possible efficiency level, the Isosceles does not lend itself well to effective flashlight use or to other required tasks. Although initial coaxiality can be achieved, it disappears the moment the gun fires, requiring the shooter to take time to reestablish it.

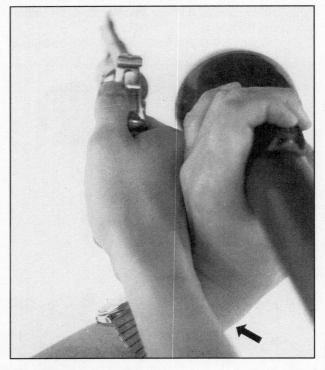

The Weaver is not only more controllable but more adaptable to effective flashlight technique, such as the Harries method, shown here. Note that except for the wrists being placed back to back and the weak hand being curled over the firing hand, it is identical to a standard Weaver. This means superior weapon control and faster shot-to-shot recovery times.

niques work at least adequately under controlled conditions, none equals or exceeds the control and tactical flexibility of the Weaver. Sure, the Isosceles can be quickly assumed from the holster, no question about it. But the locking of both arms integral to it causes muzzle flip instead of minimizing it, and the stiffness of the stance in general makes fast, balanced movement a difficult proposition. Nothing personal, you understand. I have no animosity toward those writers who are advocates of the Isosceles, but the hard truth is that the stance we now call the Weaver works better in the widest variety of circumstances.

Perhaps we'd better define the term "tactical flexibility." As applied to combat pistolcraft, it means that a given technique must perform well under stress, in the rain, *in the dark*, etc.

I realize that many shooters have been born and raised on competition and the Isosceles, but as training tools used to prepare people for the rigors of real-world handgun encounters, the record shows both competition and the Isosceles to be, at best, only marginally effective.

Traditionally, most handgun fights occur in poor light. Not complete darkness, but dark enough where we cannot always clearly see our sights or readily identify the target. Over the years, various accessories have been tried to reduce this problem, but seem to have focused on the wrong issue—the sights—rather than the techniques with which the gun is used. Sights range from colored horizontal or vertical dots or bars in various color combinations to sights that are actually self-illuminating, by either tritium or a tiny battery-operated light.

When considering these, don't forget that the biggest problem we confront in a low-light environment is target identification, not whether we can clearly see our sights. Obviously, colored or illuminated sights cannot solve this problem and often actually reduce shooting efficiency during daylight hours by "cluttering" the shooter's sight picture under stress.

The Weaver stance, by virtue of its superior muscle memory, places the weapon in exactly the same place every time it rises to eye level, minimizing the negative influence of not being able to see our sights clearly in dim light. In fact, it can be irrefutably said that if it's sufficiently light to see and identify the target, we can see our sights well enough to hit it if we use the Weaver. This simply cannot be said of the Isosceles or any other stance.

HARRIES TECHNIQUE WITH WEAVER STANCE

Taylor demonstrates the Harries flashlight technique from the Ready, using a push-button-equipped Streamlight. The light is activated after the weapon is at eye level, swept in a 60-degree arc to search, but is turned off before weapon and light are lowered back to Ready to avoid "tracking." Tracking is a process by which the shooter unnecessarily discloses his location by tracing the light beam back and forth on the ground or floor between himself and the search area. Once the search is complete and the light is turned off and lowered back to Ready, the shooter quietly moves two steps to his left or right and resumes the search.

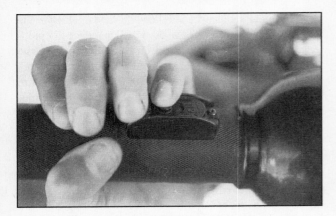

Years of testing and real-world use have shown the Weaver to provide the best results in light conditions where we don't need artificial light to detect or identify a target. The results it has produced have been so superior, in fact, that many students actually shoot better in low-light situations than they do under daylight conditions.

Another reason the Weaver is better is because it's easily

Best results are obtained with flashlights that utilize a pressure-release button, rather than a simple On/Off button (left). They will extinguish if dropped instead of rolling around on the ground while still on, illuminating the shooter. Modern mini-flashlights (below left and below) with a thumb-activated rear-located pressure switch offer an excellent combination of brightness, compactness and light weight.

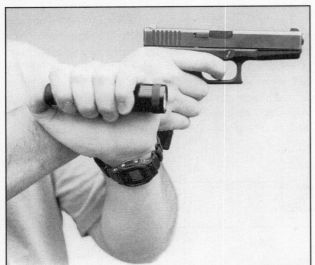

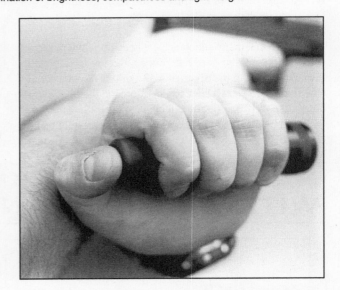

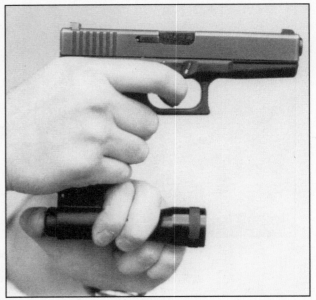

Recently, there have been a number of less-effective attempts to mount a small, powerful light on the weapon itself. Unfortunately, most of these require the shooter to sacrifice his solid hold of the gun, thus reducing or eliminating his control of it when firing. For this reason, they should be avoided.

adapted to the use of a flashlight without loss of weapon control. The technique known as the Harries flashlight method, invented by Michael Harries over twenty years ago, has no peer. Weapon control is nearly as good as with an unencumbered Weaver, something that cannot be said of any other technique.

The secret of the Harries flashlight technique is that it gets the bore of the weapon, the light beam and the shooter's line of sight as close together as possible and keeps them there even as the gun is being fired. The Isosceles and other techniques temporarily achieve similar coaxiality, but when the weapon discharges, it disappears in recoil, increasing recovery time substantially and requiring the shooter to re-establish coaxiality before he can continue.

What about laser sights? Are they a valid substitute for a good Weaver stance and Harries flashlight technique? I don't think so. From my perspective as a professional instructor/consultant, laser sights are of little or no value. Put bluntly, regardless of whether they're used in a general or special-purpose mode, their fifteen-year record shows that as a fast, effective alternative to proven conventional sights and aiming methodology, laser sights are a failure.

Logic and documented history shows five major reasons for this: 1) Keeping them zeroed is very difficult. Because of their bulk and awkward configuration, they're highly susceptible to being jostled out of zero by normal field handling. 2) This same bulk and clumsy configuration makes them awkward to handle and requires special holsters for convenient carry. 3) In most configurations, the axis of the laser beam is considerably below the axis of the weapon's bore, and due to simple geometry, the two can only converge at a single point downrange. At all other ranges, the distance between them is excessive for accurate shooting, particularly if small targets are involved. 4) The laser beam isn't sufficiently bright for use in normal light conditions. Yet, in low-light situations, it doesn't provide illumination for target detection or identification. A simple push-button, pressure-release flashlight is therefore more useful. 5) Lasers are excessively expensive in relation to their utility.

So, I vote no. Careful determination of what the shooter really needs to handle low-light situations repeatedly shows that a good Weaver stance, good training in its use in both normal and low-light situations, and a clear understanding of the elements integral to low-light encounters yield far more efficiency than any other combination.

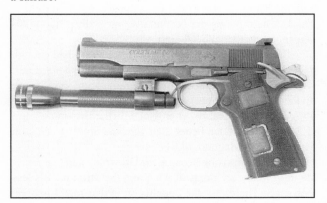

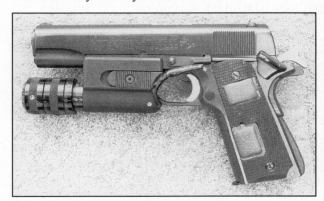

One "field expedient" and one commercial example of how to mount a light on a handgun without forcing the shooter to sacrifice control—use a stock-mounted pressure switch!

Lasers are too limited and damage-susceptible to be considered for general-purpose low-light employment. Moreover, even in their more modern compact versions, they lack the power to work in normal light.

COLD WEATHER AND SHOOTER PERFORMANCE

DURING THE 1989-90 American Small Arms Academy Arctic Weapon Evaluations, an interesting question surfaced. After nearly two years of continuous evaluation, we had collected hard data on sub-zero weapon/lubrication/ammunition performance, but we felt something was still missing.

After several hours of staff brainstorming, we realized that the missing link was how such temperatures affected the *shooter's* ability to quickly deliver hits on a target. After all, the weapon operator's role is pivotal—what difference does it make how the weapon/ammunition performs if the shooter cannot?

Hmm...an interesting—and, to me, intriguing—thought. Back to Alaska we went.

With the help of my two Alaskan staff instructors, we quickly designed a test whereby we could examine the effects of cold weather on shooter performance. The weather cooperated, and in -40-degree F. weather, we spent several days accumulating information.

Essentially, all three of us were highly proficient with the test guns, a Browning P-35 (Hi-Power) 9mm, a Colt M1911 45 ACP and a Smith & Wesson Model 27 357 Magnum, thus minimizing, if not entirely eliminating, the influence of the operator skill factor. It should be noted that both self-loaders were of the single-action type, used in the Condition One (cocked and locked) mode, while the DA revolver was utilized entirely in the DA mode.

No DA self-loaders were utilized because operator performance, rather than weapon performance, was the issue of exploration. However, if it matters, review the DA revolver performance in comparison to the SA auto and compare both the par times/scores shown in the accompanying chart. The DA auto points-per-second average will be about 20-percent lower than the SA auto.

After several days of testing, we felt that we had enough data to examine and could draw some conclusions. First, with a 5.62 points-per-second average score (raw score divided by elapsed time), shooter performance with the Colt 45 ACP was noticeably better than with the Browning 9mm (5.24) and was much better than with the Smith & Wesson Model 27 357 Magnum (4.61).

This was surprising because the Browning and Colt operate in virtually an identical way, and the 9mm recoils less than a 45. Therefore, the conclusion is that recoil matters less, and human engineering a lot *more*, than most people realize.

Although an S&W Model 27 357 exhibits considerable recoil, lower performance with the revolver was recorded

Course of Fire, Par Times	
Test	**Description**
1	1 meter Speed Rock, 2 shots, 1.0 sec.
2	1 meter Stepback, 2 shots, 1.0 sec.
3	3 meters, from Ready, 2 shots, 1.0 sec.
4	5 meters, from Ready, 2 shots, 1.2 sec.
5	7 meters, from Ready, 2 shots, 1.5 sec.
6	10 meters, from Ready, 2 shots, 2.0 sec.
7	15 meters, from Ready, 2 shots, 3.0 sec.
8	25 meters, from Ready, 2 shots, 4.0 sec.
9	50 meters, from Ready, 2 shots, 6.0 sec.

All shooters wore acrylic "space gloves," which were slippery at these temperatures.
Temperature: -40 degrees F.

Sub-Zero Shooter Performance Chart

Shooter	1	2	3	4	5	6	7	8	9	Score	Avg. Time	Pts. Per Sec.
Browning Hi-Power 9mm, 124-grain NATO ball												
1	.94	1.18	.93	1.0	1.22	1.60	2.36	3.55	3.26	81	1.78	5.05
2	1.20	.95	.87	1.5	1.31	1.85	2.06	2.39	4.70	90	1.87	5.38
3	1.14	1.20	1.0	1.0	1.30	1.73	2.36	2.49	4.80	90	1.89	5.29
											Three-shooter average:	5.24
Colt M1911 45 ACP, 230-grain U.S. ball												
1	.85	1.02	1.04	1.17	1.24	1.60	2.80	2.40	3.05	87	1.68	5.74
2	.91	1.06	1.32	1.17	1.37	1.85	2.36	2.74	4.66	90	1.94	5.14
3	1.04	1.07	.88	.94	1.30	1.63	2.39	2.24	3.69	90	1.69	5.99
											Three-shooter average:	5.62
Smith & Wesson Model 27, 4-inch bbl., 357 Magnum, 158-grain JHP												
1	.98	1.02	.99	1.34	1.58	2.05	2.22	3.07	5.35	84	2.07	4.52
2	1.17	1.17	1.20	1.34	1.73	1.92	2.10	2.64	4.66	87	1.99	4.85
3	1.34	2.06	1.23	1.34	1.59	1.74	1.90	2.32	3.93	78	1.94	4.47
											Three-shooter average:	4.61

In all tests, the possible score was 90.

more because of the effort required to operate it double action in a cold environment than by how much the handgun recoiled.

Second, with skilled shooters, the weather affected things less than expected. Look at the Overall Comparison Chart and you will see that actual times out to 10 meters were only minutely more than par. Surprisingly, the times from 15 to 50 meters ran considerably *under* par. This means that only at typical combat pistol ranges, i.e., from 0 to 10 meters, does the weather really affect things, and then to a lesser degree than previously thought.

Conversely, at longer ranges, more time with sight alignment, sight picture and particularly trigger control is required to get center hits, regardless of the weather conditions. As a result, the temperature had little effect on operator performance at these ranges.

Third, while the "space gloves" we used in the test proved to be a bit slippery, thus causing a few slower times here and there, shooter performance was remarkably consistent. This is the result of training and discipline, again proving that *operator skill is by far the most important element in winning handgun encounters, not weapons or weather conditions.*

Please don't misunderstand. No one questions that weather has an influence on gun battles. However, there is an equalizing element: All participants have the same problem to solve. The one who solves it first, wins.

Still, the weather doesn't influence things as much as many believe. Yes, there are some things about cold weather that are unique, but cold doesn't affect things to the degree that performance is altered on a "night versus day" scale. Training in such conditions will disclose everything one needs to know about the subject, just as always.

Fourth, and last, our test showed irrefutably that balancing accuracy with speed influences the outcome more than anything else. Peruse the various times and resultant scores in comparison to the test Course of Fire possible score and par times, and you will quickly see what I mean. This is as it should be, for success in handgun fights has always been the result of that careful balance. Cold or hot, wet or dry, day or night, this requirement hasn't changed in 150 years, and it never will.

Overall Comparison of Sub-Zero Performance Times

Gun	1	2	3	4	5	6	7	8	9
Brg. H-P	1.09	1.11	1.16	1.17	1.28	1.58	2.26	2.80	4.25
Colt M1911	.93	1.05	1.08	1.09	1.30	1.42	2.52	2.46	3.82
S&W M27	1.16	1.42	1.14	1.34	1.63	1.90	2.07	2.68	4.65
Average	1.01	1.19	1.13	1.20	1.40	1.63	2.28	2.67	4.24
Par	1.00	1.00	1.00	1.20	1.50	2.00	3.00	4.00	6.00
Difference	+.01	+.19	+.13	+0.0	-.10	-.37	-.72	-1.33	-1.76

All times in seconds.

COVER AND CONCEALMENT

COVER AND CONCEALMENT—the very words evoke images of desperate encounters, bringing beads of perspiration to the foreheads of those who have actually experienced deadly confrontation. Yet in spite of the dramatic connotations the two words inspire, some dangerous misconceptions about them exist.

In the military context, use of the term "cover" usually means that there is incoming fire and advises avoidance by eliminating the enemy's view of you. I won't argue that this is a good idea, but having seen considerable infantry action, I've found that, more often than not, what is available at the moment is usually "concealment," not true cover. Still, over the decades, the shout, "Take cover!" continues to connote enemy contact.

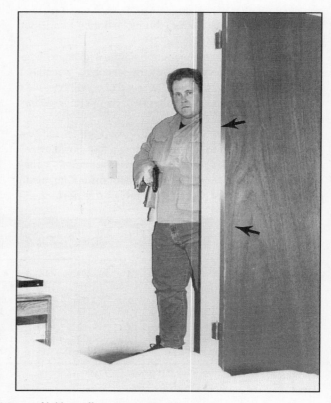

These are examples of concealment, not cover. Neither offers any protection against incoming fire.

What is cover? Simply stated, cover is anything that is proof against incoming projectiles. Easy enough, right? Or is it? I think not, because many things that we assume fall into this category are not all that effective in such a role.

For example, how resistant to gunfire is a typical automobile? Considering how much time we spend around them, wouldn't it be a good idea to know what to expect if we are fired upon while we are in or around one?

First, the kind of weapon you're confronting while crouched behind that car has a great deal of influence on the matter. In addition, where you place yourself behind that car is of equal importance. This is because very little of the vehicle is actually bulletproof, especially against potent weapons like high-power rifles.

On the other hand, even low-power arms like handguns or submachine guns can easily penetrate many portions of today's automobile. Only the shotgun represents a category of weapon against which a car is truly good cover, assuming that some form of shot is the ammunition utilized.

Generally speaking, windshield safety glass will decisively stop shot pellets, including buckshot. On those occasions where holes appear at the points of pellet impact, you are seeing what military analysts call spalling effect, not penetration. Shotgun pellets normally disintegrate upon impact, but larger shot sizes (such as buckshot) occasionally punch out small plugs of glass—which

(Above and below) This is an example of rather poor use of cover. The subject is exposed at the abdomen (through the window) and lower legs.

These examples show good use of cover, as well as a wise selection of position in relation to the available cover and not crowding the cover itself. This also minimizes the danger of being hit by ricochets and presents the toughest possible target to your adversary.

also disintegrate—from the opposite side of the plate. Field tests show that such missiles travel at low velocities and thus possess relatively low wounding potential, although if a human were struck in the eyes by them, he might well be neutralized.

Handgun, submachine gun and, of course, rifle bullets will sail right through a windshield with little reduction in effect unless the angle at which they strike becomes excessively shallow. When this happens, most projectiles will deflect, with the result being that the target is untouched.

Side glass, however, is another matter entirely, since it is

designed to shatter into small pieces upon impact. Thus, it offers no real protection. Rear window glass also falls into this category, though by virtue of its slightly tougher construction and angled configuration, multiple hits may be required to defeat it.

Bodywork is good armor against all buckshot and many handgun/submachine gun bullets, and is sometimes effective against lower powered rifle cartridges like the 5.56x45mm NATO or 30 U.S. M-1 Carbine. Quite often, but without any degree of predictability, even the various types of shotgun slugs disintegrate during passage, thus preventing any guarantee of a serious, much less incapacitating, wound. As with

Good choices but poor uses of cover due to crowding. Any incoming projectile that strikes in front of the subject will deflect directly into his face. Crowding also prevents efficient use of your own weapon because its close proximity to the cover limits its manipulation.

glass, if the slug strikes at too shallow an angle, it will deflect or fail to penetrate completely, expending itself during its passage through the outer sheet metal.

From the front, the radiator and engine offer excellent protection from virtually anything short of a large-caliber (50 or bigger) armor-piercing shell or rocket-driven charge. From the side, the engine and its compartmental structure also offer good protection. However, from the rear, only the rim of the spare tire, the horizontal cross-member beneath the rear window and the trunk surface offer any degree of protection.

Other places to avoid are the trunk area (as viewed from

This is proper use of the car as cover. The subject is well back, low and safe from ricochets. Also, he presents a difficult target.

The shotgun, especially when used with any form of shot, is relatively useless against an automobile unless the side window glass is involved. However, indoors, buckshot will sail right through typical sheetrock walls with no difficulty whatsoever. Number 4 buckshot passed easily through a double sheetrock wall from a distance of 7 feet. The target was struck by all twenty-seven pellets.

the side, there's nothing there but one layer of sheet metal) and the tires, although the wheels upon which they're mounted will usually stop everything except high-power rifle bullets. Be *very* careful about positioning yourself in such a way as to expose your legs or feet to fire transiting *beneath* the vehicle. Remember, you aren't the only one who knows that ricochet shooting can be effective. More on ricochets later.

As for buildings, fire from outside can only be stopped by dense materials like brick, concrete, stone or grouted cinder block. Aluminum siding or wood, unless uncommonly thick, offers very little resistance. Interior walls are typically constructed of sheetrock or foam and provide no protection whatsoever unless internal junction boxes or supporting studs are struck, and even these are easily penetrated by high-power rifle fire.

Furniture and appliances provide more concealment than real cover. As massive as it may appear, a refrigerator isn't all that resistant to gunfire. A few years back, my lawman friend Dalton Carr graphically proved this point by driving five out of six 250-grain 44 Special bullets completely through an old refrigerator—*at nearly 200 meters*!

Ricochets from resilient surfaces, such as an automobile hood, trunk or roof, are also a hazard. Due to simple geometry, the nearer you are to the point of initial impact and ricochet, the greater the chance of being hit by a deflected projectile. So instead, place yourself well back—never crowd your cover. By staying well back, you not only reduce the danger from ricochets, but also present the most difficult kind of target to your assailant.

Vegetation such as saplings or bushes provides some degree of protection, but, again, the location of the target behind such light cover significantly influences the effect of incoming fire. As previously mentioned, the closer the target is to the point of projectile impact and resulting deflection, the less the distance between the original flight path and the altered one. So, the farther back from intervening light cover you are, the greater your chance of avoiding being hit. Better yet, find yourself a nice thick tree, preferably at least fifteen inches in diameter.

Hard surfaces cause projectile deformation, and subsequently the projectile tends to continue on its way about 8 to 14 inches from the impact surface. However, if a rifled arm is used, the rifling twist will cause the bullet to move slightly in the direction of twist when it initially strikes. Therefore, it might be necessary to compensate by aiming slightly to the opposite side of what you are trying to hit on the ricochet.

Concealment is not bullet-proof. It is merely that which obstructs your opponent's view and is valuable because it allows you to approach or withdraw with less danger. It is not the same as cover.

The next time you're where the bullets fly, remember these points because they might save your life!

USING THE READY POSITION

THERE ARE THREE places for the defensive handgun: 1) in the holster, 2) pointed at a target, and 3) in the Ready position. The weapon is never held in both hands pointed upward, like you see in the movies. Such is pure cinematography, e.g., "Get the gun on camera." In a tactical environment, so doing not only blocks your view of the target area, but also unhinges your mind and body from one another, making quick, effective response very difficult.

Another common practice is to dangle the gun; that is, to allow it to point at the ground, held in only one hand. This, too, is common in closing scenes of the cinema, where the hero has just neutralized a dozen bad guys and is exhausted. It, too, has the effect of unhinging the mind and body, making a critical response if you are attacked all but impossible.

In order to offset these dangerous tendencies, the concept of KISS (Keep It Simple, Stupid!) dictates that as few

weapon positions as possible be used. Naturally, when your defensive handgun is carried, the most likely method of doing so is in a holster. However, if the gun is in-hand and not actually being fired at a target, the Ready position is where it belongs. The problem is that a great many shooters don't realize how important the Ready is and, as a result, tend to either ignore it entirely or perform it incorrectly.

There are two reasons for the Ready. First, if the gun is in hand and you're confronting someone—talking, for example—it places the weapon in the optimum place for a fast (less than 1/2-second) presentation to the Point position. Second, once the target is actually fired upon, the gun should be quickly returned to the Ready (for post-shooting assessment) to allow instant reengagement if required without obstructing your view of the target and target area.

Why is this such a big deal? Simple. The act of firing your defensive handgun merely proves that the *fight has begun*—not that it is over or that the target is successfully neutralized. This being the case, you simply cannot afford to relax until you have the answers to a number of questions:

1) Is the target hit? Or did I somehow miss him with my first shots or place them poorly?

2) Is he down? Did he collapse when hit or fall to the ground in reaction, etc.? While the target falling down is a positive sign of a possible incapacitation, it isn't the only sign. We need to look at him for several seconds as he lies on the ground.

3) Is he incapable of further lethal aggression? Occasion-

Search procedures are more efficient and less hazardous when the correct Ready position is used. Its combination of complete target area visibility, mental control and weapon presentation speed is hard to beat.

(Left and above) If there is a failure to stop, the correct Ready position will allow you to know it immediately and quickly reengage. Note also that a failure to stop isn't just when the target fails to fall down. It is a common occurrence for someone who has been shot to collapse, but continue to fight from the ground. The so-called Contact Ready, where the weapon is held just below eye level, blocks your view of the target area and is thus a potentially deadly error.

The correct Ready position entails the weapon being held down below eye level at about 45 degrees, with the trigger finger held straight alongside the frame of the weapon. Presentation speed from Ready to Point is under half a second.

This is the correct Close Ready position, for use when moving through confined areas such as doorways or when exiting aircraft. The weapon is held closer to the body, but is still under complete control and ready for instant presentation.

ally, people who are shot and collapse somehow "come back to life" and continue to fight from ground level.

4) Does he have friends in the area? Very few criminals now operate alone.

The Ready position offers us the best combination of target and target area visibility, before and after actually shooting or if a reengagement is required, without loss of presentation speed in the process. This is why it is so important.

So, how do we perform the Ready? The weapon is kept in both hands (the arms are in the stance of your choice, usually Weaver or Isosceles), but pointed at the ground about 45 degrees below horizontal. It is not pointed at the target's hip area, legs or feet (this just-below-horizontal position is common in the police profession and is called the "Contact Ready"), nor is it pointed at the ground just in front of your own feet. The trigger finger is kept outside the trigger guard, lying alongside the frame of the weapon.

If you're using a single-action auto and the Ready is being used in conjunction with an initial target confrontation, the thumb safety is On, but with the firing thumb held on top of it for instant deactivation during presentation from Ready to Point. However, if you're at the Ready because you've fired on a target and you're assessing the results

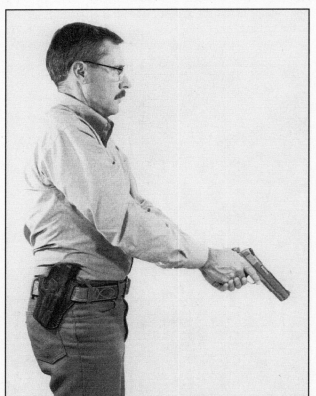

The proper Ready position with the Isosceles stance. The trigger finger is kept outside the trigger guard regardless of stance used or circumstances. A correct Ready position allows lightning-fast weapon presentation, especially under stress, and should be taught and practiced as part of any serious shooting/tactical program.

(post-shooting assessment), the thumb safety remains Off until you decide to holster the piece.

The so-called Contact Ready is the deadly product of not thinking things through to their ultimate conclusion tactically, e.g., the firing-range mentality. But it is attractive to the poorly informed because it appears to satisfy the need to address a potential target while keeping the weapon ready for instant presentation. Actually: 1) it blocks your clear view of the target; 2) it is considered "brandishing," a misdemeanor in many states, and one of the issues used to determine if you used "reasonable restraint" during the altercation (criminal and civil liability); 3) it too often has the effect of preventing the person at whom you're pointing the gun from responding to your verbal instructions because he's focused on your gun and isn't really listening to you. In other words, you can actually start a fight by doing this, rather than possibly preventing it, a situation often unknowingly precipitated by police officers who use the Contact Ready.

Those who profess that the Contact Ready is superior claim that they only use/recommend/teach it as an initial confrontation position and that once the target is actually engaged and fired upon, they advocate using the correct, classic Ready for post-shooting assessment. Unfortunately,

the subconscious mind doesn't function that way, particularly under stress. Invariably, the shooter returns to the Ready he began with—the Contact Ready, obscuring his view of the target and target area, especially if the target has collapsed or moved in any way.

To teach two different kinds of Ready position therefore smacks of the firing-range mentality in that it allows officers to make the times required during qualifications, but at the price of teaching them to do something that may well get them killed in the field if they have a failure to stop. In fact, I personally know of several instances where this has actually happened and several more where the officer was seriously injured as a result.

So, then, the importance of a correct Ready position should now be clear, as should the reasons why the so-called Contact Ready is potentially deadly to anyone who uses it. Again, we see how the firing-range mentality can get you killed or injured because those who advocate techniques created from it fail to extrapolate the use of the technique in a tactical environment. What works on firing ranges—i.e. under controlled conditions—is academic. What works in the real world, where a gunfight is anything but a controlled environment, is another matter entirely.

Don't be fooled or get lazy. The price can be terminal.

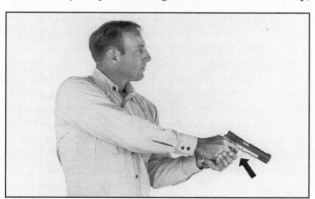

Some common mistakes include keeping your finger on trigger, pointing the gun skyward in best Hollywood style, and removing one hand from the gun. All these give loss of weapon control and presentation speed.

POST-SHOOTING ASSESSMENT

ONCE YOU'VE ENGAGED your target, it is critical that you know as soon as possible whether or not he's been successfully incapacitated, or "stopped." This phase of the tactical engagement is called post-shooting assessment. During this, as the term implies, the shooter evaluates the results of his shots. The only way he can do this is to look—to visually evaluate his target after shooting it. This gives you data critical to your subsequent actions. Perhaps he wasn't hit. Maybe he's hit, but not collapsing. Maybe he has collapsed, but is able to continue to project lethal aggression toward you from the ground. Finally, perhaps he has friends in the area, accomplices who may at any moment appear and enter the fray. Criminals these days rarely operate alone.

Here's what you do. Once you've engaged and finished firing on your target, *bring your weapon down to Ready* as quickly as possible without losing control of it and look downrange at the target itself. Evaluate his body language. Is he collapsing, reeling about, demonstrating controlled physical movement or just standing there? Is he down? Is he finished, incapacitated, out of the fight? Is he able to continue to fight?

Once you've done this, *assess the target* for at least four seconds, perhaps more, depending upon what you see and the tactical nature of the altercation. Then, if you're satisfied that he's incapable of further lethal aggression, *check slowly to the right and left* to ensure there are no other targets.

Keep the gun directly below your line of sight as you do this—don't relax or collapse your stance. *Stay in a proper Ready position during the entire process.* If you see additional targets, then you're in an ideal position to deal with them. If not, then *return your focus to the downed target* and reevaluate. If, based on this, there is then no further need for the weapon, then it is safe to relax and holster it, *but not until then.*

Too many trainers, especially if they're from a competition or less than state-of-the-art background, teach their students to simply shoot and relax. This, too, is the firing-range mentality rearing its ugly head, because in the real world, it can get you killed in a heartbeat. Remember that the act of firing your weapon merely indicates that the fight has begun, not that it is over or that you have won.

The shoot-and-relax syndrome came from shooting paper (non-reactive) silhouettes on a pistol range, a controlled environment. A gunfight is anything but controlled! If it were, you either wouldn't be there or would be using a more potent weapon—such as a rifle, shotgun or submachine gun—not a mere handgun. To shoot and relax, just because those silhouettes don't respond when hit, programs your subconscious to do the same thing out on the street, where it places you in a situation of potentially deadly proportions.

This also is why it's a good idea to use reactive targets like knockdown steel silhouettes in training. Either they fall when hit or they don't. If not, then the shooter must reengage them, firing until they do. If two solid hits don't knock them over, then the shooter should consider the situation to be a failure to stop and go for the head.

However, be careful here. Reactive targets should be reasonably sized silhouettes or half-silhouettes, not some irrelevant shape like an IPSC Pepper Popper or simple disks.

Post-shooting assessment is not just another phase of combat shooting. It is just as important as deciding you need to shoot and the actual shooting itself, because it provides you with information necessary to make intelligent, even critical, tactical and legal decisions. For this reason, it should not be overlooked or deemphasized. Practice it carefully and make certain your procedure is right—every time—because you're programming your subconscious mind here. And since the subconscious doesn't make value judgments (it merely records, wrong or right), sloppy procedure can be highly dangerous—a time bomb, if you will, waiting to explode.

FAILURE TO STOP: WHAT NOW?

FAILURE TO STOP—the self-defense handgunner's ultimate nightmare. You've done everything right; you've chosen the best weapon for your needs, the best ammo. Your holster and ancillary equipment, too, was selected with your lifestyle and normal social/cultural/natural environment at all times kept in mind.

You practiced to achieve proficiency with your gear, obtained formal training, and worked hard to learn as much as possible and develop your skill. After all, life-and-death matters are serious business—especially your own.

You did all of those things, and then, suddenly one rain-swept night, in the "Stop n' Rob" convenience store where you went for a quick loaf of bread, there he was. He was brandishing a cheap 38 Special revolver in one hand, a fist-ful of stolen money in the other. The clerk was lying on the floor in an ever-spreading pool of blood, unconscious, help-less...maybe even dead.

The gunman looks at you with feral eyes and you know—he's going to kill you. As the gun in his hand begins to move, your hand flashes inside your jacket, obtains a proper firing grip, and the weapon moves like lightning to intercept your supporting hand, forming a textbook Ready position. Halfway between the holster and the intercept point, the thumb safety is disengaged, making your 9mm Browning Hi-Power ready to roll. You know all this has happened, even though your eyes haven't left his. You know because you've dry-practiced it hundreds of times in your own living room.

His eyes widen a bit as he realizes you're not the sucker he thought you were, but although you challenge him and tell him to drop his weapon, it continues menacingly upward. As it rises in front of his snarling face, your firing eye picks up the Browning's front sight, sharp and clear.

And although you don't remember pressing the trigger,

the gun speaks twice, sending its deadly message to the thug now doing his level best to blow off your head. Something tugs at your collar as it passes, but as the mind-rending concussion dies away, the Browning quickly lowers to Ready. Your eyes focus on him, looking for results.

Curiously, the silence is deafening.

He staggers slightly, but remains erect. His gun, now with a faint wisp of smoke delicately curling from its muzzle, stays in his sagging, but still upraised, hand. His eyes fade, then refocus. He lurches, but stays on his feet, the gun in his hand again rising as he glares at you in a snarl born of unremitting sociopathic hatred....

Oh my God!—Failure to stop!

And you, pilgrim. What are *you* going to do...?

The next two seconds will see the most important decision you'll ever make—one that will quite literally mean the difference between life and death—yours.

In the movies or on TV, it rarely happens; in the Western novels, never. But in the real world, the one you and I inhabit, the failure to stop happens all the time. How could it be? You did everything right. Simple. Handguns just aren't that powerful, that's all. If they were, we wouldn't be able to handle them, due to the laws of physics.

What *is* a failure to stop? It's when your attacker isn't neutralized by your deadly force response to his assault, no matter how quickly or proficiently it may be delivered. His wounds may even be lethal, but death isn't on his mind—you are. And, although he may expire in minutes, hours or days from his wounds, he remains sufficiently mobile to continue his efforts to achieve his goal, which is your demise.

You can kill a man yet not stop him. If that happens, you'll die. As their last vestiges of life left them, many have asked what they did wrong, wondering how they could have won the fight. *Lethality*—the ability to cause death—has been given disproportionate emphasis for far too long when the real issue is *incapacitation*, which is rendering your attacker incapable of further lethal aggression.

You can also stop a man yet not kill him, although such wounds are also often lethal. Which would you rather bet your life on? Equally important, what can you do to minimize the danger of having a failure to stop in the first place?

First, select the most potent and mechanically reliable handgun you can effectively handle. I don't mean in casual or competitive shooting, either. I mean flat-out, hard-drivin' *combat* shooting, friend—fast, close and decisive—because that's what it takes when the chips are down.

Learn how to best use it and each piece of its accompanying equipment. Get some *professional* training. Not only

does it work in a gunfight, but it helps in the courtroom scenes that sometimes follow, too. Then and only then will you have done everything possible to minimize the danger, for the best insurance against a failure to stop is a fast, sure weapon presentation, followed by quick, accurate marksmanship.

But what if, in spite of all your efforts to prevent it, a failure occurs?

You then have a decision to make, and a controversial one at that. The first, and most obvious, reaction is to continue shooting the attacker in the chest, a tactic espoused by many law-enforcement agencies and several less well-informed or less experienced "experts." However, when considering this idea, we should remember that there are hundreds of case studies showing that if the first two or three hits in the chest fail to incapacitate, then, due to the fact that

A failure to stop is a common occurrence with handguns and has been historically documented for over a hundred years. In fact, this is where the old gunfighter's slogan of "Hit 'em twice, no matter what!" came from.

the subject's nervous system is shut down by the initial trauma, six more won't have much immediate effect, either. To me, this fact alone invalidates the concept and removes it from further consideration.

As well, this is where the initial controversy began, remember? Police officers in particular were literally emptying their weapons into their attackers, without decisive effect. Obviously, a better tactic was needed, yet nothing has happened to change this requirement.

As a result, several ideas on how to handle the problem have emerged. The first entails shooting the attacker's legs out from under him, in the hope that the femur (thigh bone) or knees would be broken or the femoral artery severed.

The problem is that the legs are usually moving after the attacker is initially shot, making them extremely difficult targets. On top of this, the chance of severing the femoral

A failure to stop is the ultimate nightmare—you've done everything right, but the subject isn't neutralized and still presents a deadly threat. Proper use of the Ready position and subconsciously programmed post-shooting assessment procedures give you the ability to reengage in less than half a second.

artery is fairly small, and even if it were cut, the resulting blood loss would not incapacitate the attacker quickly enough to matter.

The idea of shooting the attacker in the pelvis then surfaced. A far better concept than trying to hit the legs, it had the effect of eliminating the attacker's means of locomotion by causing him to fall down—a great idea if he is attempting to use a contact weapon (a knife or club) against you.

However, it fails to take into consideration that if the attacker is armed with a gun, the act of falling down from a pelvic hit in no way eliminates his ability to fire the weapon.

Someone finally realized that shooting the assailant in the head would quickly neutralize both his mobility and his ability to use a deadly weapon. At first, many thought that few had the skill to make such a shot. However, data on handgun confrontations has, for over thirty years, shown that the average pistol confrontation takes place at seven to ten *feet*. Thus, the marksmanship problem is, in truth, relatively easy, so easy that in a recent study I conducted of five different skill levels of shooters, the head shot proved a whopping 97-percent easier than attempting to strike a decisive blow to the assailant's legs.

Even today, some of those who espouse the pelvic-hit idea claim that the assailant will see that you're pointing a gun at his head and try to evade its bullet, twisting and dodging like a snake. *Excuse me?* Such a thing is preposterous, especially considering that the subject has already been shot at least twice in the thorax.

Besides, if this were possible, he could not advance or utilize a deadly weapon of any kind against me while so doing. In order for this to happen, the head must first stabilize, making it at that moment both highly vulnerable and easy to hit.

Tough to defend in court? I don't think so.

Your job as the intended victim is to bring the fight to a conclusion in your favor in as little time and with as few shots fired as possible, *not just make the attacker fall down*. You're supposed to present minimal risk to bystanders at the same time, remember? The head shot clearly offers the best means of accomplishing all of these goals, thus best protecting you against what I call the three forms of liability, tactical, criminal and civil.

So, there you have it—the best ways of preventing the problem, and the most common methods of dealing with it, should the unthinkable happen. I make no bones about recommending the head shot in preference to the legs or pelvic response because, of the three, it is the only one that offers instantly decisive results.

Results are what its all about. If you don't get them with Plan A, two or three quick shots to the chest, you'd better have some form of Plan B to fall back on. For me, the head shot is the best Plan B possible because it makes the most sense.

TACTICAL HOME-DEFENSE HINTS

THESE DAYS IT seems like we can't pick up a newspaper, listen to the radio or watch television without being exposed to a story about someone being bashed in the head for their Social Security check, brutalized in their own bedroom or killed in a surprise encounter with a burglar. Indeed, in these turbulent times, only a fool would ignore the fact that home security and defense is a real—even critical—concern.

Yet, at the same time, a naive, almost childish attitude toward home defense also often exists—an attitude of defiance, yes, but naive nonetheless. It's certainly true that the invasion of one's home, not to mention those who reside therein, is a *personal* thing, something that evokes a sense

of outrage. Still, considering its complexities—the law, psychology, tactics, weapons, etc.—it is surprising that so few take home defense seriously enough to actually plan its successful execution.

In order for such success to be achieved, one must first view the subject objectively. While without question serious business, home defense is, as the term implies, both *civilian* and *defensive*, not a military operation or police function. Nor is it a gentleman's duel or saloon gunfight. Therefore, it requires a different view to be taken if an accurate perspective is to be attained and a viable home defense strategy conceived.

Too often, I hear statements like, "If I see 'em comin'

Use—really *use*—your eyes! Intruders often slip outside to evaluate the situation when disturbed by the returning resident. Don't think for a moment that the threat cannot be just outside, waiting for the right opportunity.

through the window, I'll shoot 'em right there, drag 'em inside, make up a story and then call the cops." Or, "I'll shoot 'em outside and drag 'em inside...." Comments like these are dangerously irresponsible and reflect a complete lack of understanding of what home defense is all about.

Go ahead—shoot that guy on your front lawn or coming in your window, drag him inside and make up a story—and watch what happens when the police forensics team arrives on the scene and starts investigating. In about ten minutes, they'll determine exactly what really happened and be reading you your rights.

Right after they arrest you, that is.

Successful home defense, like everything else, must be

conducted with not only *weapons* and *tactics* in mind, but *the law* as well. To shoot someone on your property or coming in the window is highly questionable unless they are somehow clearly presenting a deadly threat to you in the process, a claim that is often difficult to prove. At the very least, concocted stories reduce your credibility, even if your actions during the incident were justifiable by law. Thus, they only complicate the investigation and make it tougher on you.

When can you use deadly force? In most states, only when you feel that the intruder's actions threaten you or your family with either *imminent death* or *great bodily injury*. You cannot kill him simply because he is stealing the family silverware or making off with your prized stereo.

Use your ears, too. When under stress, most people tend to firmly plant their feet on the floor and their back to the wall, and scoot along when moving, emitting a scraping sound that discloses both location and covert intent. Listening for these sounds can provide an effective early warning system. However, remember, too, that tactical principles are a double-edged sword—if you commit these errors, they give the advantage to your adversary.

Outrageous? Upsetting? Sure. We all work hard for our personal possessions and resent someone helping himself to them without permission. Still, legally, that's the way it is. Unless you're looking for trouble, you've got to accept it and factor it into your home-defense strategy.

What if you get the drop on an intruder who proves to be unarmed and he announces his intention to walk away? What would you do? Would you shoot him, or perhaps fire a warning shot to make your point, or would you let him walk?

As maddening as it would be, I'd advise you to *let him go*, unless you can find some other way to restrain him. You can't legally use deadly force unless you feel threatened by deadly force. So, unless he then attacks and is physically able to kill you, the use of your gun is highly restricted. Warning shots? You're wasting your time and increasing both your criminal and civil liability with them.

What do you do if you confront an intruder and for whatever reason, do not shoot him? First, *stay away from him!* The closer to him you get, the quicker and easier it is for him to disarm you. *Speak to him in clear, concise tones and in simple language.* Screaming and shouting prevents effective control and, because he might feel that you are going to kill him anyway, can cause him to initiate action.

Instruct him to place his hands, fingers interlocked, behind his head and get on his knees. If movement to the telephone to call the police would cause you to lose sight of him, then make him walk on his knees in the direction

you wish. Again, stay away from him. *Do not search him.* Simply keep him under control until the authorities arrive.

During this period, he may well attempt conversation with you, which *you should avoid*. He is doing this to size you up and deescalate the situation, quite possibly with the intention of moving against you.

Do not discuss his rights with him. You are under no obligation to do so. Let the police handle that.

When they arrive, *do not be caught in any posture which might be interpreted as being threatening to the responding officers.* Remember, at this point, they know only that an intruder is being held at a certain address by an armed resident. They do not know who you are or that you are the "good guy." Point the weapon away from them, advise them who you are and repeat that you have an intruder in your custody. Ask them to take over and, as soon as possible or upon direction from them, put the weapon away.

If you are forced to shoot an intruder, understand that you are under no legal or moral obligation to render emergency first-aid or CPR. Again, stay away from him, call the police, give them all the information they request, and wait.

During this time, you should continue to keep an eye on the intruder. This precludes the chance of being surprised, disarmed and perhaps killed if he was only feigning death or unconsciousness and was waiting for an opportunity to jump you.

CHUCK TAYLOR'S SURVIVAL TACTICS

Use your eyes and ears: Most people listen but don't hear, and look but don't see, because they are shutting out the rest of the world from their own sphere of existence. This is common with those who live in large urban areas. Watch the hands of a potential attacker. If he is going to act, the first thing that will happen must take place with his hands. When searching an area, indoors or out, scan systematically using the inline method. Don't miss anything—what you don't see can kill you! Listen for out-of-the-ordinary sounds as well.

Stay away from corners: Don't play "Starsky & Hutch" and be caught leaping around a corner. At such close range, you are totally at the mercy of an assailant who may be lurking on the other side, even if he has an edged or blunt weapon. Instead, play the "angles," and when you must expose yourself to danger from the corner, you will be ready for it and at maximum distance from it. This way, your assailant must react to you instead of the other way around.

Maximize the range between you and a potential danger area as much as the terrain or structure allows: Remember that the closer you are to your attacker, the easier it is for him to get you. If you must negotiate two opposite corners, then split the difference between them until you can place yourself in a position to clear one of them and use it as a base to engage the other.

Never turn your back on anything you haven't checked out first: If you must search a structure or dwelling, be certain that you have seen the right, left and rear walls of each room before continuing your search. In areas such as closets and bathrooms, it is also advisable to check the ceilings and any cupboards that might be large enough to conceal a human. You cannot be too careful when your life is at stake! For this reason you must be thorough and systematic in your search. Take your time and do it right.

Keep your balance: Don't be caught leaping around! You cannot bring accurate fire upon your attacker unless

Stay away from corners! Who knows what's lurking around the bend. If anything happens, it will be too close and too fast for you to successfully respond.

Here is the wrong way to handle a corner. Notice how this entails holding the weapon out of position for effective response. The extremely close proximity to the apex of the corner eliminates your reaction/response time if attacked.

The right way keeps you well back from the corner while you move carefully forward, ready to respond, allowing you to "play the angles" of the corner itself.

your body is balanced properly. Move in a sideways shuffle and never cross your legs. Resist the tendency to scrape your back along a wall and to drag your feet. These create noise that can give you away to an unseen attacker.

Watch your front sight: Your mind will be directing your eyes to focus on the source of trauma or excitement. Don't do it! If you watch your front sight, let the target "fuzz out" in the background and control the trigger, you will hit him. If you do not...care to gamble with your life?

Doorways:

- Ascertain which way the door opens before attempting to actually open it. If the hinges show on the outside, the door opens outward. If not, then it opens inward. If the hinges are on the right side, the door moves from left to right, if they are on the left side, then it opens from right to left. The location of the doorknob or handle is often an indicator as well.

- When you move through the door, give it a sufficient push to move it all the way against the wall. This will force any hidden assailant to take action prematurely.

- Get through the doorway and get to one side or the other quickly. Don't silhouette yourself. Always be at the

Ready. If you are not surprised, you will nearly always win the fight.

Windows:

- Resist the impulse to peek through windows. Treat them the same as corners—*Danger!*

- Keep maximum distance from them at all times.

- Remember that just because you are inside, your assailant can be anywhere, including outside. Don't limit the use of your eyes and ears to indoors only.

Reloading:

- Don't drop your magazines or speed-loaders on the floor unless the need to reload comes in the middle of an exchange of fire.

- Even if you only shoot once and down your attacker, *reload!* You don't know what might happen next and it is better to have a fully loaded weapon at the ready.

- Don't shoot your weapon empty unless the tactical situation demands it. It will take longer to reload that way.

Malfunctions:

- If you have a stoppage, take cover to clear it. Don't stand there like a target and "diddle around" with your gun.

- Rehearse the stoppage-clearance drills until you are completely familiar with them. This practice could save your life.

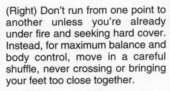

(Above) The entry team member at the left has only one foot on the ground at a time when he may have to take instant action. He is dangerously off balance.

(Right) Don't run from one point to another unless you're already under fire and seeking hard cover. Instead, for maximum balance and body control, move in a careful shuffle, never crossing or bringing your feet too close together.

Keep your balance. You cannot effective defend yourself if you're dancing around.

Don't assume anything! When searching, be sure to *see everything*— behind furniture, in closets, etc. People can, and will, hide wherever they feel they must to avoid detection. Other areas of concern include under kitchen sinks, in bathroom shower stalls and even on closet shelves.

You are well within your rights to *call your attorney* and even to refrain from answering any questions by the police until he has arrived. Just tell the interviewing officer that you'd rather not answer any questions without your lawyer and that he is enroute. Doing this is not an admission of guilt. Having said this, however, don't be surprised if you find yourself handcuffed and taken downtown which, in an increasing number of jurisdictions, is becoming standard policy anyway. Don't be unduly alarmed if this happens to you—it will all be sorted out within the next few hours.

The police are not out to get you. However, everything you say to them is *on the record*, so refrain from letting off steam by ranting and raving. Doing so only makes you look like a fool and can undermine your credibility as well. *When you talk to the police, tell them exactly what happened* and let *them* conduct the investigation.

If you have shot someone, they will want your weapon, so don't be surprised if they ask you for it. However, your attorney will want you to *get a receipt for it*.

As for weapon/ammo selection, tactics and techniques, take a good look at the photography that accompanies this text. As you do, remember that everyone's lifestyle is different, meaning that there is no universal solution for everyone.

When you must traverse doorways, place yourself on the side opposite the hinges and carefully ascertain by slow knob manipulation whether or not the door is locked. With a corner, play the angles until you've seen all you can see without actually entering. Then, briskly enter with the weapon at the Ready, checking whatever areas you haven't seen as you do. Don't linger! You'll be framing yourself in a backlit opening—an attractive target.

Be especially careful in channeled areas such as stairways, hallways, etc. These "fatal funnels," as they're called by law enforcement officers, limit your mobility and make reaction/response times super-critical.

The photos and captions here will give you considerable information, provide an accurate perspective and allow you to make intelligent choices.

In conclusion, we do indeed live in turbulent times, where it often appears that civilization is crumbling around us. However, let's not lose our perspective. We still have the legal right and physical means to defend our homes and loved ones from the criminal menace that stalks too many of our streets. For this we should be thankful, because this isn't the case in most countries. In other words, as bad as it sometimes seems, things could be a *lot* worse!

Realistically *determine your needs*, based on an objective appraisal of your lifestyle. Then and only then should you begin the process of determining what kind of weapon, ammunition, tactics and ancillary equipment you and your family will need to ensure their safety and security.

As one who has "shot for blood," I sincerely hope you never have to share the experience. Good luck.

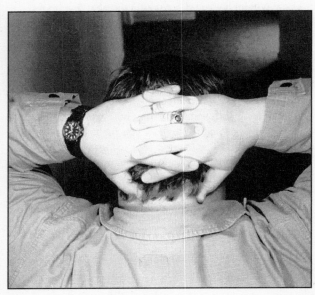

If you take someone into custody and hold them until the police arrive, stay away from them. Then, separate them from their weapon, get them down on their knees with ankles overlapped as shown and have them interlace their fingers together and place their hands behind their neck. If you must move to another location to use the telephone to call the police, allow them only to uncross their feet and "walk" them in this position (on their knees) to wherever you want them. Avoid all conversation with the subject, but issue your commands to him briskly and in a firm, controlled, businesslike manner. Don't scream at him or curse him, for this can actually escalate the situation.

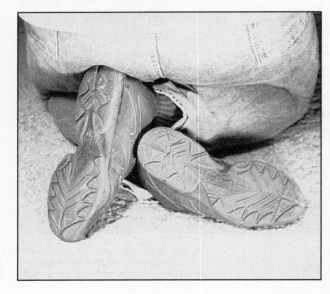

ADDRESSING MULTIPLE TARGETS

FOR MORE THAN 150 years, it has been the rule to always shoot a single target twice. There are good reasons for this, which have been proven legitimate time and time again. This method delivers the maximum trauma to the target's central nervous system before it involuntarily shuts down to protect itself, a phenomenon which is commonplace with all mammals and is intended to delay and minimize the effects of systemic shock. Provided the two hits are delivered quickly, say within 1½-2 seconds, twice as much shock is transmitted because the two hits cause twice as much damage prior to system shutdown. Thus, they provide twice the potential of quickly stopping the attacker.

It's also cheap life insurance—everyone misses now and then, especially under the stresses common to deadly force confrontations. By shooting twice, the chances are that at least one of the shots will strike the target.

Many experts say that accuracy and speed must be balanced for optimum effect, and this is absolutely true. However, when there is more than one target, the time factor alters substantially. In simple words, the more targets you have, the less time you have to deal with them. Look at it this way: All of them are focusing on you; yet, you only have the capacity to focus on one of them at a time.

This means that if you want to do everything possible to prevent that second, third or fourth target from having too much time to get you, a compromise between tactics and stopping power is required. Shooting each target twice, while totally legitimate against a single target, simply takes too long when multiple targets are involved. Instead, shoot each attacker only once. Then, quickly bring your gun down to Ready and assess the effect of your shots.

If you detect anyone still projecting lethal aggression, then reengage him, but on a failure-to-stop basis. Yep, go for that cranial shot, because he feels nothing now and shooting him in the chest again is a waste of time and ammo. Your initial shot into his chest certainly delivered shock, but in insufficient quantity to incapacitate him. Now, several seconds have passed and his nervous system has shut down, thus he feels nothing. He may become incapacitated and even die in a few seconds or minutes, but at this juncture, you can't afford to wait.

IPSC competition shooting constantly requires two hits on every target, regardless of the tactical implications, and this is where the idea of "always hit 'em twice" got off the track and became disproportionately emphasized. On a firing range it matters little, but in a firefight it can quite literally make the difference between life and death. Again, we see that techniques from this particular sector exert serious negative—even potentially fatal—influence if used in the wrong environment.

A gunfight is without question the wrong environment.

Which target do you engage first? Well, the military says the nearest target poses the most serious threat. Logically, this can't be refuted, but consider that they're talking primarily about a military battlefield, where opponents are scattered at much longer ranges than typically experienced with handguns. In such an environment, you may encounter several enemy soldiers, all armed with serious offensive weapons (not pistols) at various ranges. Perhaps one target is 50 meters distant, while another is 200 meters away, and still another is out at 400 meters.

Clearly, the nearest one can get you the quickest and should be engaged first, then the one at 200 and finally the one at 400. However, in typical handgun confrontations, only rarely does such a target configuration present itself in a civilian, law enforcement or even a military environment. With handguns, it's far more typical to have all targets within what can only be regarded as "point-blank" range.

Many police trainers advocate shooting the most dangerous target first, and at first glance, this makes perfect sense. However, consider how difficult it is to determine this under stress. Moreover, you have no time for careful analysis. Handgun fights usually take place in less than three seconds. Look how subjective the issue is: How can we decide which weapon is the most dangerous, when they're all deadly? If they weren't, we wouldn't be shooting at the person holding it.

Is a 38 Special revolver any less deadly at 3 meters than a 12-gauge shotgun? I think not. So, unless an edged or blunt weapon is involved, and its bearer is obviously located at sufficient distance to preclude it being an immediate deadly threat (in which case you cannot legally shoot him), quick determination of which weapon is the most dangerous simply takes too long.

My rule of thumb is simple. Shoot anyone who is attempting to use a deadly weapon against you, regardless of what it may be. This way, the problem is kept simple and is much less time-consuming to solve.

I also support the thesis that you should shoot the target on your strong side first, then swing *toward* your body to engage any additional ones. You're much stronger this way than if you swing away from the body, with the added advantage of *allowing better target visibility* as well.

Another hint: Watch your front sight the entire time you're shooting and swinging from target to target, waiting until you've finished and your weapon is on the way down to Ready before shifting your optical focus from the front sight to the target area. To try and focus back and forth from the front sight to each target as you shoot it, then begin your swing toward the next target, is asking too much in too little available time.

As this is written, the majority of firearms trainers have failed to realize the significance of why multiple targets require a different approach. Unfortunately, a number of their students have been killed because they did what they were trained to do—shoot each target twice—and simply ran out of time. How could it happen? Easy. Their trainers weren't innovative or historically astute, and remained committed to something dangerously obsolete, even though ample data showing its obsolescence has surfaced. Don't fall into this same trap, too. It's just not worth the risk.

In contrast to the rule of single-target engagement in which the target is always shot twice, multiple targets are hit only once each. The shooter then brings his weapon down to Ready and assesses the effect of his shots. Any target that still presents a deadly threat should be reengaged, but as a failure to stop. Several seconds have passed and the subject's nervous system is now shut down—in other words, he feels nothing. Thus, to shoot him in the chest again is a waste of time and ammunition. Better to go for the cranio-ocular cavity shot and finish the fight quickly. Here, the author has just presented his weapon from a concealed holster, hit his first target solidly in the chest, and is beginning his swing to the next target on the left. Always swing toward your body if possible to maintain strength and to prevent obscuring your view of the target(s) with your shooting arm and gun.

One of the deadly delusions of competition or so-called "practical" shooting is the constant requirement to shoot all targets twice, even when there are two, three or even four of them. No matter how fast and accurate you are, you're giving at least one of your adversaries too much time to get you. One shot apiece—then assess the situation and reengage if necessary.

HANDLING HOSTAGES AND SMALL TARGETS

ALONG WITH TRAINING on full-size silhouettes of paper and/or steel, it's a good idea to train with small targets, too. Granted, the typical handgun confrontation is a pretty "stand-up" affair, generally entailing: 1) fewer than three shots fired, total; 2) a time frame of less than three seconds; 3) a single attacker, unprotected and in the open; however, in the last five years, the statistics have indicated a trend toward dual assailants. Within the next few years, this probably will become the norm, but both targets will still present themselves upright and in the open.

Exceptions to the norm *do* occur, and it is always a good idea to plan for them, though not to the extent they're disproportionately emphasized. Sometimes opponents utilize cover or concealment, thus presenting only small, partial targets to us. As well, it is not by any means unheard of for them to use another human—perhaps your wife, husband or child—as a shield.

In order to build the most efficient repertoire of defensive handgun skills possible, about 25 percent of your training emphasis should be on small targets, partially obscured targets and hostage situations. No, I'm not advocating that you deal with a hostage situation if you don't have to—by all means wait for the police to arrive, if you can. But what if the actions of the hostage-taker *force* you to respond? What if it becomes obvious that he's going to kill the hostage before the cops get there?

Obviously, you can't just stand there and do nothing, because the odds are that once he's killed the hostage, he'll kill you, too. So, use your imagination a bit when you train. Create realistic hostage situations and practice dealing with them.

As well, consult with your family and decide on a plan of action if such a scenario does in fact take place. A pre-arranged code causing the hostage to go limp and drop to the floor, thus giving you a clear shot, is but one example of how you can preplan for this awful contingency. Don't just talk about it. *Practice it!* Under stress, people often forget anything they haven't programmed into their subconscious, the very reason for serious training in the first place.

If you find yourself facing a hostage situation, *don't ever give up your weapon*, a lesson many police departments have learned so often that it is now standard policy. *Stay at the Ready position* and stay conscious of the hostage-holder's facial expressions and general body language as well as his actual verbal statements. Don't provoke him, but don't give up any position of tactical advantage you may have, either.

If he has a weapon poised for immediate use against the hostage, such as a knife at the throat or a gun "screwed into the ear," *wait*! Sooner or later the weapon will come away, thus eliminating the danger of its inadvertent use, even with a perfect hit in the hostage-holder's cranio-ocular cavity, the obvious target for quick incapacitation.

The FBI for some time recommended shot placement in certain areas to "guarantee" instant paralysis, but found out the hard way that it didn't work, unfortunately to the detriment of several hostages who were killed by the hostage-taker after he was hit perfectly in the prescribed spot. When the brain is shattered, it sends out wild impulses through the nervous system and the muscles respond. It's all too easy for an involuntary contraction to occur, thus pressing the trigger of a gun or causing an arm to jerk, slashing the throat of the hostage.

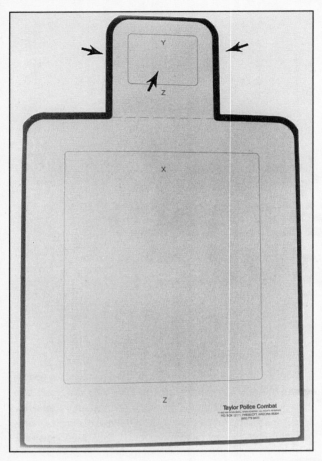

Taylor Police Combat

There is another reason to practice on small targets, and that is to be able to deal with the failure to stop. Generally speaking, handguns are only about 50-percent effective manstoppers, making the need for a quick, accurate cranio-ocular shot graphically apparent. Practice presentations from both the Ready and the holster to ensure a broad base of skill, and change the range occasionally. I practice head shots at 3, 5, and 7 meters regularly, and occasionally at 10, just to keep my perspective. Such practice pays big dividends if you experience a failure to stop and are forced to execute Plan B, the head shot.

Changing target angles, too, adds to the realism and exposes your subconscious mind to what a target looks like when it takes that particular form. I like to lean targets out to the right and left of imaginary cover, incorporating varying degrees of visual obstruction. After all, sometimes people lean out from around corners like that or stick their heads above the hood of a car or something.

The smart trainer extrapolates past the shooting range or classroom. He projects his techniques and tactics into the street or battlefield, or into the master bedroom at 3 a.m. Based upon a realistic appraisal of the threat, he then creates his training curriculum with this in mind, emphasizing the various responses commensurate with the threat. Small and obscure targets are overlooked by many trainers, but continue to be encountered in the field on a regular basis, meaning that they should be addressed in serious measure, not ignored. Make them a part of *your* training regimen—you won't be sorry.

(Above) Many times, your adversary will use a hostage, cover and/or concealment to his advantage. So, you'll need to know how to quickly hit small targets, too. The author recommends that you seriously practice high-speed engagements of the head only, as well as the normal body of a silhouette. This will allow successful target engagement if such a situation is encountered. For training purposes, shots that strike inside the box marked Y should be treated as effective. Hits outside it, but still on the head itself are regarded as being peripheral (marginal) hits. If this happens, reengage, shooting until you get a hit in the box.

The actual marksmanship problem involved with a hostage being used as a shield isn't difficult—it's the accompanying psychological hazard of shooting past a living human being that makes the shot hard. The solution is practice, like you see here. Place the target in different positions sticking out from behind the hostage to the right and/or left. Also, you can fold the head of the "hostage" down and regard the front target as being "cover."

OPTIMIZING YOUR DOUBLE-ACTION REVOLVER

IN SPITE OF the increased popularity of self-loading pistols, the revolver continues to be not only alive, but as satisfactory as ever. Although many have been swayed by the large-capacity self-loader because of its increased "firepower," the ubiquitous wheelgun just keeps right on doing its job, just like it has since 1836.

Revolver sales, although temporarily down due to the blitz of self-loaders currently offered, have remained consistent for many years. In fact, Smith & Wesson's LadySmith line reflects the fact that fully 40 percent of the handguns purchased these days are bought by women.

In a high-quality example, the DA revolver is at its historic zenith and is as reliable as a machine can be, and that's more than enough to accomplish most any reasonable function. They're accurate, too. More than one of my "wheelies" print 2-inch or better Ransom Rest groups at 50 meters.

In the 1989-90 American Small Arms Academy arctic tests, the S&W Model 27 used as a control gun functioned flawlessly throughout, even at -40 degrees Fahrenheit.

Whether you're contemplating the purchase of a new revolver or considering what might be done to enhance the efficiency of the one you already have, here are some commonsense, tactically proven thoughts to keep in mind.

Most important is KISS (Keep It Simple, Stupid!), meaning that you shouldn't do anything to your gun that doesn't truly increase its ability to perform its intended function. Complexity reduces reliability, so the addition of unnecessary aftermarket accessories isn't always a good idea. As a matter of fact, it often results in a less efficient gun than originally came out of the factory box.

The second principle is DCOI (Don't Cut On It). Reliable revolver function is dependent upon predesignated spring tension, so leave the spring modifications to someone who truly knows what they're doing. As well, don't partially unscrew the strain screw on the hammer spring to get the illusion of a lighter trigger pull. In so doing, you'll just make the gun go out of time, which in turn causes failures to fire and other stoppages.

To get the best from your DA revolver, consider these items:

Barrel Length: This should be determined by a careful analysis of what you are going to do with the gun. Is concealment important? Bullet expansion? Practical accuracy? Snubbies are at their best only in the hands of an expert. If you're *not* an expert, then you must limit their use to very close ranges.

Sights: Fixed or adjustable? Again, ask yourself exactly what you want from the gun. If self-defense is the primary object, then adjustable sights, with their greater fragility, aren't as good as plain fixed sights. The main requirement is that your sights are visible at high speed, so if you don't intend to be constantly changing your zero, you don't really need adjustability. Front sights can be even more bewildering in that so many different configurations are available. In general, unless you have a vision problem, colored sights are unnecessary and can actually detract from quick sight acquisition during high-speed presentations and multiple-target situations. If the piece is to be drawn from a carrying device of some sort, then the blade itself should be ramped, with no square or sharp edges on its rear surfaces to snag or accumulate foreign matter.

Finish: Blue is pretty, but not very serviceable. If you live in a humid environment or intend to carry the gun on your person, you need to understand that humidity, perspiration, skin acids and simple holster wear will quickly ruin bluing, itself a form of oxidation. Metalife, Armoloy, Nitex, hard chrome, electroless nickel and NP3 all resist these elements and reduce friction with moving parts as well. If you intend serious carry, selection of one of these finishes is an excellent idea.

Stocks: Large target-type stocks, while aesthetically attractive, are not very efficient if the gun must be drawn from a holster because they do not provide a quick index of the gun to the firing hand. Small stocks, often in conjunction with a grip adapter, provide a better option for self-defense work unless the shooter's hand is extraordinarily large.

Round or Square Butt: Many people find that a round butt fits their hand better, while others feel that it makes little difference. Still, the options are worth considering.

Target Hammers: These are functionally unnecessary, but are desirable from a collector's standpoint. For defensive use, the smaller the hammer, the better, so as to avoid snagging on clothing or abrading skin.

Target Triggers: These, too, should be avoided because they reduce the shooter's feel of the trigger under stress. Really good revolver shooters prefer a narrow, smooth trigger for maximum control.

Removal of Edges: Like the self-loader, the revolver comes from the box with a number of sharp edges that can actually draw blood and rip clothing. This is annoying and creates a psychological obstacle to skill development. It's also a good idea to remove the sharp edges from the cylinder release latch to prevent binding the speed-loader. In addition, relieving the left side stock panel to allow speed-loader clearance can be a big help, too. Another area usually in need of square-edge removal is the rear edge of each chamber. A slight "breaking" of these edges will greatly enhance fast loading, particularly under stress.

Grip Adapters: Unless your hands are very large, a grip

SIGHTS

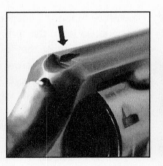

The best front sight configuration for combat shooting is the Baughman "quick-draw" serrated ramp. It allows quick weapon presentations without snagging or wearing unduly, and gives excellent high-speed sight acquisition.

A simple groove sight along the top of the frame is a fine choice, as long as the groove is wide enough to allow quick visual acquisition of the front sight. As well, it is very rugged.

Adjustable sights are often more convenient on DA revolvers due to the wide variety of ammunition available and the resulting variations in points of impact versus point of aim. However, they are more fragile due to their number of small moving parts. Shown here are typical adjustable sights from Smith & Wesson and Colt.

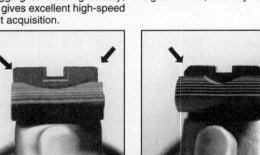

Sharp edges on each side of any adjustable or fixed sight should be removed to avoid abrasion of clothing and snagging during weapon presentations, especially from concealed carry.

Inserts, although popular, are of minimal value for combat shooting because of their fragility. Even in combination with an outlined rear notch, they often confuse rather than enhance sight alignment at the high speeds typical of deadly encounters.

FACTORY AND TARGET STOCKS

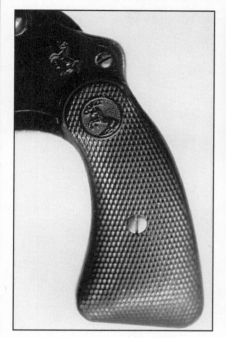

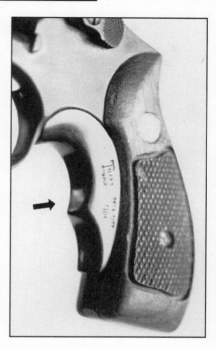

Unless you have extremely large hands and long fingers, standard factory stocks work very well for combat shooting, especially in conjunction with a grip adapter (right). In addition, they make the gun more concealable than larger stocks allow.

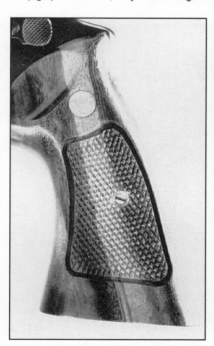
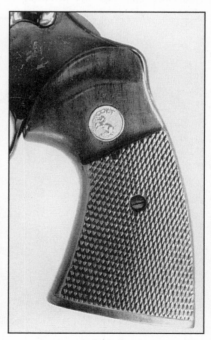

Target stocks typically found on commercial Smith & Wesson and Colt DA revolvers are fine for plinking, hunting and target shooting, but are a poor selection for combat because they eliminate the shooter's feel of the front- and backstrap, and allow serious slippage of the weapon in the hand during fast DA work.

RUBBER AND CUSTOM STOCKS

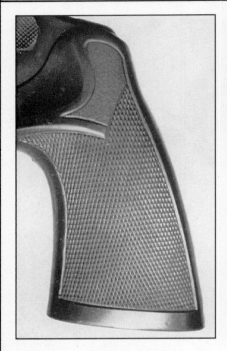  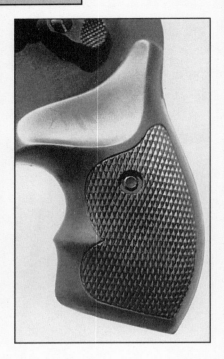

Like target stocks, rubber stocks can be taken to extremes as well. Properly designed rubber stocks can enhance performance considerably. Carefully analyze your needs before you buy, however.

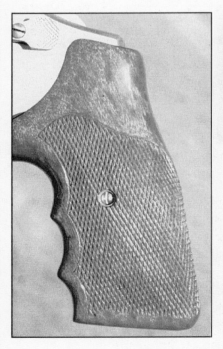 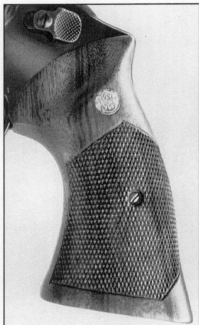 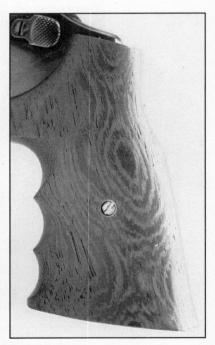

Custom stocks require careful consideration. They should be narrower at the bottom than at the top and not so thick as to reduce or eliminate proper feel of the grip frame with the shooting hand.

adaptor is a good idea. They provide an excellent grip index and prevent the knuckle of the middle finger from being struck by the rear of the trigger guard when the gun is fired.

Old or New Gun: I would not recommend acquiring a pre-turn-of-the-century DA revolver for defensive use, but any serviceable piece made by a major manufacturer after

that time is quite satisfactory, provided it's in good shape. In fact, many, such as the 38-44 Heavy Duty, are excellent guns. The key word here is serviceable.

Muzzlebrakes: Either Mag-Na-Porting or Keeperizing is a good idea for any magnum. Any increase in weapon control is worth pursuing.

HAMMERS

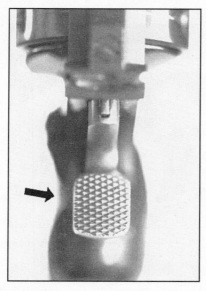

Target hammers are excessively large for defensive use. As well, they snag on clothing during rapid weapon presentations, particularly from concealed carry.

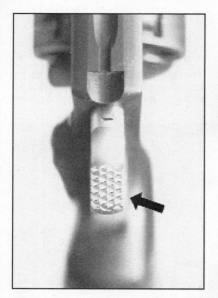

A standard hammer provides all the utility needed for any field handgun, including those used for self-defense.

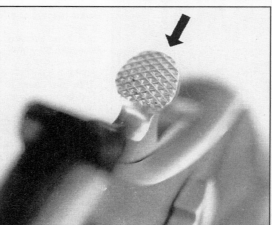

(Above and left) Many shooters have their hammers recountoured to suit their own needs. Some even have the spur removed entirely. This is not as radical as one might at first think because the vast majority of DA revolver combat shooting entails trigger, rather then thumb, cocking.

(Below) If concealment in a pocket is an issue, a shrouded hammer is a good choice. If not, then little is gained.

The selection of holsters, speed-loaders, carriers and other ancillary equipment is of equal importance to the choice of gun itself. Therefore, *careful consideration of purpose* prior to selection remains paramount. After all, the neatest revolver in the world isn't much good to you if, for example, you are unable to get it out of the holster.

Ammunition, too, is often overlooked. Few revolvers with barrel lengths of 4 inches or less produce the velocities needed to give reliable bullet expansion in humans. A heavy, SWC-type slug that provides optimum penetration with a full-caliber wound channel is my choice for use in such guns.

Last, accuracy must be defined. *Intrinsic* accuracy is that which the gun is capable of producing, exclusive of human

TRIGGERS

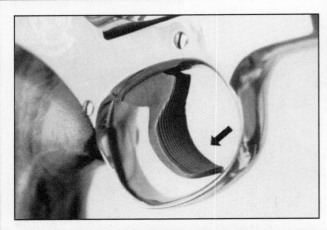

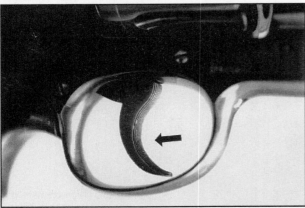

Wide triggers and trigger shoes should be avoided because they give the illusion of a lighter trigger pull. They also cause a loss of trigger feel. Narrow triggers, especially if they're smooth and/or highly polished, provide far better efficiency in fast DA sequences.

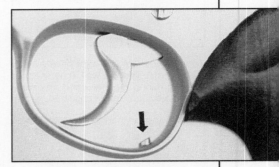

(Above) A worthwhile target shooting accessory, the trigger stop has no place on a fighting handgun and should be avoided.

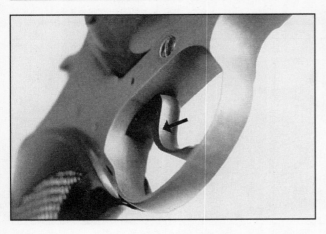

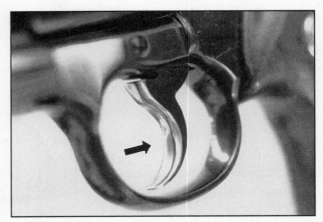

REMOVING SHARP EDGES

Removal of sharp edges at the entry to each chamber greatly enhances cartridge insertion for both speed and tactical reloading. Light polishing of the recoil plate also aids in smooth cylinder rotation, thus enhancing DA shooting.

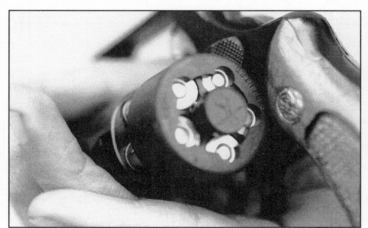

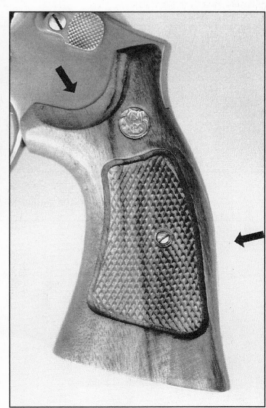

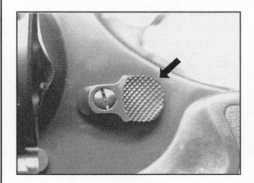

Make certain that your DA revolver allows snag-free insertion and operation of a speed-loader. If not, remove any sharp edges from the cylinder release latch and either relieve the left-hand stock panel or replace the factory stocks with some designed to be used with a speed-loader.

participation. *Practical* accuracy is that which we can actually produce under field conditions.

Obviously, the latter is more important. Practical accuracy is influenced not only by the intrinsic accuracy of the gun itself, but by its human engineering, and the efficiency of its shooter and the accessory equipment as well.

This is why careful evaluation of purpose is so critical.

So, in order to ensure that you've done everything possible to get the best from your revolver, you must never forget that there can be no correct answers without first identifying your needs. If you accomplish this goal first, and then carefully select your modifications, you'll find that the wheelgun is still perfectly capable of doing any job you ask of it.

BARREL IMPROVEMENTS

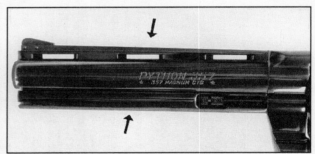

A shrouded ejection rod is far less susceptible to damage from carrying and handling the weapon. However, it increases the weight of the gun. This is particularly true when encountered with a full-length barrel lug. Although this combination gives the gun more weight up front, thus reducing muzzle flip, the extra weight contributes to fatigue from carrying the weapon and slows down presentations from the holster.

A simple heavy barrel, such as shown here on this S&W M13 357 Magnum, aids in control with only a small increase in weight. For some, this is a worthwhile compromise, but only a careful evaluation of your needs can tell you if it's right for you.

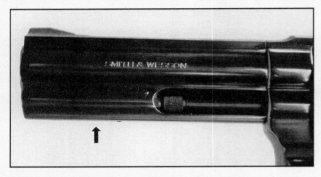

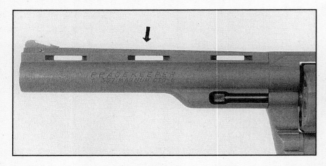

Ventilated ribs, such as on the Colt Peacekeeper and Python, are target shooting accessories and totally useless for combat. Thus, their extra expense is not justified.

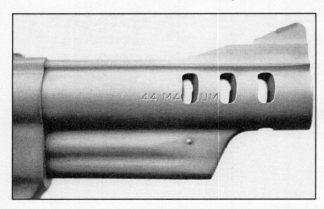

Muzzlebrakes, if properly designed, reduce muzzle flip. However, they also increase muzzle flash and redirect it upward in front of the shooter's face, a tactically negative characteristic. In general, Taylor feels that if your revolver is chambered for a cartridge so potent that it really needs a muzzlebrake, then perhaps you should opt instead for something more controllable.

OPTIMIZING YOUR DOUBLE-ACTION SELF-LOADER

WITHOUT QUESTION, THE double-action (DA) auto is enjoying unprecedented popularity these days. In fact, with the newer handgunning enthusiasts, it actually personifies the term, "self-loader," an honor previously held for more than seventy years by the Colt M1911 45 ACP.

Generally speaking, the current breed of DA auto is the best ever offered, with Smith & Wesson, SIG, Beretta, Ruger and a host of European manufacturers competing feverishly for a burgeoning market. Still, as well made and well engineered as these guns might be, they aren't by any means perfect. Unfortunately, due to the costs involved or perhaps through not realizing what is required to produce an efficient defensive pistol, most of the gunmakers have left some loose ends that need to be dealt with in order for their guns to reach full potential.

This should not be interpreted as being a condemnation of their efforts, for such is not my intent. For the most part, the DA autos produced in the last thirty years are good guns, deserving of our appreciation and certainly worthy of our confidence in them.

Nevertheless, they *do* have some shortcomings that should be addressed. Perhaps their most universal deficiency is *sharp edges*. In the world of machining, such razor-sharp edges mean correct tolerances and craftsmanship. However, in the world of combat handgunning, where people bet their lives on their pistols, sharp edges are pure poison. They abrade skin and clothing, thus preventing maximum operator efficiency from being attained. After all, who wants to bleed every time they practice hard with their pistol, and who wants to constantly replace clothing because their weapon has worn through it?

A good gunsmith I once knew summed it up: "A good combat handgun should feel in your hand like a bar of well-used soap."

Nicely put. The defensive handgun is a kind of life preserver—it's there to save your life. In order for it to accomplish this mission, you must *really practice* with it. This means fast presentations from the holster, tactical and speed reloads, shooting single/multiple/partial targets and the use of full-power ammunition.

If the gun carves you up every time you push yourself hard with it, you'll quickly develop a subconscious resistance to the weapon. It doesn't take a genius to realize that, when this happens, you'll practice less and, when you do, achieve less than your full potential with it. Take a careful look at the accompanying photos and you'll get a pretty good idea of where to look. Wherever you find sharp edges, remove them.

Then, briskly rub your hands all over the piece. You'll immediately find a few more places you missed visually. Keep doing this until no more edges are found. Yes, it might well result in refinishing the weapon, but considering that most guns are blued these days (a poor finish for daily carry and use, especially in humid environments), you'd be well advised to refinish it in a more wear- and corrosion-resistant finish anyway.

A second across-the-board trend with DA autos is that their triggers are excessively wide, often having coarse grooves or sharp corners that make proper trigger manipulation under stress very difficult. This can be corrected by narrowing and rounding the trigger and then highly polishing its front surface. Doing so provides the best feel

REMOVING SHARP EDGES

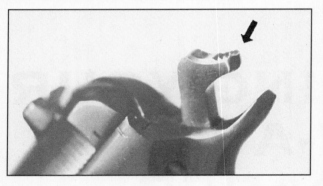

If the hammer of your DA self-loader bites you, reshaping it or reducing its spur protrusion, as shown here, may alleviate the problem.

for your trigger finger for that critical first DA shot, as well as the subsequent SA shots that follow. Trigger control is one of the three essential elements of effective marksmanship, so this modification cannot be overemphasized.

Stocks, too, are important, but unfortunately, few DA autos come from the factory with stocks that allow the weapon control needed for successful high-speed combat shooting. Many aftermarket styles are available, but be careful—fancy or target stocks should be avoided because they are intended for a completely different kind of shooting from that being addressed here. In fact, there is no similarity whatsoever.

The key to stock selection lies in remembering that quick indexing of the firing hand on the butt of the gun is absolutely mandatory, especially if presentation from a holster is involved. Therefore, any stocks that prevent this should be immediately eliminated from consideration. Palm

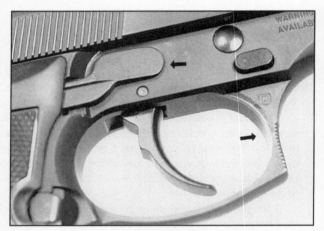

Sharp edges should be removed to prevent destruction of clothing and skin abrasion. Here is where to look for them on several popular DA autos.

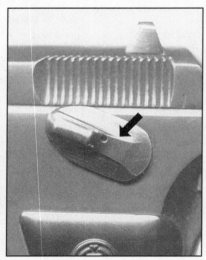

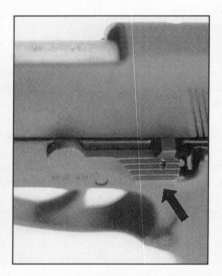

swells, mushy rubber stocks and those with strange configurations negatively affect grip index, thereby reducing control. Avoid them.

While most recently manufactured DA autos have good high-visibility fixed sights, few have sights suitable for low-light shooting. In the real world, low-light situations are so common that they are almost the norm, meaning that the ability to quickly engage and hit targets in that environment cannot be ignored.

Some manufacturers have addressed this by placing painted dots, vertical or horizontal bars, or outlines on the sights of their guns. However, since they do not generate light of their own, these do little to assist in quick sight alignment and sight picture. Better to replace them with tritium sights, of which Trijicons are probably the best. Personally, I prefer a horizontal dot pattern, but some experimentation on your part will disclose what works best for you.

Weapon control is further improved by either checkering or stippling the frontstrap and backstrap. Whichever you choose, don't make it too coarse, or it will be excessively abrasive.

Ammunition selection is important, too. Overpowered ammo offers little improvement in actual stopping power, but vastly complicates the problems of weapon control and overpenetration. In addition, increases in multiple-assailant attacks over the last few years make the need for maximum control even more critical.

Select your ammo based upon an intelligent analysis of the scenarios in which your defensive handgun is most likely to be used. For example, if your primary need is home defense, then perhaps the Glaser Safety Slug, with its enhanced short-range stopping power and reduced penetration, is the best option. On the other hand, if your requirements are more generalized, a JHP that expands reliably but offers good penetration, such as the Winchester Black Talon, might be a better choice.

Avoid gimmicks like muzzlebrakes, extended slide stops

STOCKS

As with DA revolvers and SA autos, keep stock design simple, as shown here. Utility comes from simplicity, not substituting irrelevant concepts for operator skill.

Thumb-swell stocks like this reduce grip efficiency due to a loss of feel of the grip frame by the firing hand.

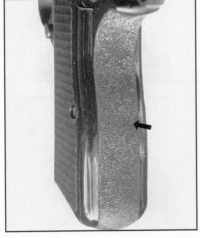

Stippling or checkering on the front- and backstraps will increase your grip efficiency. Just don't get carried away and make it too abrasive.

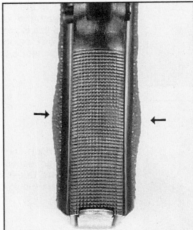

Palm swells also reduce your grip index.

SIGHTS

Vibrations during fast shooting work often cause the rear sights of DA autos to wander. A setscrew like this one will completely eliminate the problem.

and overly long magazine release buttons. These are intended for competition shooting and negatively affect both weapon reliability and operator efficiency if placed in any other environment. You'd feel pretty silly if that extended slide stop locked your slide open because the thumb of your supporting hand touched it while firing, or if that extended magazine release button released your magazine during the first shot, causing a stoppage.

That is, if you live....

Muzzlebrakes vent hot gases upward in front of your face, causing an alteration in the flash size and pattern that destroys low-light vision. In return, only minimal improvement in weapon control is received, making a brake a poor choice. Good shooting techniques can give you more control without the hazards such gadgetry imposes.

About DCOI—Don't Cut On It: *Leave the operational springs in your weapon intact.* Mechanical reliability is the single most important characteristic in a self-defense hand-

Exotic front sight configurations, such as on this Walther P-38 9mm, may provide high visibility at speed, but at the expense of snagging and being highly susceptible to damage.

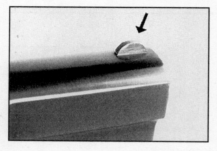

Many DA service autos come from the box with a relatively small front sight. These should be replaced immediately with a higher visibility type.

A fixed high-visibility rear sight, too, is a definite improvement. Adjustable sights are not as useful on self-loaders as they are on revolvers because they utilize ammunition that produces much less variation in point of impact versus point of aim.

(Left and right) The most common European sight illumination concept features a white dot in the front sight and a vertical bar beneath the rear notch. For low-light shooting, this is certainly better than nothing, but isn't especially efficient as far as quick alignment is concerned.

(Left and right) The most difficult combination to align, especially at speed, is three vertical bars. Due to its extreme inefficiency, this concept should be avoided at all costs.

gun. Reducing spring tension for the sake of a lighter trigger is a poor tradeoff. Smoothing up internal bearing parts, however, is not a bad idea because it reduces friction, making the gun easier to operate. Just don't overdo it.

Finally, get some *competent* professional training. Learn the best weapon handling and shooting techniques. There are many ways to shoot a gun, but some are better than others. Only a full-time professional weapons and tactics instructor/consultant has the insight into this highly specialized form of shooting to give you what you need.

Target shooters, gunshop clerks and beer-can busters have little understanding of the elements present in a life-and-death encounter. Their perspective on the subject tends to be academic, rather than practical, making it useless for our needs. Moreover, there is much more to being a professional than simply taking money for services rendered, so *carefully* examine the part-time instructor before you sign up.

Another reason to seek a full-time professional is that not only will his training be superior, but he can also more successfully testify on your behalf in court in the event of a civil suit. Like it or not, liability is a fact of life these days, although it is more of an issue in certain parts of the country than others.

These, then, are the things you should address in order to get the most from your DA auto. Above all, *don't do anything to your pistol that doesn't make it better able to accomplish its intended task!* Removing sharp edges, installing good sights, getting a properly shaped trigger and good stocks, making an intelligent ammo selection, avoiding gimmicks and getting professional training are all you need to attain maximum effectiveness when your life is on the line.

Anything else is just so much window dressing and was created for marketing reasons, not to provide superior performance. You've got to know the difference. The price for being wrong may be far too high.

The best combination for low-light work is to use tritium inserts, such as shown here. Because they produce their own illumination, they're far more useful than painted dots. These, made by Trijicon, are mounted on a Browning P-35 9mm.

ACCESSORIES

A number of DA autos feature a loaded chamber indicator, as shown here. Don't depend upon them. This one indicates a loaded chamber, but the gun is actually empty. When in doubt whether the piece is loaded or not, check and see.

Many DA autos had their beginning as military service pistols and have a lanyard hook because military specifications often require it. However, though unnecessary for most self-defense functions, it need not be removed unless it interferes with speed or tactical reloading procedures.

Though popular with competition shooters because their events overemphasize speed loading, an extended magazine release button is a dangerous accessory for a combat gun. It tends to cause unseating of the magazine during strenuous activity, causing a Type One stoppage. The sharp edges on any magazine release button should be removed.

OPTIMIZING YOUR COLT MODEL 1911

FOR MORE THAN seven decades, the Browning-designed Colt 45 auto has been, as the song says, "taking care of business." Yet in spite of its unsurpassed performance record, this classic handgun can be improved with an intelligent selection of aftermarket modifications.

The 1911, while a beautifully engineered gun from both a human and mechanical standpoint, can stand upgrading in a few areas—for example, its sights. Although the 1911-A1 was an improvement, its sights remain too small to be seen quickly during high-speed target engagements.

Aftermarket sight availability for the 1911 is nothing less than terrific, with myriad fixed or adjustable sights readily available. While certainly not as pretty to look at, fixed sights offer the best compromise between longevity and functionality because they provide faster sight acquisition without the fragility that comes with adjustable types. Remember, if self-defense is the primary object, then the simplest option is preferable.

In addition, virtually every unmodified 1911-pattern gun I've ever seen has sharp edges on the thumb safety, grip safety tang, hammer and corresponding frame areas. These quickly abrade clothing and skin, making practice with "old ugly" a less than pleasant experience. In turn, *this means that you practice less often*, preventing attainment of maximum skill. Thus, such edges must be removed, a process called "dehorning." Even if it causes you to have the gun refinished, this upgrade should not be ignored.

Rather than dehorning, many prefer to replace the standard spur hammer with a rounded Commander burr type, although strictly speaking this may be more of an aesthetic personal preference than a necessity.

One additional problem with most military-issue 1911/1911-A1 and out-of-the-box commercial Government Models is that their trigger pulls are, to say the least,

uninspiring. This, too, constitutes a critical obstacle to the development of maximum weapon efficiency and operator skill.

Commercial Colt Government Models manufactured after 1970 also feature a collet bushing in preference to the old standard, solid GI type. Legitimately claimed to increase accuracy (if correctly fitted), the collet fits so tightly when the slide/barrel are in full battery that the slightest amount of foreign matter (grit, unburned powder, etc.) will cause a Type Four (failure to go into battery) stoppage. This also applies to custom-fitted, target-type solid bushings. When viewed from the self-defense standpoint, this is entirely unsatisfactory. *A defensive handgun must, above all else, possess the highest possible degree of functional reliability.*

Another problem with the collet is that to perform as intended it must be *carefully* fitted, a time-consuming operation. If the collet is not aligned almost perfectly, uneven pressures are exerted upon the collet fingers, causing metal fatigue and eventual breakage. In a combat situation, this can be downright dangerous, since a broken finger is quite large and will lodge in the slide, causing a complete and true *jam*, as opposed to a simple stoppage that can be cleared in seconds without weapon disassembly or the use of tools.

Over the years, I have found that guns equipped with a solid bushing are not only more reliable, but are also inherently accurate enough to hit a man in the chest at 50 meters. This is more accuracy than one could ever need for a self-defense situation, especially when we consider the reduction in operator skill that accompanies extreme stress. Clearly, replacement of the collet with a solid bushing is a smart move.

Trigger pull is a critical factor with any firearm but especially so for the defensive handgun. From a mechanical

BUSHINGS

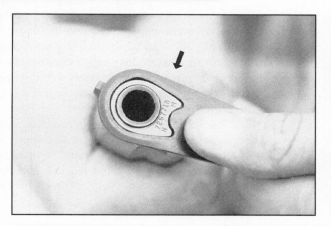

Tight bushings cause more stoppages with the M1911 than any other accessory. Installed by many gunsmiths who erroneously believe that accuracy is only a function of bushing tightness, they eliminate tolerances critical to reliable functioning under field conditions.

Whether a match-type solid version or a collet, these should be avoided. The bushing should be finger removable.

REMOVING SHARP EDGES

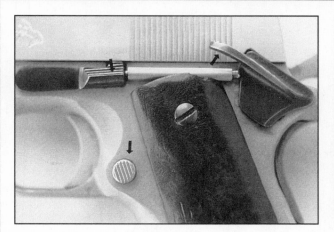

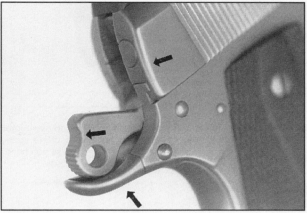

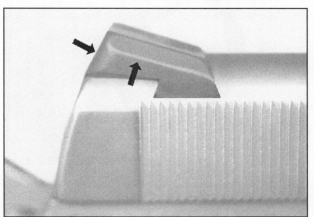

Sharp edges are the bane of the M1911 as it comes from the box. These cut skin and abrade concealment clothing and should be removed wherever encountered. The best way to locate them is to simply rub your hands briskly all over the weapon. As one old-time gunsmith put it, "A serious fighting handgun should feel like a bar of well-used soap." Taylor agrees completely. A burr, or Commander-type, hammer is readily available. Many shooters prefer the burr type to alleviate hammer bite or to eliminate snagging in concealment clothing. However, if you choose the burr type, be certain to relieve a space for it in the grip tang or the gun won't work.

standpoint, it is generally felt—and I agree—that reduction of any 1911-type trigger to less than 3.0 pounds is ill-advised and potentially dangerous. On the other hand, trigger pulls from 3.0 (for highly skilled shooters) to around 5.0 pounds, with a *crisp* letoff, are mechanically safe and provide optimum efficiency.

All 1911-A1s and commercial Government Models come with an arched mainspring housing, whereas straight 1911s, Gold Cups and Officers Models have a flat housing. In recent years, it has become the vogue for gunsmiths to arbitrarily replace the arched housing with a flat one, but for nineteen out of twenty shooters this is a poor idea.

The reason the arched housing was substituted for the flat one in the first place (which occurred in 1923) was to improve the index of the gun in the firing hand, thus increasing its pointability. Only shooters with extraordinarily large palms should consider the flat mainspring housing.

In conjunction with the arched housing, 1911-A1s come with a short trigger, another improvement over the long trigger of the original 1911. This substitution originated from the legitimate criticism that the long trigger does not allow proper trigger finger placement for operators with average-length fingers. So, only those with very long fingers should consider the long trigger.

The Gold Cup is intended for target shooting with light loads, not defensive or hunting use with full-power ammo. Sustained use of such will result in reduced sear/hammer service life and a rapid loosening of the sights. In addition, the long, wide trigger of the Gold Cup

TRIGGERS

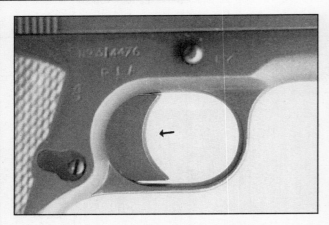

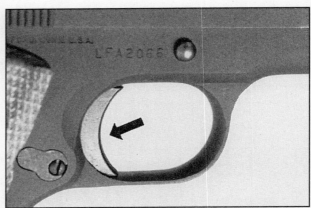

The long trigger is best used by shooters with very long fingers. For the vast majority of us, the short trigger offers superior operation. Don't let your gunsmith talk you into a long trigger unless you have long fingers or you'll receive less efficiency for your trouble and expense.

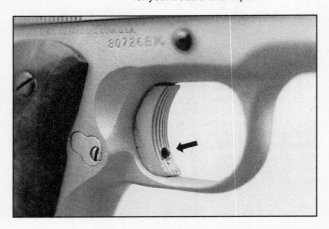

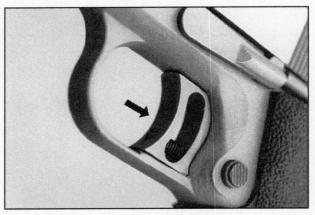

Wide and/or adjustable triggers can cause problems for the combat shooter and should be avoided. Both are target-shooting accessories with no place on a fighting weapon.

SIGHTS

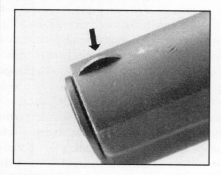

(Left and right) The typical M1911 or commercial Government Model comes with sights too small to use well at the high speeds typical of deadly confrontations. These should be replaced with larger versions allowing quicker, more positive alignment and a better sight picture under such conditions.

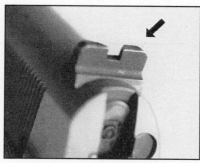

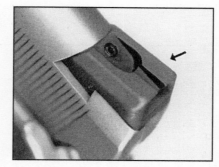

King, Novak and MMC are three examples of well-designed fixed high-visibility M1911 rear sights.

Examples of well-designed front sights for M1911-series autos. Note the ramped configurations which precludes snagging.

(Above and below) The best low-light sight configuration for the M1911 is the horizontal three-dot pattern, preferably with Tritium inserts for maximum visibility.

(Left) Adjustable sights are generally unnecessary on a self-defense M1911. Extra parts mean fragility compared to fixed sights, and due to little variation in point of aim versus point of bullet impact with the 45 ACP cartridge, adjustable sights present no real asset. However, they remain relatively popular, especially in a low-profile version, as shown here.

is anathema to the serious self-defense shooter because it negatively affects the feel of the trigger against the trigger finger.

It has also become popular to automatically change the stocks of any new 1911, substituting custom types like rubber wrap-arounds, flared/flanged stocks and even some with thumbrests. Remember that your gun's mission must be the determining factor as to what kind of options you will install. It has been repeatedly proven that, under stress, stocks of this type seriously reduce the grip index of the gun in your hand during high-speed presentations.

Humid natural environments cause almost immediate damage to blued guns, as does their carry near the skin where perspiration and skin acids come into play. Constant use/carry of the weapon under these conditions requires a finish that can resist, if not completely prevent, deterioration from these elements. Hard chrome, Metalife, Roguard, NP3, Armoloy, Nitex, electroless nickel and, lately, an improved version of black chrome, all offer good protection and also reduce friction and the resultant wear of moving parts.

Parkerizing offers a reduction in glare and, by virtue of its ability to absorb and hold preservative elements, provides some protection against the elements, but does not offer the reduction of wear and tear to mating parts.

Due to the emphasis on rapid loading in IPSC competition, many believe that it is essential to bevel the magazine well or install some sort of funneling device on any 1911-style gun to enhance speed-loading capability. With this I disagree, because only *practice*, not gimmicks, will give you skill.

ACCESSORIES

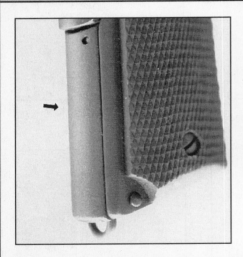

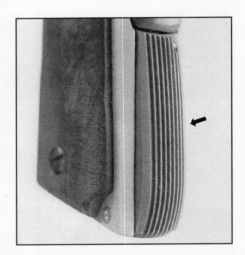

(Left and right) The flat mainspring housing is best for those with very large palms, while the arched housing is a better choice for the average person. Again, don't let your gunsmith talk you into a flat housing unless you really need it—the weapon's pointability will be reduced, making it more difficult to shoot quickly and accurately under stress.

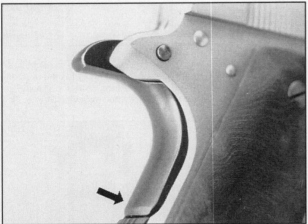

For liability reasons, pinning of the grip safety is not recommended unless your palm is too small to allow proper deactivation of the device when your hand is in a proper firing grip on the pistol.

For those who have fleshy hands and are constantly bitten by the hammer, the beavertail grip safety is a good addition. However, care in its fitting and careful edge removal remain important.

At one time, I was one of a half-dozen or so men in the world who could perform a one-second speed load, and I did it without any bevels or funnels. However, if you feel the need for beveling, be certain that you have it performed correctly with a 60-degree bevel, not less. As well, ensure that the bevel rolls over into the well, with no edges in the funnel for the magazine to bind on.

Many shooters insist that their gun have a polished feedway and relieved ejection port, both modifications that are specialized in scope and not universally necessary. I have yet to find a 1911 that would not feed ball ammunition, so unless you're going to play with exotic bullet shapes, feedway polishing doesn't really matter much.

Likewise, unless you handload a great deal, relief of the ejection port isn't essential. It in no way enhances the gun's functional reliability; it just prevents the denting of ejected cases, thus eliminating the annoying step of straightening them during the reloading process.

In reality, your 1911-style pistol needs only a few improvements to realize its maximum potential: 1) a solid bushing; 2) sharp edges removed; 3) a trigger job; and 4) high-visibility, not necessarily adjustable, sights. Other modifications should be considered only after careful analysis of your gun's intended function.

If its mission is defensive, then the KISS principle should be of supreme concern. Under no circumstances should such gadgets as extended magazine release buttons or slide stops be installed, because not only are they unnecessary, they actually reduce the reliability of the gun.

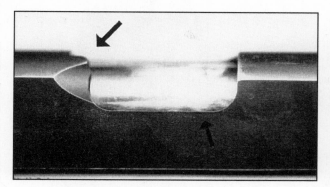

"Porting" or relieving of the ejection port to allow better ejection is more useful for a handloader than for someone who exclusively uses factory ammo. In truth, it merely prevents the expended case from being dented during the ejection cycle and has little effect on the operation of the weapon itself.

Extended slide stops are a deathtrap because they often cause the slide to lock back, due to the shooter unknowingly pressing it upward, while firing is in progress. Effective, fast slide stop operation is a function of proper technique, not gadgetry.

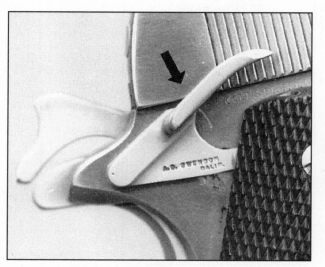

Ambidextrous thumb safeties are needed by left-handed shooters, *but no one else.* Intrinsically weaker and more failure prone, they offer no real advantage to a right-handed shooter.

Also, while popular, ambidextrous thumb safeties should be used only by left-handers, who have no choice since there is no way, short of extensive rebuilding of the gun, to provide left-hand-only safety manipulation. Ambi-safeties are inherently weaker than standard types because of their male/female configuration, making them more susceptible to failure. Remember Murphy's Law?

A last option to avoid is the extended recoil spring guide, with its erroneously claimed kinking prevention. Particularly when used in conjunction with the various buffers now offered, this device unnecessarily complicates field-stripping procedures and offers no increase whatsoever in either spring longevity or weapon/shooter efficiency.

In conclusion, 1) clearly define the mission of your gun, while remembering the KISS principle and 2) consider only those options that provide a real increase in effectiveness.

Last, but perhaps most important, remember that gadgetry, however interesting it may be, is not a legitimate substitute for skill. Learn how to properly use your piece and maintain your skill with regular dry- and live-fire practice. Only then can you truthfully say that you've done your best.

STOCKS

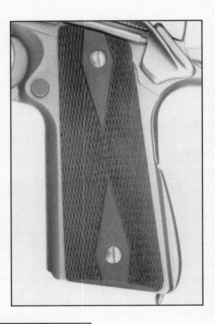

(Left and right) Keep your stocks flat, rigid and thin for the best grip index. This is critical for effective high-speed weapon presentations from a holster.

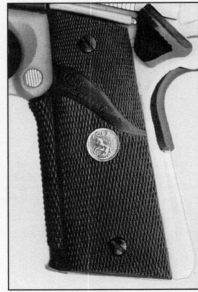

Though popular, rubber stocks reduce the proper feel (grip index) of the firing hand on the frontstrap and backstrap of the gun, slowing down presentations from the holster and increasing the potential for grip-index error ("bobbling").

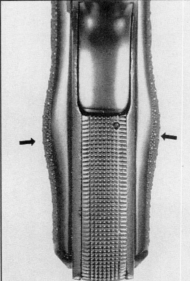

Palm-swell stocks also reduce grip indexing and should be avoided. Checkering or stippling of the frontstrap and/or backstrap can enhance indexing, but care should be taken not to make them excessively rough and abrasive.

PICKING THE PROPER HOLSTER

WHILE MANY PROSPECTIVE self-defense handgunners are bewildered about choosing a holster, perhaps because of the vast selection of holsters available, it isn't really as complex or difficult to deal with as it appears. A holster, regardless of its design, must fulfill several functions. Commensurate with its wearer's needs, it is intended to provide: 1) weapon protection against the elements; 2) security against weapon loss during physical movement; and 3) fast, consistent weapon acquisition and presentation when needed.

When I say "commensurate with its wearer's needs," I mean that, within each category, all of us have different requirements. We each live a different lifestyle and thus require varying combinations or degrees of emphasis of these three elements.

For example, a uniformed police officer has a multifaceted job, including sitting, running, walking, wrestling with suspects, concerns about having his handgun taken from behind, etc. His needs are more stringent and difficult to satisfy than those of, say, a typical civilian with a carry concealed weapon (CCW) permit. Such a person would carry his or her handgun in a more relaxed mode. Though the gun would be concealed, the holster wouldn't be required to retain it during extreme physical movement or prevent someone from snatching the weapon from behind.

As a result, holster and ancillary equipment selection is easier for civilians than for police, but still should reflect very careful examination and consideration of the various characteristics of the wearer's lifestyle. In short, your selection should reflect cognizance of what you want from your equipment. Consider your own needs, write them down and only then go shopping. Otherwise, you'll be almost immediately overwhelmed by what's available.

Don't let anyone sell you a bill of goods. No gunshop clerk, cop or gun writer—no one—can guarantee you that his holster preferences will be appropriate for you. Only you can determine that. Ulterior motives like profits and egos are often the bases for those recommendations, and the clerk won't have to pay the ultimate price if they're wrong. Don't relinquish the responsibility of holster choice to anyone.

There are two characteristics that any serious holster must possess in order to accomplish its three functions. Both are perhaps so simple that they've often been overlooked or ignored by most of the commercial, and even some custom, designers and manufacturers. Put simply, any holster that doesn't exhibit these two critical characteristics should be instantly disqualified: 1) exhibit sufficient clearance of the grip frame of the holstered weapon to allow a correct firing grip to be established; 2) cover enough of the trigger guard of the holstered weapon to prevent inadvertent weapon actuation by either an improperly placed trigger finger or some outside projection, such as brush, tree branches, etc.

Once these two criteria are satisfied, you can then consider what kind of security device best satisfies your needs. Many prefer a simple leather form-fitted rig, but these wear rather quickly, reducing weapon security against loss, and must be replaced perhaps twice a year, a costly process.

Fortunately, in the last three years, a polycarbonate material known as Kydex has become available, solving the problem nicely. Kydex holsters retain their shape and resiliency very well against heat, moisture, wear and body chemicals, making them far superior to leather. In addition, they're more economical to produce and are, therefore, lower priced. They also have considerably less bulk and weight than their leather counterparts.

Some feel that the thumb-break type is the best compromise between weapon acquisition/presentation speed and security against loss. If you choose a thumb break, make certain that it: 1) breaks toward your torso when pressed by the firing thumb, 2) incorporates a reinforced tab to keep it rigid, and 3) utilizes a high-quality snap that releases crisply when the tab bends under thumb pressure.

Others opt for a friction lock, a simple device that utilizes a piece of plastic or leather placed so as to contact either the muzzle or trigger guard of the gun, thereby holding it in place by friction. A screw allows the wearer to set whatever withdrawal force he feels is appropriate.

For many years, holsters that featured a snap-strap were widely seen. Often called Border Patrol rigs because the design was used by that agency in the 1940s and '50s, they prevent loss from physical movement and protect the weapon reasonably well, but at the expense of being dreadfully slow. Curiously, this weakness wasn't noticed for several decades due to the fact that almost every law enforcement agency in the country practiced and qualified with their straps unfastened. By the early 1960s, enough officers had been killed or injured because of this error that weapon presentation training was upgraded to include release of the security device.

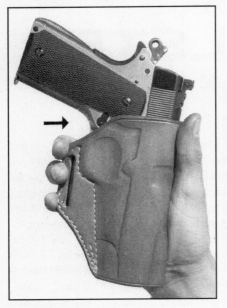

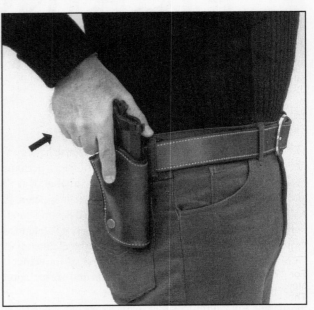

(Left and right) There are two characteristics required of a good holster: 1) it must provide adequate clearance of the grip frame to allow quick, easy acquisition by the firing hand, and 2) it must protect enough of the weapon's trigger guard to prevent inadvertent engagement by either the trigger finger or objects like brush, branches, etc.

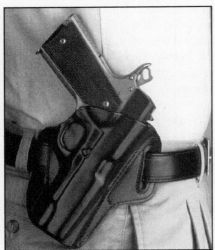

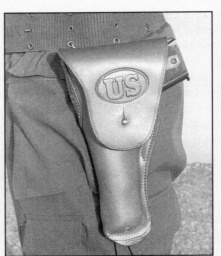

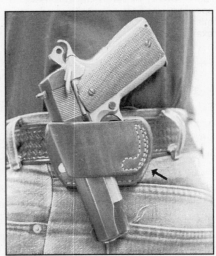

Due to ignorance, many self-defense shooters incorrectly place their holsters on their belts, thus causing them to be too far forward for fast, easy weapon acquisition. Most strong-side rigs are intended to be worn behind the point of the hip, allowing proper weapon presentation without body posturing. A good rule of thumb is to place the holster on the belt so that it is just behind the trousers seam, as shown here.

For centuries, the most common field holster was the full-flap type. Intended to provide full protection in abusive (military) environments, it prevents fast grip acquisition, making it a poor choice for either civilian or police self-defense use.

For casual carry, the simple belt slide is quite popular. Designed for those who wear their weapons only in specified places, its primary asset is that it doesn't look like a holster when there is no gun in it. From a practical standpoint, it provides poor security and weapon protection.

Naturally, the inherent slowness of the system quickly became apparent, and its popularity waned rapidly thereafter. Thank goodness, because although the design is satisfactory for "boondocking" or other forms of casual carry, its lack of presentation speed makes it obsolete.

In law enforcement circles, concerns about weapon retention are often so intense that the element of security overrides all other considerations. This results in the creation of holsters that require multiple release movements to be accomplished before the gun can be withdrawn. Not surpris-

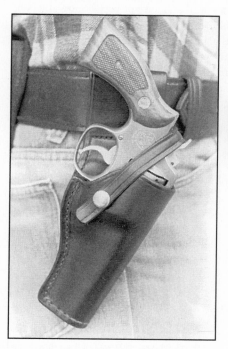

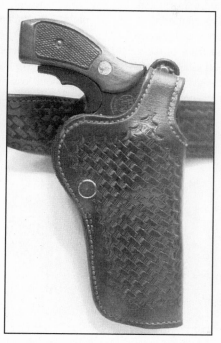

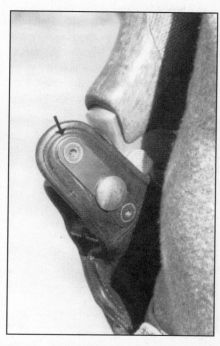

For about six decades, the snap-strap holster was considered to be status quo. Though it provides adequate security for "boondocking," it offers poor presentation speed, making it marginal for self-defense missions. Note also that this particular example does not cover the trigger guard.

Provided it is properly designed, the thumbbreak holster offers perhaps the best compromise of security and speed. However, it still must adhere to the two fundamental holster criteria—clearance for grip acquisition and a covered trigger guard.

The properly designed thumbbreak should release toward the body and be reinforced to maintain rigidity. The snap must keep a crisp release over a long period of time. Otherwise, you could get killed while trying to release it, a sad event that has happened to many police officers over the years.

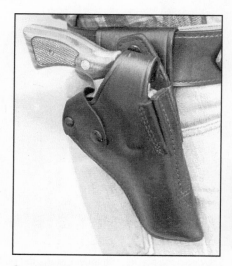

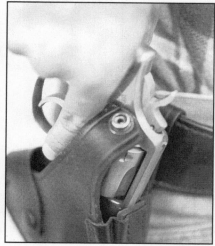

Occasionally, security somehow becomes more important than acquisition and presentation speed. In law enforcement circles, where there is legitimate concern about gun security, this is sometimes taken to extremes. This rig requires the thumbbreak to be released, then the weapon to be rocked forward in the holster before it can be withdrawn—a deathtrap in a handgun fight. The best police duty holsters offer a reasonable combination of both speed and security.

ingly, these take far too much time, considering the short time frames of handgun encounters, making such rigs virtual deathtraps. One police-officer friend of mine summed it up nicely: "These damned holsters are *so* secure that I might as well leave the gun at home!"

To his poignant, yet absolutely accurate appraisal, I can only add that when you need a handgun, you need it *now!* A reasonable degree of weapon security is without doubt needed; however, any holster that prevents you from quickly bringing your weapon into action can get you killed just as quickly as one that allows the weapon to be easily lost.

How much of the weapon the holster covers depends on the degree of protection against the elements you seek. Storekeepers often choose a simple belt-slide because when they remove the gun and leave the shop, it doesn't look like a holster, so no one knows that they're armed when working. In this case, the fact that belt-slides don't protect the gun very well and are not very secure aren't of particular concern.

The majority of plainclothes policemen and civilians prefer a holster that covers the gun to a point about an inch or so below the grip frame, providing better protection and security without loss of presentation speed. Again, consider your needs before selection.

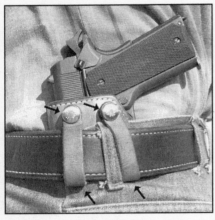

Inside-the-pants rigs have minimal "signature," making them a good choice where concealed carry is of particular importance. However, to prevent presenting the weapon with the holster still wrapped around it—a potentially fatal event—make certain that the retention loops encircle the belt completely.

This rig is a potential deathtrap. Can you tell why? Years ago Denver detective Ray Pezolt had some spring-clip holsters made with the clip inverted, so the holster couldn't be pulled out when the gun was drawn. They worked.

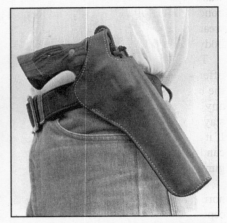

For those who spend most of their time seated, a crossdraw rig is a good choice. Crossdraws, too, must adhere to basic holster criteria.

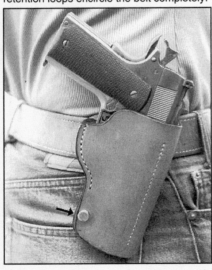

Friction-lock holsters have become quite popular in the last thirty years. They hold the gun in the holster via an adjustable plastic or leather friction device and allow the wearer to control how much pull pressure is required to withdraw the weapon. These are good holsters; however, set the friction lock carefully to maintain the proper balance between presentation speed and weapon security. If it's too loose, the gun may be lost with only minimal physical exertion; if too tight, it may not come free when you need it.

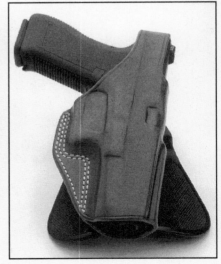

In recent years, the paddle holster has eliminated the act of sliding the weapon on and off the belt. As well, it provides rigidity and prevents the holster from moving from its correct location on the wearer.

How concealable should the holster be? It depends entirely on you. Inside-the-pants holsters provide extreme concealment, but are often fitted only with a simple spring clip to hold them in place. This often results in drawing the holster with the gun, a potentially fatal mishap, and makes such rigs a poor choice. A few makers put the spring clip on upside down, so the holster stays in place. If you prefer the inside-the-pants concept, ensure that the holster is secured to the belt via either one or two snap straps or a one-piece loop.

Shoulder holsters are widely seen in the movies and on TV, but are so uncomfortable in comparison to modern waistband holsters that they bear little consideration. Though concealable, they are such at the expense of binding the wearer's clothing to his body, preventing air flow and raising body temperatures to unreasonable levels.

To solve this problem, several holster makers now offer shoulder rigs that do not bind the harness tightly to the body, but this also causes them to flop around during any amount of physical movement. The weapon must stay at the location where the firing hand is trained to go. If it has moved, a "bobble" is guaranteed, something you can ill afford in the short time frames of the typical handgun fight.

Should the gun be held vertically, or should it be placed horizontally or upside down? Over the years, all three concepts have been embraced, but without any one in particular showing superiority. Because they're usually not secured to the wearer's belt, horizontal and upside-down holsters tend to wander rearward, printing the outline of the gun butt against concealment clothing and making grip acquisition a real chore. As if this weren't enough of a problem, many vertical and all upside-down rigs usually require three hands to reholster the gun, yet another complication to an already difficult situation.

Should you carry your defensive handgun on your strong side or crossdraw? If you spend most of your time seated at a desk or in a car, the crossdraw has much to offer because it allows quick and easy weapon access. In contrast, the strong-side rig is often inaccessible when you're seated, forcing you to withdraw the weapon and place it somewhere else for quick access, such as beneath your leg or stuck between the seats of the car.

Avoid Special Ops holsters that ride on the thigh. They're intended for someone who is wearing a great deal of equipment and using a weapon other than a handgun—usually an assault rifle, submachine gun or shotgun—as his primary arm. The handgun is thus an ancillary weapon and is placed on the thigh to make it accessible in the event the individual experiences a stoppage with his primary weapon. He can then abandon it on a carry sling, grab the handgun and return to action, clearing the stoppage later.

If you carry your gun in a purse, be sure to use one which is designed for that purpose. We've all seen what a woman's purse looks like inside and marvel at how she managed to get all that stuff into such a small container. The gun must be kept separate from everything else or it won't be accessible when needed. So ladies, don't just toss it in your bag and expect to find it on a dark, cold, rainy night when you're accosted by a would-be armed robber or rapist. Instead, get

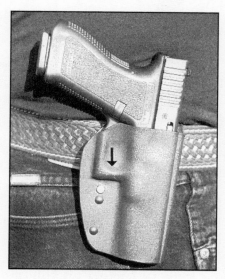

Polycarbonate (now called Kydex) holsters have existed for a long time, but only reached the point where they are truly the state of the art in the last three years. However, beware of those that "break" the gun through the front. Better to use an upward withdrawal, which allows the trigger guard to lock securely into the holster. It releases with a brisk tug.

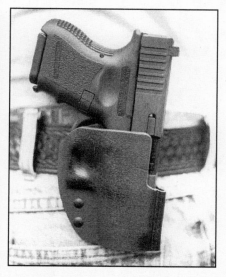

The best Kydex holster made is the Taylor Thunderbolt, by M-D Labs. Designed by the author, it provides excellent weapon security and presentation speed without loss of weapon protection in the process, and is a favorite of many plainclothes police officers and self-defense-minded civilians.

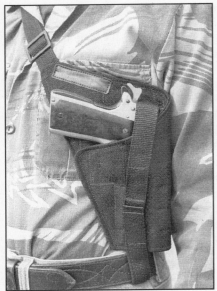

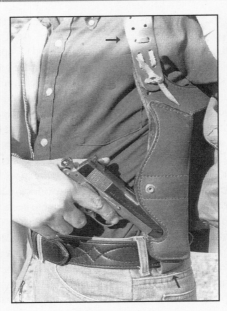

The simplest of the shoulder holsters—the military style. Intended for wear by armored vehicle and aircraft crewmen, it is light and compact, and provides relatively good weapon protection. However, it places considerable strain on the off-side shoulder and trapezius muscle, resulting in undue fatigue. Also, due to the strap crossing the torso rather than encircling it, is not very concealable.

These are examples of typical commercially offered shoulder rigs. All "break" the gun forward, a required characteristic because the weapon is mounted high on the torso. Security varies, depending upon how efficient the retention method might be. Some rigs use spring steel rods to each side of the holster; some use elastic. Still, shoulder holsters are hot and generally uncomfortable except in air-conditioned environments, and offer marginal presentation speed. Both of these are relatively efficient designs, providing adequate concealment and proper rigidity by attaching the holster to the belt.

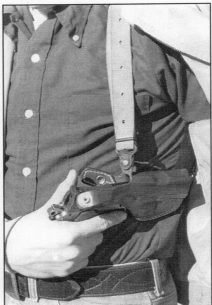

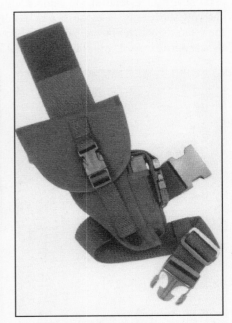

The upside-down shoulder holster was intended as a replacement for the standard vertical rig. However, since it isn't attached to the belt to maintain its location, it tends to wander rearward, printing the butt of the gun against the concealment garment. As well, once the weapon is withdrawn, it requires "three hands" to reinsert it.

In recent years, comfort has often overshadowed shoulder-holster efficiency. Note that this rig configures the gun horizontally, rather than vertically, and is not attached to the belt. Comfortable? Yes, as much as any shoulder rig can be. But it flops around with even the slightest physical activity, making it only marginally concealable and difficult to work with under stress.

The Special Operations rig is intended to carry a handgun that is being used as an ancillary weapon. Usually mounted low on the wearer's thigh, it places the weapon where it can be accessed with relative ease if the wearer experiences a malfunction with his primary weapon, which is normally an assault rifle, submachine or shotgun.

yourself a purse that features a separate gun and spare ammo compartment that is configured in such a way as to allow you to quickly find it, get it out and bring it into action when you're under stress. (Read that as being terrified.) There are several designs that accomplish this goal, but my lady friends like the Galco in particular.

Likewise, the fanny pack requires careful cogitation because it is subject to the same criteria as a purse. And like the purse, make sure that your weapon and spare ammo are kept separate from the cargo compartment. A bag that makes the gun and its spare ammo readily accessible with the simple crosswise and downward rip of a zipper, rather than fumbling

with trying to unzip it in the conventional manner, is definitely the way to go. Again, Galco seems to have gotten there first with their Fast Action Gun System, so give them a look.

There you have it, an overview of holsters in general. I've refrained from recommending any particular style as being the best because there is no such thing—what's best for me might be completely unsuitable for you. Still, regardless of type and style, all holsters have a multi-faceted mission and must satisfy certain criteria in order to accomplish it. You now know both the missions and criteria and can use them in conjunction with a careful appraisal of your needs to find which one works best for you.

Properly designed purses and fanny packs keep the gun and its spare ammo separate from the cargo compartment, and position them to allow quick, easy access and weapon presentation under stress. Here is the Galco Fast Action Gun System in action. With its fast across-and-down rip-open action, this shooter can present her 40 S&W Glock and get two center hits at 7 meters in two seconds.

Taylor believes this is one of the best leather holster/spare magazine combinations available—the Davis #1145 holster and 45MP spare magazine carrier. The weight of the two magazines helps to balance that of the gun.

CARRYING SPARE AMMO

LIKE HOLSTERS, MAGAZINE carriers, speed-loaders and other means of carrying spare ammunition are often relegated to being low-priority items. Yet, like holsters, they represent a serious part of your life-saving equipment, just as serious as any other part of it. As such, their selection requires serious thought.

Rapid reloading has never been a deciding factor in a gunfight in the overwhelming majority of the cases I've reviewed (more than 4000). Therefore, spending excessive amounts of time and energy practicing the technique might be a mistake.

As a result, unlike many of my colleagues, I cannot in good conscience recommend speed-loaders as being the solution to all revolver reloading problems *per se*. I will, however, say what I have already said repeatedly—only a careful analysis of *your* needs can tell you what best satisfies your requirements. Actually, speed-loaders were created to

Attempts to encapsulate ammunition date back to before WWI. These are half- and full-moon clips used with S&W and Colt Model 1917 45 ACP revolvers.

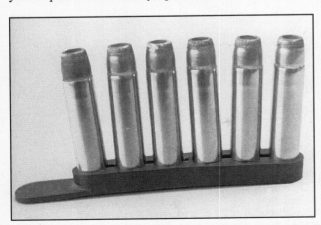

First appearing in the 1960s and continuing in production as this is written, the Speed Strip holds six rounds in line and allows the loading of two cartridges at a time. However, since it is made of soft neoprene, it offers poor cartridge retention.

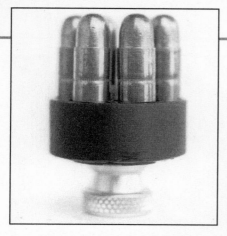

So-called speed-loaders, holding six cartridges, were first used in the 1890s, but disappeared until the middle 1960s. Early contemporary examples, made of rubber, offered poor ammo retention and were quite fragile. This, however, is the HKS, one of the best. Utilizing a turn-handle operated ratchet to hold and release cartridges, it is perhaps the most rugged of its kind.

The fastest speed-loader is the JFS, marketed by Safariland. Cartridge release is facilitated by pressing the unit forward against the ejector ratchet mounted in the rear of the revolver cylinder.

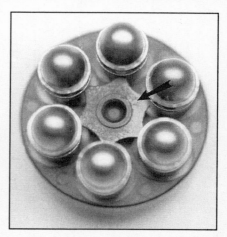

However, it can be tricky to load because it requires the cartridges to be inserted and the front-located release button to be pressed and simultaneously twisted.

beat the 7-yard, twelve-shots-in-25-seconds stage of the old PPC course, not as tactical devices, so it should be no surprise that, in every instance in which they were used in an actual handgun fight, they failed to influence the outcome to any significant degree. The sad truth is that the shooter was missing too much, not that he lacked enough ammunition to get the job done.

Therefore, other means of carrying spare ammo—loops, dump pouches—might well offer you exactly what you need. Perhaps when you go down to the Stop 'n' Rob for a quart of milk and a loaf of bread, you don't want to carry the bulk of one or two speed-loader pouches, instead preferring the compactness of a simple six-round loop carrier or 2x2x2 pouch. Maybe you don't feel that you need two spare seventeen-shot magazines for your Glock M17 9mm. That's a lot of ammunition, isn't it? Especially when the statistics repeatedly show that it isn't needed in the vast majority of gunfights.

On the other hand, assuming that an evaluation of your needs has determined that you actually *need* sizable quantities of spare ammo, you might prefer the light weight and ruggedness of a Kydex magazine carrier instead of a leather one. Or perhaps you "just feel better" when you carry a dual-cell leather carrier. Although those who want to sell you things are loathe to admit it, there is no set of rules that demands any specific way to carry spare ammo. If it works for you, then it's the right solution.

So, in the photography that accompanies this text, examine the choices, but in doing so take a broad overview approach. There are dozens of manufacturers who offer excellent quality of workmanship. Unfortunately, there are only a few who really understand the art and science of combat handgunning, which narrows the field considerably.

How do I prefer to carry spare ammo? It depends on how I'm carrying my defensive handgun. Ordinarily, I carry a

(Left) For casual carry, a simple aluminum snap-on-the-belt speed-loader carrier is favored by many. However, due to its marginal security, it should be used with great caution.

(Right) Whether concealed or not, all speed-loaders should be carried in some kind of belt-mounted carrier. Mounting configurations include back-to-back, upside-down (shown here), or a single/double cell pouch protruding forward from the belt or mounted on top. Of these designs, the latter is the most efficient because it presents the least bulk.

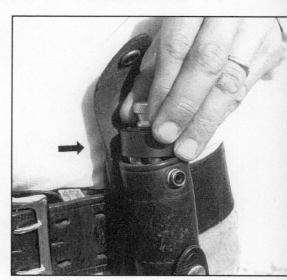

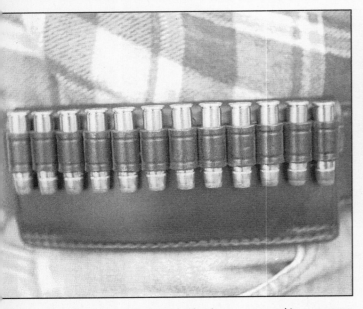

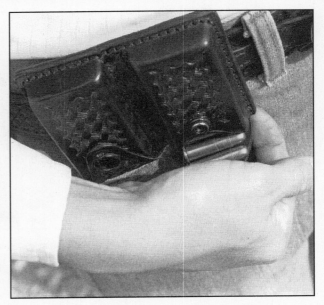

For over sixty years, simple leather loops were used to carry spare revolver ammo. While simple in concept and perfectly suitable for tactical reloading, they don't protect the cartridges from exposure to the elements. As well, since they are made of leather, they loosen up fairly quickly, reducing ammo retention capability.

Also popular in the 1950s, the dump pouch dropped six cartridges into the hand by merely releasing a flap-snap. However, since they were loose in the hand, subsequent loading into the weapon without loss was a tricky affair.

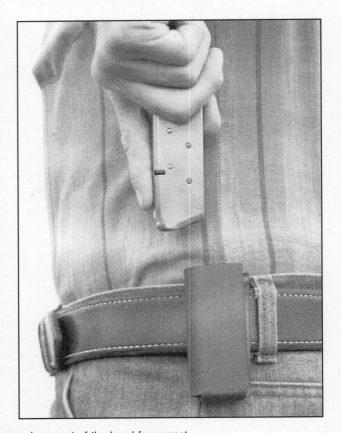

Spare magazine carriers should allow proper placement of the hand for correct speed and tactical reloading, but also offer a good compromise of protection and retention (security). Generally, those which "break" the mag through the front of the carrier (left) should be avoided in preference to those from which the magazine is withdrawn upward (right).

Glock M22 40 or Colt lightweight Commander 45 ACP in an M-D Labs Taylor Thunderbolt Kydex holster, concealed beneath either a BDU-type blouse or a large, baggy shirt. Since the Glock M22 holds ten to fifteen rounds, depending upon which magazines are used, I usually carry only a single spare mag, in an M-D Labs Kydex carrier.

However, since the Colt Commander holds a total of eight rounds, I feel better when I carry two spare seven-shot mags. See what I mean? It depends upon the circumstances—in other words, my analysis of what I think I need—as to the number of spare mags I carry and how I carry them.

On the other hand, when it gets especially hot or I figure that the environment in which I'll being operating is more casual, I carry my pistol in a Galco Fast Action Gun System fanny pack, either draped over my left shoulder, zipper release tab pointed upward, or around my waist. I don't worry about a separate spare mag carrier, because there's one integral to the pack itself. Besides, if I can't get it done with the ten to fifteen rounds of 40 S&W already in my M22 Glock or the eight of 45 ACP in my LW Commander...I'm *dead!* It's as simple as that.

Again, look carefully at your needs before you select any particular means of carrying your spare ammo and let me leave you with this, my only absolute recommendation: *If you carry a gun at all, then carry some spare ammo for it, too!* Carry it in whatever location you feel works best for you, but carry some. From the tactical viewpoint, it can't hurt and you sacrifice very little in the process.

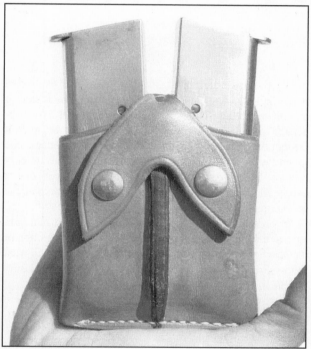

(Above) All early spare magazine carriers were made of leather. However, leather doesn't resist wear or moisture well and requires replacement fairly often, unlike modern materials like Kydex. This leather dual-cell carrier utilizes a leather friction strap to retain the magazines in place.

(Above) Flap carriers are common on many police duty rigs and shoulder holsters. Though slower to operate, they protect the magazines well and prevent their loss when extreme physical movement is involved. However, properly fitted Kydex carriers will also do this without slowing you down.

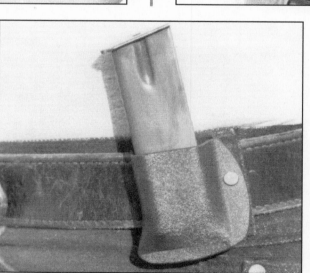

Taylor favors the low-cut M-D Labs carrier shown here.

CHOOSING THE RIGHT FINISH

ONE OF THE most important, yet very often overlooked, decisions you'll make when maximizing the efficiency of your combat handgun is what finish to put on it. Most self-defense-minded shooters will research what sights they need and how much trigger poundage works best for them. Many even tackle the job of ridding their handgun of bothersome sharp edges.

This is all fine and good—necessary, in fact—but interestingly, most forget that their defensive handgun must be carried or stored and used in some form of natural environment. They unwittingly go forth into the world of heat, cold, dust, rain, snow, mud, salt air and, of course, varying amounts of humidity, not realizing that, if the gun isn't well protected, in only a short time those elements will exert a pronounced effect on it.

Indeed, many who have spent considerable time and money preparing their handgun for combat are disconcerted when they discover that their pet carry gun has rusted or exhibits premature internal wear. "How could it have happened?" they cry. The answer is simple. They failed to realize that the elements of nature are always on the attack, and given the slightest opportunity, the elements will quickly ruin any finish that isn't proof against them. As well, due to simple friction, the more you practice with your weapon, the quicker its working parts wear.

In order to properly protect your defensive handgun against the elements and prolong its service life, selection of the best finish for your needs is an absolute must. So in what follows, we'll discuss the various types of finish, disclosing the strengths and weaknesses of each.

First, we have regular **bluing**. Especially in conjunction with the 600-grit polishing that precedes its application, blu-

Traditionally, bluing has been the finish on most handguns as they come from the factory. However, though eye-pleasing, bluing is itself a form of rust and thus will not protect the weapon from corrosion or wear. As well, it tends to wear on the high points of the weapon—muzzle, finger contact surfaces, sharp edges—very quickly. As a result, it is the least desirable finish for a gun that will be carried and used daily in a wide variety of environmental conditions.

ing is by far the most common finish available. Unfortunately, although it is aesthetically pleasant, it totally fails to protect the handgun from anything. As a matter of fact, bluing is itself a form of rust—oxidation with color control, but rust nonetheless.

Many who carry handguns comment that bluing wears off of the high points of their piece very quickly, especially if presentations from a holster are practiced to any degree, as they should be. They also rightly claim that if not immediately wiped down with some form of preservative the gun will quickly show signs of corrosion, even overnight. Third, some complain that a highly polished blued gun attracts attention, and they'd prefer a finish not so shiny.

Most factory handguns are blued because it is an economically feasible, eye-pleasing finish. After all, some kind of finish is required or the gun would quite literally rust while we watch. It is intended primarily to prevent mottling or other discoloration from occurring, not resist the elements. Moreover, shiny guns are pretty, and that stimulates sales.

We can sandblast (sharp granules) or beadblast (round, dull granules) our handgun and then reblue it, but so doing only solves the problem of light reflection. Moisture damage and wear are not in the least inhibited, meaning that any gun so finished will still require frequent examination and maintenance.

The military often applies a manganese phosphate coating (lately often with Teflon included) to their weapons. **Parkerizing,** as it's known, is a non-reflective, matte gray or black finish with a honeycomb-like internal structure that traps lubricants and preservatives, thus sealing the pores of the host metal to which it is applied from moisture, body chemicals, etc. However, it demonstrates serious surface accretion (growth), and this can cause stoppages due to reduction of critical parts tolerances. Last, like bluing, it offers no resistance to wear.

As an alternative, we can apply some form of **chrome** or **nickel plating**, and these will indeed resist corrosion and, to a degree, wear. However, application of either finish requires that the weapon first be plated with copper, causing serious surface accretion that can negatively affect critical tolerances and cause malfunctions. Both chrome and nickel finishes can be brushed or sand/beadblasted to prevent them from being excessively shiny, but both are relatively soft. Eventually, scratches and even peeling can result if they are exposed to the elements to any serious degree.

The first viable alternative to bluing, Parkerizing and chrome or nickel plating appeared in the mid-1960s—**stainless steel.** First pioneered by Smith & Wesson, stainless initially offered substantial resistance to both wear and corrosion, but proved to be excessively expensive to machine. As a result, a good deal of ferrous metal has since been added to the alloy, thus making it softer and easier to machine. Unfortunately, this act also made it far less rust- and wear-resistant, with the result that modern "stainless" guns are not really stainless at all. They will rust and even pit if not maintained on a regular basis.

Perhaps the best choice is one of the **industrial hard finishes** that have surfaced during the last twenty years. First utilized in the petroleum industry to protect high-pressure valves from corrosive chemicals, these offer an excellent combination of wear- and rust-resistance. These utilize chrome or nickel as a basis, but are applied via processes that differ considerably from those used in simple chrome or nickel plating. The resulting surface accretion is so negligible as to be unimportant. **Metalife,** for example, demonstrates only 2 microns (a micron is .001mm) surface buildup and completely seals the pores of the host metal to which it is applied. As if this weren't spectacular enough, these finishes are *hard,* often nearly twice as hard as ordnance steel. This means that they resist wear quite well.

Parkerizing is an economical matte finish that traps lubricants and preservatives, thus assisting in resisting wear and corrosion. It is therefore often the choice of many military organizations.

Though both are considered "white" finishes, **Armoloy** and Metalife are chrome-based and exhibit a slight bluish hue, while **electroless nickel** and **Nitex** demonstrate a mild straw-colored look. Most who carry a defensive handgun do so with it concealed and don't mind "white" guns, but some disagree, preferring instead a darker color.

Last, **Teflon** has finally made the grade in the form of what is known as NP3. Initially too soft and therefore showing immediate wear when applied to both external and internal surfaces, it has now been refined sufficiently to offer excellent protection against both rust and wear, and is therefore worth considering. NP3 is a pleasant gray color, and though not as tough as the industrial hard finishes, it is considerably superior to both bluing and Parkerizing. It is actually a form of electroless nickel plating that incorporates Teflon.

There you have it, the most common types of finish and the strengths and weaknesses of each. Which one is best? I like Metalife, all thing considered. If you carefully consider your needs, you'll find that one of them is just right for you.

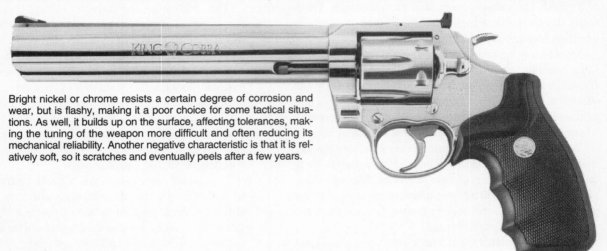

Bright nickel or chrome resists a certain degree of corrosion and wear, but is flashy, making it a poor choice for some tactical situations. As well, it builds up on the surface, affecting tolerances, making the tuning of the weapon more difficult and often reducing its mechanical reliability. Another negative characteristic is that it is relatively soft, so it scratches and eventually peels after a few years.

Stainless steel, pioneered by Smith & Wesson in the 1960s and now offered by virtually all gunmakers, is a good from-the-box alternative. However, remember that manufacturing costs have forced the addition of a fair amount of ferrous metal to make the steel easier to machine, e.g., the alloy is not truly stainless and will corrode if reasonable maintenance is not maintained.

(Below) Industrial hard nickel- or chrome-based finishes such as Metalife and Armoloy are actually harder than the metal to which they are applied, exhibit virtually no surface buildup, and resist wear and corrosion magnificently. They are, however, all "white," making them less desirable to many shooters for tactical reasons. On the plus side, white guns look big in the dark and can be somewhat more intimidating.

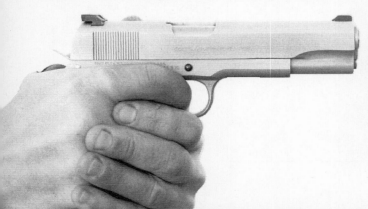

CONSIDERING LASER SIGHTS

FROM MY PERSPECTIVE as a professional weapons and tactics instructor/consultant, laser sights are of minimal value. Put bluntly, regardless of whether they're employed in a general or special-purpose mode, their fifteen-year record to date shows that, as a fast, effective alternative to conventional sights and aiming methodology, they're a failure.

Logic and documented history show five major reasons why: 1) Keeping laser sights zeroed is very difficult. Because of their odd configuration and bulk, they are highly susceptible to being jostled out of zero by normal field handling. 2) This same bulk and odd configuration makes them awkward to handle and usually requires special holsters for convenient carry. 3) In most configurations, the axis of the laser beam is considerably below the axis of the bore. The two can only converge at a single point. At all other ranges, the distance between them is excessive for efficient general-purpose use. "General purpose," means that, in addition to the ability to quickly and accurately hit targets of typical size and shape at normal pistol ranges (0 to 50 meters), we must also be able to hit small targets at close range, or oddly shaped or partially exposed targets. Lasers don't have the capability to satisfy this need. 4) The laser beam isn't sufficiently bright for normal daylight conditions. Yet, in low-light environments, it doesn't provide illumination for target detection and identification. A simple push-button flashlight is more efficient. 5) Laser sights are excessively expensive in relation to their limited utility.

Careful determination of what the shooter really needs from his weapon, a properly set-up gun and proper training in its fast, effective use yields far greater efficiency and liability protection. I vote **NO** on lasers. They're just too limited.

Author Taylor believes laser sights, even when small and unobtrusive like this Lasergrip from Crimson Trace Corp., have no place on defensive handguns.

THE STREETWISE SNUBBIE

FOR THE LAST three decades, we have seen considerable political attack upon firearms ownership. In particular, the private ownership of handguns has been selected as the initial issue by the anti-gun lobby. Claimed by these individuals to have "no sporting purpose"—and therefore no reason to exist in the hands of private citizens—the short-barreled, or "snubbie," revolver has become the symbol of evil to the anti-gunners.

Curiously, considering our highly technological times, much of this prejudice comes from both misinformation and simple ignorance. Yet, however unjustified it may be, the snubbie now has a reputation of being the "bad boy" of the

Though not intended for general-purpose defensive use, snubbies are compact and light, making them easy to carry. Here are three of the best 38 Special snubs ever made: (top to bottom) the S&W Model 15, S&W Model 12 Airweight and the Colt Detective Special, with hammer shroud. All are fitted with the Tyler T-Grip adapter to aid in quick grip acquisition without loss of compactness.

(Below) Two legendary lightweight 38 snubs: the Colt Cobra (top) and S&W Airweight Chiefs Special, also fitted with Tyler T-Grip grip adapters.

gun world. Depicted during the salad days of television ("Just the facts, ma'am, just the facts.") as the kind of handgun often carried by plainclothes police officers, revolvers with barrel lengths of under 3½ inches are now shown more often in the hands of the TV criminal. This has slurred its social reputation and further inflamed the "antis," whose knowledge and opinion of firearms is based almost entirely upon television and the cinema.

Thanks to the news media, we're all aware of the snubbie's socio-political stigma, but even from a technical standpoint, the short-barreled revolver continues to receive a good deal of criticism of its suitability as a defensive weapon.

For example, we are often told that snubbies are inaccurate or that their effective range is so short that you can't hit your hat with one past arm's length. Such statements are patently untrue. Snubs, like any other firearm with a rifled barrel, are intrinsically accurate. I've often heard the same statement made about submachine guns, too, and then I laughingly proceeded to knock down steel silhouettes with one at 100-plus meters.

Accuracy is defined in both intrinsic and practical terms. Any rifled arm is intrinsically accurate. However, from a practical standpoint, the degree of accuracy actually obtained is the result of operator skill. Thus, when someone vehemently tells you that a certain kind of gun is inaccurate or that its effective range is highly limited, what he is actually saying is that his shooting skills are insufficient to utilize the intrinsic accuracy of the weapon. In short, we're talking here about the "because I can't do it, it cannot be done" syn-

drome. There is, in fact, nothing wrong with the firearm—the fellow shooting it is just a poor marksman.

The real issue is that the snubbie's short sight radius amplifies sight alignment error, which has a potentially negative effect on practical accuracy. To overcome this, extra concentration upon sight alignment and sight picture is required, nothing more. We are dealing with simple geometry here—the closer two points of alignment are, the more effect misalignment of those two points will have when the axis of alignment must coincide with a third point.

We also hear that snubs lack stopping power. In some calibers, this is true. However, this is also true of many long-barrelled guns of the same caliber. It can't legitimately be claimed that a 2- or 3-inch 44 or 45 lacks stopping power. And while it can be said that a 2-inch 38 Special lacks stopping power, it must also be said that the 38 Special lacks punch from longer barrels, too.

Ballistically, shorter barrels reduce projectile velocities an average of nearly 100 fps per inch below standard length (about 4 inches). However, this doesn't necessarily reduce stopping power, because there is considerably more to that issue than velocity alone.

In fact, the only cartridge seriously affected is the 357 Magnum, whose claimed velocities are generally obtained from barrel lengths of 6 inches or more. The status quo 357 barrel length these days is 4 inches, with 3 $1/2$- and even $2^1/2$-inch tubes being encountered ever more frequently. The classic 1500 fps (158-grain bullet) claim of the 357 was obtained with an $8^3/8$-inch barrel. This same load rarely produces 1100 fps from the 4-inch tubes typical of today. Velocities in this range are insufficient to produce reliable JHP/JSP bullet expansion, thus further barrel reduction to $2^1/2$ inches, while making the gun more handy, only exacerbates an already serious problem.

While the problem can theoretically be solved by using lighter bullets, even 110-grain JHPs aren't reliable ex-

panders from a $2^1/2$-inch barrel, meaning that very careful ammunition selection is essential if maximum efficiency is to be achieved.

A careful analysis of the potential circumstances under which your snubbie is to be used will do much to alleviate most of its real and imagined deficiencies. Once this is accomplished, you can also select the best type of ammunition for your needs. For example, the stopping power of the 38 Special can be upgraded by avoiding round-nosed bullet configurations, opting instead for semi-wadcutters for best nerve/tissue destruction.

Or if the circumstances under which you intend to use your snubbie do not include possible targets behind cover, Glaser ammunition is a viable alternative. A word of caution, however. The Glaser Safety Slug is highly specialized in that it is intended for use against unprotected targets in the open. As such, it is unsuitable for general-purpose employment.

Except for exceptional circumstances, the claim that snubbies are easy to conceal (and therefore evil) is more myth than fact. Unless barrel lengths exceed 6 inches, concealment is hardly affected at all by barrel length. On the other hand, cylinder diameter, frame and stock size have considerable influence on the issue.

To illustrate, neither a Model 24 S&W 44 Special nor a Colt Python 357 with $2^1/2$-inch barrels are easy to hide. Conversely, self-loaders such as the SIG P225, Browning P-35, Beretta M92, Walther P-38, S&W Model 39 and Colt M1911 are easy to hide, by virtue of their lesser width, and offer increased ammunition capacity as an additional bonus.

Snubbies are a specialized kind of fighting handgun, not really intended for general-purpose use. Thus, they are best employed either as backup guns for police officers or by civilians for either casual carry or home-defense functions.

Yet, considering that few handgun fights require the expenditure of more than a few rounds of ammunition, the increased ammo capacity of the self-loader may not be important. To me, this decision hinges upon the situations I anticipate encountering with my weapon. In other words, for general-purpose defensive employment, ammo capacity might be an issue, but for specialized use like home defense, a 2-inch five-shot S&W Bodyguard loaded with Glasers will likely suffice, as long as the limitations of the Glaser are kept in mind.

There is another reason people like snubbies. They offer a good compromise between size, simplicity and power. The true pocket pistol (22, 25, 32 or 380) is indeed smaller, but the cartridges they utilize have a deservedly dismal reputation for poor target incapacitation.

These are the major elements that so often go overlooked when the short-barreled wheelgun is discussed. When we intelligently analyze the issue, we find that its biggest single disadvantage is its reduced sight radius, which makes it tougher to shoot under stress. Also, in those instances where the cartridge it fires lacks stopping power, careful ammo selection is a necessity.

Last, while snubbies aren't automatically easier to conceal, they do fit nicely into tight places like glove compartments, purses and the like. This is why history vindicates the snubbie, and it continues to be one of the most popular types of firearm available. In addition, its characteristics make it a viable backup gun for police officers.

While I am without question one of the most vehement proponents of the big-bore self-loader, I must admit that I, too, have occasionally succumbed to the snubbie's siren song. On those dark, stormy nights when I go down to the corner store for something, I've been known to slip a S&W M38 Airweight Bodyguard 38 Special into my jacket pocket in preference to my 40 Glock or Colt 45 Commander. It's loaded with Glasers, of course.

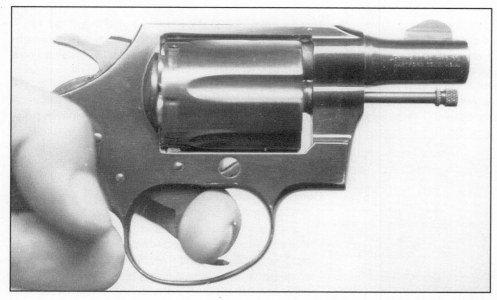

The original version of the famous Colt Detective Special is perhaps the most photographed snubbie of all time. Due to its frequent appearances in early police TV shows like "Dragnet," "The Asphalt Jungle" and "Naked City," it was commonly recognized throughout the 1950s and early 1960s.

In order to achieve the high velocities required to expect reliable bullet expansion, at least a 5-inch barrel is needed with any magnum. This makes semi-wadcutters like the three at the right better choices for snubbies. Taylor also likes the Glaser (arrow) within its limitations.

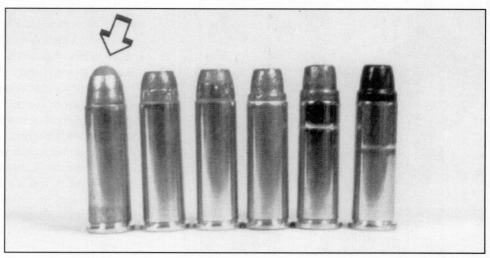

THE SWAT HANDGUN

WITH THE TEN o'clock news nightly featuring some sort of Special Weapons And Tactics (SWAT) team, the general public has long accepted the image of an elite group of men, clad in black or dark blue coveralls, wearing body armor and carrying exotic weapons as they deal with a criminal or terrorist. Yet that same public—and the vast majority of the shooting fraternity as well—is largely unaware that in spite of the presence of ultra-accurate precision (counter-sniper) rifles, submachine guns, gas launchers and stun grenades, the simple handgun is as often as not the primary weapon of the men who deal "up close and personal" with a violent suspect.

True, there are definitely occasions where a precision rifleman will bring the problem to a conclusion from a distance. And without question, the submachine gun is utilized with ever-increasing frequency, especially by assault/entry teams. But regardless of what assigned weapon each team member carries, *everyone also carries a handgun*, sometimes even more than one.

Why? In the theoretical sense, they have them for the same reasons that military personnel in combat zones scramble to obtain them—extra security in case of that unforeseen emergency. In the practical sense, these men carry handguns because smart SWAT commanders realize that a good handgun in skilled hands is often an excellent primary weapon as well, capable of dealing with many of the situations commonly encountered in SWAT operations.

Although the submachine gun is a fine choice for generalized indoor "haunted house" scenarios, the option of having several men armed with handguns is worth examination. Entry teams so equipped can function well within a wider variety of circumstances. For example, if particularly tight quarters are encountered—and make no mistake, they often are—the handgun-armed team member can take over and the SMG-armed members can cover him from a distance. Places where this is a good move include on stairways, in attics and during window entries, to name but a few. In addition, the use of an unattached flashlight is better accomplished with a handgun, especially when a good Harries flashlight technique is utilized.

Another, perhaps less well known, reason for arming cer-

(Left) One of the most popular SWAT handguns is the Colt Model 1911 45 ACP. Used by some of the more elite teams such as the famous LAPD SWAT, they've served with distinction for decades.

Another SWAT favorite—the SIG SAUER P220 45 ACP. With teams whose departments favor the big-bore DA auto, it leads the pack.

tain team members with handguns involves the delivery of diversionary munitions—so-called "stun grenades." Being a professional weapons and tactics instructor, I spend a great deal of time working with special teams in both conventional SWAT and counter-terrorist environments. During these endeavors, I've noticed repeatedly that team members often tend to handle and deliver stun grenades with considerable trepidation—meaning that they are often so glad to finally throw the device that when the actual toss takes place, they throw it so hard that they get tangled up in their equipment, usually a shotgun or submachine gun. Often, the delivery is performed with such strength that they actually miss their intended target—the doorway—resulting in a mad scramble to escape the close-range effects of the explosion that immediately follows. In addition, during the arming of the grenade, it's nice to be able to keep that pistol comfortably in your hand while pulling the pin, just in case the gun is needed in a hurry. This just cannot be done efficiently when any kind of shoulder weapon is involved.

The unexpected emergency occurs more often than most SWAT teams would like. Quite often, a suspect appears literally out of nowhere, sometimes because he has been hiding in a particularly exotic location or because the intelligence data upon which the team is basing its operational plan is, to one degree or another, inaccurate. When a man with a gun starts "climbing up your nose," that handgun suddenly become mighty important!

The type of handgun used for SWAT ops isn't inflexibly cast, either. Other than the fact that it should be of high quality and chambered for a cartridge offering the best percentages in the stopping-power department, virtually anything goes. In my travels, I encounter about an equal number of DA revolvers, DA autos and SA autos, although the DA auto is beginning to appear more often. Interestingly, most

The Browning P-35 9mm Hi-Power is perhaps the most prolific Special Ops handgun, being the favorite of many non-U.S. teams.

A relative newcomer, the H&K USP (shown here with light attached) in slightly modified form was the choice of U.S. Special Operations Command, but it can also be found in the hands of a number of U.S. SWAT teams in both 40 S&W and 45 ACP versions.

of the better teams seem to opt for the SA self-loader, the Browning Hi-Power and Colt 1911 45 ACP in particular, or the Glock in 9mm or 40 S&W. I've also noticed an increase in the use of the Beretta M92, SIG SAUER P226 and SIG SAUER P220 in departments that do not feel comfortable with the SA auto or semi-DA Glock.

Other than the 45 ACP and 9mm Parabellum, the calibers I most often encounter are the 38 Special and 357 Magnum, but lately the 40 S&W has been coming on quite strongly.

Fortunately, I have not encountered many departments that force their SWAT teams to operate under the same firearms policies used for regular officers. Thus even in many departments that do now allow a SA auto or Glock for uniformed or plainclothes carry, SWAT team members are often authorized to use them, at least when on SWAT duty.

The issue of stopping power is of paramount importance with any handgun, but it becomes critical in SWAT operations. It is mandatory that a team realizes the exact capabilities and limitations of their weapons, including handguns. Otherwise, false confidence and disaster would inevitably result. SWAT is, after all, a team event, with the object being to solve a given problem despite the close proximity of a number of your team members. If the problem is not solved instantly when the shooting starts, that means there will be more bullets flying around and more people hurt. Stopping power is therefore of extreme importance, and it ought to be maximized for best team results.

Concerning stopping power, I admit I prefer the Colt M1911 45 or Glock 40. The superiority of these two weapons/calibers can be successfully demonstrated upon demand, not only by me, but by thousands of others. In the case of the 45, there is more than eighty years of recorded history testifying to its effectiveness. There are, of course, other calibers with a good reputation for stopping power that don't sacrifice weapon controllability or demonstrate excess penetration. Among these are the 41 Magnum with the police load, the 44 Special and the 45 Colt. Although claimed to be a satisfactory manstopper, the 357 Magnum 125-grain JHP is beginning to rapidly wane in popularity because its bright muzzle blast, poor controllability and tendency toward overpenetration present too many problems in both tactical and legal environments.

The 38 Special has had stopping-power woes for a long time, but the all-time record for the number of hits sustained without the suspect becoming incapacitated belongs to the

The revolver is not dead in SWAT operations. Many teams still use them because they're satisfied with their performance. Here, an officer armed with a Smith & Wesson M67 38 Special prepares to deliver a stun grenade through a closed doorway during one of Taylor's SWAT operations training courses.

The relatively new Glock M26 or M27 in 9mm or 40 S&W (left) is a popular second gun in SWAT ops, as is the Colt LW Officer's Model 45 ACP (right). This one is Taylor's, as are the decorations.

9mm—a whopping thirty-three rounds! With the increased law enforcement service the nine has seen in the last ten years, it is again beginning to be identified as being a marginal cartridge, a repeat performance of decades past. Regardless of what some writers claim to the contrary or what they promote in print as being the ultimate, I can't help but point out that when they have a choice, almost all of them seem to opt for a 40 or 45 when the chips are down.

Only an intelligent analysis of recorded history can give us the proper perspective on what happens when people shoot each other, not theoretical tests conducted solely on artificial media. No, I'm not saying that the big bore is infallible; of course it isn't. Nevertheless, it does offer the best combination of stopping power, weapon control and manageable penetration. A realistic perspective on the subject comes from experience as well as expertise, a combination that not all so-called "experts" possess these days.

By the way, machine pistols—due to their "neither fish nor fowl" concept, their unwieldiness and general inflexibility—should be avoided for SWAT applications. They accomplish nothing that can't be better accomplished with a handgun or submachine gun.

Specialized ammunition, such as the Glaser and Exploder, is rarely encountered in SWAT operations. In my experience, the most commonly used ammo is quite normal and includes most premium brands of jacketed hollowpoints in all calibers.

In 9mm Parabellum, cartridges range from the Winchester Silvertip 115-grain JHP to the Federal Hydra-Shok 147-grain JHP, with Remington and Speer also contributing. In 357 Magnum, no one seems to use bullets that are heavier than 125 grains, the Remington version being quite popular. Some 110-grain Winchester JHPs get used as well.

In 40 S&W, we see the Federal Hydra-Shok in both 155 and 180 grains, and also the Winchester Ranger in 180 grains.

The 45 ACP guns get loaded with the Remington and Winchester 185-grainers, and also with the Federal Hydra-Shok, Winchester Ranger and Speer Gold Dot, all three in 230-grain versions.

SWAT handgun training should include the maximum use of a variety of different graphic (picture) targets, with the emphasis on close, fast engagement. Preference should also be given to shooting in crowded areas, hostage situations, small and/or partially obscured targets, multiple targets, failures to stop and malfunction clearance drills. Weapon presentations should be from the Ready, preferably the Weaver, not the deadly erroneous Contact Ready. The Harries flashlight technique should be used exclusively.

Last, but without question most important, remember that the man with the ability to think on his feet is the *real* weapon when lives are on the line. The gun, whatever kind or caliber it may be, is just a tool.

(Left) A SWAT entry team makes a "dynamic entry" after delivering a stun grenade through the doorway. All three are armed with S&W 357 Magnum revolvers.

(Below) A two-man team armed with S&W Model 686 357 Magnum revolvers approaches an automobile during a car assault exercise at one of the author's SWAT training courses.

(Above) SWAT personnel are often burdened with radios, a canteen, gas mask, stun grenades and more. Short ranges and tight quarters make the handgun a reasonable choice for the primary weapon. This operator packs a 9mm SIG SAUER P226.

SOME FAMOUS FIGHTING HANDGUNS

SOME FIREARMS JUST seem to be simply better than others. They do their job better, or easier, or with more class than most of the rest. In time, these come to be the classics, those that rise above all their competitors. There are some self-defense handguns that truly excel.

What follows are some of the more famous of these, insights into why they work as well as they do and explanations why they are so popular with so many. In a few cases, the particular makeup of the gun is unavailable in any other example, fills a definite need, and has therefore found favor. In some examples, the gun is lighter than others of its type, or has a certain feel or smoothness that is not available elsewhere, and so the gun has made a significant name for itself.

Some of these are based on older designs that have stood the test of time, like the Colt 1911-based Lightweight Officer's ACP. The S&W Model 1917 is an adaptation of a still earlier model. Others are as new as yesterday, like the Glocks and SIGs, and are quickly proving themselves worthy of inclusion in this brief hall of fame. My test of the Glock Models 26 and 27 indicate these are reliable and superior alternatives to traditional pocket pistols.

Each of these self-defense handguns has gained the respect and admiration of a great many users. They are all effective tools, but each type has provided more than just simple utility. Each has something special, some characteristic or combination of qualities that has contributed to the gun's having endeared itself to its many proponents.

These are some of the best of the best, all good fighting tools, most of them still viable and none of them actually obsolete, even though some may no longer be in production.

BROWNING'S P-35

THE LAST DESIGN of John Moses Browning, the P-35, was patented in 1927 and first appeared in 1935, its first official version going to the French. Built at Fabrique Nationale in Herstal, Belgium, it also sports the designations HP, Model 88 and, commercially, Hi-Power. As well, in its earlier days, it was also occasionally fitted with an adjustable tangent rear sight and its grip frame slotted for a shoulder stock.

The P-35 was the result of Browning's attempt to simplify his basic M1911 design. In some ways he was successful. The detachable muzzle bushing of the 1911 was eliminated. However, in return for incorporating a large-capacity magazine, a trigger linkage considerably more complex than that of the M1911 was required. The net result of the fixed bushing is that many gunsmiths complain that the P-35 isn't as accurate as the M1911 and is much more difficult to accurize.

During WWII, the Germans quickly overran Belgium,

forcing many FN personnel to flee the country to avoid capture. A good many of these highly skilled employees found their way to Canada, where they were instrumental in setting up the John Inglis Co. tooling for production of their version of the pistol. The Germans held the P-35 in high esteem as a military pistol and continued to have it produced at the captured FN plant in Belgium. In fact, under their control, some 200,000 P-35s were made.

Commercial versions of the P-35 have always been popular, perhaps due to their tremendous proliferation worldwide. It is the most commonly encountered 9mm auto in the world and is used officially by over fifty nations.

Produced for civilian sale in its typical military configuration (fixed sights, burr hammer) for two decades following WWII, it was offered in the late 1960s with high-visibility adjustable sights, an addition much appreciated by most shooters. About the same time, FN began subcontracting its

In its several variations, the P-35 Browning Hi-Power is one of the best SA autos in the world.

From the time of its appearance in the mid-1930s until the mid-1980s, the P-35 came with rather small sights. For the best sight acquisition speed under the stresses typical of handgun fights, it was advisable to replace them with larger high-visibility sights.

Beginning in the 1970s, a so-called target version of the P-35 appeared. Although it featured a larger, ramped front sight, its adjustable rear sight proved too fragile for serious self-defense needs, especially when the weapon was carried on a daily basis.

weapons to a Japanese company, an act that outraged many Browning fans and caused a sharp decline in U.S. sales for several years. Nevertheless, the Japanese-made Brownings are perfectly serviceable, not bad looking and, because they have a lower collector value, can often be purchased at low prices, something not possible with their Belgian-made counterparts.

In the late 1980s, due to inflated labor costs, FN began producing P-35s in Argentina, using FN-made parts and under FN supervision. Guns produced from this source (known as the Model 88) generally have either a Parkerized or black-oxide military finish, ambidextrous extended thumb safety tabs and high-visibility fixed sights.

As this is written, the P-35 can be found in three configurations: 1) a blued commercial type, with small "thumbnail" military sights and a tiny thumb-safety tab; 2) a blued commercial type with high-visibility adjustable sights (the small thumb-safety tab remained); and 3) the Model 88 just described.

My P-35s function well with the vast majority of bullet styles and demonstrate Ransom Rest accuracy of about 4 inches at 50 meters. One oft-heard criticism of the weapon is that is doesn't always feed exotic JHP/JSP bullet shapes very well, thus requiring major reshaping and polishing of the feed ramp. Based on my considerable experience with the P-35, I see no reason for such a claim. Mine seem to gobble up whatever I stuff into 'em. Still, it is heard sufficiently often to warrant consideration. The best accuracy is obtained from my guns with Winchester Silvertip and Remington 115-grain JHPs, followed by typical European 124-grain military ball.

While not generally realized by the uninformed, the 9mm Parabellum cartridge is highly temperamental in handloaded form. Therefore, best results are usually obtained with some form of factory ammo.

During the recent ASAA cold weather tests, in which the major types of self-loaders were tested at sub-zero temperatures, the P-35 was one of only four handguns that successfully completed the 750-round program without a single malfunction.

In conclusion, I find the P-35 to be a fine pistol, well worthy of its reputation. It's one of the best large-capacity 9mm autos, certainly the best 9mm SA auto available, and ranks among the very best of the service autos.

Appearing in the late 1980s, the most recent edition of the P-35 has a durable military finish, fixed high-visibility sights and even a large-tabbed ambidextrous thumb safety, thus correcting its few real weaknesses and bringing it to its full potential as a combat handgun.

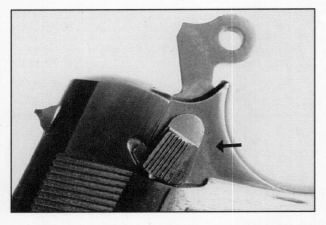

Additional criticism of the original P-35 was that its thumb safety tab was too small to be quickly and efficiently operated. Fortunately, several companies began to market replacement thumb safeties (below) that alleviated the problem.

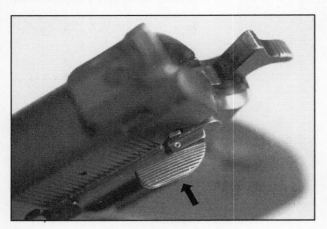

COLT'S LIGHTWEIGHT COMMANDER

BACK IN 1948, a precedent-setting experiment took place at the Colt plant in Hartford, Connecticut. Quoting from *The American Rifleman,* September of that same year:

> Early in 1948, the Colt Company, in the course of development work for a more universal acceptance of light-weight, heavy caliber automatic pistols, decided to see what would happen if a receiver was made from aluminum rather than from the standard alloy-steel forgings. Working with the Aluminum Corporation of America, it was decided, after experimentation, to try one of the high-tensile-strength aluminum alloys. Several forgings of this amazingly light metal were specially made and issued to the Colt receiver-making department, and some one hundred and forty-odd machining operations were performed on them. The result was a half-dozen 45-caliber automatic pistol receivers that seemed to jump over one's head when picked up off the bench. These were assembled into pistols chambered for the 9mm Parabellum, 38 Super and 45 ACP cartridges.
>
> The new slide was fashioned from gun steel as before, but was shortened from 7³/₈ inches to 6⁵/₈ inches...the barrel was correspondingly cut down from 5 inches to 4¹/₂ inches...a Mauser-like (burr) hammer was built (and various internal alterations instituted)...sight heights were altered to conform with the reduced lengths of barrel and slide and to conform to the ballistics of the test-caliber cartridges. The new lightweight, with magazine, "weighed in" at about 26¹/₂ ounces compared to its all-steel counterpart's 40 ounces. An anodizing process produced a blued finish on the receiver and housing that was comparable to the standard blue of the steel parts...A new gun has been born....

The "new" gun has been with us ever since. Named the Commander, it has not only survived, but has become so sought after as to amaze all but the most jaded shooting enthusiast. Light, strong, accurate, reliable and—especially in its 45 ACP chambering—powerful, the LW Commander has become the favorite carry gun of many military personnel worldwide, and of plainclothes and narcotics officers as well. Serial numbers began with 001 to 0065, then from 66L to 66277LW. In 1968, new designations were adopted and a CLW prefix will be found on those guns made since.

Contrary to the belief of the uninitiated, the alloy-framed Commander does not suffer from a reduced service life in comparison to a steel-framed gun. Several of my own LW Commanders have fired more than 30,000 rounds of full-power ammo and are still going strong. In fact I have seen and experienced more failures (cracked frames) with steel-framed Commanders, Government Models and military M1911s.

From the holster, there is no handgun faster to the first

Colt's adventure into lightweight big-bore firearms design led to one of Chuck Taylor's all-time favorite handguns, the Lightweight Commander (bottom). The author says they hold up better than steel-frame versions. That's a full-size Government Model on top.

shot than a LW Commander, illustrating one of the major reasons for its popularity as a defensive handgun. Once the first shot is fired, recoil is not so excessive that it prevents excellent control of subsequent shots. Add to this the fact that its inherent light weight makes it so pleasant to carry that one often forgets he's wearing it and it becomes easy to see why so many have come to prefer it.

As it comes from the factory, the LW Commander, like most "as issued" Colt 45 autos, needs a couple of improvements to bring it to its full potential. Among these are high-visibility fixed sights (I prefer MMCs), a trigger job, removal of a few sharp edges and a finish appropriate to the environment in which it is to be carried. However, these modifications are not prohibitively expensive, time-consuming or difficult to accomplish.

My carry Commander typically shoots into 4 to 5 inches at 50 meters from a Ransom Rest and produces its best accuracy with standard 230-grain ball, although Winchester Black Talon JHPs run a close second. It shoots Federal Hydra-Shok 230-grain JHPs very well, too.

In conclusion, if you're in the market for a highly efficient self-defense auto, the LW Commander in 45 ACP provides an unbeatable combination. And I don't make such a statement lightly, either. I carried one every day, hot or cold, rain, dust or shine, for nearly twenty years and it never—ever—let me down.

COLT'S LIGHTWEIGHT OFFICER'S MODEL

CERTAINLY THE POCKET pistol is far from an unknown commodity in the gun world, having been what can only be described as a thriving category of weapon for in excess of a hundred years. Yet, in all of that time, we can also say that the generic pocket pistol has some serious drawbacks that make a great deal of difference when life and limb are on the line.

Among these—which in and of themselves cause some serious limitations in the effective employment of the weapon—are the following negative characteristics: 1) poor sights or none at all; 2) small size, which can cause grip-indexing problems; 3) calibers which possess *very* limited stopping-power potential; 4) poor trigger pulls that are often unresponsive to gunsmithing.

Make no mistake, pocket pistols have been responsible for quite a number of deaths during their 100-plus-year lifespan thus far. However, the reliable, efficient incapacitation of one's attacker generally requires more than eventual lethality. It is well known that about half of those shot and "stopped" are not killed. Yet, it is also entirely possible to inflict a mortal wound on an assailant and not stop him, resulting in his continued aggression against his intended victim. It's easy to see how one could get clobbered if the latter occurred. The fact that our assailant dies minutes, hours, days, weeks or months after he defeats us is little consolation. This means that the parameters within which the pocket pistol should be utilized are very narrow, typically in shooting for the cranial/ocular cavities at point-blank range.

Over the last few decades, there have been attempts to bolster the stopping power of the small handgun without unduly increasing its weight and bulk beyond reasonable limits. Two examples are the S&W Bodyguard and Colt Cobra, but the basic difficulties of effectively using a pocket pistol remain.

Back in 1988, Colt introduced the Officer's Model ACP, a compact 45 self-loader intended to cure the pocket pistol's ills. This gun presented an intriguing alternative to the typical pocket pistol. Chambered for the 45 ACP cartridge, it solves the stopping-power problem. It also features excellent high-visibility fixed sights and a decent trigger, making the gun a potentially excellent choice for concealed carry.

Based upon the time-proven Colt Model 1911, the Officer's Model demonstrates reliable functioning and excellent accuracy. It is surprisingly easy to master. Indeed, even small females, once they understand the principles of the SA auto and Condition One carry, encounter little difficulty in achieving a fast, accurate solution to the problems of self-defense.

Great, right?

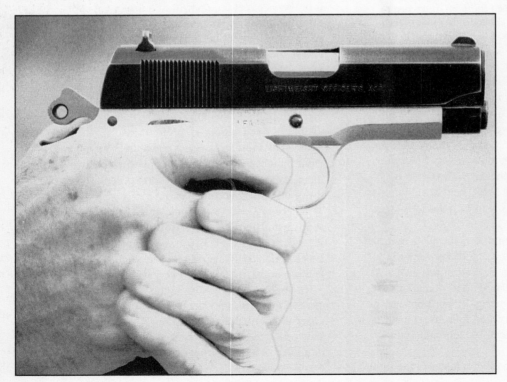

Taylor's LWOM 45 in action, using his recommended weak-hand finger placement—all under the trigger guard. Women like this gun.

Not quite, because the standard, steel-frame Officer's Model does have one drawback—weight. Empty, it weighs 32.5 ounces, a full 7.5 ounces more than a Lightweight (aluminum-frame) Commander. To me, this prevents the excellent concept upon which the gun is based from reaching its full potential.

Why? Because when we compare it to the LW Commander, we find that with the regular Officer's Model we have lost $1/2$-inch of barrel, about $3/4$-inch of sight radius and $3/8$-inch from the butt of the piece. We also have lost one cartridge from the magazine. In return for this, we gain only a reduction in size, not weight. This is not as good a tradeoff as it might at first appear to be.

However, an aluminum-framed Officer's Model is also available. The LW Officer's Model is an excellent alternative to the typical pocket pistol. Visually identical to the steel-frame OM, the LW version sports a nice matte finish as well as the same high-visibility fixed sights and amenable trigger as its heavier counterpart.

The story gets even better. The LWOM weighs 26 ounces empty, nearly the same as a LW Commander. Loaded, it weighs about half an ounce less than the LWC.

For the edification of those who are thinking that a light, compact 45 is too tough to handle, a couple of ladies armed with LWOMs, both of whom are less than 5 feet, 3 inches tall and weigh less than 110 pounds, shot better than 90 percent scores with the LWOM on the very tough ASAA Handgun Qualification course. As well, both commented that they liked the LWOM very much and found it easy to carry and shoot.

Why do people insist upon steel frames? Who knows, but my guess is that they feel that aluminum, while advantageous from a weight-reduction standpoint, won't last as long or wear as well as steel. I disagree, having carried and shot a LW Commander 45 for over twenty years. In fact, I have experienced more cracked *steel* than aluminum frames, a fact directly contradictory to the assumed norm. To illustrate, my favorite LW Commander has digested more than 30,000 rounds of full-power service ammo and is still going strong.

Light, compact, with good sights and trigger, and in a caliber famous for excellent manstopping ability, the lightweight Officer's ACP is indeed the world's best pocket pistol. Colt deserves lots of credit for creating this excellent self-defense gun. On demand, it will save the lives of, and deliver much peace of mind to, those who choose it.

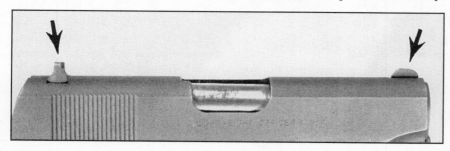

(Above) High-visibility fixed sights are standard on the Officer's Model and offer excellent sight acquisition at high speed without sacrificing ruggedness.

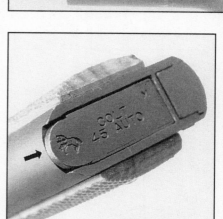

(Right) The Officer's ACP has an enlarged muzzle to aid in consistent muzzle-to-bushing fit. In spite of its small size and potent chambering, the gun shoots extremely well.

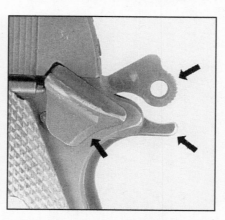

An enlarged ejection port is standard on the LWOM and aids in extracting a loaded cartridge from the chamber during the unloading process.

A large thumb safety, an extended grip-safety tang and a burr hammer show that Colt demonstrated considerable awareness of the best features to have on a fighting Model 1911-type self-loader.

Only real weakness in the LW Officer's ACP "from the box" is that it utilizes a magazine with a shortened floorplate, thus preventing fast, efficient removal of a stuck magazine.

GLOCK'S MODELS 26 AND 27

UNTIL VERY RECENTLY, undercover and plainclothes police officers were forced to make do with pocket pistols, a situation shared by uniformed officers when considering the purchase of a second or backup gun. Unfortunately, for virtually their entire history, pocket pistols have exhibited certain characteristics that make them less than satisfactory self-defense weapons.

Traditional pocket pistols have either no sights at all or sights so small as to be worthless. A second problem is that they lack ammunition capacity, most carrying from five to seven shots. Yet another problem with pocket pistols is that they're almost always chambered for cartridges that lack stopping power, the 22, 25, 32 and 380 being the most typical. For more than ninety years, this deficiency was accepted

as simply the price one had to pay for small size and convenient concealability. The trouble is, *stopping power is the very heart of the defensive handgun!*

Some tried to solve the problem by carrying small-frame 38 Special snubbies, such as the Colt Cobra or Smith & Wesson Chiefs Special. After all, they have adequate sights, and the 38 Special cartridge for which they are chambered is considerably more potent than any 380. Cylinder thickness made comfortable concealment an irritating task, but there simply was no better option.

Those with a job requiring effective concealment of a handgun didn't have that many choices. One just accepted that fact and did his best to live with it, based on the premise that *any gun* beat no gun at all. This is true, with-

Glock's small new M26 and M27, available in 9mm or 40 S&W, are good choices for undercover or backup service. The author gives them his unequivocal endorsement.

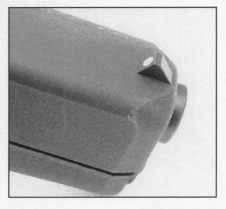

Adjustable high-visibility sights come standard with both the M26 and M27, allowing fast acquisition under extreme stress. While adjustable sights are generally unnecessary on a self-defense handgun, this particular version is highly compact and relatively rugged, thus not presenting any special weakness.

out question, but...Ugh! What a lousy choice to be forced to make.

That's the way it was, decade after decade...until August 1995.

At that time, Glock introduced their solution to the pocket-pistol problem in the form of two guns, the 9mm Model 26 and the 40 S&W Model 27. Identical in configuration and appearance, the two new guns are pocket pistols in every sense of the word.

But there is a difference. Though small and thus highly concealable, the new Glocks feature excellent high-visibility, low-profile sights, with a white-dot front and adjustable white outline rear configuration for low-light use.

They also hold more ammunition than most pocket pistols, without suffering from a loss of concealability. Not including the additional round that would be chambered during carry, the Model 26 (9mm) holds ten rounds, while the Model 27 (40 S&W) holds nine, more than enough to solve any tactical handgun problem.

They also have that same military-spec matte finish, the awesome toughness of which I've come to admire over these last few years.

Best of all, they're both chambered for service-pistol cartridges, thus satisfying the most critical requirement for any fighting handgun—adequate stopping power.

I recently concluded a thirty-day field evaluation of both pistols that included firing 2500 rounds of varying power and bullet configurations through each; 100 high-speed presentations from the holster; 100 tactical reloads; 100 speed reloads; and daily carry in the widest possible variety of environmental conditions.

The results didn't surprise me. I've been trying to wear out a Glock M17 9mm since 1990, and though it has digest-ed over 125,000 rounds so far, it shows no signs of quitting. In these recent tests, the 26 and 27 showed minimal finish wear, visible as a slight burnishing on the high points. The guns exhibited minimal denting of the magazine well areas from rapid magazine insertions. They functioned without mishap with all types of ammunition utilized in all weather conditions encountered.

Both guns shot as accurately at the end of the test as they did initially. Ransom Rest groups fired at the beginning and end of the test were identical.

The new guns handled well enough using the superb M-D Labs Thunderbolt holster that I was able to "clean" the highly challenging American Small Arms Academy (ASAA) Advanced Defensive Handgun course evaluation drill.

One more thing—during the test, I noticed that, in spite of the Model 26/27's very short grip frame, weapon control in fast presentation and shooting sequences was nearly as good as with a full-size Glock of the same caliber. Considering the power of the 40 S&W in particular, I found this to be a pleasant surprise.

Am I impressed? I'm *so* impressed with the Glock Model 26 and 27 that I give them my *unequivocal endorsement*. At last, undercover and plainclothes officers have a better choice. The new Glocks are light, small, accurate, functionally reliable, powerful and highly concealable, making them excellent alternatives to previous choices. Uniformed officers considering a backup gun will also like them.

I have no doubt that the Glock Models 26 and 27 will become very popular. I suggest that anyone with a need for a weapon of this kind take a hard look at them. But you'd better do it soon. Unless I miss my guess, they're going to sell like hotcakes.

The front of the slide is radiused all around for quick holstering without looking at the holster itself. This is an important, yet often overlooked, part of combat handgunning.

The magazine well is heavily relieved to assist in maximum concealment. Yet, it doesn't hinder effective magazine manipulation.

The slide lock and magazine release buttons are well located and easily manipulated. The thumb and finger grooves to aid proper firing-hand indexing are another nice touch.

SMITH & WESSON'S MODEL 12

FIRST SURFACING IN the early 1950s as a U.S. Air Force crewman's sidearm, the Model 12 was unique in that it featured not only an aluminum frame, but an aluminum cylinder as well. Designated by the USAF as the "M13," S&W did not assign a number to the gun, which weighed a mere 14³/₈ ounces.

Within a year of its adoption, problems were encountered with the aluminum cylinder, and in 1954, a steel cylinder was substituted, bringing the weight of the piece to 18 ounces in the snub version. With its then-new designation of Model 12, no further problems were encountered, and the gun subsequently continued in this same form throughout its career. It was available with a barrel length of 2 or 4 inches. The short version had a round butt; the longer, square.

Model 12s saw service and were quite popular with not only USAF crews, but also with U.S. Army helicopter pilots during the Vietnam War, and the guns were credited with the demise of a number of North Vietnamese troops who were attempting to storm U.S. helicopters on "hot" landing zones. The favored ammunition for these functions seems to have been the Remington 125-grain JHP, which was issued

by the USAF in spite of the Hague Accords restrictions on the use of frangible-bullet ammo.

Because of its alloy frame, the Model 12 is technically a "carry often, but shoot seldom" gun, and a steady diet of +P loads is not recommended. However, the gun itself is well made, shoots more accurately than its mission requires and generally presents itself as an excellent member of the S&W K-frame family.

The Model 12's short barrel offers poor potential for bullets to expand. So, Glasers or 158-grain lead SWCs provide the best combination of stopping power, accuracy and penetration. The best accuracy in my Model 12 was obtained with Remington 125-grain JHPs, which produced 25-meter, three-shot Ransom Rest groups of under 2 inches. Glasers, unfortunately, demonstrated poor accuracy in my gun at ranges past 10 meters. On the other hand, Remington, Federal and Winchester 158-grain lead SWCs shot quite decently and would be my choice for general-purpose use.

Though now discontinued, the Model 12 is a delightful little snubbie, quite well made, reliable and indeed a joy to carry due to its light weight. I highly recommend it for typical snubbie situations.

Originally fitted with an aluminum cylinder, the Model 12 features an aluminum frame but steel cylinder. It was offered in 2- or 4-inch versions. The Air Force got 'em first.

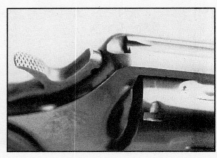

(Left and right) Using a ramped front and wide-notched rear high visibility sight system, the Model 12 allows fast, accurate DA work, something not especially common with snub revolvers. As well, to minimize the potential for snagging in concealment clothing, it features a narrow, low-profile hammer.

SMITH & WESSON'S MODEL 15

ALTHOUGH THE MODEL 15 designation first appeared when S&W began to number their guns in 1957, its basic K-frame configuration evolved from the old 38 Hand Ejector series of 1900. Advertised as one of the Combat Masterpiece series introduced in 1949 (that included barrel lengths of 4, 6, and 8³/₈ inches), the Model 15 with 2-inch barrel appeared in 1962 as a special production run for the U.S. Air Force with a heavy barrel and full-length rib extending to the front sight.

To delineate these from regular Model 15s, Smith designated them as the "Model 56." Some 15,205 such guns were built, and they soon became so popular that the Model 56 designation was dropped and the gun added to the regular Model 15 series. The "Model 56" was never again made.

To the present day, the 2-inch Model 15, though now out of production, remains one of the most sought-after 38 Special snubbies in the world and has earned a reputation for reliability and accuracy to date unsurpassed by any other revolver. It is indeed a "sweet piece" by anyone's standards. Its balance is exceptional; its sights, excellent.

With Winchester 125-grain +P JHP ammo, my 2-inch Model 15 consistently punches 25-meter Ransom Rest groups of a mere inch, more than justifying its near-legendary reputation for accuracy.

For self-defense applications, JHP ammo is a poor choice in a snubbie due to the lack of reliable bullet expansion at the low velocities they produce. However, Glaser Safety Slugs alleviate this problem, even if accuracy with them from a 2-inch barrel, while adequate for most snubbie situations, is only satisfactory. Should you prefer more general-purpose capability, a good, stout SWC load offers the best combination of penetration, accuracy and stopping power.

In short, the Model 15 2-inch is a slick gun, suitable for a wide variety of self-defense missions (something that most snubs are not!). If you can find one, grab it. Then go get yourself a box or two of 158-grain lead SWCs and enjoy.

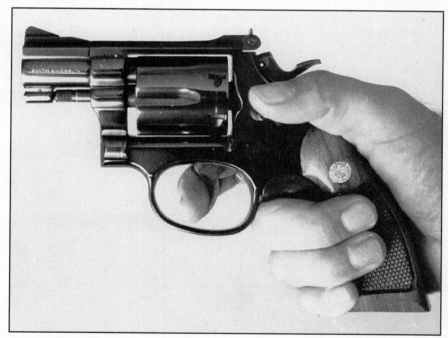

The S&W Model 15 snub is a very much sought-after item, one Taylor says is exceptionally accurate. His gun prints 1-inch groups at 25 meters.

(Left and right) Regarded by many as the most sophisticated snubbie ever made, the Model 15 has excellent, adjustable, high-visibility sights that, though more fragile than fixed styles, allow perfect high-speed sight acquisition.

SMITH & WESSON'S MODEL 20

BECAUSE OF INCREASED criminal mobility and the heavy sheet-metal bodywork of automobiles during the "Roaring Twenties," law enforcement agencies voiced a need to Smith & Wesson for a revolver chambered for a cartridge more potent than the standard 38 Special. The result of this request was the 38/44 Heavy Duty, later to become the Model 20 when S&W assigned model numbers to their firearms in 1957.

Built on the "44" (later to become the "S" and then "N") frame due to the higher pressure of the 38/44 cartridge, the Heavy Duty fast became the lawman's lifetime friend. Production commenced on April 1, 1930, and a total of 11,111 had been manufactured when World War II forced the cessation of production in 1941.

Production was resumed in 1946, but the increased popularity of the 357 Magnum cartridge (introduced in 1935) caused diminishing interest in the 38/44. Manufacture ceased in 1966, by which time an additional 20,604 post-war Model 20s had been built. Total production was 31,715 guns built from 1930 to 1966.

During the 1930s, the Model 20 was by far the most popular and best-selling Smith & Wesson revolver, and was the mainstay of many police officers, who praised its balance (a product of its 5-inch barrel and 40-ounce weight), high-visibility fixed sights, excellent penetration and fine accuracy. However, many special-order guns with 3½-, 4-, 6- and even 8⅜-inch barrels were produced.

The 38/44 cartridge for which it was chambered proved

The Model 20 is the most recent designation for the 38/44 Heavy Duty, a very useful 38-caliber sidearm. Taylor recommends acquiring the next one you find.

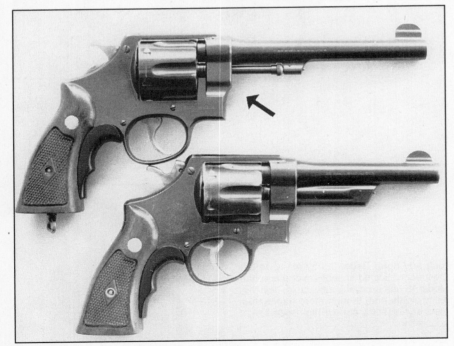

The heavy-frame 44 Special Hand Ejector (top) was the basis for the 38/44 HD. Though large, it had the needed strength to handle the high-pressure 38/44 high-velocity cartridge.

to be highly accurate; it was substantially more accurate than the 357 Magnum that eventually supplanted it. This is why Dick Tinker used 38/44—not 357 Magnum—ammunition to shoot the famous 600-yard targets in Ed McGivern's classic book, *Fast and Fancy Revolver Shooting*.

Inasmuch as 38/44 factory ammunition is no longer produced, for the Heavy Duty and its fancier companion, the Model 23 Outdoorsman, either handloading or modern 38 Special factory ammo is the order of the day. Elmer Keith's original 38/44 handload with Hercules 2400 powder and his 173-grain SWC provided the best overall performance possible with the powders available at the time.

However, we find that Hodgdon's H-4227—a powder that became available long after the 38/44's demise as a factory cartridge—provides cleaner, more consistent performance than 2400. Velocities produced with a 158-grain bullet and my best load of H-4227 slightly exceed 1100 fps from the Model 20's 5-inch barrel, making it nearly equal to modern 158-grain 357 Magnum ammunition in all respects, while being somewhat more accurate.

Today, 38 Special cases are used for such handloads, the 38/44 being dimensionally identical. However, the original ammunition utilized a large, rather than the now-standard small, pistol primer. This is because no magnum small pistol primer existed when the 38/44 was created. So for high-performance handloads, a magnum small pistol primer should be selected for best results.

Factory +P 38 Special ammo can also be used without difficulty in any 38/44. Remington, Federal and Winchester 158-grain SWCHP or JHP ammo of this type are my favorites and good choices for most personal-defense missions.

As a general-purpose self-defense weapon, the Model 20 and any of these loads are an excellent combination. Penetration and accuracy are superb, recoil and flash are moderate, and weapon reliability is nearly flawless.

I am fortunate to have not one but two 5-inch Model 20s, one of which was a gift from my dear friend and lifetime lawman Dalton Carr of Craig, Colorado, who carried it for nearly two decades and whose life it saved eleven times. The other was still in the original box when I found it at, of all things, a yard sale.

If you come across a Model 20 38/44 in good shape, especially with a 5-inch barrel, you'd be well advised to grab it. Most who own them aren't usually inclined to part with them. Whether you're a collector of law enforcement firearms or someone who just enjoys owning and shooting an important piece of American firearms history, I think you'll find the Model 20 to be a pleasant and worthwhile find.

SMITH & WESSON'S MODEL 24

A DIRECT DESCENDANT of the 44 Triple Lock revolver from early in this century, the Smith & Wesson Model 24 and its stainless counterpart, the Model 624, are among the very few non-magnum large-frame revolvers offered by Smith & Wesson in the last two decades. Having been in continuous production for three decades, the Model 24's manufacture mysteriously ceased in 1967, when the gun was on the verge of becoming the preferred police service handgun over the 38 Special.

It was reintroduced to the shooting public in the late 1980s, possibly to determine if public acceptance would be sufficient to justify its reentry into the S&W line on a permanent basis. S&W even introduced a stainless version of it. However attractive the guns were, and in spite of an

The Model 24 is the 44 Special precursor to the famous Model 29 and its 44 Magnum cartridge. The 24 is a useful and accurate handgun with enough cartridge to make it a viable self-defense package for those who favor the revolver.

excellent sales showing, for some reason manufacture of both guns ceased after less than five years.

The 44 Special is a descendant of the 44 Russian cartridge of more than a century ago and a survivor of the turn-of-the-century shift from black to smokeless powder. However, in deference to the many older guns still in service and a couple of more modern, but very small-framed and therefore fragile versions, all 44 Special factory ammunition, even +P, remains quite mild. There has never been a truly modern commercial loading for the excellent cartridge.

This gun was originally called the 1950 44 Target and was offered with a 4- or 6½-inch barrel. Perhaps the biggest feather in the 44 Special/Model 24's historical cap is that it was the basis from which the famous Model 29 and its 44 Remington Magnum cartridge were developed, under the tutelage of a now-deceased acquaintance of mine, Elmer Keith. Although interchangeable in a magnum-chambered gun, the 44 Special's case is .125-inch shorter than the Magnum, thus comparing to it in much the same way as the 38 Special does to the 357 Magnum. This prevents the more potent magnum from inadvertently being chambered and fired in a gun not designed to handle its 35,000+ psi pressures.

Keith developed high-intensity 44 Special loads that have yet to be surpassed, his favorite (and mine) being his (Lyman #429421) 245-grain SWC bullet and a maximum load of Hercules 2400 that produces 1050 fps from my 6.5-inch M24 and about 985 fps from my 4-inch. Recoil is, to say the least, "magnumesque," feeling much like the 357/125. The consensus of opinion is that a steady diet of such loads will reduce the service life of the gun considerably. This being the case and considering that such loads are no longer necessary (there now being a full-blown magnum 44), it is therefore recommended that its use be limited.

On the other hand, the Keith 245-grain SWC bullet with a top load of Hodgdon H-4227 remains the best performer from both an accuracy and penetration standpoint. Recoil and muzzle flip are also much more manageable, and flash is reduced to minimal levels. My Models 24 and 624 perform beautifully, printing three-shot, 25-meter groups with standard of +P factory 44 Special ammo (246-grain RNL) averaging about 1.75 inches.

It is my hope that Smith & Wesson sees its way clear to again produce the Model 24 and keep it available on a permanent basis. The offering of a few decent commercial loads would enhance its popularity and potential as a fighting handgun.

In short, the Model 24 is a heck of a nice defensive handgun and, while a bit slow from a holster due to its size and weight, should be seriously considered by anyone interested

SMITH & WESSON'S MODEL 25-5

ONLY A FEW years ago, Smith & Wesson, after nearly two decades of prodding from big-bore revolver aficionados, introduced a new version of their famed Model 25 1950 Target. Chambered for the 45 Colt cartridge, and featuring a 4-inch barrel and a longer cylinder to accommodate the big Keith SWC bullet, the Model 25-5 was instantly accepted by serious handgunners everywhere and hailed as being long overdue. Disappointed with the marginal stopping power of

the 38 Special, a number of law enforcement agencies around the country rushed to obtain M25-5s and quickly placed them in service.

Accuracy problems were noted with the early models, due to a manufacturing tolerance oversight, and the 25-5's fledgling reputation suffered as a result. However, S&W quickly corrected the problem, and all later versions exhibit excellent accuracy with all types of factory ammo and most handloads.

One of the handiest and potentially most powerful self-defense handguns is the S&W Model 25-5, in 45 Colt caliber. Taylor likes it for self-defense. This 4-inch version has custom stocks.

My M25-5 prints three-shot, 25-meter Ransom Rest groups of about 2½ inches with most factory fodder, with experimental +P handloads reducing group size by perhaps an additional 10 percent. Not bad! Along with this, however, I also noted that muzzle flip increased to the point where the rear sight could not be lowered enough to bring the gun onto point of aim.

Weapon control with factory 255-grain lead flatpoint (LFP) ammunition is excellent, but a handload of 10 grains of Hercules Unique and a Hornady XTP 250-grain JHP bullet, while producing velocities in the mid-800 fps range, exhibits serious though not uncontrollable recoil.

Repeatedly, stories have circulated that, because of the large diameter and long length of the 45 Colt cartridge, the 25-5 is incapable of handling heavy handloads. In order to test this idea, I put together an old Keith handload intended for the Colt Model P (Single Action Army) consisting of a 250-grain SWC bullet and 18 grains of Hercules 2400 powder, and fired fifty rounds, with no ill effects.

Then I tried fifty more of an even heavier load for use in the super-strong Ruger SA revolver. This was 20 grains of Hercules 2400 with the Keith 250-grain SWC bullet. It gave no problems. In both instances, fired cases dropped freely from the cylinder at the first touch of the ejector rod. My shooting hand, though, demonstrated symptoms of "magnumitis," from the heavy recoil produced by both loads.

While sustained use of such heavy loads is not recommended, the 25-5 is strong enough to withstand any kind of reasonable load and is capable of a long, trouble-free service life.

The Model 25-5's reputation suffered another bashing about ten years ago because of some spectacular law enforcement failures to stop with so-called +P JHP ammo, resulting in a number of departments abandoning the weapon like a hot potato. This is too bad, because the problem lay with the ammo, not the gun.

Like the 44 Special, the 45 Colt is a survivor from the blackpowder era, when its factory load punched out a 255-grain bullet at about 900 fps from a 7.5-inch Colt SA revolver. While the generic modern factory load retains the original bullet shape, concerns about blowing up Granddaddy's old Colt SAA have kept pressure—and resulting muzzle velocity—to a minimum, *even in so-called "+P" loads!"*

With decent ammunition, the M25-5 is a fine general-purpose defensive handgun, even if the 45 Colt cartridge it fires is a bit large for its performance level. Unfortunately, the ammunition problem has yet to be solved, so I suggest the regular factory 255-grain LFP load as a middle-of-the-road alternative. It is, after all, a huge bullet, even if it is traveling at fairly low velocity, and is still a good manstopper.

SMITH & WESSON'S MODEL 27

SINCE THE 357 Magnum cartridge first appeared in 1935, there have been myriad handguns chambered for it. Of all the guns sporting the 357 Magnum stamp, only one can be called the Cadillac of the breed—the Model 27.

Considered at the time to be the world's most powerful handgun cartridge, the 357 Magnum mandated that Smith & Wesson build a special handgun for it. On April 8, 1935, the first "Three-Fifty-Seven" was presented to FBI founder and director, J. Edgar Hoover.

Based upon S&W's highly successful S-frame, the new gun was finely checkered on both its topstrap and barrel rib, offered with seven different combinations of front and rear

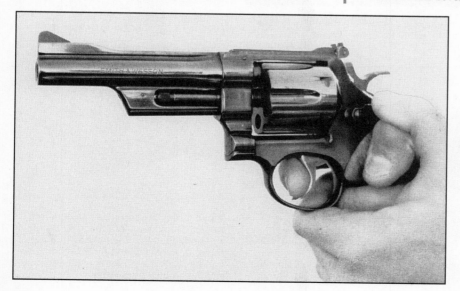

The first and probably the finest 357, S&W's Model 27 was recently discontinued. This gun began the era of the magnum in 1935.

sights and shipped from the factory with barrel lengths from 3½ to a full 8¾ inches long. Shortly after the gun's introduction, maximum barrel length was reduced to 8⅜ inches.

Sales of the new revolver were brisk and outstripped S&W's 120 gun-per-month capacity to build them, a condition that persisted until the onset of World War II. Along with many of their other handguns, it was temporarily discontinued to allow S&W's full attention to wartime military contracts. Total prewar production of the "Three-Fifty-Seven" was 6642 guns. When manufacture again commenced in 1948, barrel length was standardized at 3½, 5, 6½ and 8⅜ inches.

Sales continued to be very strong, with an additional 6322 guns sold by June 1952, and in 1957 when S&W assigned model numbers to their guns, the "Three-Fifty-Seven" became the Model 27, the designation it retained until its discontinuation in 1995.

Throughout the next two decades, S&W made continuous improvements on the Model 27. By September 1975, it was offered with a target hammer, target trigger, checkered Goncalo Alves target stocks and a mahogany presentation case. Several years ago, the barrel lengths of 3½, 5 and 6½ inches were dropped, and lengths of 4, 6 and 8⅜ inches became standard.

Accuracy with my two M27s, both early 3½- and 6½-inch versions, is excellent, with 50-meter Ransom Rest groups of around 2 inches being the norm. Generally speaking, the Model 27 is a forgiving handgun, meaning that it shoots well with pretty much anything one cares to stuff into it. Nonetheless, best accuracy in my guns is achieved with a near-maximum handload with Hodgdon's H-110, a Remington magnum small pistol primer and the Nosler 158-grain JHP bullet.

If you're not a handloader, nearly equal performance can be obtained with the Norma 158-grain JSP, Winchester or Remington 125-grain JHP, or the Federal 158-grain JSP.

The highest velocity factory 357 Magnum load is the ultra-lightweight Glaser Safety Slug, but for more general-purpose defensive missions, the highly frangible Glaser might not suffice. Thus, the honor of the highest velocity obtained with a conventional bullet goes to the Winchester 125-grain JHP.

In spite of its recent discontinuation, the Smith & Wesson Model 27 remains the Cadillac of 357 Magnum revolvers and produces excellent results with virtually any kind of ammunition. It is aesthetically pleasing, functionally reliable, very accurate and well worth whatever price you may have to pay to get one...if you can find one for sale anywhere.

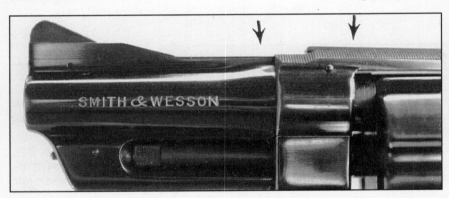

The checkered top strap and sight rib were hallmarks of the Model 27. The 3½-inch version was perhaps the most commonly encountered in law enforcement circles and was the favorite of the FBI for many years.

The gun was offered in numerous barrel lengths, but the 5-inch version was much sought after because of its excellent balance.

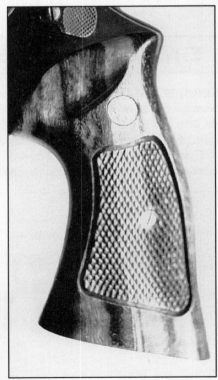

Target stocks to absorb the heavier recoil of the 357 cartridge quickly became standard on the Model 27. These are of Goncalo Alves, a wood favored by S&W for more than three decades. Stocks were also available in walnut and rosewood.

A legendary fighting handgun, the S&W Model 27 (bottom) is shown for size comparison with another famous 357, the Colt Python. Note the screw at the top of the sideplate, just under the rear sight, marking this as an early gun.

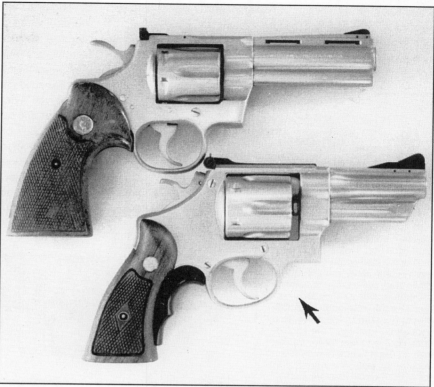

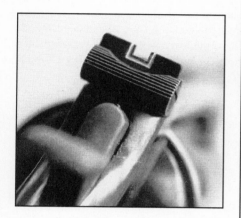

A white-outlined rear sight and a host of front sight options were available on the Model 27.

SMITH & WESSON'S MODEL 1917

OFFICIALLY TERMED THE "45 Hand Ejector U.S. Service Model of 1917," this classic example of the early S&W large-frame revolver first appeared on September 6, 1917, and was the result of a successful attempt to mate the highly effective—but rimless—45 ACP cartridge with a DA revolver.

As the probability of U.S. involvement in WWI loomed larger, military demands for M1911 45 ACP handguns exceeded Colt's capacity to manufacture them. Thus, the government turned to Smith & Wesson for additional guns, and although S&W's new Willow Street plant was not yet completed, production of what employees called the "S&W Government Model" began.

Using essentially the 44 Hand Ejector, Second Model, as its basis, the Model 1917 was built with a 5.5-inch barrel, blued finish, checkered walnut stocks and a lanyard ring in the butt. In spite of S&W's attempts to provide sufficient quantities of the new revolver, the U.S. government took over the plant on September 13, 1917, and managed production of the weapon from that point on, hoping to increase output.

By 1918, monthly manufacture had risen from 5000 to 14,000 guns per month, with a total wartime production of 163,476. S&W offered the M1917 commercially until Janu-

ary 5, 1921, but sales were relatively slow, and it was discontinued at that time. It was replaced by a virtually identical commercial version that featured full-size walnut stocks, rather than the thin military type.

Although sales were slow, production of this commercial version was boosted in 1937 by an order from the Brazilian government for 25,000 guns. These were supplied with the Brazilian seal on the sideplate and delivered between February and October, 1938. Many of these same guns have recently become available for civilian sale here in the United States.

Production was again suspended with the onset of WWII and resumed in May 1946. A total of 991 new M1917s were built before it was permanently discontinued in 1949 to allow Smith & Wesson to concentrate upon a successor, the much-improved Model 1950 45 Target.

Light, reliable and accurate, the Model 1917 shoots quite well, especially considering the "thumbnail"-type front sight and narrow rear notch typical of most guns of that era. The DA pull is crisp and smooth, and fast DA work is relatively easy. If a Tyler T-Grip adapter and more substantial stocks are installed, the M1917 is a quite viable 25-meter general-purpose revolver.

My M1917 consistently produces fine accuracy, with 50-

meter Ransom Rest groups hovering around 3 inches with most any factory jacketed load I put through it. Although its rifling is quite shallow in deference to jacketed bullets, it also shoots cast bullets well. With bullet weights over 200 grains, recoil is noticeable—the result of its light barrel.

(Above) To allow the use and extraction of rimless 45 ACP ammunition, so-called "half-moon" three-round clips were created. Since then, two-round (the author's preference because they allow correct tactical reloading) and "full-moon" six-round clips have also appeared. However, if the shooter doesn't care to use these, he can instead use 45 Auto Rim ammunition, which functions normally in the M1917 and in its more modern descendants.

Over the years, I've often carried my M1917 as a boon-docking gun and found it entirely suitable for defense against the generality of two-legged and most four-legged critters one might encounter during such endeavors. A 44 Magnum it isn't, but then, a 45 isn't exactly anemic, either.

Provided you can find one in good condition and at a fair price, you'll find that it will give you many hours of shooting pleasure and can double quite well in the self-defense mode. The M1917 continues to receive attention from both serious combat shooters and collectors alike.

Like a good man, a good gun isn't all that easy to find, but this one is without doubt a winner. Should you encounter one of these famous S&W big-bores, grab it. I don't think you'll be sorry.

The S&W Model 1917 (bottom), shown with the SIG SAUER P220 for size comparison, is a light yet powerful 45 ACP revolver that can serve well in the self-defense role. If you find a good one, grab it, says the author.

SIG SAUER'S P220

FIRST APPEARING ALMOST two decades ago as the Browning BDA, the P220 in its current American version is regarded by many as being *the* state-of-the-art 45 auto. Indeed, its popularity is exceeded only by that of the Colt M1911 Government Model, whose king-of-the-hill status the P220 is now seriously challenging, especially in law enforcement circles.

This is not due solely to the fact that the P220 is a nice pistol, but also because of many police administrator's real and imagined fears about the 1911's cocked-and-locked (Condition One) carry mode. Thus, part of the P220's claim

to fame is due to it being in the right place at the right time. It's the right caliber, the 45 ACP, and there are no public relations concerns, as with the single-action M1911.

The P220 is a simple design, perhaps as simple as a handgun can be and still work. Its human engineering is excellent because, like its baby 9mm brothers, the P225 and P226, its controls are placed where they can be readily operated, something exceptional for a DA auto. Furthermore, its mechanical performance leaves nothing to be desired. It is probably the best DA self-loader around.

From the box, it comes with high-visibility fixed sights

featuring the white-dot insert front and horizontal-bar rear low-light combination so popular in Europe. In truth, one of the few improvements I would recommend for the P220 would be to replace these with a simpler and faster three-dot horizontal pattern.

Field-stripping is perhaps the fastest of all autos: 1) lock the slide to the rear, 2) turn the takedown lever 90 degrees downward, 3) grasp the slide firmly, 4) release the slide lock, 5) withdraw the slide from the frame, 6) remove the recoil spring guide and barrel from the slide.

That's it! My average time for this procedure is less than five seconds, as opposed to a bit over seven seconds for my Colt 1911 or Commander.

My P220 shoots very well indeed, with three-shot Ransom Rest 25-meter groups averaging slightly over 2 inches. I've also had no functioning problems whatsoever with the gun, although in some of the earlier versions, some problems were reported with several styles of JHP bullet. SIG SAUER, to their credit, immediately relieved the front of the magazine body to allow better bullet clearance, which solved the problem nicely. Trigger pulls, both SA and DA, are acceptable and typical of a weapon of this type.

In summary, the P220 is an excellent example of how good a DA auto can be. As such, it is well worth its not-inconsequential price and clearly a handgun upon which one could with confidence bet his life.

The P220 is a 45-caliber double action which author Taylor believes to be the best of the breed. The P220 is very well made, reliable and accurate, he says, and well worth its hefty price tag.

SIG SAUER'S P226

AS THE DOUBLE-ACTION, large-magazine-capacity 9mm craze began to grip the U.S. a decade ago, a *bunch* of new self-loading pistols appeared. And while this phenomenon was largely based on an unjustified fear of cocked-and-locked single-action autos, it quickly spread throughout the law enforcement community in particular.

The result has been a trend toward what has been incorrectly been termed "firepower." I say *incorrectly* because the term has no application whatsoever to handguns. After all, when was the last time you saw an infantry squad armed

with handguns storming a fortified objective or conducting ambush/counter-ambush drills? Yep, you've guessed it—*never!* So much for "firepower" in handguns, eh?

The only sound tactical and legal solution to non-military anti-personnel encounters, especially with handguns, is to hit what you're shooting at. Suppressive fire and indiscriminate bullet launching not only waste time and ammunition, but vastly complicate both the tactical and legal situation as well. Remember that in a non-military environment, we have laws—both of nature (what goes up must come down and guess who's responsible) and the kind we see in civil and criminal court. Simply stated, we must incorporate this glaring fact into our defensive strategy and tactics or run the risk of getting ourselves into big trouble. So, while I feel the concept around which the modern high-capacity auto is based to be dreadfully ill-advised, I also feel that the P226 is one of the best-designed and best-built examples of the breed.

It is extremely well made and finished, featuring a black-anodized frame and Parkerized slide, and presents a formidable appearance, backed by solid functionality. It is one of the most accurate self-loaders I have ever fired and possesses well-conceived human engineering features.

Its decocking lever and slide lock/release are all centrally located for quick, easy manipulation. In addition, it feeds most anything you care to stuff into the magazine, including the latest exotic JHP designs. It field-strips in less than five seconds. A rebounding hammer and white-dot-front, white-outline-rear sight combination complete its formidable package.

Much of the above is due to the fact that it was originally designed to satisfy the criteria of the infamous U.S. military Joint Service Small Arms Program handgun trials, wherein many "in the know" claim that the P226 actually outperformed the eventual choice, the Beretta M92. One of the most user-friendly large-capacity DA autos produced, the P226 also points well and presents few edges to cut skin and abrade concealment clothing.

So, if you're one of those who prefers a large-capacity DA auto, you can't really go wrong with the P226. In fact, while its certainly no secret that I'm not an advocate of the concept, I find the P226 to be a pleasant gun to shoot and prefer it hands-down over all other large-capacity DA 9mm pistols. It isn't a cheap gun, but it's well worth its price.

The P226 (top) in size comparison to the Browning P-35 9mm. For those who like the high-capacity DA 9mms, the SIG SAUER is one of the best.

(Below) Exhibiting excellent accuracy, the P226 is one of the most efficient 9mm fighting handguns in the world. Here is a fourteen-shot group from offhand Weaver at 25 meters, using 124-grain military ball ammo.

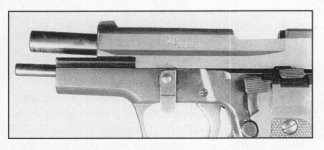

Field-stripping is accomplished in less than five seconds. Just turn the lever from horizontal to vertical, grasp the slide, release the slide lock and ease it forward, off the gun. Then remove the recoil spring/spring guide and barrel. That's it!

GLOSSARY OF TERMS

Action: Breech mechanism of a gun by which it is loaded and unloaded.

Air space: Space in a loaded cartridge not occupied by propellant powder or a seated bullet.

Ammunition: A generic term used to describe the complete package of bullet, case, primer and propellant powder. Also known as a *cartridge*.

Anvil: In a primer or cartridge case, a fixed point against which the priming mixture is compressed and thereby detonated by the action of the firing pin or striker.

AP: Armor piercing.

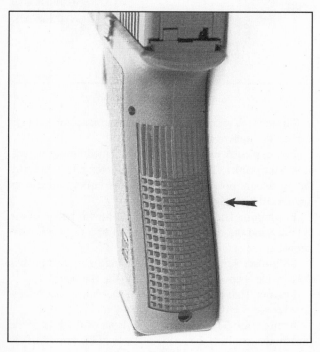

Backstrap.

Backstrap: The rear portion of the firearm's frame that contacts the palm of the shooting hand.

Ball: Early term for *bullet,* still used in military descriptions of issued ammunition utilizing bullets that are fully jacketed.

Ballistics: The science of projectiles in motion.

Barrel: A tube through which the projectile (bullet) is accelerated into flight. The standard length of handgun barrels varies from 2 to as long as 14 inches. Service or combat handguns usually feature barrel lengths of 6.5 inches or shorter.

Battery: The position of readiness of a gun for firing.

Blowback: A type of semi-automatic action in which the breech is not locked closed, but simply held shut by recoil spring tension and inertia, and then blown open as the cartridge fires and breech pressure increases.

Blackpowder: A mixture of charcoal, sulfur and potassium nitrate used as a propellant. It produces much smoke and fouling when burned.

Bore: The interior surface of the barrel.

Bore diameter: In rifled arms, the diametrical measurement, in either millimeters or thousandths of an inch, between the tops of the rifling lands.

Bullet: A single projectile launched from a small arm. (A contemporary error often encountered is the use of the term to describe a cartridge.)

Bullet jacket: A capsular covering of metal harder than lead and softer than steel which encloses a bullet's core. It is intended to take and hold rifling at velocities that would strip lead.

Bullet mold: Metallic device with a cavity or cavities into which molten lead alloy is poured and allowed to harden into projectiles (bullets).

Butt: That part of a handgun which is grasped by the firing hand. It is composed of the lower rear portion of the frame, together with the stocks.

Breech bolt: The part of a breech that resists the rearward force of the combustion that occurs when a chambered cartridge fires.

Caliber: The diameter of the bore, measured in either millimeters or hundredths or thousandths of an inch, to the depth of the rifling grooves.

Cannelure: Circumferential serrated groove(s) around a bullet or cartridge case to allow proper seating and crimping of the bullet.

Cartridge: A complete round of ammunition, made up of a case, bullet, powder and primer.

Cartridge case: The container in which the bullet, propellant powder and primer are housed. Often referred to as *brass*.

CF: Centerfire. Those cartridges which are ignited by means of a separate and replaceable primer.

Chamber: That portion of the bore (or revolver cylinder) at the breech, formed to accept the cartridge.

Chronograph: An instrument which measures the velocity at which a projectile travels.

Clip: A device, usually of metal, used to hold several cartridges together to facilitate packaging or loading. A "stripper clip" is one from which cartridges are forced by hand into the magazine. A clip is *not* a magazine.

Cock: Originally a noun denoting the swinging arm of a flintlock that scraped the flint against the frizzen. Now a verb describing the act of forcing the hammer or striker against the mainspring to prepare the gun for firing.

Cordite: A nitroglycerine smokeless propellant used in England prior to 1960.

Crimp: The bending inward of the case mouth perimeter in order to grip and hold a bullet.

Cylinder: In a revolver, a cartridge container that rotates around an axis parallel to and below the barrel. Each time

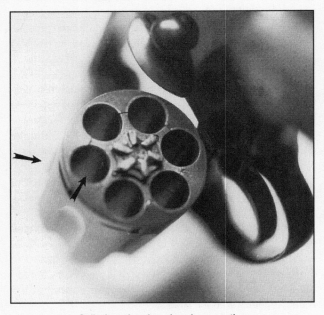

Cylinder, showing chamber mouths.

the weapon is cocked, a chamber containing a cartridge is brought into line with the barrel.

Disconnector: Any device that takes part of a mechanism out of action with another so as to render that mechanism inoperative.

Double action: A firing system which permits a firearm to be fired in two ways—either from a cocked or uncocked condition. Today, the term denotes trigger cocking.

Drift: A bullet's movement during flight, to right or left, away from the line of the bore, caused by the bullet's rotation.

Ejector: The device at the breech or within the action that knocks the fired case from the gun.

Energy: In projectiles, the amount of work done at given ranges, as expressed in foot-pounds, also known as kinetic energy. It is obtained by multiplying the mass of a moving object by one-half the square of its velocity. Energy is only one of several means of measuring the so-called power of a firearm.

Erosion: The gradual wearing away of rifling in the barrel by combustion gases.

Extractor: The device that withdraws the fired case from the chamber.

Extractor.

Firearm: A weapon that employs internal combustion to initiate the flight of its missile.

Firing pin: A pin which, when actuated by the trigger, strikes the primer of the cartridge, thus detonating it to ignite the propellant powder and causing the bullet to begin its movement through the bore.

Flash gap: The space between the forward edge of the cylinder and the rear end of the barrel of a revolver. Also known as the *cylinder gap*.

Follower: A metal platform in a magazine that pushes the cartridges upward for feeding into the chamber.

Frame: That part of the firearm that houses all operational parts.

Frontstrap: That portion of the front of the butt of the firearm that contacts the inside surfaces of the fingers of the firing hand.

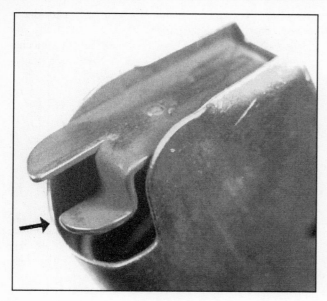

Follower.

Full cock: The condition of the gun when the mainspring (hammer spring) is fully compressed and the gun is ready to fire.

Gas check: A cup, usually of copper, used at the base of a lead-alloy bullet to protect it from hot powder gases during its passage through the bore.

Gas operation: In small arms, an automatic or semi-automatic action in which the barrel and breechblock are positively locked together and stationary during discharge, and in which a portion of combustion gas is diverted to unlock the breech and operate the action.

Gilding metal: An alloy of copper and nickel used as a bullet jacket.

Grip: The method of placing the hand(s) upon the gun to allow its efficient firing and control.

Grip adapter: A contoured piece of metal or plastic used to fill the space behind the trigger guard and in front of the frontstrap of a revolver. It prevents painful impact of the rear of the trigger guard with the middle knuckle of the middle finger of the firing hand and improves pointing of the gun.

Grip safety: A device designed to prevent a pistol from firing unless it is properly gripped in the firing hand.

Groove diameter: In rifled arms, the diametrical measurement between bottoms of grooves.

Grooves: Spiral cuts in a bore which cause the bullet to spin as it travels through the barrel.

Group: The pattern of a number of shots fired into a target, usually with one sight setting.

Gun: Loosely stated, any firearm. English use, a shotgun. Military use, a flat-trajectory cannon, as opposed to a howitzer or mortar.

Hammer: A part of the action that drives the firing pin against the primer, thus igniting the powder charge and firing the weapon.

Handgun: A small firearm with a short barrel and no buttstock that can be worn upon the person. It may be fired with either one or both hands.

Hang-fire: An abnormal delay in cartridge ignition after the primer is struck by the firing pin, usually caused by defective priming or powder.

HP: Hollowpoint. A form of expanding bullet, also known as *JHP*, for jacketed hollowpoint.

Headspace: For rimmed cartridges, the distance from the face of the breechblock to the support surface for the forward edge of the case rim. For a rimless cartridge, the distance from the face of the breechblock to a predetermined point on the shoulder of the chamber.

Holster: A handgun carrying device that is worn on the person.

Lands: That portion of the bore remaining after the rifling grooves have been cut.

Leading: Lead deposited on bore surfaces by bullets passing through.

Load: A specific cartridge or the exact specifications for a cartridge. Also the act of placing a cartridge into the firing chamber of a firearm. A gun with an empty chamber and a loaded magazine in place is not actually loaded.

Locked breech: A firearm action in which the breech is positively and mechanically locked during firing.

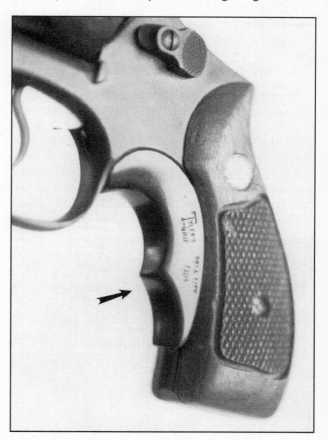

Grip adapter.

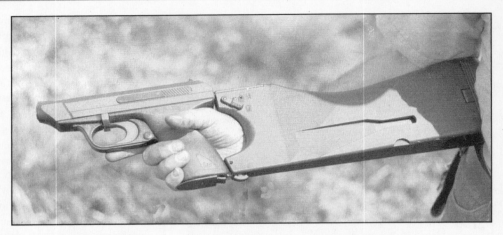

Machine pistol, showing automatic fire selector.

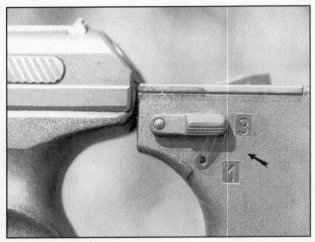

Machine pistol: A self-operating handgun capable of fully automatic fire. These often utilize a detachable buttstock that doubles as a holster. Tactically, the MP, as it's called, is a relatively useless arm, containing all the weaknesses of the handgun but none of its assets. Although handguns and MPs both utilize pistol cartridges, a machine pistol is not a submachine gun. It is a handgun, whereas a submachine gun is a shoulder weapon with an integral buttstock.

Magazine: A device or reservoir to hold extra cartridges, usually residing within the firearm itself. A magazine always incorporates a follower spring whereas a clip does not. Thus a magazine is not a clip.

Magazine release: A lever or button mounted either on the butt of the handgun or on the side of its grip frame that positively locks the magazine in place. When actuated, it releases the magazine to drop free or to be withdrawn from the gun.

Magazine well: A receptacle in the butt of a pistol into which the magazine is placed.

Magnum: A contemporary term for a cartridge or a handgun intended to utilize higher-pressure loads than normally used for the caliber. The increased pressure produces higher bullet velocities.

Mainspring: The spring which drives the firing mechanism of a firearm. It is not necessarily the largest spring in the gun.

MC: Metal case. A form of bullet completely covered with gilding metal.

ME: Muzzle energy.

Mid-range: Usually used in connection with trajectory, referring to a point midway between the muzzle and target.

Misfire: A cartridge that does not fire when struck by the firing pin.

Magazine release button.

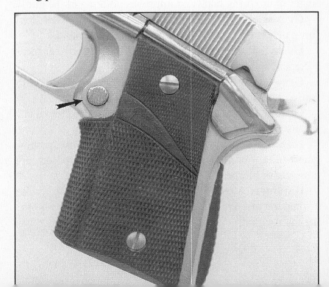

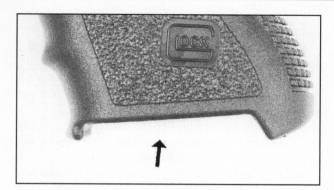

Magazine well.

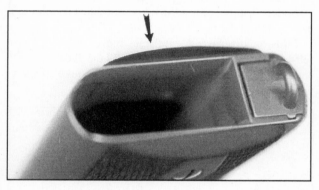

Momentum: The property of a moving body that tends to keep it in motion. Momentum is obtained by multiplying the mass of a projectile by its velocity. Momentum is a more satisfactory means of measuring handgun power than simple kinetic energy.

MP: Machine pistol.

MRT: Mid-range trajectory.

Mushroom: The act of expansion of certain bullets upon impact and/or during passage through the target.

Muzzle: The end of the barrel (opposite the breech) from which the bullet exits into free flight.

Muzzle flash: A fireball created as burning propellant gases follow the bullet from the muzzle and contact cool, oxygen-laden air.

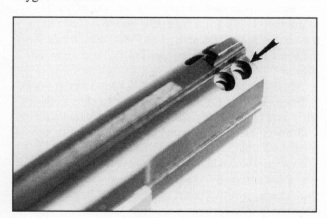

Muzzlebrake.

Muzzlebrake: A device which redirects burning propellant gases through vents to reduce the upward climb of a small arm when fired; also known as a *compensator*.

MV: Muzzle velocity. The velocity of a fired bullet measured at, or very near, the muzzle of the gun.

Piece: Any small arm. Derived from *piece of ordnance*.

Pistol: Loosely stated, any handgun. Properly stated, a self-loading handgun.

Power: The force developed by a cartridge when fired in a specific firearm. This is often measured by comparisons of kinetic energy, but is more correctly measured by comparing the momentum generated by the bullets.

Pressure: The gas pressure generated in a cartridge when fired, usually expressed in either pounds per square inch (psi) or copper units of pressure (CUP).

Primer: The small cup containing a detonating mixture that is seated in a recess in the base of the cartridge case. In a rimfire, a similar mixture is housed inside the rim of the case.

Range: The distance to which a missile is thrown. In small arms, *maximum range* is the absolute distance a bullet will travel before landing. In the practical sense, it denotes how far away one can effectively hit his target. Also, it is an abbreviation of *firing range,* e.g., a place where shooting takes place.

Ranson Rest.

Ransom Rest: A handgun accuracy testing device, produced by Ransom International, that positively locks a handgun in place, thus eliminating human sighting and grip error during firing.

Ready position.

Ready position: A position taken by a person with weapon in the hand for imminent use. The firearm is kept down at about 45 degrees below horizontal. The trigger finger is kept outside the trigger guard. The so-called Contact Ready, in which the weapon is held just below the line of sight to the target, is tactically dangerous and presents many legal problems.

Recoil: Newton's Third Law of Motion. For every action, there is an equal and opposite reaction; also known as *kick*. The rearward thrust of a firearm caused by the reaction to powder gases pushing the bullet through the bore.

Recoil operation: An automatic or semi-automatic action in which barrel and breech are positively locked together during the firing cycle, and move rearward while still locked, until gas pressure has dropped enough to allow the action to open without blowing the cartridge case apart.

Recoil spring: The spring or springs that return the gun into battery after firing.

Revolver: A multi-shot handgun that utilizes a revolving cylinder as a cartridge container.

RF: Rimfire.

Rifling: Spiral grooves cut into the bore which impart a spin to the projectile, thereby keeping it point-on and stable during flight.

RN: Round-nose.

Round: One cartridge.

Sear: That part of a firing mechanism which holds the hammer or striker in the cocked position. When the sear is forced out of engagement by the trigger, the hammer or striker falls, firing the gun.

Shell: An explosive artillery projectile. Slang term for small-arms ammunition.

Shot: The discharge of a firearm. Also, round pellets used as projectiles in shotguns.

Sidearm: A weapon that can be easily worn upon the person, leaving both hands free when the weapon is not in actual use.

Sight: A device used to align the shooter's firing eye as nearly as possible with the trajectory of the bullet and the target. May be either fixed or adjustable.

Sight radius: The distance between the front and rear sights. The longer this distance, the more precise the alignment can be.

Slide: That part of a self-loading pistol that reciprocates back and forth during the firing cycle.

Slide lock/release: A mechanical lever found on most self-loading pistols that positively holds the slide rearward and then releases the slide, allowing it to move forward, when actuated.

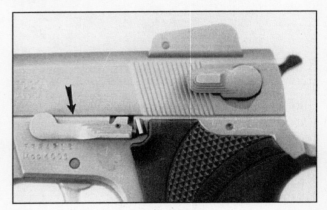

Slide lock/release.

Small arms: In general, those arms intended to be carried and operated by one man. Specifically, any firearm of less than 50-caliber.

Smokeless powder: Gunpowder which produces either no or very little smoke during combustion.

Sound suppressor: A mechanical device either integral to the barrel of a firearm or attached to it that radically reduces the sound of discharge. In some cases, it eliminates the sonic boom of a supersonic bullet. Also known as a *silencer*.

SP: Softpoint. Also known as *JSP*, for jacketed softpoint.

Speed-loader: A mechanical device used to simultaneously load multiple cartridges into a double-action revolver.

Stance: The configuration in which the body is held when discharging or handling a firearm.

Stocks: The wood, plastic or rubber portions of a small arm that contact the hands and support recoil. Handgun stocks are usually two-piece, thus the plural. These are often erroneously called *grips*.

Striker: A firing element (gun part) that moves in a

Sound suppressor.

Thumb safety.

straight line to strike the primer and fire the weapon. A *hammer* swings in an arc.

SWC: Semi-wadcutter. A bullet having both a flat point and a pronounced sharp shoulder.

Target: The object at which one is shooting.

Thumb safety: A mechanical safety device manipulated by the firing thumb, used primarily with single-action self-loaders, such as the Colt M1911 and Browning P-35.

Trajectory: The path of the bullet from the gun to the target.

Transfer bar: A safety device used in modern revolvers that prevents the hammer from contacting the firing pin or primer unless the trigger is pressed, thus reducing the potential for an accidental discharge.

Trigger: The finger piece of a small arm which, when pressed, allows the sear to release the hammer, thus firing the gun.

Trigger cocking: That form of firing which utilizes trigger manipulation to raise and release the hammer, causing the weapon to fire. The term is used with double-action revolvers or DA self-loading pistols.

Trigger guard: An approximately circular appendage on the frame of a firearm that protects the trigger from inadvertent operation.

Twist: The angle of the rifling relative to the axis of the bore; normally expressed in terms of turns per centimeter or inch.

WC: Wadcutter. A bullet having a completely flat front surface that extends to the full bullet diameter.

Velocity: Projectile speed, measured in feet per second or meters per second.

Zero: That sight setting which results in a bullet group on target exactly at the point of aim.

Stances (from left): FBI, isosceles and Weaver.

MANUFACTURERS' DIRECTORY

A

A&B Industries, Inc. (See Top-Line USA, Inc.)

A.A. Arms, Inc., 4811 Persimmont Ct., Monroe, NC 28110/704-289-5356, 800-935-1119; FAX: 704-289-5859

Abel Safe & File, Inc., 124 West Locust St., Fairbury, IL 61739/800-346-9280, 815-692-2131; FAX: 815-692-3350

AC Dyna-tite Corp., 155 Kelly St., P.O. Box 0984, Elk Grove Village, IL 60007/847-593-5566; FAX: 847-593-1304

Acadian Ballistic Specialties, P.O. Box 61, Covington, LA 70434

Acculube II, Inc., 4366 Shackleford Rd., Norcross, GA 30093-2912

Accupro Gun Care, 15512-109 Ave., Surrey, BC U3R 7E8, CANADA/604-583-7807

Accuracy Gun Shop, 7818 Wilkerson Ct., San Diego, CA 92111/619-282-8500

Accuracy International, 9115 Trooper Trail, P.O. Box 2019, Bozeman, MT 59715/406-587-7922; FAX: 406-585-9434

Accuracy Unlimited, 7479 S. DePew St., Littleton, CO 80123

Accuracy Unlimited, 16036 N. 49 Ave., Glendale, AZ 85306/602-978-9089; FAX: 602-978-9089

Accurate Arms Co., Inc., 5891 Hwy. 230 West, McEwen, TN 37101/615-729-4207, 800-416-3006; FAX 615-729-4211

Accuright, RR 2 Box 397, Sebeka, MN 56477/218-472-3383

Accu-Tek, 4525 Carter Ct., Chino, CA 91710/909-627-2404; FAX: 909-627-7817

Ace Custom 45's, Inc., 1880½ Upper Turtle Creek Rd., Kerrville, TX 78028/210-257-4290; FAX: 210-257-5724

Action Bullets, Inc., 1811 W. 13th Ave., Denver, CO 80204/303-595-9636; FAX: 303-595-4413

Action Products, Inc., 22 N. Mulberry St., Hagerstown, MD 21740/301-797-1414; FAX: 301-733-2073

Action Target, Inc., P.O. Box 636, Provo, UT 84603/801-377-8033; FAX: 801-377-8096

Actions by "T", Teddy Jacobson, 16315 Redwood Forest Ct., Sugar Land, TX 77478/713-277-4008

AcuSport Corporation, 1 Hunter Place, Bellefontaine, OH 43311-3001/513-593-7010; FAX: 513-592-5625

Ad Hominem, RR 3, Orillia, Ont. L3V 6H3, CANADA/705-689-5303

Adair Custom Shop, Bill, 2886 Westridge, Carrollton, TX 75006

Adams & Son Engravers, John J., 87 Acorn Rd., Dennis, MA 02638/508-385-7971

Adams Jr., John J., 87 Acorn Rd., Dennis, MA 02638/508-385-7971

Adaptive Technology, 939 Barnum Ave, Bridgeport, CT 06609/800-643-6735; FAX: 800-643-6735

ADCO International, 10 Cedar St., Unit 17, Woburn, MA 01801/617-935-1799; FAX: 617-935-1011

Adkins, Luther, 1292 E. McKay Rd., Shelbyville, IN 46176-9353/317-392-3795

Advance Car Mover Co., Rowell Div., P.O. Box 1, 240 N. Depot St., Juneau, WI 53039/414-386-4464; FAX: 414-386-4416

Adventure 16, Inc., 4620 Alvarado Canyon Rd., San Diego, CA 92120/619-283-6314

Adventurer's Outpost, P.O. Box 70, Cottonwood, AZ 86326/800-762-7471; FAX: 602-634-8781

African Import Co., 20 Braunecker Rd., Plymouth, MA 02360/508-746-8552

AFSCO Ammunition, 731 W. Third St., P.O. Box L, Owen, WI 54460/715-229-2516

Ahlman Guns, Rt. 1, Box 20, Morristown, MN 55052/507-685-4243; FAX: 507-685-4247

Ahrends, Kim, Custom Firearms, Box 203, Clarion, IA 50525/515-532-3449; FAX: 515-532-3926

Aimpoint, Inc., 580 Herndon Parkway, Suite 500, Herndon, VA 22070/703-471-6828; FAX: 703-689-0575

Aimtech Mount Systems, P.O. Box 223, 101 Inwood Acres, Thomasville, GA 31799/912-226-4313; FAX: 912-227-0222

Airguns-R-Us, 101 7th Ave., Columbia, TN 38401/615-381-4428; FAX: 615-381-1218

Airrow (See Swivel Machine Works, Inc.)

Ajax Custom Grips, Inc., 9130 Viscount Row, Dallas, TX 75247/214-630-8893; FAX: 214-630-4942

Aker Leather Products, 2248 Main St., Suite 6, Chula Vista, CA 91911/619-423-5182; FAX: 619-423-1363

Alaska Bullet Works, P.O. Box 54, Douglas, AK 99824/907-789-3834

Alco Carrying Cases, 601 W. 26th St., New York, NY 10001/212-675-5820; FAX: 212-691-5935

Aldis Gunsmithing & Shooting Supply, 502 S. Montezuma St., Prescott, AZ 86303/602-445-6723; FAX: 602-445-6763

Alessi Holsters, Inc., 2465 Niagara Falls Blvd., Amherst, NY 14228-3527/716-691-5615

Alfano, Sam, 36180 Henry Gaines Rd., Pearl River, LA 70452/504-863-3364; FAX: 504-863-7715

All Rite Products, Inc., 5752 N. Silverstone Circle, Mountain Green, UT 84050/801-876-3330; 801-876-2216

Allard, Gary, Creek Side Metal & Woodcrafters, Fishers Hill, VA 22626/703-465-3903

Allen Co., Inc., 525 Burbank St., Broomfield, CO 80020/303-469-1857, 800-876-8600; FAX: 303-466-7437

Allen Mfg., 6449 Hodgson Rd., Circle Pines, MN 55014/612-429-8231

Allen, Richard L., 339 Grove Ave., Prescott, AZ 86301/602-778-1237

Alliant Techsystems, Smokeless Powder Group, 200 Valley Rd., Suite 305, Mt. Arlington, NJ 07856/800-276-9337; FAX: 201-770-2528

Alpha 1 Drop Zone, 2121 N. Tyler, Wichita, KS 67212/316-729-0800

Alpha Gunsmith Division, 1629 Via Monserate, Fallbrook, CA 92028/619-723-9279, 619-728-2663

Alpha Precision, Inc., 2765-B Preston Rd. NE, Good Hope, GA 30641/770-267-6163

Alpine's Precision Gunsmithing & Indoor Shooting Range, 2401 Government Way, Coeur d'Alene, ID 83814/208-765-3559; FAX: 208-765-3559

Altamont Co., 901 N. Church St., P.O. Box 309, Thomasboro, IL 61878/217-643-3125, 800-626-5774; FAX: 217-643-7973

Alumna Sport by Dee Zee, 1572 NE 58th Ave., P.O. Box 3090, Des Moines, IA 50316/800-798-9899

AmBr Software Group Ltd., P.O. Box 301, Reistertown, MD 21136-0301/410-526-4106; FAX: 410-526-7212

American Ammunition, 3545 NW 71st St., Miami FL 33147/305-835-7400; FAX: 305-694-0037

American Arms & Ordnance, Inc., P.O. Box 2691, 1303 S. College Ave., Bryan, TX 77805/409-822-4983

American Arms, Inc., 715 Armour Rd., N. Kansas City, MO 64116/816-474-3161; FAX: 816-474-1225

American Derringer Corp., 127 N. Lacy Dr., Waco, TX 76705/800-642-7817, 817-799-9111; FAX: 817-799-7935

American Display Co., 55 Cromwell St., Providence, RI 02907/401-331-2464; FAX: 401-421-1264

American Gas & Chemical Co., Ltd., 220 Pegasus Ave., Northvale, NJ 07647/201-767-7300

American Gripcraft, 3230 S. Dodge 2, Tucson, AZ 85713/602-790-1222

American Handgunner Magazine, 591 Camino de la Reina, Suite 200, San Diego, CA 92108/619-297-5350; FAX: 619-297-5353

American Pioneer Video, P.O. Box 50049, Bowling Green, KY 42102-2649/800-743-4675

American Products Co., 14729 Spring Valley Road, Morrison, IL 61270/815-772-3336; FAX: 815-772-7921

American Sales & Kirkpatrick, P.O. Box 677, Laredo, TX 78042/210-723-6893; FAX: 210-725-0672

American Security Products Company, 11925 Pacific Ave., Fontana, CA 92337/909-685-9680, 800-421-6142; FAX: 909-685-9685

American Small Arms Academy, P.O. Box 12111, Prescott, AZ 86304/602-778-5623

American Target, 1328 S. Jason St., Denver, CO 80223/303-733-0433; FAX: 303-777-0311

American Whitetail Target Systems, P.O. Box 41, 106 S. Church St., Tennyson, IN 47637/812-567-4527

Americase, P.O. Box 271, 1610 E. Main, Waxahachie, TX 75165/800-880-3629; FAX: 214-937-8373

Ames Metal Products, 4324 S. Western Blvd., Chicago, IL 60609/312-523-3230; FAX: 312-523-3854

Amherst Arms, P.O. Box 1457, Englewood, FL 34295/941-475-2020; FAX: 941-473-1212

Ammo Load, Inc., 1560 E. Edinger, Suite G, Santa Ana, CA 92705/714-558-8858; FAX: 714-569-0319

Amrine's Gun Shop, 937 La Luna, Ojai, CA 93023/805-646-2376

AMT, 6226 Santos Diaz St., Irwindale, CA 91702/818-334-6629; FAX: 818-969-5247

Amtec 2000, Inc., 84 Industrial Rowe, Gardner, MA 01440/508-632-9608; FAX: 508-632-2300

Anderson Manufacturing Co., Inc., 22602 53rd Ave. SE, Bothell, WA 98021/206-481-1858; FAX: 206-481-7839

Anics Firm, Inc., 3 Commerce Park Square, 23200 Chagrin Blvd., Suite 240, Beechwood, OH 44122/216-292-4363, 800-550-1582; FAX: 216-292-2588

Anschutz GmbH, Postfach 1128, D-89001 Ulm, Donau, GERMANY (U.S. importers—Accuracy International; AcuSport Corporation; Champion Shooters' Supply; Champion's Choice; Gunsmithing, Inc.)

Ansen Enterprises, Inc., 1506 W. 228th St., Torrance, CA 90501-5105/310-534-1837; FAX: 310-534-3162

Answer Products Co., 1519 Westbury Drive, Davison, MI 48423/810-653-2911

Anthony and George Ltd., Rt. 1, P.O. Box 45, Evington, VA 24550/804-821-8117

Antique American Firearms (See Carlson, Douglas R.)

Antique Arms Co., 1110 Cleveland Ave., Monett, MO 65708/417-235-6501

Aplan Antiques & Art, James O., HC 80, Box 793-25, Piedmont, SD 57769/605-347-5016

Arco Powder, HC-Rt. 1, P.O. Box 102, County Rd. 357, Mayo, FL 32066/904-294-3882; FAX: 904-294-1498

Arkfeld Mfg. & Dist. Co., Inc., 1230 Monroe Ave., Norfolk, NE 68702-0054/402-371-9430; 800-533-0676

Armament Gunsmithing Co., Inc., 525 Rt. 22, Hillside, NJ 07205/908-686-0960

Armi San Paolo, via Europa 172-A, I-25062 Concesio, 030-2751725 (BS) ITALY

Armite Laboratories, 1845 Randolph St., Los Angeles, CA 90001/213-587-7768; FAX: 213-587-5075

Armor Metal Products, P.O. Box 4609, Helena, MT 59604/406-442-5560

Armory Publications, P.O. Box 4206, Oceanside, CA 92052-4206/619-757-3930; FAX: 619-722-4108

Armoury, Inc., The, Rt. 202, Box 2340, New Preston, CT 06777/203-868-0001

Arms & Armour Press, Ltd., Wellington House, 125 Strand, London WC2R 0BB ENGLAND/0171-420-5555; FAX: 0171-240-7265

Arms Corporation of the Philippines, Bo. Parang Marikina, Metro Manila, PHILIPPINES/632-941-6243, 632-941-6244; FAX: 632-942-0682

Arms, Peripheral Data Systems (See Arms Software)

Arms Software, P.O. Box 1526, Lake Oswego, OR 97035/800-366-5559, 503-697-0533; FAX: 503-697-3337

Arms United Corp., 1018 Cedar St., Niles, MI 49120/616-683-6837

Armscorp USA, Inc., 4424 John Ave., Baltimore, MD 21227/410-247-6200; FAX: 410-247-6205

Armsport, Inc., 3950 NW 49th St., Miami, FL 33142/305-635-7850; FAX: 305-633-2877

Arnold Arms Co., Inc., P.O. Box 1011, Arlington, WA 98223/800-371-1011, 360-435-1011; FAX: 360-435-7304

Aro-Tek, Ltd., 206 Frontage Rd. North, Suite C, Pacific, WA 98047/206-351-2984; FAX: 206-833-4483

Arratoonian, Andy (See Horseshoe Leather Products)

Art Jewel Enterprises Ltd., Eagle Business Ctr., 460 Randy Rd., Carol Stream, IL 60188/708-260-0400

Arundel Arms & Ammunition, Inc., A., 24 Defense St., Annapolis, MD 21401/301-224-8683

Aspen Outdoors, Inc., 1059 W. Market St., York, PA 17404/717-846-0255, 800-677-4780; FAX: 717-845-7447

Astra Sport, S.A., Apartado 3, 48300 Guernica, Espagne, SPAIN/34-4-6250100; FAX: 34-4-6255186 (U.S. importer—E.A.A. Corp.; P.S.M.G. Gun Co.)

A-Tech Corp., P.O. Box 1281, Cottage Grove, OR 97424

Atlantic Mills, Inc., 1325 Washington Ave., Asbury Park, NJ 07712/800-242-7374

Atlantic Rose, Inc., P.O. Box 1305, Union, NJ 07083

Auto Arms, 738 Clearview, San Antonio, TX 78228/512-434-5450

Auto-Ordnance Corp., Williams Lane, West Hurley, NY 12491/914-679-4190; FAX: 914-679-2698

AWC Systems Technology, P.O. Box 41938, Phoenix, AZ 85080-1938/602-780-1050

Aztec International Ltd., P.O. Box 1384, Clarkesville, GA 30523/706-754-7263

B

B&D Trading Co., Inc., 3935 Fair Hill Rd., Fair Oaks, CA 95628/800-334-3790, 916-967-9366; FAX: 916-967-4873

Badger Shooters Supply, Inc., P.O. Box 397, Owen, WI 54460/800-424-9069; FAX: 715-229-2332

Baer Custom, Inc., Les, 29601 34th Ave., Hillsdale, IL 61257/309-658-2716; FAX: 309-658-2610

Bagmaster Mfg., Inc., 2731 Sutton Ave., St. Louis, MO 63143/314-781-8002; FAX: 314-781-3363

Bain & Davis, Inc., 307 E. Valley Blvd., San Gabriel, CA 91776-3522/818-573-4241, 213-283-7449

Baker's Leather Goods, Roy, P.O. Box 893, Magnolia, AR 71753/501-234-0344

Bald Eagle Precision Machine Co., 101-K Allison St., Lock Haven, PA 17745/717-748-6772; FAX: 717-748-4443

Ballard Built, P.O. Box 1443, Kingsville, TX 78364/512-592-0853

Ballistic Engineering & Software, Inc., 185 N. Park Blvd., Suite 330, Lake Orion, MI 48362/313-391-1074

Ballistic Products, Inc., 20015 75th Ave. North, Hamel, MN 55340-9456/612-494-9237; FAX: 612-494-9236

Ballistic Program Co., Inc., The, 2417 N. Patterson St., Thomasville, GA 31792/912-228-5739, 800-368-0835

Ballistic Research, 1108 W. May Ave., McHenry, IL 60050/815-385-0037

Ballistica Maximus North, 107 College Park Plaza, Johnstown, PA 15904/814-266-8380

Ballisti-Cast, Inc., Box 383, Parshall, ND 58770/701-862-3324; FAX: 701-862-3331

Bandcor Industries, Div. of Man-Sew Corp., 6108 Sherwin Dr., Port Richey, FL 34668/813-848-0432

Bang-Bang Boutique (See Holster Shop, The)

Banks, Ed, 2762 Hwy. 41 N., Ft. Valley, GA 31030/912-987-4665

Bansner's Gunsmithing Specialties, 261 East Main St. Box VH, Adamstown, PA 19501/800-368-2379; FAX: 717-484-0523

Barami Corp., 6689 Orchard Lake Rd. No. 148, West Bloomfield, MI 48322/810-738-0462; FAX: 810-855-4084

Barnes Bullets, Inc., P.O. Box 215, American Fork, UT 84003/801-756-4222, 800-574-9200; FAX: 801-756-2465; WEB: http://www.itsnet.com/home/bbullets

Baron Technology, 62 Spring Hill Rd., Trumbull, CT 06611/203-452-0515; FAX: 203-452-0663

Barraclough, John K., 55 Merit Park Dr., Gardena, CA 90247/310-324-2574

Barsotti, Bruce (See River Road Sporting Clays)

Bar-Sto Precision Machine, 73377 Sullivan Rd., P.O. Box 1838, Twentynine Palms, CA 92277/619-367-2747; FAX: 619-367-2407

Bartlett, Don, P.O. Box 55, Colbert, WA 99005/509-467-5009

Bartlett Engineering, 40 South 200 East, Smithfield, UT 84335-1645/801-563-5910; FAX: 801-563-8416

Bates Engraving, Billy, 2302 Winthrop Dr., Decatur, AL 35603/205-355-3690

Baumannize Custom, 4784 Sunrise Hwy., Bohemia, NY 11716/800-472-4387; FAX: 516-567-0001

Bauska Barrels, 105 9th Ave. W., Kalispell, MT 59901/406-752-7706

Bear Hug Grips, Inc., 17230 County Rd. 338, Buena Vista, CO 81211/800-232-7710

Bear Mountain Gun & Tool, 120 N. Plymouth, New Plymouth, ID 83655/208-278-5221; FAX: 208-278-5221

Bear Reloaders, P.O. Box 1613, Akron, OH 44309-1613/216-920-1811

Beartooth Bullets, P.O. Box 491, Dept. HLD, Dover, ID 83825-0491/208-448-1865

Beauchamp & Son, Inc., 160 Rossiter Rd., P.O. Box 181, Richmond, MA 01254/413-698-3822; FAX: 413-698-3866

Beaver Lodge (See Fellowes, Ted)

Beeline Custom Bullets Limited, P.O. Box 85, Yarmouth, Nova Scotia CANADA B5A 4B1/902-648-3494; FAX: 902-648-0253

Beeman Precision Airguns, 5454 Argosy Dr., Huntington Beach, CA 92649/714-890-4800; FAX: 714-890-4808

Behlert Precision, Inc., P.O. Box 288, 7067 Easton Rd., Pipersville, PA 18947/215-766-8681, 215-766-7301; FAX: 215-766-8681

Beitzinger, George, 116-20 Atlantic Ave., Richmond Hill, NY 11419/718-847-7661

Bell Originals, Inc., Sid, 7776 Shackham Rd., Tully, NY 13159-9333/607-842-6431

Bell Reloading, Inc., 1725 Harlin Lane Rd., Villa Rica, GA 30180

Bellm Contenders, P.O. Box 459, Cleveland, UT 84518/801-653-2530

Belltown, Ltd., 11 Camps Rd., Kent, CT 06757/860-354-5750

Belt MTN Arms, 107 10th Ave. SW, White Sulphur Springs, MT 59645/406-586-4495

Ben's Machines, 1151 S. Cedar Ridge, Duncanville, TX 75137/214-780-1807; FAX: 214-780-0316

Benchmark Guns, 12593 S. Ave. 5 East, Yuma, AZ 85365

Bengtson Arms Co., L., 6345-B E. Akron St., Mesa, AZ 85205/602-981-6375

Benjamin/Sheridan Co., Crossman, Rts. 5 and 20, E. Bloomfield, NY 14443/716-657-6161; FAX: 716-657-5405

Bentley, John, 128-D Watson Dr., Turtle Creek, PA 15145

Beomat of America Inc., 300 Railway Ave., Campbell, CA 95008/408-379-4829

Beretta S.p.A., Pietro, Via Beretta, 18-25063 Gardone V.T. (BS) ITALY/XX39/30-8341.1; FAX: XX39/30-8341.421 (U.S. importer—Beretta U.S.A. Corp.)

Beretta U.S.A. Corp., 17601 Beretta Drive, Accokeek, MD 20607/301-283-2191; FAX: 301-283-0435

Bergman & Williams, 2450 Losee Rd., Suite F, Las Vegas, NV 89030/702-642-1901; FAX: 702-642-1540

Bernardelli S.p.A., Vincenzo, 125 Via Matteotti, P.O. Box 74, Gardone V.T., Brescia ITALY, 25063/39-30-8912851-2-3; FAX: 39-30-8910249

Berry's Bullets, Div. of Berry's Mfg., Inc., 401 N. 3050 E., St. George, UT 84770-9004

Berry's Mfg., Inc., 401 North 3050 East St., St. George, UT 84770/801-634-1682; FAX: 801-634-1683

Bersa S.A., Gonzales Castillo 312, 1704 Ramos Mejia, ARGENTINA/541-656-2377; FAX: 541-656-2093 (U.S. importer—Eagle Imports, Inc.)

Bertram Bullet Co., P.O. Box 313, Seymour, Victoria 3660, AUSTRALIA/61-57-922912; FAX: 61-57-991650

Bestload, Inc., Carl Vancini, P.O. Box 4354, Stamford, CT 06907/203-978-0796; FAX: 203-978-0796

Bianchi International, Inc., 100 Calle Cortez, Temecula, CA 92590/909-676-5621; FAX: 909-676-6777

Biesen, Al, 5021 Rosewood, Spokane, WA 99208/509-328-9340

Biesen, Roger, 5021 W. Rosewood, Spokane, WA 99208/509-328-9340

Big Spring Enterprises "Bore Stores", P.O. Box 1115, Big Spring Rd., Yellville, AR 72687/501-449-5297; FAX: 501-449-4446

Bill's Custom Cases, P.O. Box 2, Dunsmuir, CA 96025/916-235-0177; FAX: 916-235-4959

Bill's Gun Repair, 1007 Burlington St., Mendota, IL 61342/815-539-5786

Billingsley & Brownell, P.O. Box 25, Dayton, WY 82836/307-655-9344

Birchwood Casey, 7900 Fuller Rd., Eden Prairie, MN 55344/800-328-6156, 612-937-7933; FAX: 612-937-7979

Birdsong & Assoc., W.E., 1435 Monterey Rd., Florence, MS 39073-9748/601-366-8270

Black Belt Bullets, Big Bore Express Ltd., 7154 W. State St., Suite 200, Boise, ID 83703

Black Hills Ammunition, Inc., P.O. Box 3090, Rapid City, SD 57709-3090/605-348-5150; FAX: 605-348-9827

Black Hills Shooters Supply, P.O. Box 4220, Rapid City, SD 57709/800-289-2506

Black Sheep Brand, 3220 W. Gentry Parkway, Tyler, TX 75702/903-592-3853; FAX: 903-592-0527

Blackhawk East, Box 2274, Loves Park, IL 61131

Blackhawk West, Box 285, Hiawatha, KS 66434

Blacksmith Corp., 830 N. Road No. 1 E., P.O. Box 1752, Chino Valley, AZ 86323/520-636-4456; FAX: 520-636-4457

BlackStar Accurizing, 11501 Brittmoore Park Drive, Houston, TX 77041/713-849-9999; FAX: 713-849-5445

BlackStar AccuMax Barrels (See BlackStar Accurizing)

BlackStar Barrel Accurizing (See BlackStar Accurizing)

Blacktail Mountain Books, 42 First Ave. W., Kalispell, MT 59901/406-257-5573

Blackwell, W. (See Load From a Disk)

Blair Engraving, J.R., P.O. Box 64, Glenrock, WY 82637/307-436-8115

Blammo Ammo, P.O. Box 1677, Seneca, SC 29679/803-882-1768

Bleile, C. Roger, 5040 Ralph Ave., Cincinnati, OH 45238/513-251-0249

Blocker Holsters, Inc., Ted, Clackamas Business Park Bld. A, 14787 S.E. 82nd Dr./Clackamas, OR 97015/503-557-7757; FAX: 503-557-3771

Blue and Gray Products, Inc. (See Ox-Yoke Originals, Inc.)

Blue Book Publications, Inc., One Appletree Square, Minneapolis, MN 55425/800-877-4867, 612-854-5229; FAX: 612-853-1486

Blue Ridge Machinery & Tools, Inc., P.O. Box 536-GD, Hurricane, WV 25526/800-872-6500; FAX: 304-562-5311

Bob's Gun Shop, P.O. Box 200, Royal, AR 71968/501-767-1970

Bob's Tactical Indoor Shooting Range & Gun Shop, 122 Lafayette Rd., Salisbury, MA 01952/508-465-5561

Boessler, Erich, Am Vogeltal 3, 97702 Munnerstadt, GERMANY/9733-9443

Boggs, Wm., 1816 Riverside Dr. C, Columbus, OH 43212/614-486-6965

Bohemia Arms Co., 17101 Los Modelos, Fountain Valley, CA 92708/619-442-7005; FAX: 619-442-7005

Bo-Mar Tool & Mfg. Co., Rt. 12, Box 405, Longview, TX 75605/903-759-4784; FAX: 903-759-9141

Bond Custom Firearms, 8954 N. Lewis Ln., Bloomington, IN 47408/812-332-4519

Bondini Paolo, Via Sorrento, 345, San Carlo di Cesena, ITALY I-47020/0547 663 240; FAX: 0547 663 780

Bone Engraving, Ralph, 718 N. Atlanta, Owasso, OK 74055/918-272-9745

Boone's Custom Ivory Grips, Inc., 562 Coyote Rd., Brinnon, WA 98320/206-796-4330

Bowen Classic Arms Corp., P.O. Box 67, Louisville, TN 37777/615-984-3583

Boyds' Gunstock Industries, Inc., 3rd & Main, P.O. Box 305, Geddes, SD 57342/605-337-2125; FAX: 605-337-3363

Boyt, 509 Hamilton, P.O. Drawer 668, Iowa Falls, IA 50126/515-648-4626; FAX: 515-648-2385

Brace, Larry D., 771 Blackfoot Ave., Eugene, OR 97404/503-688-1278

Brass Eagle, Inc., 7050A Bramalea Rd., Unit 19, Mississauga, Ont. L4Z 1C7, CANADA/416-848-4844

Brass-Tech Industries, P.O. Box 521-v, Wharton, NJ 07885/201-366-8540

Bratcher, Dan, 311 Belle Air Pl., Carthage, MO 64836/417-358-1518

Brauer Bros. Mfg. Co., 2020 Delman Blvd., St. Louis, MO 63103/314-231-2864; FAX: 314-249-4952

Braun, M., 32, rue Notre-Dame, 2440 LUXEMBURG

Braverman Corp., R.J., 88 Parade Rd., Meridith, NH 03293/800-736-4867

Break-Free, Inc., P.O. Box 25020, Santa Ana, CA 92799/714-953-1900; FAX: 714-953-0402

Bridgers Best, P.O. Box 1410, Berthoud, CO 80513

Briese Bullet Co., Inc., RR1, Box 108, Tappen, ND 58487/701-327-4578; FAX: 701-327-4579

Briganti & Co., A., 475 Rt. 32, Highland Mills, NY 10930/914-928-9573

Briley Mfg., Inc., 1230 Lumpkin, Houston, TX 77043/800-331-5718, 713-932-6995; FAX: 713-932-1043

British Antiques, P.O. Box 7, Latham, NY 12110/518-783-0773

BRNO (See U.S. importers—Bohemia Arms Co.; Magnum Research, Inc.)

Broad Creek Rifle Works, 120 Horsey Ave., Laurel, DE 19956/302-875-5446

Brobst, Jim, 299 Poplar St., Hamburg, PA 19526/215-562-2103

Brockman's Custom Gunsmithing, P.O. Box 357, Gooding, ID 83330/208-934-5050

Broken Gun Ranch, 10739 126 Rd., Spearville, KS 67876/316-385-2587; FAX: 316-385-2597

Brolin Arms, 2755 Thompson Creek Rd., Pomona, CA 91767/909-392-2352; FAX: 909-392-2354

Brooker, Dennis, Rt. 1, Box 12A, Derby, IA 50068/515-533-2103

Brooks Tactical Systems, 279-A Shorewood Ct., Fox Island, WA 98333/800-410-4747; FAX: 206-572-6797

Brown Co., E. Arthur, 3404 Pawnee Dr., Alexandria, MN 56308/612-762-8847

Brown, H.R. (See Silhouette Leathers)

Brown Products, Inc., Ed, Rt. 2, Box 492, Perry, MO 63462/573-565-3261; FAX: 573-565-2791

Brownell Checkering Tools, W.E., 9390 Twin Mountain Circle, San Diego, CA 92126/619-695-2479; FAX: 619-695-2479

Brownells, Inc., 200 S. Front St., Montezuma, IA 50171/515-623-5401; FAX: 515-623-3896

Browning Arms Co. (Gen. Offices), One Browning Place, Morgan, UT 84050/801-876-2711; FAX: 801-876-3331

Browning Arms Co. (Parts & Service), 3005 Arnold Tenbrook Rd., Arnold, MO 63010-9406/314-287-6800; FAX: 314-287-9751

BRP, Inc. High Performance Cast Bullets, 1210 Alexander Rd., Colorado Springs, CO 80909/719-633-0658

Bruno Shooters Supply, 111 N. Wyoming St., Hazleton, PA 18201/717-455-2281; FAX: 717-455-2211

Brunton U.S.A., 620 E. Monroe Ave., Riverton, WY 82501/307-856-6559; FAX: 307-856-1840

Brynin, Milton, P.O. Box 383, Yonkers, NY 10710/914-779-4333

BSA Guns Ltd., Armoury Rd. Small Heath, Birmingham, ENGLAND B11 2PX/011-021-772-8543; FAX: 011-021-773-0845

B-Square Company, Inc., P.O. Box 11281, 2708 St. Louis Ave., Ft. Worth, TX 76110/817-923-0964, 800-433-2909; FAX: 817-926-7012

Bucheimer, J.M., Jumbo Sports Products, 721 N. 20th St., St. Louis, MO 63103/314-241-1020

Buck Stix—SOS Products Co., Box 3, Neenah, WI 54956

Buckhorn Gun Works, 8109 Woodland Dr., Black Hawk, SD 57718/605-787-6472

Buckskin Bullet Co., P.O. Box 1893, Cedar City, UT 84721/801-586-3286

Buffalo Arms, 123 S. Third, Suite 6, Sandpoint, ID 83864/208-263-6953; FAX: 208-265-2096

Bull Mountain Rifle Co., 6327 Golden West Terrace, Billings, MT 59106/406-656-0778

Bullberry Barrel Works, Ltd., 2430 W. Bullberry Ln. 67-5, Hurricane, UT 84737/801-635-9866

Bullet, Inc., 3745 Hiram Alworth Rd., Dallas, GA 30132

Bullet Swaging Supply, Inc., P.O. Box 1056, 303 McMillan Rd, West Monroe, LA 71291/318-387-7257; FAX: 318-387-7779

BulletMakers Workshop, The, RFD 1 Box 1755, Brooks, ME 04921

Bullseye Bullets, 1610 State Road 60, No. 12, Valrico, FL 33594/813-654-6563

Bull-X, Inc., 520 N. Main, Farmer City, IL 61842/309-928-2574, 800-248-3845 orders only; FAX: 309-928-2130

Burgess, Byron, P.O. Box 6853, Los Osos, CA 93412/805-528-1005

Burgess & Son Gunsmiths, R.W., P.O. Box 3364, Warner Robins, GA 31099/912-328-7487

Burris Co., Inc., P.O. Box 1747, 331 E. 8th St., Greeley, CO 80631/970-356-1670; FAX: 970-356-8702

Bushmaster Firearms (See Quality Parts Co./Bushmaster Firearms)

Bushmaster Hunting & Fishing, 451 Alliance Ave., Toronto, Ont. M6N 2J1 CANADA/416-763-4040; FAX: 416-763-0623

Bushnell (See Bausch & Lomb)

Bushwacker Backpack & Supply Co. (See Counter Assault)

Bustani, Leo, P.O. Box 8125, W. Palm Beach, FL 33407/305-622-2710

Butler Creek Corporation, 290 Arden Dr., Belgrade, MT 59714/800-423-8327, 406-388-1356; FAX: 406-388-7204

Butler Enterprises, 834 Oberting Rd., Lawrenceburg, IN 47025/812-537-3584

Butterfield & Butterfield, 220 San Bruno Ave., San Francisco, CA 94103/415-861-7500

Buzztail Brass (See Grayback Wildcats)

B-West Imports, Inc., 2425 N. Huachuca Dr., Tucson, AZ 85745-1201/602-628-1990; FAX: 602-628-3602

C

C3 Systems, 678 Killingly St., Johnston, RI 02919

C&D Special Products (See Claybuster Wads & Harvester Bullets)

Cabela's, 812-13th Ave., Sidney, NE 69160/308-254-6644; FAX: 308-254-6669

Cabinet Mtn. Outfitters Scents & Lures, P.O. Box 766, Plains, MT 59859/406-826-3970

Cache La Poudre Rifleworks, 140 N. College, Ft. Collins, CO 80524/303-482-6913

Calibre Press, Inc., 666 Dundee Rd., Suite 1607, Northbrook, IL 60062-2760/800-323-0037; FAX: 708-498-6869

Calico Light Weapon Systems, 405 E. 19th St., Bakersfield, CA 93305/805-323-1327; FAX: 805-323-7844

California Sights (See Fautheree, Andy)

Camdex, Inc., 2330 Alger, Troy, MI 48083/810-528-2300; FAX: 810-528-0989

Cameron's, 16690 W. 11th Ave., Golden, CO 80401/303-279-7365; FAX: 303-628-5413

Camilli, Lou, 4700 Oahu Dr. NE, Albuquerque, NM 87111/505-293-5259

Campbell, Dick, 20,000 Silver Ranch Rd., Conifer, CO 80433/303-697-0150

Camp-Cap Products, P.O. Box 173, Chesterfield, MO 63006/314-532-4340; FAX: 314-532-4340

Cannon's Guns, Box 1036, 320 Main St., Polson, MT 59860/406-887-2048

Cannon Safe, Inc., 9358 Stephens St., Pico Rivera, CA 90660/310-692-0636, 800-242-1055; FAX: 310-692-7252

Canons Delcour, Rue J.B. Cools, B-4040 Herstal, BELGIUM 32.(0)41.40.61.40; FAX: 32(0)412.40.22.88

Canyon Cartridge Corp., P.O. Box 152, Albertson, NY 11507/FAX: 516-294-8946

Cape Outfitters, 599 County Rd. 206, Cape Girardeau, MO 63701/314-335-4103; FAX: 314-335-1555

Caraville Manufacturing, P.O. Box 4545, Thousand Oaks, CA 91359/805-499-1234

Carbide Checkering Tools (See J&R Engineering)

Carbide Die & Mfg. Co., Inc., 15615 E. Arrow Hwy., Irwindale, CA 91706/818-337-2518

Carlson, Douglas R., Antique American Firearms, P.O. Box 71035, Dept. GD, Des Moines, IA 50325/515-224-6552

Carnahan Bullets, 17645 110th Ave. SE, Renton, WA 98055

Carter's Gun Shop, 225 G St., Penrose, CO 81240/719-372-6240

Carvajal Belts & Holsters, 422 Chestnut, San Antonio, TX 78202/210-222-1634

Cascade Bullet Co., Inc., 2355 South 6th St., Klamath Falls, OR 97601/503-884-9316

Case & Sons Cutlery Co., W.R., Owens Way, Bradford, PA 16701/814-368-4123, 800-523-6350; FAX: 814-768-5369

Cash Mfg. Co., Inc., P.O. Box 130, 201 S. Klein Dr., Waunakee, WI 53597-0130/608-849-5664; FAX: 608-849-5664

Caspian Arms Ltd., 14 North Main St., Hardwick, VT 05843/802-472-6454; FAX: 802-472-6709

Caswell International Corp., 1221 Marshall St. NE, Minneapolis, MN 55413-1055/612-379-2000; FAX: 612-379-2367

Cathey Enterprises, Inc., P.O. Box 2202, Brownwood, TX 76804/915-643-2553; FAX: 915-643-3653

CBC, Avenida Humberto de Campos, 3220, 09400-000 Ribeirao Pires-SP-BRAZIL/55-11-742-7500; FAX: 55-11-459-7385

CCI, Div. of Blount, Inc., Sporting Equipment Div., 2299 Snake River Ave.,, P.O. Box 856/Lewiston, ID 83501/800-627-3640, 208-746-2351; FAX: 208-746-2915

Celestron International, P.O. Box 3578, 2835 Columbia St., Torrance, CA 90503/310-328-9560; FAX: 310-212-5835

Centaur Systems, Inc., 1602 Foothill Rd., Kalispell, MT 59901/406-755-8609; FAX: 406-755-8609

Center Lock Scope Rings, 9901 France Ct., Lakeville, MN 55044/612-461-2114

CenterMark, P.O. Box 4066, Parnassus Station, New Kensington, PA 15068/412-335-1319

Central Specialties Ltd., 1122 Silver Lake Road, Cary, IL 60013/708-639-3900; FAX: 708-639-3972

Century Gun Dist., Inc., 1467 Jason Rd., Greenfield, IN 46140/317-462-4524

Century International Arms, Inc., P.O. Box 714, St. Albans, VT 05478-0714/802-527-1252; FAX: 802-527-0470; WEB: http://www.generation.net/~century

CF Ventures, 509 Harvey Dr., Bloomington, IN 47403-1715

C-H Tool & Die Corp. (See 4-D Custom Die Co.)

CHAA, Ltd., P.O. Box 565, Howell, MI 48844/800-677-8737; FAX: 313-894-6930

Chace Leather Products, 507 Alden St., Fall River, MA 02722/508-678-7556; FAX: 508-675-9666

Chadick's Ltd., P.O. Box 100, Terrell, TX 75160/214-563-7577

Chambers Flintlocks Ltd., Jim, Rt. 1, Box 513-A, Candler, NC 28715/704-667-8361

Champion Target Co., 232 Industrial Parkway, Richmond, IN 47374/800-441-4971

Champion's Choice, Inc., 201 International Blvd., LaVergne, TN 37086/615-793-4066; FAX: 615-793-4070

Champlin Firearms, Inc., P.O. Box 3191, Woodring Airport, Enid, OK 73701/405-237-7388; FAX: 405-242-6922

Chapman Academy of Practical Shooting, 4350 Academy Rd., Hallsville, MO 65255/573-696-5544, 573-696-2266

Chapman Manufacturing Co., 471 New Haven Rd., P.O. Box 250, Durham, CT 06422/203-349-9228; FAX: 203-349-0084

Checkmate Refinishing, 370 Champion Dr., Brooksville, FL 34601/904-799-5774

Cheddite France, S.A., 99, Route de Lyon, F-26500 Bourg-les-Valence, FRANCE/33-75-56-4545; FAX: 33-75-56-3587

Chelsea Gun Club of New York City, Inc., 237 Ovington Ave., Apt. D53, Brooklyn, NY 11209/718-836-9422, 718-833-2704

Chem-Pak, Inc., 11 Oates Ave., P.O. Box 1685, Winchester, VA 22604/800-336-9828, 703-667-1341; FAX: 703-722-3993

CheVron Bullets, RR1, Ottawa, IL 61350/815-433-2471

CheVron Case Master (See CheVron Bullets)

Choate Machine & Tool Co., Inc., P.O. Box 218, 116 Lovers Ln., Bald Knob, AR 72010/501-724-6193, 800-972-6390; FAX: 501-724-5873

Chopie Mfg., Inc., 700 Copeland Ave., LaCrosse, WI 54603/608-784-0926

Christie's East, 219 E. 67th St., New York, NY 10021/212-606-0400

Christman Jr., David, 937 Lee Hedrick Rd., Colville, WA 99114/509-684-5686 days; 509-684-3314 evenings

Chronotech, 1655 Siamet Rd. Unit 6, Mississauga, Ont. L4W 1Z4 CANADA/905-625-5200; FAX: 905-625-5190

Chuck's Gun Shop, P.O. Box 597, Waldo, FL 32694/904-468-2264

Churchill, Winston, Twenty Mile Stream Rd., RFD P.O. Box 29B, Proctorsville, VT 05153/802-226-7772

Churchill Glove Co., James, P.O. Box 298, Centralia, WA 98531

Cimarron Arms, P.O. Box 906, Fredericksburg, TX 78624-0906/210-997-9090; FAX: 210-997-0802

C.J. Ballistics, Inc., P.O. Box 132, Acme, WA 98220/206-595-5001

Clark Co., Inc., David, P.O. Box 15054, Worcester, MA 01615-0054/508-756-6216; FAX: 508-753-5827

Clark Custom Guns, Inc., 336 Shootout Lane, Princeton, LA 71067/318-949-9884; FAX: 318-949-9829

Clark Firearms Engraving, P.O. Box 80746, San Marino, CA 91118/818-287-1652

Classic Brass, 14 Grove St., Plympton, MA 02367/FAX: 617-585-5673

Classic Guns, Inc., Frank S. Wood, 3230 Medlock Bridge Rd., Suite 110, Norcross, GA 30092/404-242-7944

Claybuster Wads & Harvester Bullets, 309 Sequoya Dr., Hopkinsville, KY 42240/800-922-6287, 800-284-1746, 502-885-8088; FAX: 502-885-1951

Clearview Mfg. Co., Inc., 413 S. Oakley St., Fordyce, AR 71742/501-352-8557; FAX: 501-352-8557

Clements' Custom Leathercraft, Chas, 1741 Dallas St., Aurora, CO 80010-2018/303-364-0403

Clenzoil Corp., P.O. Box 80226, Sta. C, Canton, OH 44708-0226/330-833-9758; FAX: 330-833-4724

Clerke Co., J.A., P.O. Box 627, Pearblossom, CA 93553-0627/805-945-0713

Clift Mfg., L.R., 3821 Hammonton Rd., Marysville, CA 95901/916-755-3390; FAX: 916-755-3393

Clift Welding Supply & Cases, 1332-A Colusa Hwy., Yuba City, CA 95993/916-755-3390; FAX: 916-755-3393

Clymer Manufacturing Co., Inc., 1645 W. Hamlin Rd., Rochester Hills, MI 48309-1530/810-853-5555, 810-853-5627; FAX: 810-853-1530

C-More Systems, P.O. Box 1750, 7553 Gary Rd., Manassas, VA 22110/703-361-2663; FAX: 703-361-5881

Coats, Mrs. Lester, 300 Luman Rd., Space 125, Phoenix, OR 97535/503-535-1611

Cobra Gunskin, 133-30 32nd Ave., Flushing, NY 11354/718-762-8181; FAX: 718-762-0890

Cobra Sport s.r.l., Via Caduti Nei Lager No. 1, 56020 San Romano, Montopoli v/Arno (Pi), ITALY/0039-571-450490; FAX: 0039-571-450492

Cogar's Gunsmithing, P.O. Box 755, Houghton Lake, MI 48629/517-422-4591

Cole's Gun Works, Old Bank Building, Rt. 4, Box 250, Moyock, NC 27958/919-435-2345

Cole-Grip, 16135 Cohasset St., Van Nuys, CA 91406/818-782-4424

Collings, Ronald, 1006 Cielta Linda, Vista, CA 92083

Colonial Arms, Inc., P.O. Box 636, Selma, AL 36702-0636/334-872-9455; FAX: 334-872-9540

Colonial Repair, P.O. Box 372, Hyde Park, MA 02136-9998/617-469-4951

Colorado Gunsmithing Academy Lamar, 27533 Highway 287 South, Lamar, CO 81052/719-336-4099

Colorado School of Trades, 1575 Hoyt St., Lakewood, CO 80215/800-234-4594; FAX: 303-233-4723

Colorado Shooter's Supply, 1163 W. Paradise Way, Fruita, CO 81521/303-858-9191

Colorado Sutlers Arsenal (See Cumberland States Arsenal)

Colt Blackpowder Arms Co., 5 Centre Market Place, New York, NY 10013/212-925-2159; FAX: 212-966-4986

Colt's Mfg. Co., Inc., P.O. Box 1868, Hartford, CT 06144-1868/800-962-COLT, 203-236-6311; FAX: 203-244-1449

Combat Military Ordnance Ltd., 3900 Hopkins St., Savannah, GA 31405/912-238-1900; FAX: 912-236-7570

Competition Electronics, Inc., 3469 Precision Dr., Rockford, IL 61109/815-874-8001; FAX: 815-874-8181

Competitor Corp., Inc., Appleton Business Center, 30 Tricnit Road, Unit 16, New Ipswich, NH 03071-0508/603-878-3891; FAX: 603-878-3950

Conetrol Scope Mounts, 10225 Hwy. 123 S., Seguin, TX 78155/210-379-3030, 800-CONETROL; FAX: 210-379-3030

CONKKO, P.O. Box 40, Broomall, PA 19008/215-356-0711

Cook Engineering Service, 891 Highbury Rd., Vermont VICT 3133 AUSTRALIA

Coonan Arms (JS Worldwide DBA), 1745 Hwy. 36 E., Maplewood, MN 55109/612-777-3156; FAX: 612-777-3683

Cooper-Woodward, 3800 Pelican Rd., Helena, MT 59601/406-458-3800

Corbin, Inc., 600 Industrial Circle, P.O. Box 2659, White City, OR 97503/541-826-5211; FAX: 541-826-8669

Cor-Bon Bullet & Ammo Co., 1311 Industry Rd., Sturgis, SD 57785/800-626-7266; FAX: 800-923-2666

Corkys Gun Clinic, 4401 Hot Springs Dr., Greeley, CO 80634-9226/970-330-0516

Corry, John, 861 Princeton Ct., Neshanic Station, NJ 08853/908-369-8019

Costa, David, Island Pond Gun Shop, P.O. Box 428, Cross St., Island Pond, VT 05846/802-723-4546

Counter Assault, Box 4721, Missoula, MT 59806/406-728-6241; FAX: 406-728-8800

Country Armourer, The, P.O. Box .308, Ashby, MA 01431-0308/508-827-6797; FAX: 508-827-4845

Cousin Bob's Mountain Products, 7119 Ohio River Blvd., Ben Avon, PA 15202/412-766-5114; FAX: 412-766-5114

CQB Training, P.O. Box 1739, Manchester, MO 63011

Craftguard, 3624 Logan Ave., Waterloo, IA 50703/319-232-2959; FAX: 319-234-0804

Craig Custom Ltd., Research & Development, 629 E. 10th, Hutchinson, KS 67501/316-669-0601

Crandall Tool & Machine Co., 19163 21 Mile Rd., Tustin, MI 49688/616-829-4430

Crane & Crane Ltd., 105 N. Edison Way 6, Reno, NV 89502-2355/702-856-1516; FAX: 702-856-1616

Crawford Co., Inc., R.M., P.O. Box 277, Everett, PA 15537/814-652-6536; FAX: 814-652-9526

CRDC Laser Systems Group, 3972 Barranca Parkway, Ste. J-484, Irvine, CA 92714/714-586-1295; FAX: 714-831-4823

Creative Cartridge Co., 56 Morgan Rd., Canton, CT 06019/203-693-2529

Creedmoor Sports, Inc., P.O. Box 1040, Oceanside, CA 92051/619-757-5529

Creek Side Metal & Woodcrafters (See Allard, Gary)

Crit'R Call, Box 999G, La Porte, CO 80535/970-484-2768; FAX: 970-484-0807

Crosman Airguns, Rts. 5 and 20, E. Bloomfield, NY 14443/716-657-6161; FAX: 716-657-5405

Crosman Products of Canada Ltd., 1173 N. Service Rd. West, Oakville, Ontario, L6M 2V9 CANADA/905-827-1822

Crouse's Country Cover, P.O. Box 160, Storrs, CT 06268/860-423-8736

Cullity Restoration, Daniel, 209 Old County Rd., East Sandwich, MA 02537/508-888-1147

Cumberland Arms, 514 Shafer Road, Manchester, TN 37355/800-797-8414

Cumberland Knife & Gun Works, 5661 Bragg Blvd., Fayetteville, NC 28303/919-867-0009

Cumberland States Arsenal, 1124 Palmyra Road, Clarksville, TN 37040

Cummings Bullets, 1417 Esperanza Way, Escondido, CA 92027

Cunningham Co., Eaton, 607 Superior St., Kansas City, MO 64106/816-842-2600

Cupp, Alana, Custom Engraver, P.O. Box 207, Annabella, UT 84711/801-896-4834

Curtis Custom Shop, RR1, Box 193A, Wallingford, KY 41093/703-659-4265

Curtis Gun Shop, Dept. ST, 119 W. College, Bozeman, MT 59715/406-587-4934

Custom Checkering Service, Kathy Forster, 2124 SE Yamhill St., Portland, OR 97214/503-236-5874

Custom Chronograph, Inc., 5305 Reese Hill Rd., Sumas, WA 98295/360-988-7801

Custom Firearms (See Ahrends, Kim)

Custom Gun Products, 5021 W. Rosewood, Spokane, WA 99208/509-328-9340

Custom Gunsmiths, 4303 Friar Lane, Colorado Springs, CO 80907/719-599-3366

Custom Products (See Jones Custom Products, Neil A.)

Custom Tackle and Ammo, P.O. Box 1886, Farmington, NM 87499/505-632-3539

Cutsinger Bench Rest Bullets, RR 8, Box 161-A, Shelbyville, IN 46176/317-729-5360

CVA, 5988 Peachtree Corners East, Norcross, GA 30071/800-251-9412; FAX: 404-242-8546

Cylinder & Slide, Inc., William R. Laughridge, 245 E. 4th St., Fremont, NE 68025/402-721-4277; FAX: 402-721-0263

CZ (See U.S. importer—Magnum Research, Inc.)

D

D&D Gunsmiths, Ltd., 363 E. Elmwood, Troy, MI 48083/810-583-1512; FAX: 810-583-1524

D&H Precision Tooling, 7522 Barnard Mill Rd., Ringwood, IL 60072/815-653-4011

D&H Prods. Co., Inc., 465 Denny Rd., Valencia, PA 16059/412-898-2840, 800-776-0281; FAX: 412-898-2013

D&J Bullet Co. & Custom Gun Shop, Inc., 426 Ferry St., Russell, KY 41169/606-836-2663; FAX: 606-836-2663

D&L Industries (See D.J. Marketing)

D&L Sports, P.O. Box 651, Gillette, WY 82717/307-686-4008

Dade Screw Machine Products, 2319 NW 7th Ave., Miami, FL 33147/305-573-5050

Daewoo Precision Industries Ltd., 34-3 Yeoeuido-Dong, Yeongdeungoo-GU, 15th, Fl./Seoul, KOREA (U.S. importer—Nationwide Sports Distributors)

Daisy Mfg. Co., P.O. Box 220, Rogers, AR 72757/501-636-1200; FAX: 501-636-1601

Dakota Arms, Inc., HC 55, Box 326, Sturgis, SD 57785/605-347-4686; FAX: 605-347-4459

Dan's Whetstone Co., Inc., 130 Timbs Place, Hot Springs, AR 71913/501-767-1616; FAX: 501-767-9598

Dangler, Homer L., Box 254, Addison, MI 49220/517-547-6745

Dapkus Co., Inc., J.G., Commerce Circle, P.O. Box 293, Durham, CT 06422

Dara-Nes, Inc. (See Nesci Enterprises, Inc.)

Data Tech Software Systems, 19312 East Eldorado Drive, Aurora, CO 80013

Datumtech Corp., 2275 Wehrle Dr., Buffalo, NY 14221

Davidson, Jere, Rt. 1, Box 132, Rustburg, VA 24588/804-821-3637

Davis, Don, 1619 Heights, Katy, TX 77493/713-391-3090

Davis Co., R.E., 3450 Pleasantville NE, Pleasantville, OH 43148/614-654-9990

Davis Industries, 15150 Sierra Bonita Ln., Chino, CA 91710/909-597-4726; FAX: 909-393-9771

Davis Leather Co., G. Wm., 3990 Valley Blvd., Unit D, Walnut, CA 91789/909-598-5620

Davis Products, Mike, 643 Loop Dr., Moses Lake, WA 98837/509-765-6178, 509-766-7281 orders only

Davis Service Center, Bill, 7221 Florin Mall Dr., Sacramento, CA 95823/916-393-4867

Day & Sons, Inc., Leonard, P.O. Box 122, Flagg Hill Rd., Heath, MA 01346/413-337-8369

Dayson Arms Ltd., P.O. Box 532, Vincennes, IN 47591/812-882-8680; FAX: 812-882-8446

Dayton Traister, 4778 N. Monkey Hill Rd., P.O. Box 593, Oak Harbor, WA 98277/206-679-4657; FAX:206-675-1114

DBI Books, Division of Krause Publications, 4092 Commercial Ave., Northbrook, IL 60062/847-272-6310; FAX: 847-272-2051; For consumer orders, see Krause Publications

D.C.C. Enterprises, 259 Wynburn Ave., Athens, GA 30601

Dead Eye's Sport Center, RD 1, Box 147B, Shickshinny, PA 18655/717-256-7432

Decker Shooting Products, 1729 Laguna Ave., Schofield, WI 54476/715-359-5873

Defense Training International, Inc., 749 S. Lemay, Ste. A3-337, Ft. Collins, CO 80524/303-482-2520; FAX: 303-482-0548

deHaas Barrels, RR 3, Box 77, Ridgeway, MO 64481/816-872-6308

Del Rey Products, P.O. Box 91561, Los Angeles, CA 90009/213-823-0494

Delhi Gun House, 1374 Kashmere Gate, Delhi, INDIA 110 006/(011)237375 239116; FAX: 91-11-2917344

Delorge, Ed, 2231 Hwy. 308, Thibodaux, LA 70301/504-447-1633

Delta Arms Ltd., P.O. Box 1000, Delta, VT 84624-1000

Delta Frangible Ammunition, LLC, 1111 Jefferson Davis Hwy., Suite 508, Arlington, VA 22202/703-416-4928; FAX: 703-416-4934

Dem-Bart Checkering Tools, Inc., 6807 Bickford Ave., Old Hwy. 2, Snohomish, WA 98290/360-568-7356; FAX: 360-568-1798

Denver Bullets, Inc., 1811 W. 13th Ave., Denver, CO 80204/303-893-3146; FAX: 303-893-9161

Denver Instrument Co., 6542 Fig St., Arvada, CO 80004/800-321-1135, 303-431-7255; FAX: 303-423-4831

DeSantis Holster & Leather Goods, Inc., P.O. Box 2039, 149 Denton Ave., New Hyde Park, NY 11040-0701/516-354-8000; FAX: 516-354-7501

Desert Industries, Inc., P.O. Box 93443, Las Vegas, NV 89193-3443/702-597-1066; FAX: 702-871-9452

Desert Mountain Mfg., P.O. Box 2767, Columbia Falls, MT 59912/800-477-0762, 406-892-7772; FAX: 406-892-7772

Desquesnes, Gerald (See Napoleon Bonaparte, Inc.)

Detroit-Armor Corp., 720 Industrial Dr. No. 112, Cary, IL 60013/708-639-7666; FAX: 708-639-7694

Dever Co., Jack, 8590 NW 90, Oklahoma City, OK 73132/405-721-6393

Dewey Mfg. Co., Inc., J., P.O. Box 2014, Southbury, CT 06488/203-264-3064; FAX: 203-262-6907

DGR Custom Rifles, RR1, Box 8A, Tappen, ND 58487/701-327-8135

DGS, Inc., Dale A. Storey, 1117 E. 12th, Casper, WY 82601/307-237-2414

Diamond Mfg. Co., P.O. Box 174, Wyoming, PA 18644/800-233-9601

Diamondback Supply, 2431 Juan Tabo, Suite 163, Albuquerque, NM 87112/505-237-0068

Diana (See U.S. importer—Dynamit Nobel-RWS, Inc.)

Dibble, Derek A., 555 John Downey Dr., New Britain, CT 06051/203-224-2630

Dietz Gun Shop & Range, Inc., 421 Range Rd., New Braunfels, TX 78132/210-885-4662

Dilliott Gunsmithing, Inc., 657 Scarlett Rd., Dandridge, TN 37725/615-397-9204

Dillon Precision Products, Inc., 8009 East Dillon's Way, Scottsdale, AZ 85260/602-948-8009, 800-762-3845; FAX: 602-998-2786

Dixie Gun Works, Inc., Hwy. 51 South, Union City, TN 38261/901-885-0561, order 800-238-6785; FAX: 901-885-0440

Dixon Muzzleloading Shop, Inc., RD 1, Box 175, Kempton, PA 19529/610-756-6271

D.J. Marketing, 10602 Horton Ave., Downey, CA 90241/310-806-0891; FAX: 310-806-6231

DKT, Inc., 14623 Vera Drive, Union, MI 49130-9744/616-641-7120; FAX: 616-641-2015

D-Max, Inc., RR1, Box 473, Bagley, MN 56621/218-785-2278

Dohring Bullets, 100 W. 8 Mile Rd., Ferndale, MI 48220

Dolbare, Elizabeth, P.O. Box 222, Sunburst, MT 59482-0222

Doskocil Mfg. Co., Inc., P.O. Box 1246, 4209 Barnett, Arlington, TX 76017/817-467-5116; FAX: 817-472-9810

Double A Ltd., Dept. ST, Box 11306, Minneapolis, MN 55411

Dowtin Gunworks, Rt. 4, Box 930A, Flagstaff, AZ 86001/602-779-1898

Drain, Mark, SE 3211 Kamilche Point Rd., Shelton, WA 98584/206-426-5452

Dremel Mfg. Co., 4915-21st St., Racine, WI 53406

Dropkick, 1460 Washington Blvd., Williamsport, PA 17701/717-326-6561; FAX: 717-326-4950

Duane's Gun Repair (See DGR Custom Rifles)

Dubber, Michael W., P.O. Box 312, Evansville, IN 47702/812-424-9000; FAX: 812-424-6551

Duffy (See Guns Antique & Modern DBA/Charles E. Duffy)

Du-Lite Corp., Charles E., 171 River Rd., Middletown, CT 06457/203-347-2505; FAX: 203-347-9404

Duncan's Gun Works, Inc., 1619 Grand Ave., San Marcos, CA 92069/619-727-0515

DuPont (See IMR Powder Co.)

Dutchman's Firearms, Inc., The, 4143 Taylor Blvd., Louisville, KY 40215/502-366-0555

Dykstra, Doug, 411 N. Darling, Fremont, MI 49412/616-924-3950

Dynamit Nobel-RWS, Inc., 81 Ruckman Rd., Closter, NJ 07624/201-767-7971; FAX: 201-767-1589

Dyson & Son Ltd., Peter, 29-31 Church St., Honley Huddersfield, W. Yorkshire HD7 2AH, ENGLAND/44-1484-661062; FAX: 44-1484-663709

E

E&L Mfg., Inc., 4177 Riddle by Pass Rd., Riddle, OR 97469/541-874-2137; FAX: 541-874-3107

E.A.A. Corp., P.O. Box 1299, Sharpes, FL 32959/407-639-4842, 800-536-4442; FAX: 407-639-7006

Eagan, Donald V., P.O. Box 196, Benton, PA 17814/717-925-6134

Eagle Imports, Inc., 1750 Brielle Ave., Unit B1, Wanamassa, NJ 07712/908-493-0333; FAX: 908-493-0301

Eagle International, Inc., 5195 W. 58th Ave., Suite 300, Arvada, CO 80002/303-426-8100; FAX: 303-426-5475

Eagle Mfg. & Engineering, 2648 Keen Dr., San Diego, CA 92139/619-479-4402; FAX: 619-472-5585

E-A-R, Inc., Div. of Cabot Safety Corp., 5457 W. 79th St., Indianapolis, IN 46268/800-327-3431; FAX: 800-488-8007

Easy Pull Outlaw Products, 316 1st St. East, Polson, MT 59860/406-883-6822

Echols & Co., D'Arcy, 164 W. 580 S., Providence, UT 84332/801-753-2367

Ed's Gun House, Rt. 1, Box 62, Minnesota City, MN 55959/507-689-2925

Eezox, Inc., P.O. Box 772, Waterford, CT 06385-0772/860-447-8282, 800-462-3331; FAX: 860-447-3484

EGW Evolution Gun Works, 4050 B-8 Skyron Dr., Doylestown, PA 18901/215-348-9892; FAX: 215-348-1056

Eichelberger Bullets, Wm., 158 Crossfield Rd., King of Prussia, PA 19406

Ekol Leather Care, P.O. Box 2652, West Lafayette, IN 47906/317-463-2250; FAX: 317-463-7004

El Dorado Leather, P.O. Box 2603, Tucson, AZ 85702/520-586-4791; FAX: 520-586-4791

El Paso Saddlery Co., P.O. Box 27194, El Paso, TX 79926/915-544-2233; FAX: 915-544-2535

Electronic Shooters Protection, Inc., 11997 West 85th Place, Arvada, CO 80005/303-456-8964; 800-797-7791

Electronic Trigger Systems, Inc., P.O. Box 13, 230 Main St. S., Hector, MN 55342/612-848-2760

Eley Ltd., P.O. Box 705, Witton, Birmingham, B6 7UT, ENGLAND/021-356-8899; FAX: 021-331-4173

Elkhom Bullets, P.O. Box 5293, Central Point, OR 97502/541-826-7440

Elko Arms, Dr. L. Kortz, 28 rue Ecole Moderne, B-7060 Soignies, BELGIUM/(32)67-33-29-34

Ellicott Arms, Inc./Woods Pistolsmithing, 3840 Dahlgren Ct., Ellicott City, MD 21042/410-465-7979

Elliott Inc., G.W., 514 Burnside Ave., East Hartford, CT 06108/203-289-5741; FAX: 203-289-3137

Emerging Technologies, Inc. (See Laseraim Technologies, Inc.)

EMF Co., Inc., 1900 E. Warner Ave. Suite 1-D, Santa Ana, CA 92705/714-261-6611; FAX: 714-756-0133

Engineered Accessories, 1307 W. Wabash Ave., Effingham, IL 62401/217-347-7700; FAX: 217-347-7737

Engraving Artistry, 36 Alto Rd., RFD 2, Burlington, CT 06013/203-673-6837

Enguix Import-Export, Alpujarras 58, Alzira, Valencia, SPAIN 46600/(96) 241 43 95; FAX: (96) (241 43 95) 240 21 53

Epps, Ellwood (See "Gramps" Antique Cartridges)

Erhardt, Dennis, 3280 Green Meadow Dr., Helena, MT 59601/406-442-4533

Erickson's Mfg., C.W., Inc., 530 Garrison Ave. N.E., P.O. Box 522, Buffalo, MN 55313/612-682-3665; FAX: 612-682-4328

Erma Werke GmbH, Johan Ziegler St., 13/15/FeldiglSt., D-8060 Dachau, GERMANY (U.S. importers—Amtec 2000, Inc.; Mandall Shooting Supplies, Inc.)

Essex Arms, P.O. Box 345, Island Pond, VT 05846/802-723-4313

Essex Metals, 1000 Brighton St., Union, NJ 07083/800-282-8369

Euroarms of America, Inc., P.O. Box 3277, Winchester, VA 22601/540-662-1863; FAX: 540-662-4464

Eutaw Co., Inc., The, P.O. Box 608, U.S. Hwy. 176 West, Holly Hill, SC 29059/803-496-3341

Evans Engraving, Robert, 332 Vine St., Oregon City, OR 97045/503-656-5693

Eversull Co., Inc., K., 1 Tracemont, Boyce, LA 71409/318-793-8728; FAX: 318-793-5483

Exe, Inc., 18830 Partridge Circle, Eden Prairie, MN 55346/612-944-7662

Executive Protection Institute, Rt. 2, Box 3645, Berryville, VA 22611/540-955-1128

Eyster Heritage Gunsmiths, Inc., Ken, 6441 Bishop Rd., Centerburg, OH 43011/614-625-6131

E-Z-Way Systems, P.O. Box 4310, Newark, OH 43058-4310/614-345-6645, 800-848-2072; FAX: 614-345-6600

F

F&A Inc., 50 Elm St., Richfield Springs, NY 13439/315-858-1470; FAX: 315-858-2969

Fagan & Co., William, 22952 15 Mile Rd., Clinton Township, MI 48035/313-465-4637; FAX: 313-792-6996

Faith Associates, Inc., 1139 S. Greenville Hwy., Hendersonville, NC 28792/704-692-1916; FAX: 704-697-6827

Fanzoj GmbH, Griesgasse 1, 9170 Ferlach, AUSTRIA 9170/(43) 04227-2283; FAX: (43) 04227-2867

FAS, Via E. Fermi, 8, 20019 Settimo Milanese, Milano, ITALY/02-3285846; FAX: 02-33500196 (U.S. importer—Nygord Precision Products)

Faust, Inc., T.G., 544 Minor St., Reading, PA 19602/610-375-8549; FAX: 610-375-4488

Fautheree, Andy, P.O. Box 4607, Pagosa Springs, CO 81157/303-731-5003

Feather Industries, Inc., 37600 Liberty Dr., Trinidad, CO 81082/719-846-2699; FAX: 719-846-2644

Federal Cartridge Co., 900 Ehlen Dr., Anoka, MN 55303/612-323-2300; FAX: 612-323-2506

Federated-Fry (See Fry Metals)

FEG, Budapest, Soroksariut 158, H-1095 HUNGARY (U.S. importers—Century International Arms, Inc.; K.B.I., Inc.)

Feken, Dennis, Rt. 2 Box 124, Perry, OK 73077/405-336-5611

Fellowes, Ted, Beaver Lodge, 9245 16th Ave. SW, Seattle, WA 98106/206-763-1698

Feminine Protection, Inc., 10514 Shady Trail, Dallas, TX 75220/214-351-4500; FAX: 214-352-4686

Ferdinand, Inc., P.O. Box 5, 201 Main St., Harrison, ID 83833/208-689-3012, 800-522-6010 (U.S.A.), 800-258-5266 (Canada); FAX: 208-689-3142

Ferguson, Bill, P.O. Box 1238, Sierra Vista, AZ 85636/520-458-5321; FAX: 520-458-9125

Ferris Firearms, 30115 U.S. Hwy. 281 North, Suite 158, Bulverde, TX 78163/210-980-4811

Finch Custom Bullets, 40204 La Rochelle, Prairieville, LA 70769

Fiocchi Munizioni s.p.a. (See U.S. importer—Fiocchi of America, Inc.)

Fiocchi of America, Inc., 5030 Fremont Rd., Ozark, MO 65721/417-725-4118, 800-721-2666; FAX: 417-725-1039

Firearm Training Center, The, 9555 Blandville Rd., West Paducah, KY 42086/502-554-5886

Firearms Academy of Seattle, P.O. Box 2814, Kirkland, WA 98083/206-820-4853

Firearms Engraver's Guild of America, 332 Vine St., Oregon City, OR 97045/503-656-5693

Fire'n Five, P.O. Box 11 Granite Rt., Sumpter, OR 97877

First, Inc., Jack, 1201 Turbine Dr., Rapid City, SD 57701/605-343-9544; FAX: 605-343-9420

Fish, Marshall F., Rt. 22 N., P.O. Box 2439, Westport, NY 12993/518-962-4897

Fisher, Jerry A., 553 Crane Mt. Rd., Big Fork, MT 59911/406-837-2722

Fisher Custom Firearms, 2199 S. Kittredge Way, Aurora, CO 80013/303-755-3710

Fisher Enterprises, Inc., 1071 4th Ave. S., Suite 303, Edmonds, WA 98020-4143/206-771-5382

Fisher, R. Kermit (See Fisher Enterprises, Inc.)

Fitz Pistol Grip Co., P.O. Box 610, Douglas City, CA 96024/916-778-0240

Flaig's, 2200 Evergreen Rd., Millvale, PA 15209/412-821-1717

Flambeau Products Corp., 15981 Valplast Rd., Middlefield, OH 44062/216-632-1631; FAX: 216-632-1581

Flannery Engraving Co., Jeff W., 11034 Riddles Run Rd., Union, KY 41091/606-384-3127

Flayderman & Co., N., Inc., P.O. Box 2446, Ft. Lauderdale, FL 33303/305-761-8855

Fleming Firearms, 7720 E 126th St. N, Collinsville, OK 74021-7016/918-665-3624

Flents Products Co., Inc., P.O. Box 2109, Norwalk, CT 06852/203-866-2581; FAX: 203-854-9322

Flintlocks, Etc. (See Beauchamp & Son, Inc.)

Flitz International Ltd., 821 Mohr Ave., Waterford, WI 53185/414-534-5898; FAX: 414-534-2991

Floatstone Mfg. Co., 106 Powder Mill Rd., P.O. Box 765, Canton, CT 06019/203-693-1977

Flores Publications, Inc., J., P.O. Box 830131, Miami, FL 33283/305-559-4652

Fluoramics, Inc., 18 Industrial Ave., Mahwah, NJ 07430/800-922-0075, 201-825-7035

FN Herstal, Voie de Liege 33, Herstal 4040, BELGIUM/(32)41.40.82.83; FAX: (32)41.40.86.79

Fobus International Ltd., Kfar Hess, ISRAEL 40692/972-9-911716; FAX: 972-9-911716

Ford, Jack, 1430 Elkwood, Missouri City, TX 77489/713-499-9984

Forgett Jr., Valmore J., 689 Bergen Blvd., Ridgefield, NJ 07657/201-945-2500; FAX: 201-945-6859

Forgreens Tool Mfg., Inc., P.O. Box 990, 723 Austin St., Robert Lee, TX 76945/915-453-2800

Forkin, Ben (See Belt MTN Arms)

Forrest, Inc., Tom, P.O. Box 326, Lakeside, CA 92040/619-561-5800; FAX: 619-561-0227

Forster, Kathy (See Custom Checkering Service)

Forster, Larry L., P.O. Box 212, 220 First St. NE, Gwinner, ND 58040-0212/701-678-2475

Forster Products, 82 E. Lanark Ave., Lanark, IL 61046/815-493-6360; FAX: 815-493-2371

Fort Hill Gunstocks, 12807 Fort Hill Rd., Hillsboro, OH 45133/513-466-2763

Fort Knox Security Products, 1051 N. Industrial Park Rd., Orem, UT 84057/801-224-7233, 800-821-5216; FAX: 801-226-5493

Forty Five Ranch Enterprises, Box 1080, Miami, OK 74355-1080/918-542-5875

Fountain Products, 492 Prospect Ave., West Springfield, MA 01089/413-781-4651; FAX: 413-733-8217

4-D Custom Die Co., 711 N. Sandusky St., P.O. Box 889, Mt. Vernon, OH 43050-0889/614-397-7214; FAX: 614-397-6600

Foy Custom Bullets, 104 Wells Ave., Daleville, AL 36322

Francesca, Inc., 3115 Old Ranch Rd., San Antonio, TX 78217/512-826-2584; FAX: 512-826-8211

Francolini, Leonard, 106 Powder Mill Rd., P.O. Box 765, Canton, CT 06019/203-693-1977

Frank Custom Classic Arms, Ron, 7131 Richland Rd., Ft. Worth, TX 76118/817-284-9300; FAX: 817-284-9300

Frank Knives, Box 984, Whitefish, MT 59937/406-862-2681; FAX: 406-862-2681

Frazier Brothers Enterprises, 1118 N. Main St., Franklin, IN 46131/317-736-4000; FAX: 317-736-4000

Freedom Arms, Inc., P.O. Box 1776, Freedom, WY 83120/307-883-2468, 800-833-4432 (orders only); FAX: 307-883-2005

Freeman Animal Targets, 5519 East County Road, 100 South, Plainsfield, IN 46168/317-487-9482; FAX: 317-487-9671

Fremont Tool Works, 1214 Prairie, Ford, KS 67842/316-369-2327

French, J.R., 1712 Creek Ridge Ct., Irving, TX 75060/214-254-2654

Frielich Police Equipment, 211 East 21st St., New York, NY 10010/212-254-3045

Frontier, 2910 San Bernardo, Laredo, TX 78040/210-723-5409; FAX: 210-723-1774

Frontier Arms Co., Inc., 401 W. Rio Santa Cruz, Green Valley, AZ 85614-3932

Frontier Products Co., 164 E. Longview Ave., Columbus, OH 43202/614-262-9357

Frontier Safe Co., 3201 S. Clinton St., Fort Wayne, IN 46806/219-744-7233; FAX: 219-744-6678

Fry Metals, 4100 6th Ave., Altoona, PA 16602/814-946-1611

Fullmer, Geo. M., 2499 Mavis St., Oakland, CA 94601/510-533-4193

Fulmer's Antique Firearms, Chet, P.O. Box 792, Rt. 2 Buffalo Lake, Detroit Lakes, MN 56501/218-847-7712

Fury Cutlery, 801 Broad Ave., Ridgefield, NJ 07657/201-943-5920; FAX: 201-943-1579

Fusilier Bullets, 10010 N. 6000 W., Highland, UT 84003/801-756-6813

FWB, Neckarstrasse 43, 78727 Oberndorf a. N., GERMANY/07423-814-0; FAX: 07423-814-89 (U.S. importer—Beeman Precision Airguns)

G

G96 Products Co., Inc., River St. Station, P.O. Box 1684, Paterson, NJ 07544/201-684-4050; FAX: 201-684-3848

G&C Bullet Co., Inc., 8835 Thornton Rd., Stockton, CA 95209/209-477-6479; FAX: 209-477-2813

Gage Manufacturing, 663 W. 7th St., San Pedro, CA 90731

Galati International, P.O. Box 326, Catawissa, MO 63015/314-257-4837; FAX: 314-257-2268

Galazan, P.O. Box 1692, New Britain, CT 06051-1692/203-225-6581; FAX: 203-832-8707

GALCO International Ltd., 2019 W. Quail Ave., Phoenix, AZ 85027/602-258-8295, 800-874-2526; FAX: 602-582-6854

Gamba-Societa Armi Bresciane Srl., Renato, Via Artigiani, 93, 25063 Gardone Val Trompia (BS), ITALY/30-8911640; FAX: 30-8911648 (U.S. importer—The First National Gun Bank Corp.)

Gammog, Gregory B. Gally, 14608 Old Gunpowder Rd., Laurel, MD 20707-3131/301-725-3838

Gamo (See U.S. importers—Daisy Mfg. Co.; Dynamit Nobel-RWS, Inc.)

Gamo USA, Inc., 3721 S.W. 47th Ave., Suite 304, Ft. Lauderdale, FL 33314

Gander Mountain, Inc., P.O. Box 128, Hwy. "W", Wilmot, WI 53192/414-862-2331,Ext. 6425

GAR, 590 McBride Avenue, West Paterson, NJ 07424/201-754-1114; FAX: 201-742-2897

Garcia National Gun Traders, Inc., 225 SW 22nd Ave., Miami, FL 33135/305-642-2355

Garthwaite, Jim, Rt. 2, Box 310, Watsontown, PA 17777/717-538-1566

Gaucher Armes, S.A., 46, rue Desjoyaux, 42000 Saint-Etienne, FRANCE/77 33 38 92; FAX: 77 61 95 72

G.B.C. Industries, Inc., P.O. Box 1602, Spring, TX 77373/713-350-9690; FAX: 713-350-0601

GDL Enterprises, 409 Le Gardeur, Slidell, LA 70460/504-649-0693

Gehmann, Walter (See Huntington Die Specialties)

Gene's Custom Guns, P.O. Box 10534, White Bear Lake, MN 55110/612-429-5105

Gentex Corp., 5 Tinkham Ave., Derry, NH 03038/603-434-0311; FAX: 603-434-3002

George, Tim, Rt. 1, P.O. Box 45, Evington, VA 24550/804-821-8117

Getz Barrel Co., P.O. Box 88, Beavertown, PA 17813/717-658-7263

GFR Corp., P.O. Box 1439, New London, NH 03257-1439

G.G. & G., 3602 E. 42nd Stravenue, Tucson, AZ 85713/520-748-7167; FAX: 520-748-7583

G.H. Enterprises Ltd., Bag 10, Okotoks, Alberta T0L 1T0 CANADA/403-938-6070

Giron, Robert E., 1328 Pocono St., Pittsburgh, PA 15218/412-731-6041

Glaser Safety Slug, Inc., P.O. Box 8223, Foster City, CA 94404-8223/800-221-3489, 415-345-7677; FAX: 415-345-8217

Glass, Herb, P.O. Box 25, Bullville, NY 10915/914-361-3021

Glimm, Jerome C., 19 S. Maryland, Conrad, MT 59425/406-278-3574

Glock GmbH, P.O. Box 50, A-2232 Deutsch Wagram, AUSTRIA (U.S. importer—Glock, Inc.)

Glock, Inc., P.O. Box 369, Smyrna, GA 30081/770-432-1202; FAX: 770-433-8719

GML Products, Inc., 394 Laredo Dr., Birmingham, AL 35226/205-979-4867

Goddard, Allen, 716 Medford Ave., Hayward, CA 94541/510-276-6830

Goergen's Gun Shop, Inc., Rt. 2, Box 182BB, Austin, MN 55912/507-433-9280

GOEX, Inc., 1002 Springbrook Ave., Moosic, PA 18507/717-457-6724; FAX: 717-457-1130

Goldcoast Reloaders, Inc., 2421 NE 4th Ave., Pompano Beach, FL 33064/305-783-4849

Golden Age Arms Co., 115 E. High St., Ashley, OH 43003/614-747-2488

Golden Bear Bullets, 3065 Fairfax Ave., San Jose, CA 95148/408-238-9515

Gonzalez Guns, Ramon B., P.O. Box 370, Monticello, NY 12701/914-794-4515

Goodwin, Fred, Silver Ridge Gun Shop, Sherman Mills, ME 04776/207-365-4451

Gordie's Gun Shop, 1401 Fulton St., Streator, IL 61364/815-672-7202

Gotz Bullets, 7313 Rogers St., Rockford, IL 61111

Gould & Goodrich, P.O. Box 1479, Lillington, NC 27546/910-893-2071; FAX: 910-893-4742

Gournet, Geoffroy, 820 Paxinosa Ave., Easton, PA 18042/215-559-0710

Gozon Corp., U.S.A., P.O. Box 6278, Folson, CA 95763/916-983-2026; FAX: 916-983-9500

Grace, Charles E., 6943 85.5 Rd., Trinchera, CO 81081/719-846-9435

Grace Metal Products, Inc., P.O. Box 67, Elk Rapids, MI 49629/616-264-8133

"Gramps" Antique Cartridges, Box 341, Washago, Ont. L0K 2B0 CANADA/705-689-5348

Grand Falls Bullets, Inc., P.O. Box 720, 803 Arnold Wallen Way, Stockton, MO 65785/816-229-0112

Granite Custom Bullets, Box 190, Philipsburg, MT 59858/406-859-3245

Grant, Howard V., Hiawatha 15, Woodruff, WI 54568/715-356-7146

Graphics Direct, P.O. Box 372421, Reseda, CA 91337-2421/818-344-9002

Graves Co., 1800 Andrews Ave., Pompano Beach, FL 33069/800-327-9103; FAX: 305-960-0301

Grayback Wildcats, 5306 Bryant Ave., Klamath Falls, OR 97603/541-884-1072

Graybill's Gun Shop, 1035 Ironville Pike, Columbia, PA 17512/717-684-2739

Great Lakes Airguns, 6175 S. Park Ave., Hamburg, NY 14075/716-648-6666; FAX: 716-648-5279

Green, Arthur S., 485 S. Robertson Blvd., Beverly Hills, CA 90211/310-274-1283

Green Bay Bullets, 1638 Hazelwood Dr., Sobieski, WI 54171/414-826-7760

Green, Roger M., P.O. Box 984, 435 E. Birch, Glenrock, WY 82637/307-436-9804

Greenwald, Leon E. "Bud", 2553 S. Quitman St., Denver, CO 80219/303-935-3850

Greenwood Precision, P.O. Box 468, Nixa, MO 65714-0468/417-725-2330

Greider Precision, 431 Santa Marina Ct., Escondido, CA 92029/619-480-8892

Gremmel Enterprises, 2111 Carriage Drive, Eugene, OR 97408-7537/541-302-3000

Grier's Hard Cast Bullets, 1107 11th St., LaGrande, OR 97850/503-963-8796

Griffin & Howe, Inc., 33 Claremont Rd., Bernardsville, NJ 07924/908-766-2287; FAX: 908-766-1068

Griffin & Howe, Inc., 36 W. 44th St., Suite 1011, New York, NY 10036/212-921-0980

Grizzly Bullets, 322 Green Mountain Rd., Trout Creek, MT 59874/406-847-2627

Groenewold, John, P.O. Box 830, Mundelein, IL 60060/708-566-2365

GRS Corp., Glendo, P.O. Box 1153, 900 Overlander St., Emporia, KS 66801/316-343-1084, 800-835-3519

Guardsman Products, 411 N. Darling, Fremont, MI 49412/616-924-3950

Gun-Alert, 1010 N. Maclay Ave., San Fernando, CA 91340/818-365-0864; FAX: 818-365-1308

Gun City, 212 W. Main Ave., Bismarck, ND 58501/701-223-2304

Gun-Ho Sports Cases, 110 E. 10th St., St. Paul, MN 55101/612-224-9491

Gun Hunter Books, Div. of Gun Hunter Trading Co., 5075 Heisig St., Beaumont, TX 77705/409-835-3006

Gun Leather Limited, 116 Lipscomb, Ft. Worth, TX 76104/817-334-0225; 800-247-0609

Gun List (See Krause Publications, Inc.)

Gun Locker, Div. of Airmold, W.R. Grace & Co.-Conn., Becker Farms Ind. Park,, P.O. Box 610/Roanoke Rapids, NC 27870/800-344-5716; FAX: 919-536-2201

Gun Parts Corp., The, 226 Williams Lane, West Hurley, NY 12491/914-679-2417; FAX: 914-679-5849

Gun Room, The, 1121 Burlington, Muncie, IN 47302/317-282-9073; FAX: 317-282-5270

Gun Room Press, The, 127 Raritan Ave., Highland Park, NJ 08904/908-545-4344; FAX: 908-545-6686

Gun Shop, The, 5550 S. 900 East, Salt Lake City, UT 84117/801-263-3633

Gun Shop, The, 62778 Spring Creek Rd., Montrose, CO 81401

Gun-Tec, P.O. Box 8125, W. Palm Beach, FL 33407

Gun Works, The, 247 S. 2nd, Springfield, OR 97477/541-741-4118; FAX: 541-988-1097

Guncraft Books (See Guncraft Sports, Inc.)

Guncraft Sports, Inc., 10737 Dutchtown Rd., Knoxville, TN 37932/423-966-4545; FAX: 423-966-4500

Gunfitters, The, P.O. 426, Cambridge, WI 53523-0426/608-764-8128

Gunline Tools, 2950 Saturn St., Suite O, Brea, CA 92621/714-993-5100; FAX: 714-572-4128

Gunnerman Books, P.O. Box 214292, Auburn Hills, MI 48321/810-879-2779

Guns, 81 E. Streetsboro St., Hudson, OH 44236/216-650-4563

Guns Antique & Modern DBA/Charles E. Duffy, Williams Lane, West Hurley, NY 12491/914-679-2997

Guns, Div. of D.C. Engineering, Inc., 8633 Southfield Fwy., Detroit, MI 48228/313-271-7111, 800-886-7623 (orders only); FAX: 313-271-7112

GUNS Magazine, 591 Camino de la Reina, Suite 200, San Diego, CA 92108/619-297-5350; FAX: 619-297-5353

Gunsite Custom Shop, P.O. Box 451, Paulden, AZ 86334/520-636-4104; FAX: 520-636-1236

Gunsite Gunsmithy (See Gunsite Custom Shop)

Gunsite Training Center, P.O. Box 700, Paulden, AZ 86334/520-636-4565; FAX: 520-636-1236

Gunsmithing Ltd., 57 Unquowa Rd., Fairfield, CT 06430/203-254-0436; FAX: 203-254-1535

Gurney, F.R., Box 13, Sooke, BC V0S 1N0 CANADA/604-642-5282; FAX: 604-642-7859

Gusty Winds Corp., 2950 Bear St., Suite 120, Costa Mesa, CA 92626/714-536-3587

Gwinnell, Bryson J., P.O. Box 248C, Maple Hill Rd., Rochester, VT 05767/802-767-3664

GZ Paintball Sports Products (See GFR Corp.)

H

H&P Publishing, 7174 Hoffman Rd., San Angelo, TX 76905/915-655-5953

H&R 1871, Inc., 60 Industrial Rowe, Gardner, MA 01440/508-632-9393; FAX: 508-632-2300

H&S Liner Service, 515 E. 8th, Odessa, TX 79761/915-332-1021

Hafner Creations, Inc., P.O. Box 1987, Lake City, FL 32055/904-755-6481; FAX: 904-755-6595

Hale/Engraver, Peter, 800 E. Canyon Rd., Spanish Fork, UT 84660/801-798-8215

Half Moon Rifle Shop, 490 Halfmoon Rd., Columbia Falls, MT 59912/406-892-4409

Hall Plastics, Inc., John, P.O. Box 1526, Alvin, TX 77512/713-489-8709

Hallberg Gunsmith, Fritz, 33 S. Main, Payette, ID 83661/208-642-7157; FAX: 208-642-9643

Hamilton, Alex B. (See Ten-Ring Precision, Inc.)

Hamilton, Keith, P.O. Box 871, Gridley, CA 95948/916-846-2316

Hammerli USA, 19296 Oak Grove Circle, Groveland, CA 95321/209-962-5311; FAX: 209-962-5931

Hammerli Ltd., Seonerstrasse 37, CH-5600 Lenzburg, SWITZERLAND/064-50 11 44; FAX: 064-51 38 27 (U.S. importer—Hammerli USA)

Handgun Press, P.O. Box 406, Glenview, IL 60025/847-657-6500; FAX: 847-724-8831

HandiCrafts Unltd. (See Clements' Custom Leathercraft, Chas)

Hands Engraving, Barry Lee, 26192 E. Shore Route, Bigfork, MT 59911/406-837-0035

Hank's Gun Shop, Box 370, 50 West 100 South, Monroe, UT 84754/801-527-4456

Hanned Line, The, P.O. Box 2387, Cupertino, CA 95015-2387

Hanned Precision (See Hanned Line, The)

Hansen & Co. (See Hansen Cartridge Co.)

Hansen Cartridge Co., 244-246 Old Post Rd., Southport, CT 06490/203-259-6222, 203-259-7337; FAX: 203-254-3832

Hanson's Gun Center, Dick, 233 Everett Dr., Colorado Springs, CO 80911

Hardin Specialty Dist., P.O. Box 338, Radcliff, KY 40159-0338/502-351-6649

Hardison, Charles, P.O. Box 356, 200 W. Baseline Rd., Lafayette, CO 80026-0356/303-666-5171

Harrell's Precision, 5756 Hickory Dr., Salem, VA 24133/703-380-2683

Harrington & Richardson (See H&R 1871, Inc.)

Harris Engineering, Inc., Rt. 1, Barlow, KY 42024/502-334-3633; FAX: 502-334-3000

Harris Enterprises, P.O. Box 105, Bly, OR 97622/503-353-2625

Harris Gunworks, 3840 N. 28th Ave., Phoenix, AZ 85017-4733/602-230-1414; FAX: 602-230-1422

Harris Hand Engraving, Paul A., 10630 Janet Lee, San Antonio, TX 78230/512-391-5121

Harris Publications, 1115 Broadway, New York, NY 10010/212-807-7100; FAX: 212-627-4678

Harrison Bullets, 6437 E. Hobart St., Mesa, AZ 85205

Harrison-Hurtz Enterprises, Inc., P.O. Box 268, RR1, Wymore, NE 68466/402-645-3378; FAX: 402-645-3606

Hart & Son, Inc., Robert W., 401 Montgomery St., Nescopeck, PA 18635/717-752-3655, 800-368-3656; FAX: 717-752-1088

Hartford (See U.S. importer— EMF Co., Inc.)

Harvey, Frank, 218 Nightfall, Terrace, NV 89015/702-558-6998

Harwood, Jack O., 1191 S. Pendlebury Lane, Blackfoot, ID 83221/208-785-5368

Haselbauer Products, Jerry, P.O. Box 27629, Tucson, AZ 85726/602-792-1075

Hastings Barrels, 320 Court St., Clay Center, KS 67432/913-632-3169; FAX: 913-632-6554

Hawk, Inc., 849 Hawks Bridge Rd., Salem, NJ 08079/609-299-2700; FAX: 609-299-2800

Hawk Laboratories, Inc. (See Hawk, Inc.)

Hawken Shop, The (See Dayton Traister)

Haydon Shooters' Supply, Russ, 15018 Goodrich Dr. NW, Gig Harbor, WA 98329/206-857-7557

Heatbath Corp., P.O. Box 2978, Springfield, MA 01101/413-543-3381

Hebard Guns, Gil, 125-129 Public Square, Knoxville, IL 61448

HEBB Resources, P.O. Box 999, Mead, WA 99021-09996/509-466-1292

Hecht, Hubert J., Waffen-Hecht, P.O. Box 2635, Fair Oaks, CA 95628/916-966-1020

Heckler & Koch GmbH, P.O. Box 1329, 78722 Oberndorf, Neckar, GERMANY/49-7423179-0; FAX: 49-7423179-2406 (U.S. importer—Heckler & Koch, Inc.)

Heckler & Koch, Inc., 21480 Pacific Blvd., Sterling, VA 20166-8903/703-450-1900; FAX: 703-450-8160

Hege Jagd-u. Sporthandels, GmbH, P.O. Box 101461, W-7770 Ueberlingen a. Bodensee, GERMANY

Heidenstrom Bullets, Urds GT 1 Heroya, 3900 Porsgrunn, NORWAY

Heilmann, Stephen, P.O. Box 657, Grass Valley, CA 95945/916-272-8758

Heinie Specialty Products, 301 Oak St., Quincy, IL 62301-2500/309-543-4535; FAX: 309-543-2521

Hellweg Ltd., 40356 Oak Park Way, Suite H, Oakhurst, CA 93644/209-683-3030; FAX: 209-683-3422

Hendricks, Frank E., Master Engravers, Inc., HC03, Box 434, Dripping Springs, TX 78620/512-858-7828

Henigson & Associates, Steve, 2049 Kerwood Ave., Los Angeles, CA 90025/213-305-8288

Henriksen Tool Co., Inc., 8515 Wagner Creek Rd., Talent, OR 97540/541-535-2309

Hensler, Jerry, 6614 Country Field, San Antonio, TX 78240/210-690-7491

Hensley & Gibbs, Box 10, Murphy, OR 97533/541-862-2341

Heppler's Machining, 2240 Calle Del Mundo, Santa Clara, CA 95054/408-748-9166; FAX: 408-988-7711

Heritage Manufacturing, Inc., 4600 NW 135th St., Opa Locka, FL 33054/305-685-5966; FAX: 305-687-6721

Heritage/VSP Gun Books, P.O. Box 887, McCall, ID 83638/208-634-4104; FAX: 208-634-3101

Herrett's Stocks, Inc., P.O. Box 741, Twin Falls, ID 83303/208-733-1498

Hesco-Meprolight, 2139 Greenville Rd., LaGrange, GA 30240/706-884-7967; FAX: 706-882-4683

Hi-Point Firearms, 5990 Philadelphia Dr., Dayton, OH 45415/513-275-4991; FAX: 513-522-8330

Hidalgo, Tony, 12701 SW 9th Pl., Davie, FL 33325/305-476-7645

High Bridge Arms, Inc., 3185 Mission St., San Francisco, CA 94110/415-282-8358

High North Products, Inc., P.O. Box 2, Antigo, WI 54409/715-627-2331

High Performance International, 5734 W. Florist Ave., Milwaukee, WI 53218/414-466-9040

High Standard Mfg. Co., Inc., 4601 S. Pinemont, 148-B, Houston, TX 77041/713-462-4200; FAX: 713-462-6437

Highline Machine Co., 654 Lela Place, Grand Junction, CO 81504/970-434-4971

Hill Speed Leather, Ernie, 4507 N. 195th Ave., Litchfield Park, AZ 85340/602-853-9222; FAX: 602-853-9235

Hiptmayer, Armurier, RR 112 750, P.O. Box 136, Eastman, Quebec JOE 1P0, CANADA/514-297-2492

Hiptmayer, Heidemarie, RR 112 750, P.O. Box 136, Eastman, Quebec JOE 1PO, CANADA/514-297-2492

Hiptmayer, Klaus, RR 112 750, P.O. Box 136, Eastman, Quebec J0E 1P0, CANADA/514-297-2492

Hirtenberger Aktiengesellschaft, Leobersdorferstrasse 31, A-2552 Hirtenberg, AUSTRIA/43(0)2256 81184; FAX: 43(0)2256 81807

HJS Arms, Inc., P.O. Box 3711, Brownsville, TX 78523-3711/800-453-2767, 210-542-2767

H.K.S. Products, 7841 Founion Dr., Florence, KY 41042/606-342-7841, 800-354-9814; FAX: 606-342-5865

Hoag, James W., 8523 Canoga Ave., Suite C, Canoga Park, CA 91304/818-998-1510

Hobson Precision Mfg. Co., Rt. 1, Box 220-C, Brent, AL 35034/205-926-4662

Hoch Custom Bullet Moulds (See Colorado Shooter's Supply)

Hodgdon Powder Co., Inc., P.O. Box 2932, 6231 Robinson, Shawnee Mission, KS 66202/913-362-9455; FAX: 913-362-1307; WEB: http://www.unicom.net/hpc

Hoehn Sales, Inc., 75 Greensburg Ct., St. Charles, MO 63304/314-441-4231

Hoelscher, Virgil, 11047 Pope Ave., Lynwood, CA 90262/310-631-8545

Hogue Grips, P.O. Box 1138, Paso Robles, CA 93447/800-438-4747, 805-239-1440; FAX: 805-239-2553

Holland's, Box 69, Powers, OR 97466/503-439-5155; FAX: 503-439-5155

Hollis Gun Shop, 917 Rex St., Carlsbad, NM 88220/505-885-3782

Hollywood Engineering, 10642 Arminta St., Sun Valley, CA 91352/818-842-8376

Holster Shop, The, 720 N. Flagler Dr., Ft. Lauderdale, FL 33304/305-463-7910; FAX: 305-761-1483

Homak Mfg. Co., Inc., 3800 W. 45th St., Chicago, IL 60632/312-523-3100, FAX: 312-523-9455

Home Shop Machinist, The, Village Press Publications, P.O. Box 1810, Traverse City, MI 49685/800-447-7367; FAX: 616-946-3289

Hondo Ind., 510 S. 52nd St.,l04, Tempe, AZ 85281

Hoppe's Div., Penguin Industries, Inc., Airport Industrial Mall, Coatesville, PA 19320/610-384-6000

Horizons Unlimited, P.O. Box 426, Warm Springs, GA 31830/706-655-3603; FAX: 706-655-3603

Hornady Mfg. Co., P.O. Box 1848, Grand Island, NE 68802/800-338-3220, 308-382-1390; FAX: 308-382-5761

Horseshoe Leather Products, Andy Arratoonian, The Cottage Sharow, Ripon HG4 5BP ENGLAND/44-1765-605858

Horst, Alan K., 3221 2nd Ave. N., Great Falls, MT 59401/406-454-1831

House of Muskets, Inc., The, P.O. Box 4640, Pagosa Springs, CO 81157/303-731-2295

Howell Machine, 815½ D St., Lewiston, ID 83501/208-743-7418

Hoyt Holster Co., Inc., P.O. Box 69, Coupeville, WA 98239-0069/360-678-6640; FAX: 360-678-6549

Huey Gun Cases, P.O. Box 22456, Kansas City, MO 64113/816-444-1637; FAX: 816-444-1637

Hugger Hooks Co., 3900 Easley Way, Golden, CO 80403/303-279-0600

Hughes, Steven Dodd, P.O. Box 545, Livingston, MT 59047/406-222-9377

Hume, Don, P.O. Box 351, Miami, OK 74355/918-542-6604; FAX: 918-542-4340

Hungry Horse Books, 4605 Hwy. 93 South, Whitefish, MT 59937/406-862-7997

Hunkeler, A. (See Buckskin Machine Works)

Hunter Co., Inc., 3300 W. 71st Ave., Westminster, CO 80030/303-427-4626; FAX: 303-428-3980

Huntington Die Specialties, 601 Oro Dam Blvd., Oroville, CA 95965/916-534-1210; FAX: 916-534-1212

Hydrosorbent Products, P.O. Box 437, Ashley Falls, MA 01222/413-229-2967; FAX: 413-229-8743

Hyper-Single, Inc., 520 E. Beaver, Jenks, OK 74037/918-299-2391

I

ICI-America, P.O. Box 751, Wilmington, DE 19897/302-575-3000

Idaho Ammunition Service, 2816 Mayfair Dr., Lewiston, ID 83501/208-743-0270; FAX: 208-743-4930

IMI, P.O. Box 1044, Ramat Hasharon 47100, ISRAEL/972-3-5485222

IMI Services USA, Inc., 2 Wisconsin Circle, Suite 420, Chevy Chase, MD 20815/301-215-4800; FAX: 301-657-1446

Impact Case Co., P.O. Box 9912, Spokane, WA 99209-0912/800-262-3322, 509-467-3303; FAX: 509-326-5436

Imperial (See E-Z-Way Systems)

Import Sports Inc., 1750 Brielle Ave., Unit B1, Wanamassa, NJ 07712/908-493-0302; FAX: 908-493-0301

IMR Powder Co., 1080 Military Turnpike, Suite 2, Plattsburgh, NY 12901/518-563-2253; FAX: 518-563-6916

Info-Arm, P.O. Box 1262, Champlain, NY 12919

Ingle, Ralph W., 4 Missing Link, Rossville, GA 30741/404-866-5589

Innovative Weaponry, Inc., 337 Eubank NE, Albuquerque, NM 87123/800-334-3573, 505-296-4645; FAX: 505-271-2633

Innovision Enterprises, 728 Skinner Dr., Kalamazoo, MI 49001/616-382-1681; FAX: 616-382-1830

INTEC International, Inc., P.O. Box 5708, Scottsdale, AZ 85261/602-483-1708

Interarms, 10 Prince St., Alexandria, VA 22314/703-548-1400; FAX: 703-549-7826

Intermountain Arms & Tackle, Inc., 1375 E. Fairview Ave., Meridian, ID 83642-1816/208-888-4911; FAX: 208-888-4381

Intratec, 12405 SW 130th St., Miami, FL 33186/305-232-1821; FAX: 305-253-7207

Iosso Products, 1485 Lively Blvd., Elk Grove Village, IL 60007/708-437-8400; FAX: 708-437-8478

Ironside International Publishers, Inc., P.O. Box 55, 800 Slaters Lane, Alexandria, VA 22313/703-684-6111; FAX: 703-683-5486

Ironsighter Co., P.O. Box 85070, Westland, MI 48185/313-326-8731; FAX: 313-326-3378

Irwin, Campbell H., 140 Hartland Blvd., East Hartland, CT 06027/203-653-3901

Island Pond Gun Shop (See Costa, David)

I.S.S., P.O. Box 185234, Ft. Worth, TX 76181/817-595-2090

Ivanoff, Thomas G. (See Tom's Gun Repair)

J

J-4, Inc., 1700 Via Burton, Anaheim, CA 92806/714-254-8315; FAX: 714-956-4421

J&D Components, 75 East 350 North, Orem, UT 84057-4719/801-225-7007

J&J Products, Inc., 9240 Whitmore, El Monte, CA 91731/818-571-5228, 800-927-8361; FAX: 818-571-8704

J&J Sales, 1501 21st Ave. S., Great Falls, MT 59405/406-453-7549

J&L Superior Bullets (See Huntington Die Specialties)

J&R Engineering, P.O. Box 77, 200 Lyons Hill Rd., Athol, MA 01331/508-249-9241

J&S Heat Treat, 803 S. 16th St., Blue Springs, MO 64015/816-229-2149; FAX: 816-228-1135

Jackalope Gun Shop, 1048 S. 5th St., Douglas, WY 82633/307-358-3441

Jaeger, Paul, Inc./Dunn's, P.O. Box 449, 1 Madison Ave., Grand Junction, TN 38039/901-764-6909; FAX: 901-764-6503

JagerSport, Ltd., One Wholesale Way, Cranston, RI 02920/800-962-4867, 401-944-9682; FAX: 401-946-2587

Jamison's Forge Works, 4527 Rd. 6.5 NE, Moses Lake, WA 98837/509-762-2659

Jantz Supply, P.O. Box 584-GD, Davis, OK 73030-0584/405-369-2316; FAX: 405-369-3082

Jarvis, Inc., 1123 Cherry Orchard Lane, Hamilton, MT 59840/406-961-4392

Javelina Lube Products, P.O. Box 337, San Bernardino, CA 92402/714-882-5847; FAX: 714-434-6937

J-B Bore Cleaner, 299 Poplar St., Hamburg, PA 19526/610-562-2103

JBM, P.O. Box 3648, University Park, NM 88003

Jeffredo Gunsight, P.O. Box 669, San Marcos, CA 92079/619-728-2695

Jennings Firearms, Inc., 17692 Cowan, Irvine, CA 92714/714-252-7621; FAX: 714-252-7626

Jensen Bullets, 86 North, 400 West, Blackfoot, ID 83221/208-785-5590

Jensen's Custom Ammunition, 5146 E. Pima, Tucson, AZ 85712/602-325-3346; FAX: 602-322-5704

Jensen's Firearms Academy, 1280 W. Prince, Tucson, AZ 85705/602-293-8516

Jester Bullets, Rt. 1 Box 27, Orienta, OK 73737

JGS Precision Tool Mfg., 1141 S. Summer Rd., Coos Bay, OR 97420/503-267-4331; FAX:503-267-5996

J.I.T., Ltd., P.O. Box 230, Freedom, WY 83120/708-494-0937

JLK Bullets, 414 Turner Rd., Dover, AR 72837/501-331-4194

J.O. Arms Inc., 5709 Hartsdale, Houston, TX 77036/713-789-0745; FAX: 713-789-7513

John's Custom Leather, 523 S. Liberty St., Blairsville, PA 15717/412-459-6802

Johns Master Engraver, Bill, RR 4, Box 220, Fredericksburg, TX 78624-9545/210-997-6795

Johnson's Gunsmithing, Inc., Neal, 208 W. Buchanan St., Suite B, Colorado Springs, CO 80907/800-284-8671 (orders), 719-632-3795; FAX: 719-632-3493

Johnston Bros., 1889 Rt. 9, Unit 22, Toms River, NJ 08755/800-257-2595; FAX: 800-257-2534

Johnston, James (See North Fork Custom Gunsmithing)

Jonad Corp., 2091 Lakeland Ave., Lakewood, OH 44107/216-226-3161

Jonas Appraisals & Taxidermy, Jack, 1675 S. Birch, Suite 506, Denver, CO 80222/303-757-7347: FAX: 303-639-9655

Jones Co., Dale, 680 Hoffman Draw, Kila, MT 59920/406-755-4684

Jones Custom Products, Neil A., 17217 Brookhouser Road, Saegertown, PA 16433/814-763-2769; FAX: 814-763-4228

Jones Moulds, Paul, 4901 Telegraph Rd., Los Angeles, CA 90022/213-262-1510

Jones, J.D. (See SSK Industries)

Joy Enterprises (See Fury Cutlery)

J.P. Enterprises, Inc., P.O. Box 26324, Shoreview, MN 55126/612-486-9064; FAX: 612-482-0970

JRP Custom Bullets, RR2-2233 Carlton Rd., Whitehall, NY 12887/802-438-5548 (p.m.), 518-282-0084 (a.m.)

Jumbo Sports Products (See Bucheimer, J.M.)

Jungkind, Reeves C., 5001 Buckskin Pass, Austin, TX 78745-2841/512-442-1094

Jurras, L.E., P.O. Box 680, Washington, IN 47501/812-254-7698

JWH: Software, 6947 Haggerty Rd., Hillsboro, OH 45133/513-393-2402

K

K&M Industries, Inc., Box 66, 510 S. Main, Troy, ID 83871/208-835-2281; FAX: 208-835-5211

K&M Services, 5430 Salmon Run Rd., Dover, PA 17315/717-764-1461

K&S Mfg., 2611 Hwy. 40 East, Inglis, FL 34449/904-447-3571

K&T Co., Div. of T&S Industries, Inc., 1027 Skyview Dr., W. Carrollton, OH 45449/513-859-8414

Kahr Arms, P.O. Box 220, 630 Route 303, Blauvelt, NY 10913/914-353-5996; FAX: 914-353-7833

Kalispel Case Line, P.O. Box 267, Cusick, WA 99119/509-445-1121

Kamyk Engraving Co., Steve, 9 Grandview Dr., Westfield, MA 01085-1810/413-568-0457

Kane, Edward, P.O. Box 385, Ukiah, CA 95482/707-462-2937

Kane Products, Inc., 5572 Brecksville Rd., Cleveland, OH 44131/216-524-9962

Ka Pu Kapili, P.O. Box 745, Honokaa, HI 96727/808-776-1644; FAX: 808-776-1731

Kapro Mfg. Co., Inc. (See R.E.I.)

Kasenit Co., Inc., 13 Park Ave., Highland Mills, NY 10930/914-928-9595; FAX: 914-928-7292

Kasmarsik Bullets, 152 Crstler Rd., Chehalis, WA 98532

Kaswer Custom, Inc., 13 Surrey Drive, Brookfield, CT 06804/203-775-0564; FAX: 203-775-6872

K.B.I., Inc., P.O. Box 5440, Harrisburg, PA 17110-0440/717-540-8518; FAX: 717-540-8567

K-D, Inc., Box 459, 585 N. Hwy. 155, Cleveland, UT 84518/801-653-2530

KeeCo Impressions, Inc., 346 Wood Ave., North Brunswick, NJ 08902/800-468-0546

Keeler, R.H., 817 "N" St., Port Angeles, WA 98362/206-457-4702

Kehr, Roger, 2131 Agate Ct. SE, Lacy, WA 98503/360-456-0831

Keith's Bullets, 942 Twisted Oak, Algonquin, IL 60102/708-658-3520

Keith's Custom Taxidermy, 2241 Forest Ave., Rolling Meadows, IL 60008/847-255-7059

Keller Co., The, 4215 McEwen Rd., Dallas, TX 75244/214-770-8585

Kelley's, P.O. Box 125, Woburn, MA 01801/617-935-3389

Kellogg's Professional Products, 325 Pearl St., Sandusky, OH 44870/419-625-6551; FAX: 419-625-6167

Kelly, Lance, 1723 Willow Oak Dr., Edgewater, FL 32132/904-423-4933

Kel-Tec CNC Industries, Inc., P.O. Box 3427, Cocoa, FL 32924/407-631-0068; FAX: 407-631-1169

Ken's Gun Specialties, Rt. 1, Box 147, Lakeview, AR 72642/501-431-5606

Ken's Kustom Kartridges, 331 Jacobs Rd., Hubbard, OH 44425/216-534-4595

Keng's Firearms Specialty, Inc., P.O. Box 44405, 875 Wharton Dr. SW, Atlanta, GA 30336/404-691-7611: FAX: 404-505-8445

Kennebec Journal, 274 Western Ave., Augusta, ME 04330/207-622-6288

Kennedy Firearms, 10 N. Market St., Muncy, PA 17756/717-546-6695

KenPatable Ent., Inc., P.O. Box 19422, Louisville, KY 40259/502-239-5447

Kent Cartridge Mfg. Co. Ltd., Unit 16, Branbridges Industrial Estate, East, Peckham/Tonbridge, Kent, TN12 5HF ENGLAND/622-872255; FAX: 622-872645

Kesselring Gun Shop, 400 Hwy. 99 North, Burlington, WA 98233/206-724-3113; FAX: 206-724-7003

Kilham & Co., Main St., P.O. Box 37, Lyme, NH 03768/603-795-4112

Kimball, Gary, 1526 N. Circle Dr., Colorado Springs, CO 80909/719-634-1274

Kimber of America, Inc., 9039 SE Jannsen Rd., Clackamas, OR 97015/503-656-1704, 800-880-2418; FAX: 503-656-5357

Kimel Industries (See A.A. Arms, Inc.)

King & Co., P.O. Box 1242, Bloomington, IL 61702/309-473-3964

King's Gun Works, 1837 W. Glenoaks Blvd., Glendale, CA 91201/818-956-6010; FAX: 818-548-8606

Kirkpatrick Leather Co., 1910 San Bernardo, Laredo, TX 78040/210-723-6631; FAX: 210-725-0672

KJM Fabritek, Inc., P.O. Box 162, Marietta, GA 30061/404-426-8251

KK Air International (See Impact Case Co.)

K.K. Arms Co., Star Route Box 671, Kerrville, TX 78028/210-257-4718; FAX: 210-257-4891

KLA Enterprises, P.O. Box 2028, Eaton Park, FL 33840/941-682-2829; FAX: 941-682-2829

Kleen-Bore, Inc., 16 Industrial Pkwy., Easthampton, MA 01027/413-527-0300; FAX: 413-527-2522

Klein Custom Guns, Don, 433 Murray Park Dr., Ripon, WI 54971/414-748-2931

Kleinendorst, K.W., RR 1, Box 1500, Hop Bottom, PA 18824/717-289-4687

Klingler Woodcarving, P.O. Box 141, Thistle Hill, Cabot, VT 05647/802-426-3811

Kmount, P.O. Box 19422, Louisville, KY 40259/502-239-5447

Knight's Mfg. Co., 7750 9th St. SW, Vero Beach, FL 32968/407-562-5697; FAX: 407-569-2955

Kodiak Custom Bullets, 8261 Henry Circle, Anchorage, AK 99507/907-349-2282

Koevenig's Engraving Service, Box 55 Rabbit Gulch, Hill City, SD 57745

Kolpin Mfg., Inc., P.O. Box 107, 205 Depot St., Fox Lake, WI 53933/414-928-3118; FAX: 414-928-3687

Kopp, Terry K., Route 1, Box 224F, Lexington, MO 64067/816-259-2636

Korth, Robert-Bosch-Str. 4, P.O. Box 1320, 23909 Ratzeburg, GERMANY/451-4991497; FAX: 451-4993230 (U.S. importer—Interarms; Mandall Shooting Supplies, Inc.)

Korzinek Riflesmith, J., RD 2, Box 73D, Canton, PA 17724/717-673-8512

Kowa Optimed, Inc., 20001 S. Vermont Ave., Torrance, CA 90502/310-327-1913; FAX: 310-327-4177

Kramer Designs, 36 Chokecherry Ln., Clancy, MT 59634/406-933-8658; FAX: 406-933-8658

Kramer Handgun Leather, P.O. Box 112154, Tacoma, WA 98411/206-564-6652; FAX: 206-564-1214

Krause Publications, Inc., 700 E. State St., Iola, WI 54990/715-445-2214; FAX: 715-445-4087; Consumer orders only 800-258-0929

Kris Mounts, 108 Lehigh St., Johnstown, PA 15905/814-539-9751

KSN Industries, Ltd. (See U.S. importer—J.O. Arms Inc.)

Kudlas, John M., 622 14th St. SE, Rochester, MN 55904/507-288-5579

Kulis Freeze Dry Taxidermy, 725 Broadway Ave., Bedford, OH 44146/216-232-8352; FAX: 216-232-7305

Kwik Mount Corp., P.O. Box 19422, Louisville, KY 40259/502-239-5447

Kwik-Site Co., 5555 Treadwell, Wayne, MI 48184/313-326-1500; FAX: 313-326-4120

L

L&R Lock Co., 1137 Pocalla Rd., Sumter, SC 29150/803-775-6127

L&S Technologies, Inc. (See Aimtech Mount Systems)

La Clinique du .45, 1432 Rougemont, Chambly, Quebec, J3L 2L8 CANADA/514-658-1144

LaBounty Precision Reboring, P.O. Box 186, 7968 Silver Lk. Rd., Maple Falls, WA 98266/360-599-2047

LaFrance Specialties, P.O. Box 178211, San Diego, CA 92177-8211/619-293-3373

Lakewood Products, Inc., 275 June St., P.O. Box 230, Berlin, WI 54923/800-US-BUILT; FAX: 414-361-5058

Lampert, Ron, Rt. 1, Box 177, Guthrie, MN 56461/218-854-7345

Lane Bullets, Inc., 1011 S. 10th St., Kansas City, KS 66105/913-621-6113, 800-444-7468

Lane Publishing, P.O. Box 459, Lake Hamilton, AR 71951/501-525-7514; FAX: 501-525-7519

Lapua Ltd., P.O. Box 5, Lapua, FINLAND SF-62101/64-310111; FAX: 64-4388991 (U.S. importers—Champion's Choice; Keng's Firearms Specialty, Inc.

L.A.R. Mfg., Inc., 4133 W. Farm Rd., West Jordan, UT 84088/801-280-3505; FAX: 801-280-1972

LaRocca Gun Works, Inc., 51 Union Place, Worcester, MA 01608/508-754-2887; FAX: 508-754-2887

Laser Devices, Inc., 2 Harris Ct. A4, Monterey, CA 93940/408-373-0701, 800-235-2162; FAX: 408-373-0903

Laseraim, Inc. (See Emerging Technologies, Inc.)

LaserMax, 3495 Winton Place, Bldg. B, Rochester, NY 14623/716-272-5420; FAX: 716-272-5427

Lassen Community College, Gunsmithing Dept., P.O. Box 3000, Hwy. 139, Susanville, CA 96130/916-251-8809 ext. 109 or 200; FAX: 916-257-8964

Lathrop's, Inc., 5146 E. Pima, Tucson, AZ 85712/520-881-0266, 800-875-4867; FAX: 520-322-5704

Laughridge, William R. (See Cylinder & Slide, Inc.)

Law Concealment Systems, Inc., P.O. Box 3952, Wilmington, NC 28406/919-791-6656, 800-373-0116 orders

Lawrence Leather Co., P.O. Box 1479, Lillington, NC 27546/910-893-2071; FAX: 910-893-4742

Lawson Co., Harry, 3328 N. Richey Blvd., Tucson, AZ 85716/520-326-1117

Lawson, John G. (See Sight Shop, The)

LBT, HCR 62, Box 145, Moyie Springs, ID 83845/208-267-3588

Le Clear Industries (See E-Z-Way Systems)

Lea Mfg. Co., 237 E. Aurora St., Waterbury, CT 06720/203-753-5116

Leather Arsenal, 27549 Middleton Rd., Middleton, ID 83644/208-585-6212

Lebeau-Courally, Rue St. Gilles, 386, 4000 Liege, BELGIUM/041-52-48-43; FAX: 32-041-52-20-08 (U.S. importer—New England Arms Co.)

Leckie Professional Gunsmithing, 546 Quarry Rd., Ottsville, PA 18942/215-847-8594

Ledbetter Airguns, Riley, 1804 E. Sprague St., Winston Salem, NC 27107-3521/919-784-0676

Lee Precision, Inc., 4275 Hwy. U, Hartford, WI 53027/414-673-3075

Lee's Red Ramps, 4 Kristine Ln., Silver City, NM 88061/505-538-8529

LeFever Arms Co., Inc., 6234 Stokes, Lee Center Rd., Lee Center, NY 13363/315-337-6722; FAX: 315-337-1543

Legend Products Corp., 1555 E. Flamingo Rd., Suite 404, Las Vegas, NV 89119/702-228-1808, 702-796-5778; FAX: 702-228-7484

Leibowitz, Leonard, 1205 Murrayhill Ave., Pittsburgh, PA 15217/412-361-5455

Leica USA, Inc., 156 Ludlow Ave., Northvale, NJ 07647/201-767-7500; FAX: 201-767-8666

L.E.M. Gun Specialties, Inc., The Lewis Lead Remover, P.O. Box 2855, Peachtree City, GA 30269-2024/770-487-0556

Lem Sports, Inc., P.O. Box 2107, Aurora, IL 60506/815-286-7421, 800-688-8801 (orders only)

Lethal Force Institute, P.O. Box 122, Concord, MA 03302/603-226-1484; FAX: 603-226-3554

Lett Custom Grips, 672 Currier Rd., Hopkinton, NH 03229-2652

Leupold & Stevens, Inc., P.O. Box 688, Beaverton, OR 97075/503-646-9171; FAX: 503-526-1455

Lewis Lead Remover, The (See LEM Gun Specialties, Inc.)

Liberty Antique Gunworks, 19 Key St., P.O. Box 183, Eastport, ME 04631/207-853-4116

Liberty Metals, 2233 East 16th St., Los Angeles, CA 90021/213-581-9171; FAX: 213-581-9351

Liberty Safe, 1060 N. Spring Creek Pl., Springville, UT 84663/800-247-5625; FAX: 801-489-6409

Liberty Shooting Supplies, P.O. Box 357, Hillsboro, OR 97123/503-640-5518

Lightning Performance Innovations, Inc., RD1 Box 555, Mohawk, NY 13407/315-866-8819, 800-242-5873; FAX: 315-866-8819

Lind Custom Guns, Al, 7821 76th Ave. SW, Tacoma, WA 98498/206-584-6361

Lindsay, Steve, RR 2 Cedar Hills, Kearney, NE 68847/308-236-7885

Lindsley Arms Cartridge Co., P.O. Box 757, 20 College Hill Rd., Henniker, NH 03242/603-428-3127

Linebaugh Custom Sixguns, Route 2, Box 100, Maryville, MO 64468/816-562-3031

List Precision Engineering, Unit 1, Ingley Works, 13 River Road, Barking, Essex 1G11 0HE ENGLAND/011-081-594-1686

Lister, Weldon, Route 1, P.O. Box 1517, Boerne, TX 78006/210-755-2210

Lithi Bee Bullet Lube, 1885 Dyson St., Muskegon, MI 49442/616-726-3400

"Little John's" Antique Arms, 1740 W. Laveta, Orange, CA 92668

Little Trees Ramble (See Scott Pilkington, Little Trees Ramble)

Littler Sales Co., 20815 W. Chicago, Detroit, MI 48228/313-273-6889; FAX: 313-273-1099

Littleton, J.F., 275 Pinedale Ave., Oroville, CA 95966/916-533-6084

Llama Gabilondo Y Cia, Apartado 290, E-01080, Victoria, SPAIN (U.S. importer—Import Sports, Inc.)

Load From A Disk, 9826 Sagedale, Houston, TX 77089/713-484-0935

Loadmaster, P.O. Box 1209, Warminster, Wilts. BA12 9XJ ENGLAND/01044 1985 218544; FAX: 01044 1985 214111

Loch Leven Industries, P.O. Box 2751, Santa Rosa, CA 95405/707-573-8735; FAX: 707-573-0369

Lock's Philadelphia Gun Exchange, 6700 Rowland Ave., Philadelphia, PA 19149/215-332-6225; FAX: 215-332-4800

Log Cabin Sport Shop, 8010 Lafayette Rd., Lodi, OH 44254/216-948-1082

Lomont Precision Bullets, RR 1, P.O. Box 34, Salmon, ID 83467/208-756-6819; FAX: 208-756-6824

London Guns Ltd., Box 3750, Santa Barbara, CA 93130/805-683-4141; FAX: 805-683-1712

Lone Star Gunleather, 1301 Brushy Bend Dr., Round Rock, TX 78681/512-255-1805

Long, George F., 1500 Rogue River Hwy., Ste. F, Grants Pass, OR 97527/541-476-7552

Lorcin Engineering Co., Inc., 10427 San Sevaine Way, Ste. A, Mira Loma, CA 91752/909-360-1406; FAX: 909-360-0623

Lortone, Inc., 2856 NW Market St., Seattle, WA 98107/206-789-3100

Lothar Walther Precision Tool, Inc., 2190 Coffee Rd., Lithonia, GA 30058/770-482-4253; Fax: 770-482-9344

Loweth, Richard, 29 Hedgegrow Lane, Kirby Muxloe, Leics. LE9 9BN ENGLAND

L.P.A. Snc, Via Alfieri 26, Gardone V.T., Brescia, ITALY 25063/30-891-14-81; FAX: 30-891-09-51

LPS Laboratories, Inc., 4647 Hugh Howell Rd., P.O. Box 3050, Tucker, GA 30084/404-934-7800

Lucas, Edward E., 32 Garfield Ave., East Brunswick, NJ 08816/201-251-5526

Luch Metal Merchants, Barbara, 48861 West Rd., Wixon, MI 48393/800-876-5337

Lutz Engraving, Ron, E. 1998 Smokey Valley Rd., Scandinavia, WI 54977/715-467-2674

Lyman Instant Targets, Inc. (See Lyman Products Corp.)

Lyman Products Corporation, 475 Smith Street, Middletown, CT 06457-1541/860-632-2020, 800-22-LYMAN; FAX: 860-632-1699

M

M&D Munitions Ltd., 127 Verdi St., Farmingdale, NY 11735/800-878-2788, 516-752-1038; FAX: 516-752-1905

M&N Bullet Lube, P.O. Box 495, 151 NE Jefferson St., Madras, OR 97741/503-255-3750

MA Systems, P.O. Box 1143, Chouteau, OK 74337/918-479-6378

Mac-1 Distributors, 13974 Van Ness Ave., Gardena, CA 90249/310-327-3582

Mac's .45 Shop, P.O. Box 2028, Seal Beach, CA 90740/310-438-5046

Madis, George, P.O. Box 545, Brownsboro, TX 75756

Mag-Na-Port International, Inc., 41302 Executive Dr., Harrison Twp., MI 48045-1306/810-469-6727; FAX: 810-469-0425

Magma Engineering Co., P.O. Box 161, 20955 E. Ocotillo Rd., Queen Creek, AZ 85242/602-987-9008; FAX: 602-987-0148

Magnolia Sports, Inc., 211 W. Main, Magnolia, AR 71753/501-234-8410, 800-530-7816; FAX: 501-234-8117

Magnum Research, Inc., 7110 University Ave. NE, Minneapolis, MN 55432/800-772-6168, 612-574-1868; FAX: 612-574-0109

Magnus Bullets, P.O. Box 239, Toney, AL 35773/205-828-5089; FAX: 205-828-7756

MagSafe Ammo Co., 2725 Friendly Grove Rd NE, Olympia, WA 98506/360-357-6383; FAX: 360-705-4715

MAGTECH Recreational Products, Inc., 5030 Paradise Rd., Suite A104, Las Vegas, NV 89119/702-736-2043; FAX: 702-736-2140

Mahony, Philip Bruce, 67 White Hollow Rd., Lime Rock, CT 06039-2418/203-435-9341

Mahovsky's Metalife, R.D. 1, Box 149a Eureka Road, Grand Valley, PA 16420/814-436-7747

Maine Custom Bullets, RFD 1, Box 1755, Brooks, ME 04921

Mains Enterprises, Inc., 3111 S. Valley View Blvd., Suite B120, Las Vegas, NV 89102-7790/702-876-6278; FAX: 702-876-1269

Maionchi-L.M.I., Via Di Coselli-Zona Industriale Di Guamo, Lucca, ITALY 55060/011 39-583 94291

Mandall Shooting Supplies, Inc., 3616 N. Scottsdale Rd., Scottsdale, AZ 85252/602-945-2553; FAX: 602-949-0734

Marble Arms, P.O. Box 111, Gladstone, MI 49837/906-428-3710; FAX: 906-428-3711

Marchmon Bullets, 8191 Woodland Shore Dr., Brighton, MI 48116

Marent, Rudolf, 9711 Tiltree St., Houston, TX 77075/713-946-7028

Markell, Inc., 422 Larkfield Center 235, Santa Rosa, CA 95403/707-573-0792; FAX: 707-573-9867

Marksman Products, 5482 Argosy Dr., Huntington Beach, CA 92649/714-898-7535, 800-822-8005; FAX: 714-891-0782

Marmik Inc., 2116 S. Woodland Ave., Michigan City, IN 46361-7508/219-872-7231

Marple & Associates, Dick, 21 Dartmouth St., Hooksett, NH 03106/603-627-1837; FAX: 603-627-1837

Marquart Precision Co., Inc., Rear 136 Grove Ave., Box 1740, Prescott, AZ 86302/602-445-5646

Marsh, Mike, Croft Cottage, Main St., Elton, Derbyshire DE4 2BY, ENGLAND/01629 650 669

Martin Bookseller, J., P.O. Drawer AP, Beckley, WV 25802/304-255-4073; FAX: 304-255-4077

Martin's Gun Shop, 937 S. Sheridan Blvd., Lakewood, CO 80226/303-922-2184

Martz, John V., 8060 Lakeview Lane, Lincoln, CA 95648/916-645-2250

Marvel, Alan, 3922 Madonna Rd., Jarretsville, MD 21084/301-557-6545

Maryland Paintball Supply, 8507 Harford Rd., Parkville, MD 21234/410-882-5607

Masen Co., Inc., John, 1305 Jelmak, Grand Prairie, TX 75050/817-430-8732; FAX: 817-430-1715

MAST Technology, 4350 S. Arville, Suite 3, Las Vegas, NV 89103/702-362-5043; FAX: 702-362-9554

Master Class Bullets, 4209-D West 6th, Eugene, OR 97402/503-687-1263, 800-883-1263

Master Engravers, Inc. (See Hendricks, Frank E.)

Master Lock Co., 2600 N. 32nd St., Milwaukee, WI 53245/414-444-2800

Match Prep, P.O. Box 155, Tehachapi, CA 93581/805-822-5383

Matco, Inc., 1003-2nd St., N. Manchester, IN 46962/219-982-8282

Mathews & Son, Inc., George E., 10224 S. Paramount Blvd., Downey, CA 90241/310-862-6719; FAX: 310-862-6719

Mauser Werke Oberndorf Waffensysteme GmbH, Postfach 1349, 78722 Oberndorf/N. GERMANY (U.S. importer—GSI, Inc.)

Maxi-Mount, P.O. Box 291, Willoughby Hills, OH 44094-0291/216-944-9456; FAX: 216-944-9456

Maximum Security Corp., 32841 Calle Perfecto, San Juan Capistrano, CA 92675/714-493-3684; FAX: 714-496-7733

Mazur Restoration, Pete, 13083 Drummer Way, Grass Valley, CA 95949/916-268-2412

McCament, Jay, 1730-134th St. Ct. S., Tacoma, WA 98444/206-531-8832

McCann's Machine & Gun Shop, P.O. Box 641, Spanaway, WA 98387/206-537-6919; FAX: 206-537-6993

McCann's Muzzle-Gun Works, 14 Walton Dr., New Hope, PA 18938/215-862-2728

McCombs, Leo, 1862 White Cemetery Rd., Patriot, OH 45658/614-256-1714

McCormick Corp., Chip, 1825 Fortview Rd., Ste. 115, Austin, TX 78704/800-328-CHIP, 512-462-0004; FAX: 512-462-0009

McDonald, Dennis, 8359 Brady St., Peosta, IA 52068/319-556-7940

McFarland, Stan, 2221 Idella Ct., Grand Junction, CO 81505/303-243-4704

McGowen Rifle Barrels, 5961 Spruce Lane, St. Anne, IL 60964/815-937-9816; FAX: 815-937-4024

McKenzie, Lynton, 6940 N. Alvernon Way, Tucson, AZ 85718/520-299-5090

McKillen & Heyer, Inc., 35535 Euclid Ave. Suite 11, Willoughby, OH 44094/216-942-2044

McKinney, R.P. (See Schuetzen Gun Co.)

McMurdo, Lynn (See Specialty Gunsmithing)

MCRW Associates Shooting Supplies, R.R. 1 Box 1425, Sweet Valley, PA 18656/717-864-3967; FAX: 717-864-2669

MCS, Inc., 34 Delmar Dr., Brookfield, CT 06804/203-775-1013; FAX: 203-775-9462

MEC-Gar S.R.L., Via Madonnina 64, Gardone V.T., Brescia, ITALY 25063/39-30-8912687; FAX: 39-30-8910065 (U.S. importer—MEC-Gar U.S.A., Inc.)

Meier Works, P.O. Box 423, Tijeras, NM 87059/505-281-3783

Meister Bullets (See Gander Mountain)

Mele, Frank, 201 S. Wellow Ave., Cookeville, TN 38501/615-526-4860

Men-Metallwerk Elisenhuette, GmbH, P.O. Box 1263, D-56372 Nassau/Lahn, GERMANY/2604-7819

Menck, Thomas W., 5703 S. 77th St., Ralston, NE 68127-4201

Mendez, John A., P.O. Box 620984, Orlando, FL 32862/407-282-2178

Meprolight (See Hesco-Meprolight)

Mercer Custom Stocks, R.M., 216 S. Whitewater Ave., Jefferson, WI 53549/414-674-5130

Merit Corporation, Box 9044, Schenectady, NY 12309/518-346-1420

Merkuria Ltd., Argentinska 38, 17005 Praha 7, CZECH REPUBLIC/422-875117; FAX: 422-809152

Metalife Industries (See Mahovsky's Metalife)

Metaloy Inc., Rt. 5, Box 595, Berryville, AR 72616/501-545-3611

Michael's Antiques, Box 591, Waldoboro, ME 04572

Michaels of Oregon Co., P.O. Box 13010, Portland, OR 97213/503-255-6890; FAX: 503-255-0746

Micro Sight Co., 242 Harbor Blvd., Belmont, CA 94002/415-591-0769; FAX: 415-591-7531

Mid-America Guns and Ammo, 1205 W. Jefferson, Suite E, Effingham, IL 62401/800-820-5177

Mid-America Recreation, Inc., 1328 5th Ave., Moline, IL 61265/309-764-5089; FAX: 309-764-2722

Middlebrooks Custom Shop, 7366 Colonial Trail East, Surry, VA 23883/804-357-0881; FAX: 804-365-0442

Midway Arms, Inc., 5875 W. Van Horn Tavern Rd., Columbia, MO 65203/800-243-3220, 314-445-6363; FAX: 314-446-1018

Miller Co., David, 3131 E. Greenlee Rd., Tucson, AZ 85716/602-326-3117

Miller Custom, 210 E. Julia, Clinton, IL 61727/217-935-9362

Miller Enterprises, Inc., R.P., 1557 E. Main St., P.O. Box 234, Brownsburg, IN 46112/317-852-8187

Millett Sights, 16131 Gothard St., Huntington Beach, CA 92647/714-842-5575, 800-645-5388; FAX: 714-843-5707

Minute Man High Tech Industries, 10611 Canyon Rd. E., Suite 151, Puyallup, WA 98373/800-233-2734

Mirador Optical Corp., P.O. Box 11614, Marina Del Rey, CA 90295-7614/310-821-5587; FAX: 310-305-0386

Mitchell Arms, Inc., 3433-B. W. Harvard St., Santa Ana, CA 92704/714-957-5711; FAX: 714-957-5732

Mitchell's Accuracy Shop, 68 Greenridge Dr., Stafford, VA 22554/703-659-0165

MI-TE Bullets, R.R. 1 Box 230, Ellsworth, KS 67439/913-472-4575

Mittermeier, Inc., Frank, P.O. Box 2G, 3577 E. Tremont Ave., Bronx, NY 10465/718-828-3843

Mixson Corp., 7435 W. 19th Ct., Hialeah, FL 33014/305-821-5190, 800-327-0078; FAX: 305-558-9318

MJK Gunsmithing, Inc., 417 N. Huber Ct., E. Wenatchee, WA 98802/509-884-7683

MJM Mfg., 3283 Rocky Water Ln. Suite B, San Jose, CA 95148/408-270-4207

MKL Service Co., 610 S. Troy St., P.O. Box D, Royal Oak, MI 48068/810-548-5453

MKS Supply, Inc. (See Hi-Point Firearms)

MMP, Rt. 6, Box 384, Harrison, AR 72601/501-741-5019; FAX: 501-741-3104

M.O.A. Corp., 2451 Old Camden Pike, Eaton, OH 45320/513-456-3669

Modern Gun Repair School, P.O. Box 92577, Southlake, TX 76092/800-493-4114; FAX: 800-556-5112

Modern Gun School, 500 N. Kimball, Suite 105, Southlake, TX 76092/800-774-5112

Modern MuzzleLoading, Inc., 234 Airport Rd., P.O. Box 130, Centerville, IA 52544/515-856-2626; FAX: 515-856-2628

Montana Outfitters, Lewis E. Yearout, 308 Riverview Dr. E., Great Falls, MT 59404/406-761-0859

Montana Precision Swaging, P.O. Box 4746, Butte, MT 59702/406-782-7502

Monte Kristo Pistol Grip Co., P.O. Box 85, Whiskeytown, CA 96095/916-778-0240

Montgomery Community College, P.O. Box 787-GD, Troy, NC 27371/910-572-3691, 800-839-6222

Moreton/Fordyce Enterprises, P.O. Box 940, Saylorsburg, PA 18353/717-992-5742; FAX: 717-992-8775

Morini (See U.S. importers—Mandall Shooting Supplies, Inc.; Nygord Precision Products)

Morrow, Bud, 11 Hillside Lane, Sheridan, WY 82801-9729/307-674-8360

Morton Booth Co., P.O. Box 123, Joplin, MO 64802/417-673-1962; FAX: 417-673-3642

Mo's Competitor Supplies (See MCS, Inc.)

Moschetti, Mitchell R., P.O. Box 27065, Denver, CO 80227

Mountain Bear Rifle Works, Inc., 100 B Ruritan Rd., Sterling, VA 20164/703-430-0420; FAX: 703-430-7068

Mountain South, P.O. Box 381, Barnwell, SC 29812/FAX: 803-259-3227

Mountain State Muzzleloading Supplies, Box 154-1, Rt. 2, Williamstown, WV 26187/304-375-7842; FAX: 304-375-3737

Mountain States Engraving, Kenneth W. Warren, P.O. Box 2842, Wenatchee, WA 98802/509-663-6123

Mowrey's Guns & Gunsmithing, RR1, Box 82, Canajoharie, NY 13317/518-673-3483

MSC Industrial Supply Co., 151 Sunnyside Blvd., Plainview, NY 11803-9915/516-349-0330

MSR Targets, P.O. Box 1042, West Covina, CA 91793/818-331-7840

Mt. Alto Outdoor Products, Rt. 735, Howardsville, VA 24562

Mt. Baldy Bullet Co., 12981 Old Hill City Rd., Keystone, SD 57751-6623/605-666-4725

MTM Molded Products Co., Inc., 3370 Obco Ct., Dayton, OH 45414/513-890-7461; FAX: 513-890-1747

Mullins Ammo, Rt. 2, Box 304K, Clintwood, VA 24228/703-926-6772

Mullis Guncraft, 3523 Lawyers Road E., Monroe, NC 28110/704-283-6683

Multiplex International, 26 S. Main St., Concord, NH 03301/FAX: 603-796-2223

Munsch Gunsmithing, Tommy, Rt. 2, P.O. Box 248, Little Falls, MN 56345/612-632-6695

Murmur Corp., 2823 N. Westmoreland Ave., Dallas, TX 75222/214-630-5400

Murray State College, 100 Faculty Dr., Tishomingo, OK 73460/405-371-2371 ext. 238, 800-342-0698

Muscle Products Corp., 112 Fennell Dr., Butler, PA 16001/800-227-7049, 412-283-0567; FAX: 412-283-8310

Museum of Historical Arms Inc., 2750 Coral Way, Suite 204, Miami, FL 33145/305-444-9199

Mushroom Express Bullet Co., 601 W. 6th St., Greenfield, IN 46140-1728/317-462-6332

Mustra's Custom Guns, Inc., Carl, 1002 Pennsylvania Ave., Palm Harbor, FL 34683/813-785-1403

Muzzleloaders Etcetera, Inc., 9901 Lyndale Ave. S., Bloomington, MN 55420/612-884-1161

N

N&J Sales, Lime Kiln Rd., Northford, CT 06472/203-484-0247

Nagel's Bullets, 9 Wilburn, Baytown, TX 77520

Napoleon Bonaparte, Inc., Gerald Desquesnes, 640 Harrison St., Santa Clara, CA 95050

Nastoff's 45 Shop, Inc., Steve, 12288 Mahoning Ave., P.O. Box 446, North Jackson, OH 44451/216-538-2977

National Bullet Co., 1585 E. 361 St., Eastlake, OH 44095/216-951-1854; FAX: 216-951-7761

National Security Safe Co., Inc., P.O. Box 39, 620 S. 380 E., American Fork, UT 84003/801-756-7706, 800-544-3829; FAX: 801-756-8043

National Target Co., 4690 Wyaconda Rd., Rockville, MD 20852/800-827-7060, 301-770-7060; FAX: 301-770-7892

Nationwide Sports Distributors, Inc., 70 James Way, Southampton, PA 18966/215-322-2050, 800-355-3006; FAX: 702-358-2093

Naval Ordnance Works, Rt. 2, Box 919, Sheperdstown, WV 25443/304-876-0998

Navy Arms Co., 689 Bergen Blvd., Ridgefield, NJ 07657/201-945-2500; FAX: 201-945-6859

N.B.B., Inc., 24 Elliot Rd., Sterling, MA 01564/508-422-7538, 800-942-9444

N.C. Ordnance Co., P.O. Box 3254, Wilson, NC 27895/919-237-2440; FAX: 919-243-0927

NCP Products, Inc., 3500 12th St. N.W., Canton, OH 44708/330-456-5130; FAX: 330-456-5234

NECO, 1316-67th St., Emeryville, CA 94608/510-450-0420; FAX: 510-450-0421

Necromancer Industries, Inc., 14 Communications Way, West Newton, PA 15089/412-872-8722

NEI Handtools, Inc., 51583 Columbia River Hwy., Scappoose, OR 97056/503-543-6776; FAX: 503-543-6799; E-MAIL: neiht@mci-mail.com

Nelson Combat Leather, Bruce, P.O. Box 8691 CRB, Tucson, AZ 85738

Nelson, Gary K., 975 Terrace Dr., Oakdale, CA 95361/209-847-4590

Nesci Enterprises, Inc., P.O. Box 119, Summit St., East Hampton, CT 06424/860-267-2588; FAX: 860-267-2589

Nettestad Gun Works, RR 1, Box 160, Pelican Rapids, MN 56572/218-863-4301

Neumann GmbH, Am Galgenberg 6, 90575 Langenzenn, GERMANY/09101/8258; FAX: 09101/6356

Nevada Pistol Academy Inc., 4610 Blue Diamond Rd., Las Vegas, NV 89139/702-897-1100

New Advantage Arms Corp., 2843 N. Alvernon Way, Tucson, AZ 85712/602-881-7444; FAX: 602-323-0949

New England Ammunition Co., 1771 Post Rd. East, Suite 223, Westport, CT 06880/203-254-8048

New England Arms Co., Box 278, Lawrence Lane, Kittery Point, ME 03905/207-439-0593; FAX: 207-439-6726

New Orleans Jewelers Supply Co., 206 Charters St., New Orleans, LA 70130/504-523-3839; FAX: 504-523-3836

New Win Publishing, Inc., Box 5159, Clinton, NJ 08809/201-735-9701; FAX: 201-735-9703

Newell, Robert H., 55 Coyote, Los Alamos, NM 87544/505-662-7135

NgraveR Co., The, 67 Wawecus Hill Rd., Bozrah, CT 06334/203-823-1533

Nicholson Custom, Rt. 1, Box 176-3, Sedalia, MO 65301/816-826-8746

Niemi Engineering, W.B., Box 126 Center Road, Greensboro, VT 05841/802-533-7180 days, 802-533-7141 evenings

Nikon, Inc., 1300 Walt Whitman Rd., Melville, NY 11747/516-547-8623; FAX: 516-547-0309

Nitex, Inc., P.O. Box 1706, Uvalde, TX 78801/210-278-8843

Noble Co., Jim, 1305 Columbia St., Vancouver, WA 98660/206-695-1309

Noreen, Peter H., 5075 Buena Vista Dr., Belgrade, MT 59714/406-586-7383

Norma Precision AB (See U.S. importers—Dynamit Nobel-RWS Inc.; Paul Co. Inc., The)

North American Arms, Inc., 2150 South 950 East, Provo, UT 84606-6285/800-821-5783, 801-374-9990; FAX: 801-374-9998

North American Correspondence Schools, The Gun Pro School, Oak & Pawney St., Scranton, PA 18515/717-342-7701

North American Shooting Systems, P.O. Box 306, Osoyoos, B.C. V0H 1V0 CANADA/604-495-3131; FAX: 604-495-2816

North American Specialties, P.O. Box 189, Baker City, OR 97814/503-523-6954

North Devon Firearms Services, 3 North St., Braunton, EX33 1AJ ENGLAND/01271 813624; FAX: 01271 813624

North Fork Custom Gunsmithing, James Johnston, 428 Del Rio Rd., Roseburg, OR 97470/503-673-4467

North Mountain Pine Training Center (See Executive Protection Institute)

North Specialty Products, 2664-B Saturn St., Brea, CA 92621/714-524-1665

North Star West, P.O. Box 488, Glencoe, CA 95232/209-293-7010

Northern Precision Custom Swaged Bullets, 329 S. James St., Carthage, NY 13619/315-493-1711

No-Sho Mfg. Co., 10727 Glenfield Ct., Houston, TX 77096/713-723-5332

Nosler, Inc., P.O. Box 671, Bend, OR 97709/800-285-3701, 503-382-3921; FAX: 503-388-4667

Novak's, Inc., 1206½ 30th St., P.O. Box 4045, Parkersburg, WV 26101/304-485-9295; FAX: 304-428-6722

Nowlin Custom Mfg., Rt. 1, Box 308, Claremore, OK 74017/918-342-0689; FAX: 918-342-0624

NRI Gunsmith School, 4401 Connecticut Ave. NW, Washington, D.C. 20008

Nu-Line Guns, Inc., 1053 Caulks Hill Rd., Harvester, MO 63304/314-441-4500, 314-447-4501; FAX: 314-447-5018

Null Holsters Ltd., K.L., 161 School St. NW, Hill City Station, Resaca, GA 30735/706-625-5643; FAX: 706-625-9392

Nu-Teck, 30 Industrial Park Rd., Box 37, Centerbrook, CT 06409/203-767-3573; FAX: 203-767-9137

Nygord Precision Products, P.O. Box 12578, Prescott, AZ 86304/520-717-2315; FAX: 520-717-2198

O

October Country, P.O. Box 969, Dept. GD, Hayden, ID 83835/208-772-2068; FAX: 208-772-9230

Oehler Research, Inc., P.O. Box 9135, Austin, TX 78766/512-327-6900, 800-531-5125; FAX: 512-327-6903

Oglesby & Oglesby Gunmakers, Inc., RR 5, Springfield, IL 62707/217-487-7100

Oil Rod and Gun Shop, 69 Oak St., East Douglas, MA 01516/508-476-3687

Ojala Holsters, Arvo, P.O. Box 98, N. Hollywood, CA 91603/503-669-1404

Oker's Engraving, 365 Bell Rd., P.O. Box 126, Shawnee, CO 80475/303-838-6042

Oklahoma Ammunition Co., 4310 W. Rogers Blvd., Skiatook, OK 74070/918-396-3187; FAX: 918-396-4270

Oklahoma Leather Products, Inc., 500 26th NW, Miami, OK 74354/918-542-6651; FAX: 918-542-6653

OK Weber, Inc., P.O. Box 7485, Eugene, OR 97401/541-747-0458; FAX: 541-747-5927

Old Dominion Engravers, 100 Progress Drive, Lynchburg, VA 24502/804-237-4450

Old Wagon Bullets, 32 Old Wagon Rd., Wilton, CT 06897

Old West Bullet Moulds, P.O. Box 519, Flora Vista, NM 87415/505-334-6970

Old West Reproductions, Inc., 446 Florence S. Loop, Florence, MT 59833/406-273-2615

Old Western Scrounger, Inc., 12924 Hwy. A-l2, Montague, CA 96064/916-459-5445; FAX: 916-459-3944

Old World Oil Products, 3827 Queen Ave. N., Minneapolis, MN 55412/612-522-5037

Ole Frontier Gunsmith Shop, 2617 Hwy. 29 S., Cantonment, FL 32533/904-477-8074

Olson, Myron, 989 W. Kemp, Watertown, SD 57201/605-886-9787

Olson, Vic, 5002 Countryside Dr., Imperial, MO 63052/314-296-8086

Omark Industries, Div. of Blount, Inc., 2299 Snake River Ave., P.O. Box 856, Lewiston, ID 83501/800-627-3640, 208-746-2351

Ordnance Works, The, 2969 Pidgeon Point Road, Eureka, CA 95501/707-443-3252

Outa-Site Gun Carriers, 219 Market St., Laredo, TX 78040/210-722-4678, 800-880-9715; FAX: 210-726-4858

Outdoor Connection, Inc., The, 201 Cotton Dr., P.O. Box 7751, Waco, TX 76714-7751/800-533-6076; 817-772-5575; FAX: 817-776-3553

Outdoorsman's Bookstore, The, Llangorse, Brecon, Powys LD3 7UE, U.K./44-1874-658-660; FAX: 44-1874-658-650

Outers Laboratories, Div. of Blount, Inc., Sporting Equipment Div., Route 2,, P.O. Box 39/Onalaska, WI 54650/608-781-5800; FAX: 608-781-0368

Ox-Yoke Originals, Inc., 34 Main St., Milo, ME 04463/800-231-8313, 207-943-7351; FAX: 207-943-2416

Ozark Gun Works, 11830 Cemetery Rd., Rogers, AR 72756/501-631-6944; FAX: 501-631-6944

P

P&M Sales and Service, 5724 Gainsborough Pl., Oak Forest, IL 60452/708-687-7149

P&S Gun Service, 2138 Old Shepardsville Rd., Louisville, KY 40218/502-456-9346

Pachmayr, Ltd., 1875 S. Mountain Ave., Monrovia, CA 91016/818-357-7771, 800-423-9704; FAX: 818-358-7251

Pacific Pistolcraft, 1810 E. Columbia Ave., Tacoma, WA 98404/206-474-5465

Pacific Rifle Co., 1040-D Industrial Parkway, Newberg, OR 97132/503-538-7437

Paco's (See Small Custom Mould & Bullet Co.)

P.A.C.T., Inc., P.O. Box 531525, Grand Prairie, TX 75053/214-641-0049

Page Custom Bullets, P.O. Box 25, Port Moresby Papua, NEW GUINEA

Pagel Gun Works, Inc., 1407 4th St. NW, Grand Rapids, MN 55744/218-326-3003

Palmer Security Products, 2930 N. Campbell Ave., Chicago, IL 60618/800-788-7725; FAX: 312-267-8080

PanaVise Products, Inc., 1485 Southern Way, Sparks, NV 89431/702-353-2900; FAX: 702-353-2929

Para-Ordnance Mfg., Inc., 980 Tapscott Rd., Scarborough, Ont. M1X 1E7, CANADA/416-297-7855; FAX: 416-297-1289 (U.S. importer—Para-Ordnance, Inc.)

Para-Ordnance, Inc., 1919 NE 45th St., Ft. Lauderdale, FL 33308

Paragon Sales & Services, Inc., P.O. Box 2022, Joliet, IL 60434/815-725-9212; FAX: 815-725-8974

Pardini Armi Srl, Via Italica 154, 55043 Lido Di Camaiore Lu, ITALY/584-90121; FAX: 584-90122 (U.S. importers—Nygord Precision Products)

Paris, Frank J., 17417 Pershing St., Livonia, MI 48152-3822

Parker Gun Finishes, 9337 Smokey Row Rd., Strawberry Plains, TN 37871/423-933-3286

Parker, Mark D., 1240 Florida Ave. 7, Longmont, CO 80501/303-772-0214

Parsons Optical Mfg. Co., P.O. Box 192, Ross, OH 45061/513-867-0820; FAX: 513-867-8380

Parts & Surplus, P.O. Box 22074, Memphis, TN 38122/901-683-4007

Pasadena Gun Center, 206 E. Shaw, Pasadena, TX 77506/713-472-0417; FAX: 713-472-1322

Passive Bullet Traps, Inc. (See Savage Range Systems, Inc.)

PAST Sporting Goods, Inc., P.O. Box 1035, Columbia, MO 65205/314-445-9200; FAX: 314-446-6606

Paterson Gunsmithing, 438 Main St., Paterson, NJ 07502/201-345-4100

Pathfinder Sports Leather, 2920 E. Chambers St., Phoenix, AZ 85040/602-276-0016

Patrick Bullets, P.O. Box 172, Warwick QSLD 4370 AUSTRALIA

PC Bullet/ADC, Inc., 52700 NE First, Scappoose, OR 97056-3212/503-543-5088; FAX: 503-543-5990

Peacemaker Specialists, P.O. Box 157, Whitmore, CA 96096/916-472-3438

Pease Accuracy, Bob, P.O. Box 310787, New Braunfels, TX 78131/210-625-1342

Pedersen, C.R., 2717 S. Pere Marquette Hwy., Ludington, MI 49431/616-843-2061

Pedersen, Rex C., 2717 S. Pere Marquette Hwy., Ludington, MI 49431/616-843-2061

Peerless Alloy, Inc., 1445 Osage St., Denver, CO 80204-2439/303-825-6394, 800-253-1278

Pejsa Ballistics, 2120 Kenwood Pkwy., Minneapolis, MN 55405/612-374-3337; FAX: 612-374-3337

Peltor, Inc., 41 Commercial Way, E. Providence, RI 02914/401-438-4800; FAX: 401-434-1708

PEM's Mfg. Co., 5063 Waterloo Rd., Atwater, OH 44201/216-947-3721

Pence Precision Barrels, 7567 E. 900 S., S. Whitley, IN 46787/219-839-4745

Pend Oreille Sport Shop, 3100 Hwy. 200 East, Sandpoint, ID 83864/208-263-2412

Pendleton Royal, c/o Swingler Buckland Ltd., 4/7 Highgate St., Birmingham, ENGLAND B12 0XS/44 121 440 3060, 44 121 446 5898; FAX: 44 121 446 4165

Penguin Industries, Inc., Airport Industrial Mall, Coatesville, PA 19320/610-384-6000; FAX: 610-857-5980

Pennsylvania Gunsmith School, 812 Ohio River Blvd., Avalon, Pittsburgh, PA 15202/412-766-1812

Penrod Precision, 312 College Ave., P.O. Box 307, N. Manchester, IN 46962/219-982-8385

Pentax Corp., 35 Inverness Dr. E., Englewood, CO 80112/303-799-8000; FAX: 303-790-1131

Pentheny de Pentheny, 2352 Baggett Ct., Santa Rosa, CA 95401/707-573-1390; FAX: 707-573-1390

Perazone-Gunsmith, Brian, P.O. Box 275GD, Cold Spring Rd., Roxbury, NY 12474/607-326-4088; FAX: 607-326-3140

Performance Specialists, 308 Eanes School Rd., Austin, TX 78746/512-327-0119

Personal Protection Systems, RD 5, Box 5027-A, Moscow, PA 18444/717-842-1766

Peters Stahl GmbH, Stettiner Strasse 42, D-33106 Paderborn, GERMANY/05251-750025; FAX: 05251-75611 (U.S. importers—Harris Gunworks; Olympic Arms)

Petersen Publishing Co., 6420 Wilshire Blvd., Los Angeles, CA 90048/213-782-2000; FAX: 213-782-2867

Petro-Explo, Inc., 7650 U.S. Hwy. 287, Suite 100, Arlington, TX 76017/817-478-8888

Pettinger Books, Gerald, Rt. 2, Box 125, Russell, IA 50238/515-535-2239

Phillippi Custom Bullets, Justin, P.O. Box 773, Ligonier, PA 15658/412-238-9671

Phoenix Arms, 1420 S. Archibald Ave., Ontario, CA 91761/909-947-4843; FAX: 909-947-6798

Piedmont Community College, P.O. Box 1197, Roxboro, NC 27573/910-599-1181

Pierce Pistols, 2326 E. Hwy. 34, Newnan, GA 30263/404-253-8192

Pilgrim Pewter, Inc. (See Bell Originals Inc., Sid)

Pilkington, Scott, Little Trees Ramble, P.O. Box 97, Monteagle, TN 37356/615-924-3475; FAX: 615-924-3489

Pine Technical College, 1100 4th St., Pine City, MN 55063/800-521-7463; FAX: 612-629-6766

Pinetree Bullets, 133 Skeena St., Kitimat BC, CANADA V8C 1Z1/604-632-3768; FAX: 604-632-3768

Pioneer Arms Co., 355 Lawrence Rd., Broomall, PA 19008/215-356-5203

Pioneer Guns, 5228 Montgomery Rd., Norwood, OH 45212/513-631-4871

Piquette, Paul R., 80 Bradford Dr., Feeding Hills, MA 01030/413-781-8300, Ext. 682

Plaxco, J. Michael, Rt. 1, P.O. Box 203, Roland, AR 72135/501-868-9787

Plum City Ballistic Range, N2162 80th St., Plum City, WI 54761-8622/715-647-2539

PlumFire Press, Inc., 30-A Grove Ave., Patchogue, NY 11772-4112/800-695-7246; FAX:516-758-4071

PMC/Eldorado Cartridge Corp., P.O. Box 62508, 12801 U.S. Hwy. 95 S., Boulder City, NV 89005/702-294-0025; FAX: 702-294-0121

P.M. Enterprises, Inc., 146 Curtis Hill Rd., Chehalis, WA 98532/206-748-3743; FAX: 206-748-1802

Police Bookshelf, P.O. Box 122, Concord, NH 03301/603-224-6814; FAX: 603-226-3554

Policlips North America, 59 Douglas Crescent, Toronto, Ont. CANADA M4W 2E6/800-229-5089, 416-924-0383; FAX: 416-924-4375

Pomeroy, Robert, RR1, Box 50, E. Corinth, ME 04427/207-285-7721

Pony Express Reloaders, 608 E. Co. Rd. D, Suite 3, St. Paul, MN 55117/612-483-9406; FAX: 612-483-9884

Pony Express Sport Shop, Inc., 16606 Schoenborn St., North Hills, CA 91343/818-895-1231

Portus, Robert, 130 Ferry Rd., Grants Pass, OR 97526/503-476-4919

Potts, Wayne E., 912 Poplar St., Denver, CO 80220/303-355-5462

Powder Valley Services, Rt. 1, Box 100, Dexter, KS 67038/316-876-5418

Power Custom, Inc., RR 2, P.O. Box 756AB, Gravois Mills, MO 65037/314-372-5684

Practical Tools, Inc., Div. Behlert Precision, 7067 Easton Rd., P.O. Box 133, Pipersville, PA 18947/215-766-7301; FAX: 215-766-8681

Precise Metalsmithing Enterprises, 146 Curtis Hill Rd., Chehalis, WA 98532/206-748-3743; FAX: 206-748-8102

Precision Airgun Sales, Inc., 5139 Warrensville Center Rd., Maple Hts., OH 44137-1906/216-587-5005

Precision Castings & Equipment, Inc., P.O. Box 326, Jasper, IN 47547-0135/812-634-9167

Precision Components, 3177 Sunrise Lake, Milford, PA 18337/717-686-4414

Precision Components and Guns, Rt. 55, P.O. Box 337, Pawling, NY 12564/914-855-3040

Precision Delta Corp., P.O. Box 128, Ruleville, MS 38771/601-756-2810; FAX: 601-756-2590

Precision Metal Finishing, John Westrom, P.O. Box 3186, Des Moines, IA 50316/515-288-8680; FAX: 515-244-3925

Precision Munitions, Inc., P.O. Box 326, Jasper, IN 47547

Precision Reloading, Inc., P.O. Box 122, Stafford Springs, CT 06076/860-684-7979; FAX: 860-684-6788

Precision Sales International, Inc., P.O. Box 1776, Westfield, MA 01086/413-562-5055; FAX: 413-562-5056

Precision Small Arms, 9777 Wilshire Blvd., Suite 1005, Beverly Hills, CA 90212/310-859-4867; FAX: 310-859-2868

Precision Specialties, 131 Hendom Dr., Feeding Hills, MA 01030/413-786-3365; FAX: 413-786-3365

Precision Sport Optics, 15571 Producer Lane, Unit G, Huntington Beach, CA 92649/714-891-1309; FAX: 714-892-6920

Prescott Projectile Co., 1808 Meadowbrook Road, Prescott, AZ 86303

Price Bullets, Patrick W., 16520 Worthley Drive, San Lorenzo, CA 94580/510-278-1547

Prime Reloading, 30 Chiswick End, Meldreth, Royston SG8 6LZ UK/0763-260636

Pro Load Ammunition, Inc., 5180 E. Seltice Way, Post Falls, ID 83854/208-773-9444; FAX: 208-773-9441

Pro-Shot Products, Inc., P.O. Box 763, Taylorville, IL 62568/217-824-9133; FAX: 217-824-8861

Professional Gunsmiths of America, Inc., Route 1, Box 224F, Lexington, MO 64067/816-259-2636

Professional Hunter Supplies (See Star Custom Bullets)

Prolix® Lubricants, P.O. Box 1348, Victorville, CA 92393/800-248-LUBE, 619-243-3129; FAX: 619-241-0148

Protecto Plastics, Div. of Penguin Ind., Airport Industrial Mall, Coatesville, PA 19320/215-384-6000

Protector Mfg. Co., Inc., The, 443 Ashwood Place, Boca Raton, FL 33431/407-394-6011

Protektor Model, 1-11 Bridge St., Galeton, PA 16922/814-435-2442

P.S.M.G. Gun Co., 10 Park Ave., Arlington, MA 02174/617-646-8845; FAX: 617-646-2133

PWL Gunleather, P.O. Box 450432, Atlanta, GA 31145/404-822-1640; FAX: 404-822-1704

Q

Quality Firearms of Idaho, Inc., 114 13th Ave. S., Nampa, ID 83651/208-466-1631

Quality Parts Co./Bushmaster Firearms, 999 Roosevelt Trail, Bldg. 3, Windham, ME 04062/800-998-7928, 207-892-2005; FAX: 207-892-8068

Quigley's Personal Protection Strategies, Paxton, 9903 Santa Monica Blvd.,, 300/Beverly Hills, CA 90212/310-281-1762

R

Rabeno, Martin, 92 Spook Hole Rd., Ellenville, NY 12428/914-647-4567

Radical Concepts, P.O. Box 1473, Lake Grove, OR 97035/503-538-7437

Rainier Ballistics Corp., 4500 15th St. East, Tacoma, WA 98424/800-638-8722, 206-922-7589; FAX: 206-922-7854

Ram-Line, Inc., 545 Thirty-One Rd., Grand Junction, CO 81504/303-434-4500; FAX: 303-434-4004

Ranch Products, P.O. Box 145, Malinta, OH 43535/313-277-3118; FAX: 313-565-8536

Randco UK, 286 Gipsy Rd., Welling, Kent DA16 1JJ, ENGLAND/44 81 303 4118

Ranger Products, 2623 Grand Blvd., Suite 209, Holiday, FL 34609/813-942-4652, 800-407-7007; FAX: 813-942-6221

Ranging, Inc., Routes 5 & 20, East Bloomfield, NY 14443/716-657-6161; FAX: 716-657-5405

Ransom International Corp., P.O. Box 3845, 1040-A Sandretto Dr., Prescott, AZ 86302/520-778-7899; FAX: 520-778-7993; E-MAIL: ransom@primenet.com; WEB: http://www.primenet.com/~ransom

Rapine Bullet Mould Mfg. Co., 9503 Landis Lane, East Greenville, PA 18041/215-679-5413; FAX: 215-679-9795

Ravell Ltd., 289 Diputacion St., 08009, Barcelona SPAIN/34(3) 4874486; FAX: 34(3) 4881394

Raytech, Div. of Lyman Products Corp., 475 Smith Street, Middletown, CT 06457-1541/860-632-2020; FAX: 860-632-1699

RCBS, Div. of Blount, Inc., Sporting Equipment Div., 605 Oro Dam Blvd., Oroville, CA 95965/800-533-5000, 916-533-5191; FAX: 916-533-1647

Reardon Products, P.O. Box 126, Morrison, IL 61270/815-772-3155

Recoilless Technologies, Inc., 3432 W. Wilshire Dr., Suite 11, Phoenix, AZ 85009/602-278-8903; FAX: 602-272-5946

Red Cedar Precision Mfg., W. 485 Spruce Dr., Brodhead, WI 53520/608-897-8416

Red Star Target Co., P.O. Box 275, Babb, MT 59411-0275/800-679-2917; FAX: 800-679-2918

Redding Reloading Equipment, 1097 Starr Rd., Cortland, NY 13045/607-753-3331; FAX: 607-756-8445

Redfield, Inc., 5800 E. Jewell Ave., Denver, CO 80224-2303/303-757-6411; FAX: 303-756-2338

Redman's Rifling & Reboring, 189 Nichols Rd., Omak, WA 98841/509-826-5512

Redwood Bullet Works, 3559 Bay Rd., Redwood City, CA 94063/415-367-6741

Reed, Dave, Rt. 1, Box 374, Minnesota City, MN 55959/507-689-2944

R.E.I., P.O. Box 88, Tallevast, FL 34270/813-755-0085

Reloading Specialties, Inc., Box 1130, Pine Island, MN 55463/507-356-8500; FAX: 507-356-8800

Remington Arms Co., Inc., P.O. Box 700, 870 Remington Drive, Madison, NC 27025-0700/800-243-9700

Renegade, P.O. Box 31546, Phoenix, AZ 85046/602-482-6777; FAX: 602-482-1952

Reno, Wayne, 2808 Stagestop Rd., Jefferson, CO 80456/719-836-3452

R.E.T. Enterprises, 2608 S. Chestnut, Broken Arrow, OK 74012/918-251-GUNS; FAX: 918-251-0587

Retting, Inc., Martin B., 11029 Washington, Culver City, CA 90232/213-837-2412

R.G.-G., Inc., P.O. Box 1261, Conifer, CO 80433-1261/303-697-4154; FAX: 303-697-4154

Rice, Keith (See White Rock Tool & Die)

Richards, John, Richards Classic Oil Finish, Rt. 2, Box 325, Bedford, KY 40006/502-255-7222

Rickard, Inc., Pete, RD 1, Box 292, Cobleskill, NY 12043/800-282-5663; FAX: 518-234-2454

Ridgetop Sporting Goods, P.O. Box 306, 42907 Hilligoss Ln. East, Eatonville, WA 98328/360-832-6422; FAX: 360-832-6422

Riebe Co., W.J., 3434 Tucker Rd., Boise, ID 83703

Ries, Chuck, 415 Ridgecrest Dr., Grants Pass, OR 97527/503-476-5623

RIG Products, 87 Coney Island Dr., Sparks, NV 89431-6334/702-331-5666; FAX: 702-331-5669

Riggs, Jim, 206 Azalea, Boerne, TX 78006/210-249-8567

Riling Arms Books Co., Ray, 6844 Gorsten St., P.O. Box 18925, Philadelphia, PA 19119/215-438-2456; FAX: 215-438-5395

Rim Pac Sports, Inc., 1034 N. Soldano Ave., Azusa, CA 91702-2135

Ringler Custom Leather Co., 31 Shining Mtn. Rd., Powell, WY 82435/307-645-3255

R.I.S. Co., Inc., 718 Timberlake Circle, Richardson, TX 75080/214-235-0933

River Road Sporting Clays, Bruce Barsotti, P.O. Box 3016, Gonzales, CA 93926/408-675-2473

R.M. Precision, Inc., Attn. Greg F. Smith Marketing, P.O. Box 210, LaVerkin, UT 84745/801-635-4656; FAX: 801-635-4430

Robar Co.'s, Inc., The, 21438 N. 7th Ave., Suite B, Phoenix, AZ 85027/602-581-2648; FAX: 602-582-0059

Roberts/Engraver, J.J., 7808 Lake Dr., Manassas, VA 22111/703-330-0448

Roberts Products, 25328 SE Iss. Beaver Lk. Rd., Issaquah, WA 98029/206-392-8172

Robinson H.V. Bullets, 3145 Church St., Zachary, LA 70791/504-654-4029

Rochester Lead Works, 76 Anderson Ave., Rochester, NY 14607/716-442-8500; FAX: 716-442-4712

Rockwood Corp., Speedwell Division, 136 Lincoln Blvd., Middlesex, NJ 08846/908-560-7171, 800-243-8274; FAX: 980-560-7475

Rocky Fork Enterprises, P.O. Box 427, 878 Battle Rd., Nolensville, TN 37135/615-941-1307

Rocky Mountain Arms, Inc., 600 S. Sunset, Unit C, Longmont, CO 80501/303-768-8522; FAX: 303-678-8766

Rocky Mountain Target Co., 3 Aloe Way, Leesburg, FL 34788/904-365-9598

Rod Guide Co., Box 1149, Forsyth, MO 65653/800-952-2774

Rogers Gunsmithing, Bob, P.O. Box 305, 344 S. Walnut St., Franklin Grove, IL 61031/815-456-2685; FAX: 815-288-7142

Rohner, Hans, 1148 Twin Sisters Ranch Rd., Nederland, CO 80466-9600

Rohner, John, 710 Sunshine Canyon, Boulder, CO 80302/303-444-3841

Rolston, Inc., Fred W., 210 E. Cummins St., Tecumseh, MI 49286/517-423-6002, 800-314-9061 (orders only); FAX: 517-423-6002

Romain's Custom Guns, Inc., RD 1, Whetstone Rd., Brockport, PA 15823/814-265-1948

Rooster Laboratories, P.O. Box 412514, Kansas City, MO 64141/816-474-1622; FAX: 816-474-1307

Rorschach Precision Products, P.O. Box 151613, Irving, TX 75015/214-790-3487

Rosenberg & Sons, Jack A., 12229 Cox Ln., Dallas, TX 75234/214-241-6302

Rosenthal, Brad and Sallie, 19303 Ossenfort Ct., St. Louis, MO 63038/314-273-5159; FAX: 314-273-5149

Rosser, Bob, 1824 29th Ave., Suite 24, Birmingham, AL 35209/205-870-4422

Rossi S.A., Amadeo, Rua: Amadeo Rossi, 143, Sao Leopoldo, RS, BRAZIL 93030-220/051-592-5566 (U.S. importer—Interarms)

Roto Carve, 2754 Garden Ave., Janesville, IA 50647

Round Edge, Inc., P.O. Box 723, Lansdale, PA 19446/215-361-0859

Royal Arms Gunstocks, 919 8th Ave. NW, Great Falls, MT 59404/406-453-1149

Roy's Custom Grips, Rt. 3, Box 174-E, Lynchburg, VA 24504/804-993-3470

RPM, 15481 N. Twin Lakes Dr., Tucson, AZ 85737/602-825-1233; FAX: 602-825-3333

Rucker Dist. Inc., P.O. Box 479, Terrell, TX 75160/214-563-2094

Ruger (See Sturm, Ruger & Co., Inc.)

Rundell's Gun Shop, 6198 Frances Rd., Clio, MI 48420/313-687-0559

Runge, Robert P., 94 Grove St., Ilion, NY 13357/315-894-3036

Rusteprufe Laboratories, 1319 Jefferson Ave., Sparta, WI 54656/608-269-4144

Rusty Duck Premium Gun Care Products, 7785 Foundation Dr., Suite 6, Florence, KY 41042/606-342-5553; FAX: 606-342-5556

Rutgers Book Center, 127 Raritan Ave., Highland Park, NJ 08904/908-545-4344; FAX: 908-545-6686

Ruvel & Co., Inc., 4128-30 W. Belmont Ave., Chicago, IL 60641/312-286-9494; FAX: 312-286-9323

R.V.I. (See Fire'n Five)

RWS (See U.S. importer—Dynamit Nobel-RWS, Inc.)

Rybka Custom Leather Equipment, Thad, 134 Havilah Hill, Odenville, AL 35120

S

S&B Industries, 11238 McKinley Rd., Montrose, MI 48457/810-639-5491

S&K Manufacturing Co., P.O. Box 247, Pittsfield, PA 16340/814-563-7808; FAX: 814-563-7808

S&S Firearms, 74-11 Myrtle Ave., Glendale, NY 11385/718-497-1100; FAX: 718-497-1105

Sabatti S.R.L., via Alessandro Volta 90, 25063 Gardone V.T., Brescia, ITALY/030-8912207-831312; FAX: 030-8912059 (U.S. importer—E.A.A. Corp.; K.B.I., Inc.)

SAECO (See Redding Reloading Equipment)

Safari Outfitters Ltd., 71 Ethan Allan Hwy., Ridgefield, CT 06877/203-544-9505

Safari Press, Inc., 15621 Chemical Lane B, Huntington Beach, CA 92649/714-894-9080; FAX: 714-894-4949

Safariland Ltd., Inc., 3120 E. Mission Blvd., P.O. Box 51478, Ontario, CA 91761/909-923-7300; FAX: 909-923-7400

SAFE, P.O. Box 864, Post Falls, ID 83854/208-773-3624

Safesport Manufacturing Co., 1100 W. 45th Ave., Denver, CO 80211/303-433-6506, 800-433-6506; FAX: 303-433-4112

Safety Speed Holster, Inc., 910 S. Vail Ave., Montebello, CA 90640/213-723-4140; FAX: 213-726-6973

Samco Global Arms, Inc., 6995 NW 43rd St., Miami, FL 33166/305-593-9782

Sampson, Roger, 430 N. Grove, Mora, MN 55051/320-679-4868

San Francisco Gun Exchange, 124 Second St., San Francisco, CA 94105/415-982-6097

Sandia Die & Cartridge Co., 37 Atancacio Rd. NE, Albuquerque, NM 87123/505-298-5729

Sarco, Inc., 323 Union St., Stirling, NJ 07980/908-647-3800

Saunders Gun & Machine Shop, R.R. 2, Delhi Road, Manchester, IA 52057

Savage Range Systems, Inc., 100 Springdale RD., Westfield, MA 01085/413-568-7001; FAX: 413-562-1152

Savana Sports, Inc., 5763 Ferrier St., Montreal, Quebec, CANADA H4P 1N3/514-739-1753; FAX: 514-739-1755

Saville Iron Co. (See Greenwood Precision)

Scattergun Technologies Inc., 620 8th Ave. S., Nashville, TN 37203/616-254-1441; FAX: 616-254-1449; WEB: http://www.scattergun.com

Schaefer Shooting Sports, 1923 Grand Ave., Baldwin, NY 11510/516-379-4900; FAX: 516-379-6701

Scharch Mfg., Inc., 10325 Co. Rd. 120, Unit C, Salida, CO 81201/719-539-7242, 800-836-4683; FAX: 719-539-3021

Scherer, Box 250, Ewing, VA 24240/615-733-2615; FAX: 615-733-2073

Schiffman, Mike, 8233 S. Crystal Springs, McCammon, ID 83250/208-254-9114

Schmidtman Custom Ammunition, 6 Gilbert Court, Cotati, CA 94931

Schroeder Bullets, 1421 Thermal Ave., San Diego, CA 92154/619-423-3523

Schuetzen Gun Co., P.O. Box 272113, Fort Collins, CO 80527/970-223-3678

Schuetzen Pistol Works, 620-626 Old Pacific Hwy. SE, Olympia, WA 98513/360-459-3471; FAX: 360-491-3447

Schulz Industries, 16247 Minnesota Ave., Paramount, CA 90723/213-439-5903

ScopLevel, 151 Lindbergh Ave., Suite C, Livermore, CA 94550/510-449-5052; FAX: 510-373-0861

Scot Powder Co. of Ohio, Inc., Box GD96, Only, TN 37140/615-729-4207, 800-416-3006; FAX: 615-729-4217

Scott, Dwight, 23089 Englehardt St., Clair Shores, MI 48080/313-779-4735

Scott Fine Guns, Inc., Thad, P.O. Box 412, Indianola, MS 38751/601-887-5929

Scott, McDougall & Associates, 7950 Redwood Dr., Cotati, CA 94931/707-546-2264; FAX: 707-795-1911

Seattle Binocular & Scope Repair Co., P.O. Box 46094, Seattle, WA 98146/206-932-3733

Second Chance Body Armor, P.O. Box 578, Central Lake, MI 49622/616-544-5721; FAX: 616-544-9824

Seebeck Assoc., R.E., P.O. Box 59752, Dallas, TX 75229

Seligman Shooting Products, Box 133, Seligman, AZ 86337/602-422-3607

Selsi Co., Inc., P.O. Box 10, Midland Park, NJ 07432-0010/201-935-0388; FAX: 201-935-5851

Semmer, Charles, 7885 Cyd Dr., Denver, CO 80221/303-429-6947

Sentinel Arms, P.O. Box 57, Detroit, MI 48231/313-331-1951; FAX: 313-331-1456

Shanghai Airguns, Ltd. (See U.S. importer—Sportsman Airguns, Inc.)

Shaw, Inc., E.R. (See Small Arms Mfg. Co.)

Shay's Gunsmithing, 931 Marvin Ave., Lebanon, PA 17042

Shell Shack, 113 E. Main, Laurel, MT 59044/406-628-8986

Sherwood, George, 46 N. River Dr., Roseburg, OR 97470/541-672-3159

Shilen Rifles, Inc., P.O. Box 1300, 205 Metro Park Blvd., Ennis, TX 75119/214-875-5318; FAX: 214-875-5402

Shiloh Creek, Box 357, Cottleville, MO 63338/314-447-2900; FAX: 314-447-2900

Shirley Co. Gun & Riflemakers Ltd., J.A., P.O. Box 368, High Wycombe, Bucks. HP13 6YN, ENGLAND/0494-446883; FAX: 0494-463685

Shockley, Harold H., 204 E. Farmington Rd., Hanna City, IL 61536/309-565-4524

Shoemaker & Sons, Inc., Tex, 714 W. Cienega Ave., San Dimas, CA 91773/909-592-2071; FAX: 909-592-2378

Shooter Shop, The, 221 N. Main, Butte, MT 59701/406-723-3842

Shooter's Choice, 16770 Hilltop Park Place, Chagrin Falls, OH 44023/216-543-8808; FAX: 216-543-8811

Shooter's World, 3828 N. 28th Ave., Phoenix, AZ 85017/602-266-0170

Shooters Supply, 1120 Tieton Dr., Yakima, WA 98902/509-452-1181

Shootin' Accessories, Ltd., P.O. Box 6810, Auburn, CA 95604/916-889-2220

Shootin' Shack, Inc., 1065 Silver Beach Rd., Riviera Beach, FL 33403/407-842-0990

Shooting Chrony Inc., 3269 Niagara Falls Blvd., N. Tonawanda, NY 14120/905-276-6292; FAX: 905-276-6295

Shooting Components Marketing, P.O. Box 1069, Englewood, CO 80150/303-987-2543; FAX: 303-989-3508

Shooting Gallery, The, 8070 Southern Blvd., Boardman, OH 44512/216-726-7788

Shoot-N-C Targets (See Birchwood Casey)

Shotgun Shop, The, 14145 Proctor Ave., Suite 3, Industry, CA 91746/818-855-2737; FAX: 818-855-2735

Siegrist Gun Shop, 8754 Turtle Road, Whittemore, MI 48770

Sierra Bullets, 1400 W. Henry St., Sedalia, MO 65301/816-827-6300; FAX: 816-827-6300; WEB: http://www.sierrabullets.com

Sierra Specialty Prod. Co., 1344 Oakhurst Ave., Los Altos, CA 94024/FAX: 415-965-1536

SIG, CH-8212 Neuhausen, SWITZERLAND (U.S. importer—Mandall Shooting Supplies, Inc.)

SIG-Sauer (See U.S. importer—Sigarms, Inc.)

Sigarms, Inc., Corporate Park, Industrial Drive, Exeter, NH 03833/603-772-2302; FAX: 603-772-9082

Sight Shop, The, John G. Lawson, 1802 E. Columbia Ave., Tacoma, WA 98404/206-474-5465

Sightron, Inc., Rt. 1, Box 293, Franklinton, NC 27525/919-494-5040; FAX: 919-494-2612

Sile Distributors, Inc., 7 Centre Market Pl., New York, NY 10013/212-925-4111; FAX: 212-925-3149

Silencio/Safety Direct, 56 Coney Island Dr., Sparks, NV 89431/800-648-1812, 702-354-4451; FAX: 702-359-1074

Silhouette Leathers, P.O. Box 1161, Gunnison, CO 81230/303-641-6639

Silhouette, The, P.O. Box 1509, Idaho Falls, ID 83403

Silver Eagle Machining, 18007 N. 69th Ave., Glendale, AZ 85308

Silver Ridge Gun Shop (See Goodwin, Fred)

Simmons, Jerry, 715 Middlebury St., Goshen, IN 46526/219-533-8546

Simmons Gun Repair, Inc., 700 S. Rogers Rd., Olathe, KS 66062/913-782-3131; FAX: 913-782-4189

Simmons Outdoor Corp., 2120 Kilarney Way, Tallahassee, FL 32308/904-878-5100; FAX: 904-878-0300

Sinclair International, Inc., 2330 Wayne Haven St., Fort Wayne, IN 46803/219-493-1858; FAX: 219-493-2530

Sinclair, W.P., Box 1209, Warminster, Wiltshire BA12 9XJ, ENGLAND/01044-1985-218544; FAX: 01044-1985-214111

Single Shot, Inc. (See Montana Armory, Inc.)

Singletary, Kent, 2915 W. Ross, Phoenix, AZ 85027/602-582-4900

Sipes Gun Shop, 7415 Asher Ave., Little Rock, AR 72204/501-565-8480

Skaggs, R.E., P.O. Box 555, Hamilton, IN 46742/219-488-3755

SKAN A.R., 4 St. Catherines Road, Long Melford, Suffolk, CO10 9JU ENGLAND/011-0787-312942

Skeoch, Brian R., P.O. Box 279, Glenrock, WY 82637/307-436-9655; FAX: 307-436-9034

Skip's Machine, 364 29 Road, Grand Junction, CO 81501/303-245-5417

Sklany, Steve, 566 Birch Grove Dr., Kalispell, MT 59901/406-755-4257

S.L.A.P. Industries, P.O. Box 1121, Parklands 2121, SOUTH AFRICA/27-11-788-0030; FAX: 27-11-788-0030

Slings 'N Things, Inc., 8909 Bedford Circle, Suite 11, Omaha, NE 68134/402-571-6954; FAX: 402-571-7082

Slug Group, Inc., P.O. Box 376, New Paris, PA 15554/814-839-4517; FAX: 814-839-2601

Small Custom Mould & Bullet Co., Box 17211, Tucson, AZ 85731

Smires, C.L., 28269 Old Schoolhouse Rd., Columbus, NJ 08022/609-298-3158

Smith & Wesson, 2100 Roosevelt Ave., Springfield, MA 01102/413-781-8300; FAX: 413-731-8980

Smith, Art, 230 Main St. S., Hector, MN 55342/612-848-2760; FAX: 612-848-2760

Smith, Mark A., P.O. Box 182, Sinclair, WY 82334/307-324-7929

Smith, Ron, 5869 Straley, Ft. Worth, TX 76114/817-732-6768

Smith Abrasives, Inc., 1700 Sleepy Valley Rd., P.O. Box 5095, Hot Springs, AR 71902-5095/501-321-2244; FAX: 501-321-9232

Smith Saddlery, Jesse W., 3601 E. Boone Ave., Spokane, WA 99202-4501/509-325-0622

Smokey Valley Rifles (See Lutz Engraving, Ron E.)

Snapp's Gunshop, 6911 E. Washington Rd., Clare, MI 48617/517-386-9226

SOS Products Co. (See Buck Stix—SOS Products Co.)

Sotheby's, 1334 York Ave. at 72nd St., New York, NY 10021/212-606-7260

South Bend Replicas, Inc., 61650 Oak Rd., South Bend, IN 46614/219-289-4500

Southeastern Community College, 1015 S. Gear Ave., West Burlington, IA 52655/319-752-2731

Southern Ammunition Co., Inc., 4232 Meadow St., Loris, SC 29569-3124/803-756-3262; FAX: 803-756-3583

Southern Armory, The, Rt. 2, Box 134, Woodlawn, VA 24381/703-238-1343; FAX: 703-238-1453

Southern Bloomer Mfg. Co., P.O. Box 1621, Bristol, TN 37620/615-878-6660; FAX: 615-878-8761

Southern Security, 1700 Oak Hills Dr., Kingston, TN 37763/423-376-6297; 800-251-9992

Southwind Sanctions, P.O. Box 445, Aledo, TX 76008/817-441-8917

Sparks, Milt, 605 E. 44th St. No. 2, Boise, ID 83714-4800

Specialty Gunsmithing, Lynn McMurdo, P.O. Box 404, Afton, WY 83110/307-886-5535

Speedfeed, Inc., 3820 Industrial Way, Suite N, Benicia, CA 94510/707-746-1221; FAX: 707-746-1888

Speer Products, Div. of Blount, Inc., Sporting Equipment Div., P.O. Box 856, Lewiston, ID 83501/208-746-2351; FAX: 208-746-2915

Spegel, Craig, P.O. Box 3108, Bay City, OR 97107/503-377-2697

Spence, George W., 115 Locust St., Steele, MO 63877/314-695-4926

Spencer's Custom Guns, Rt. 1, Box 546, Scottsville, VA 24590/804-293-6836

S.P.G., Inc., P.O. Box 761-H, Livingston, MT 59047/406-222-8416; FAX: 406-222-8416

Sphinx Engineering SA, Ch. des Grandes-Vies 2, CH-2900 Porrentruy, SWITZERLAND/41 66 66 73 81; FAX: 41 66 66 30 90 (U.S. importer—Sphinx USA Inc.)

Sphinx USA Inc., 998 N. Colony, Meriden, CT 06450/203-238-1399; FAX: 203-238-1375

Sport Flite Manufacturing Co., P.O. Box 1082, Bloomfield Hills, MI 48303/810-647-3747

Sportsman Airguns, Inc., 17712 Carmenita Rd., Cerritos, CA 90703-8639/800-424-7486

Sportsman Supply Co., 714 East Eastwood, P.O. Box 650, Marshall, MO 65340/816-886-9393

Sportsmen's Exchange & Western Gun Traders, Inc., 560 S. "C" St., Oxnard, CA 93030/805-483-1917

Springfield, Inc., 420 W. Main St., Geneseo, IL 61254/309-944-5631; FAX: 309-944-3676

Springfield Sporters, Inc., RD 1, Penn Run, PA 15765/412-254-2626; FAX: 412-254-9173

SSK Industries, 721 Woodvue Lane, Wintersville, OH 43952/614-264-0176; FAX: 614-264-2257

Stackpole Books, 5067 Ritter Rd., Mechanicsburg, PA 17055-6921/717-234-5041; FAX: 717-234-1359

Stalker, Inc., P.O. Box 21, Fishermans Wharf Rd., Malakoff, TX 75148/903-489-1010

Stalwart Corporation, 76 Imperial, Unit A, Evanston, WY 82930/307-789-7687; FAX: 307-789-7688

Stanley Bullets, 2085 Heatheridge Ln., Reno, NV 89509

Star Bonifacio Echeverria S.A., Torrekva 3, Eibar, SPAIN 20600/43-107340; FAX: 43-101524 (U.S. importer—Interarms; P.S.M.G. Gun Co.)

Star Custom Bullets, P.O. Box 608, 468 Main St., Ferndale, CA 95536/707-786-9140; FAX: 707-786-9117

Star Machine Works, 418 10th Ave., San Diego, CA 92101/619-232-3216

Star Reloading Co., Inc., 5520 Rock Hampton Ct., Indianapolis, IN 46268/317-872-5840

Stark's Bullet Mfg., 2580 Monroe St., Eugene, OR 97405

Starlight Training Center, Inc., Rt. 1, P.O. Box 88, Bronaugh, MO 64728/417-843-3555

Starnes Gunmaker, Ken, 32900 SW Laurelview Rd., Hillsboro, OR 97123/503-628-0705; FAX: 503-628-6005

Starr Trading Co., Jedediah, P.O. Box 2007, Farmington Hills, MI 48333/810-683-4343; FAX: 810-683-3282

Starrett Co., L.S., 121 Crescent St., Athol, MA 01331/617-249-3551

State Arms Gun Co., 815 S. Division St., Waunakee, WI 53597/608-849-5800

Steffens, Ron, 18396 Mariposa Creek Rd., Willits, CA 95490/707-485-0873

Steger, James R., 1131 Dorsey Pl., Plainfield, NJ 07062

Steves House of Guns, Rt. 1, Minnesota City, MN 55959/507-689-2573

Stewart's Gunsmithing, P.O. Box 5854, Pietersburg North 0750, Transvaal, SOUTH AFRICA/01521-89401

Steyr Mannlicher AG, Mannlicherstrasse 1, P.O.B. 1000, A-4400 Steyr, AUSTRIA/0043-7252-896-0; FAX: 0043-7252-68621 (U.S. importer—GSI, Inc.; Nygord Precision Products)

Stiles Custom Guns, RD3, Box 1605, Homer City, PA 15748/412-479-9945, 412-479-8666

Stillwell, Robert, 421 Judith Ann Dr., Schertz, TX 78154

Stoeger Industries, 5 Mansard Ct., Wayne, NJ 07470/201-872-9500, 800-631-0722; FAX: 201-872-2230

Stoeger Publishing Co. (See Stoeger Industries)

Stone Enterprises Ltd., Rt. 609, P.O. Box 335, Wicomico Church, VA 22579/804-580-5114; FAX: 804-580-8421

Stone Mountain Arms, 5988 Peachtree Corners E., Norcross, GA 30071/800-251-9412

Stoney Point Products, Inc., P.O. Box 234, 1815 North Spring Street, New Ulm, MN 56073-0234/507-354-3360; FAX: 507-354-7236

Storey, Dale A. (See DGS, Inc.)

Stott's Creek Armory, Inc., RR1, Box 70, Morgantown, IN 46160/317-878-5489

Stratco, Inc., P.O. Box 2270, Kalispell, MT 59901/406-755-1221; FAX: 406-755-1226

Strawbridge, Victor W., 6 Pineview Dr., Dover, NH 03820/603-742-0013

Strong Holster Co., 39 Grove St., Gloucester, MA 01930/508-281-3300; FAX: 508-281-6321

Stuart, V. Pat, Rt.1, Box 447-S, Greenville, VA 24440/804-556-3845

Sturm, Ruger & Co., Inc., Lacey Place, Southport, CT 06490/203-259-4537; FAX: 203-259-2167

"Su-Press-On," Inc., P.O. Box 09161, Detroit, MI 48209/313-842-4222 7:30-11p.m. Mon-Thurs.

Sullivan, David S. (See Westwind Rifles, Inc.)

Sundance Industries, Inc., 25163 W. Avenue Stanford, Valencia, CA 91355/805-257-4807

Sun Welding Safe Co., 290 Easy St. No.3, Simi Valley, CA 93065/805-584-6678, 800-729-SAFE; FAX: 805-584-6169

Surecase Co., The, 233 Wilshire Blvd., Ste. 900, Santa Monica, CA 90401/800-92ARMLOC

Swampfire Shop, The (See Peterson Gun Shop, Inc., A.W.)

SwaroSports, Inc. (See JagerSport, Ltd.)

Swarovski Optik North America Ltd., One Wholesale Way, Cranston, RI 02920/401-942-3380, 800-426-3089; FAX: 401-946-2587

Swenson's 45 Shop, A.D., P.O. Box 606, Fallbrook, CA 92028

Swift Instruments, Inc., 952 Dorchester Ave., Boston, MA 02125/617-436-2960, 800-446-1116; FAX: 617-436-3232

Swivel Machine Works, Inc., 11 Monitor Hill Rd., Newtown, CT 06470/203-270-6343; FAX: 203-874-9212

T

3-D Ammunition & Bullets, 112 W. Plum St., P.O. Box J, Doniphan, NE 68832/402-845-2285, 800-255-6712; FAX: 402-845-6546

300 Gunsmith Service, Inc., at Cherry Creek State Park Shooting Center,, 12500 E. Belleview Ave./Englewood, CO 80111/303-690-3300

Tabler Marketing, 2554 Lincoln Blvd., Suite 555, Marina Del Rey, CA 90291/818-755-4565; FAX: 818-755-0972

TacStar Industries, Inc., 218 Justin Drive, P.O. Box 70, Cottonwood, AZ 86326/602-639-0072; FAX: 602-634-8781

TacTell, Inc., P.O. Box 5654, Maryville, TN 37802/615-982-7855; FAX: 615-558-8294

Tactical Defense Institute, 574 Miami Bluff Ct., Loveland, OH 45140/513-677-8229

Talley, Dave, P.O. Box 821, Glenrock, WY 82637/307-436-8724, 307-436-9315

Talmage, William G., 10208 N. County Rd. 425 W., Brazil, IN 47834/812-442-0804

Talon Mfg. Co., Inc., 575 Bevans Industrial Ln., Paw Paw, WV 25434/304-947-7440; FAX: 304-947-7447

Tamarack Products, Inc., P.O. Box 625, Wauconda, IL 60084/708-526-9333; FAX: 708-526-9353

Tanfoglio S.r.l., Fratelli, via Valtrompia 39, 41, 25068 Gardone V.T., Brescia, ITALY/30-8910361; FAX: 30-8910183 (U.S. importer—E.A.A. Corp.)

Tank's Rifle Shop, P.O. Box 474, Fremont, NE 68025/402-727-1317; FAX: 402-721-2573

Taracorp Industries, Inc., 1200 Sixteenth St., Granite City, IL 62040/618-451-4400

Tarnhelm Supply Co., Inc., 431 High St., Boscawen, NH 03303/603-796-2551; FAX: 603-796-2918

Tasco Sales, Inc., 7600 NW 26th St., Miami, FL 33156/305-591-3670; FAX: 305-592-5895

Taurus Firearms, Inc., 16175 NW 49th Ave., Miami, FL 33014/305-624-1115; FAX: 305-623-7506

Taurus International Firearms (See U.S. importer—Taurus Firearms, Inc.)

Taurus S.A., Forjas, Avenida Do Forte 511, Porto Alegre, RS BRAZIL 91360/55-51-347-4050; FAX: 55-51-347-3065

Taylor & Robbins, P.O. Box 164, Rixford, PA 16745/814-966-3233

TCCI, P.O. Box 302, Phoenix, AZ 85001/602-237-3823; FAX: 602-237-3858

TCSR, 3998 Hoffman Rd., White Bear Lake, MN 55110-4626/800-328-5323; FAX: 612-429-0526

TDP Industries, Inc., 606 Airport Blvd., Doylestown, PA 18901/215-345-8687; FAX: 215-345-6057

Tele-Optics, 5514 W. Lawrence Ave., Chicago, IL 60630/312-283-7757; FAX: 312-283-7757

Ten-Ring Precision, Inc., Alex B. Hamilton, 1449 Blue Crest Lane, San Antonio, TX 78232/210-494-3063; FAX: 210-494-3066

Tennessee Valley Mfg., P.O. Box 1175, Corinth, MS 38834/601-286-5014

Tepeco, P.O. Box 342, Friendswood, TX 77546/713-482-2702

Tetra Gun Lubricants, 1812 Margaret Ave., Annapolis, MD 21401/410-268-6451; FAX: 410-268-8377

Texas Armory, P.O. Box 154906, Waco, TX 76715/817-867-6972

Texas Longhorn Arms, Inc., 5959 W. Loop South, Suite 424, Bellaire, TX 77401/713-660-6323; FAX: 713-660-0493

Texas Platers Supply Co., 2453 W. Five Mile Parkway, Dallas, TX 75233/214-330-7168

T.F.C. S.p.A., Via G. Marconi 118, B, Villa Carcina, Brescia 25069, ITALY/030-881271; FAX: 030-881826

Theis, Terry, P.O. Box 535, Fredericksburg, TX 78624/210-997-6778

Thiewes, George W., 14329 W. Parada Dr., Sun City West, AZ 85375

Thirion Gun Engraving, Denise, P.O. Box 408, Graton, CA 95444/707-829-1876

Thomas, Charles C., 2600 S. First St., Springfield, IL 62794/217-789-8980; FAX: 217-789-9130

Thompson, Randall (See Highline Machine Co.)

Thompson Bullet Lube Co., P.O. Box 472343, Garland, TX 75047-2343/214-271-8063; FAX: 214-840-6743

Thompson/Center Arms, P.O. Box 5002, Rochester, NH 03866/603-332-2394; FAX: 603-332-5133

Thompson Precision, 110 Mary St., P.O. Box 251, Warren, IL 61087/815-745-3625

Thompson Target Technology, 618 Roslyn Ave., SW, Canton, OH 44710/216-453-7707; FAX: 216-478-4723

T.H.U. Enterprises, Inc., P.O. Box 418, Lederach, PA 19450/215-256-1665; FAX: 215-256-9718

Thunder Mountain Arms, P.O. Box 593, Oak Harbor, WA 98277/206-679-4657; FAX: 206-675-1114

Thunder Ranch, HCR 1 Box 53, Mountain Home, TX 78058/210-640-3138; FAX: 210-640-3183

Thunderbird Cartridge Co., Inc. (See TCCI)

Thurston Sports, Inc., RD 3 Donovan Rd., Auburn, NY 13021/315-253-0966

Tiger-Hunt, Box 379, Beaverdale, PA 15921/814-472-5161

Timber Heirloom Products, 618 Roslyn Ave. SW, Canton, OH 44710/216-453-7707; FAX: 216-478-4723

Time Precision, Inc., 640 Federal Rd., Brookfield, CT 06804/203-775-8343

Timney Mfg., Inc., 3065 W. Fairmont Ave., Phoenix, AZ 85017/602-274-2999; FAX: 602-241-0361

Tioga Engineering Co., Inc., P.O. Box 913, 13 Cone St., Wellsboro, PA 16901/717-724-3533, 717-662-3347

TMI Products (See Haselbauer Products, Jerry)

Tom's Gun Repair, Thomas G. Ivanoff, 76-6 Rt. Southfork Rd., Cody, WY 82414/307-587-6949

Tom's Gunshop, 3601 Central Ave., Hot Springs, AR 71913/501-624-3856

Tonoloway Tack Drives, HCR 81, Box 100, Needmore, PA 17238

Top-Line USA, Inc., 7920-28 Hamilton Ave., Cincinnati, OH 45231/513-522-2992, 800-346-6699; FAX: 513-522-0916

Torel, Inc., 1708 N. South St., P.O. Box 592, Yoakum, TX 77995/512-293-2341; FAX: 512-293-3413

Totally Dependable Products (See TDP Industries, Inc.)

TOZ (See U.S. importer—Nygord Precision Products)

TR Metals Corp., 1 Pavilion Ave., Riverside, NJ 08075/609-461-9000; FAX: 609-764-6340

Track of the Wolf, Inc., P.O. Box 6, Osseo, MN 55369-0006/612-424-2500; FAX: 612-424-9860

Traditions, Inc., P.O. Box 776, 1375 Boston Post Rd., Old Saybrook, CT 06475/860-388-4656; FAX: 860-388-4657

Trafalgar Square, P.O. Box 257, N. Pomfret, VT 05053/802-457-1911

Trammco, 839 Gold Run Rd., Boulder, CO 80302

Treso, Inc., P.O. Box 4640, Pagosa Springs, CO 81157/303-731-2295

Trijicon, Inc., 49385 Shafer Ave., P.O. Box 930059, Wixom, MI 48393-0059/810-960-7700; FAX: 810-960-7725

Trinidad State Junior College, Gunsmithing Dept., 600 Prospect St., Trinidad, CO 81082/719-846-5631; FAX: 719-846-5667

Triple-K Mfg. Co., Inc., 2222 Commercial St., San Diego, CA 92113/619-232-2066; FAX: 619-232-7675

Trophy Bonded Bullets, Inc., 900 S. Loop W., Suite 190, Houston, TX 77054/713-645-4499; FAX: 713-741-6393

Trotman, Ken, 135 Ditton Walk, Unit 11, Cambridge CB5 8PY, ENGLAND/01223-211030; FAX: 01223-212317

Tru-Square Metal Prods., Inc., 640 First St. SW, P.O. Box 585, Auburn, WA 98071/206-833-2310; FAX: 206-833-2349

True Flight Bullet Co., 5581 Roosevelt St., Whitehall, PA 18052/610-262-7630; FAX: 610-262-7806

Trulock Tool, Broad St., Whigham, GA 31797/912-762-4678

TTM, 1550 Solomon Rd., Santa Maria, CA 93455/805-934-1281

Turnbull Restoration, Inc., Doug, 6426 County Rd. 30, P.O. Box 471, Bloomfield, NY 14469/716-657-6338; WEB: http://gunshop.com/dougt.htm

Twin Pine Armory, P.O. Box 58, Hwy. 6, Adna, WA 98522/360-748-4590; FAX: 360-748-1802

Tyler Mfg.-Dist., Melvin, 1326 W. Britton Rd., Oklahoma City, OK 73114/405-842-8044, 800-654-8415

Tyler Scott, Inc., 313 Rugby Ave., Terrace Park, OH 45174/513-831-7603; FAX: 513-831-7417

U

Uberti USA, Inc., P.O. Box 469, Lakeville, CT 06039/860-435-8068; FAX: 860-435-8146

Uberti, Aldo, Casella Postale 43, I-25063 Gardone V.T., ITALY (U.S. importers—American Arms, Inc.; Cimarron Arms; Dixie Gun Works; EMF Co., Inc.; Forgett Jr., Valmore J.; Navy Arms Co; Taylor's & Co., Inc.; Uberti USA, Inc.)

Ultra Light Arms, Inc., P.O. Box 1270, 214 Price St., Granville, WV 26505/304-599-5687; FAX: 304-599-5687

Uncle Mike's (See Michaels of Oregon Co.)

Unique/M.A.P.F., 10, Les Allees, 64700 Hendaye, FRANCE 64700/33-59 20 71 93 (U.S. importer—Nygord Precision Products)

United States Products Co., 518 Melwood Ave., Pittsburgh, PA 15213/412-621-2130

Upper Missouri Trading Co., 304 Harold St., Crofton, NE 68730/402-388-4844

USAC, 4500-15th St. East, Tacoma, WA 98424/206-922-7589

USA Sporting Inc., 1330 N. Glassell, Unit M, Orange, CA 92667/714-538-3109, 800-538-3109; FAX: 714-538-1334

V

Valade Engraving, Robert, 931 3rd Ave., Seaside, OR 97138/503-738-7672

Valor Corp., 5555 NW 36th Ave., Miami, FL 33142/305-633-0127; FAX: 305-634-4536

Van Gorden & Son, Inc., C.S., 1815 Main St., Bloomer, WI 54724/715-568-2612

Van Patten, J.W., P.O. Box 145, Foster Hill, Milford, PA 18337/717-296-7069

Vancini, Carl (See Bestload, Inc.)

Vann Custom Bullets, 330 Grandview Ave., Novato, CA 94947

Varner's Service, 102 Shaffer Rd., Antwerp, OH 45813/419-258-8631

Vega Tool Co., c/o T.R. Ross, 4865 Tanglewood Ct., Boulder, CO 80301/303-530-0174

Venco Industries, Inc. (See Shooter's Choice)

Venus Industries, P.O. Box 246, Sialkot-1, PAKISTAN/FAX: 92 432 85579

Vest, John, P.O. Box 1552, Susanville, CA 96130/916-257-7228

VibraShine, Inc., P.O. Box 577, Taylorsville, MS 39168/601-785-9854; FAX: 601-785-9874

Vibra-Tek Co., 1844 Arroya Rd., Colorado Springs, CO 80906/719-634-8611; FAX: 719-634-6886

Vic's Gun Refinishing, 6 Pineview Dr., Dover, NH 03820-6422/603-742-0013

Victory USA, P.O. Box 1021, Pine Bush, NY 12566/914-744-2060; FAX: 914-744-5181

Vihtavuori Oy, FIN-41330 Vihtavuori, FINLAND/358-41-3779211; FAX: 358-41-3771643

Vihtavuori Oy/Kaltron-Pettibone, 1241 Ellis St., Bensenville, IL 60106/708-350-1116; FAX: 708-350-1606

Viking Leathercraft, Inc., 1579A Jayken Way, Chula Vista, CA 91911/800-262-6666; FAX: 619-429-8268

Vincent's Shop, 210 Antoinette, Fairbanks, AK 99701

Vintage Arms, Inc., 6003 Saddle Horse, Fairfax, VA 22030/703-968-0779; FAX: 703-968-0780

Vintage Industries, Inc., 781 Big Tree Dr., Longwood, FL 32750/407-831-8949; FAX: 407-831-5346

Viramontez, Ray, 601 Springfield Dr., Albany, GA 31707/912-432-9683

Vitt/Boos, 2178 Nichols Ave., Stratford, CT 06497/203-375-6859

Voere-KGH m.b.H., P.O. Box 416, A-6333 Kufstein, Tirol, AUSTRIA/0043-5372-62547; FAX: 0043-5372-65752 (U.S. importers—JagerSport, Ltd.)

Volquartsen Custom Ltd., 24276 240th Street, P.O. Box 271, Carroll, IA 51401/712-792-4238; FAX: 712-792-2542; E-MAIL: vcl@netins.net

Von Minden Gunsmithing Services, 2403 SW 39 Terrace, Cape Coral, FL 33914/813-542-8946

Vorhes, David, 3042 Beecham St., Napa, CA 94558/707-226-9116

Vortek Products, Inc., P.O. Box 871181, Canton, MI 48187-6181/313-397-5656; FAX:313-397-5656

VSP Publishers (See Heritage/VSP Gun Books)

Vulpes Ventures, Inc., Fox Cartridge Division, P.O. Box 1363, Bolingbrook, IL 60440-7363/708-759-1229

W

Wagoner, Vernon G., 2325 E. Encanto, Mesa, AZ 85213/602-835-1307

Waldron, Herman, Box 475, 80 N. 17th St., Pomeroy, WA 99347/509-843-1404

Walker Arms Co., Inc., 499 County Rd. 820, Selma, AL 36701/334-872-6231

Wallace, Terry, 385 San Marino, Vallejo, CA 94589/707-642-7041

Walt's Custom Leather, Walt Whinnery, 1947 Meadow Creek Dr., Louisville, KY 40218/502-458-4361

Walters Industries, 6226 Park Lane, Dallas, TX 75225/214-691-6973

Walters, John, 500 N. Avery Dr., Moore, OK 73160/405-799-0376

Walther GmbH, Carl, B.P. 4325, D-89033 Ulm, GERMANY (U.S. importer—Champion's Choice; Interarms; P.S.M.G. Gun Co.)

WAMCO, Inc., Mingo Loop, P.O. Box 337, Oquossoc, ME 04964-0337/207-864-3344

WAMCO—New Mexico, P.O. Box 205, Peralta, NM 87042-0205/505-869-0826

Ward & Van Valkenburg, 114 32nd Ave. N., Fargo, ND 58102/701-232-2351

Wardell Precision Handguns Ltd., 48851 N. Fig Springs Rd., New River, AZ 85027-8513/602-465-7995

Warenski, Julie, 590 E. 500 N., Richfield, UT 84701/801-896-5319; FAX: 801-896-5319

Warne Manufacturing Co., 9039 SE Jannsen Rd., Clackamas, OR 97015/503-657-5590, 800-683-5590; FAX: 503-657-5695

Warren Muzzleloading Co., Inc., Hwy. 21 North, P.O. Box 100, Ozone, AR 72854/501-292-3268

Warren, Kenneth W. (See Mountain States Engraving)

Washita Mountain Whetstone Co., P.O. Box 378, Lake Hamilton, AR 71951/501-525-3914

Wayne Firearms for Collectors and Investors, James, 2608 N. Laurent, Victoria, TX 77901/512-578-1258; FAX: 512-578-3559

WD-40 Co., 1061 Cudahy Pl., San Diego, CA 92110/619-275-1400; FAX: 619-275-5823

Weaver Arms Corp. Gun Shop, RR 3, P.O. Box 266, Bloomfield, MO 63825-9528

Weber & Markin Custom Gunsmiths, 4-1691 Powick Rd., Kelowna, B.C. CANADA V1X 4L1/604-762-7575; FAX: 604-861-3655

Webley and Scott Ltd., Frankley Industrial Park, Tay Rd., Rubery, Rednal, Birmingham B45 0PA, ENGLAND/011-021-453-1864; FAX: 021-457-7846 (U.S. importer—Beeman Precision Airguns; Groenewold, John)

Webster Scale Mfg. Co., P.O. Box 188, Sebring, FL 33870/813-385-6362

Weigand Combat Handguns, Inc., P.O. Box 239, Crestwood Industrial Park, Mountain Top, PA 18707/717-474-9804; FAX: 717-474-9987

Weihrauch KG, Hermann, Industriestrasse 11, 8744 Mellrichstadt, GERMANY/09776-497-498 (U.S. importers—Beeman Precision Airguns; E.A.A. Corp.)

Weisz Parts, P.O. Box 20038, Columbus, OH 43220-0038/614-45-70-500; FAX: 614-846-8585

Welch, Sam, CVSR 2110, Moab, UT 84532/801-259-8131

Wells Custom Gunsmith, R.A., 3452 1st Ave., Racine, WI 53402/414-639-5223

Wells, Rachel, 110 N. Summit St., Prescott, AZ 86301/520-445-3655

Welsh, Bud, 80 New Road, E. Amherst, NY 14051/716-688-6344

Werner, Carl, P.O. Box 492, Littleton, CO 80160

Werth, T.W., 1203 Woodlawn Rd., Lincoln, IL 62656/217-732-1300

Wescombe, P.O. Box 488, Glencoe, CA 95232/209-293-7010

Wessinger Custom Guns & Engraving, 268 Limestone Rd., Chapin, SC 29036/803-345-5677

West, Robert G., 3973 Pam St., Eugene, OR 97402/541-344-3700

Western Design (See Alpha Gunsmith Division)

Western Missouri Shooters Alliance, P.O. Box 11144, Kansas City, MO 64119/816-597-3950; FAX: 816-229-7350

Western Nevada West Coast Bullets, 2307 W. Washington St., Carson City, NV 89703/702-246-3941; FAX: 702-246-0836

Westfield Engineering, 6823 Watcher St., Commerce, CA 90040/FAX: 213-928-8270

Westrom, John (See Precision Metal Finishing)

Westwind Rifles, Inc., David S. Sullivan, P.O. Box 261, 640 Briggs St., Erie, CO 80516/303-828-3823

Whildin & Sons Ltd., E.H., RR2, Box 119, Tamaqua, PA 18252/717-668-6743; FAX: 717-668-6745

Whinnery, Walt (See Walt's Custom Leather)

White Laboratory, Inc., H.P., 3114 Scarboro Rd., Street, MD 21154/410-838-6550; FAX: 410-838-2802

White Owl Enterprises, 2583 Flag Rd., Abilene, KS 67410/913-263-2613; FAX: 913-263-2613

White Rock Tool & Die, 6400 N. Brighton Ave., Kansas City, MO 64119/816-454-0478

White Shooting Systems, Inc., 25 E. Hwy. 40, Box 330-12, Roosevelt, UT 84066/801-722-3085, 800-213-1315; FAX: 801-722-3054

Whitehead, James D., 204 Cappucino Way, Sacramento, CA 95838

Whitestone Lumber Corp., 148-02 14th Ave., Whitestone, NY 11357/718-746-4400; FAX: 718-767-1748

Whitetail Design & Engineering Ltd., 9421 E. Mannsiding Rd., Clare, MI 48617/517-386-3932

Wichita Arms, Inc., 923 E. Gilbert, P.O. Box 11371, Wichita, KS 67211/316-265-0661; FAX: 316-265-0760

Wick, David E., 1504 Michigan Ave., Columbus, IN 47201/812-376-6960

Widener's Reloading & Shooting Supply, Inc., P.O. Box 3009 CRS, Johnson City, TN 37602/615-282-6786; FAX: 615-282-6651

Wideview Scope Mount Corp., 13535 S. Hwy. 16, Rapid City, SD 57701/605-341-3220; FAX: 605-341-9142

Wiebe, Duane, 33604 Palm Dr., Burlington, WI 53105-9260

Wilcox All-Pro Tools & Supply, 4880 147th St., Montezuma, IA 50171/515-623-3138; FAX: 515-623-3104

Wild Bill's Originals, P.O. Box 13037, Burton, WA 98013/206-463-5738

Wild West Guns, 7521 Old Seward Hwy, Unit A, Anchorage, AK 99518/907-344-4500; FAX: 907-344-4005

Wilderness Sound Products Ltd., 4015 Main St. A, Springfield, OR 97478/503-741-0263, 800-437-0006; FAX: 503-741-7648

Wildey, Inc., P.O. Box 475, Brookfield, CT 06804/203-355-9000; FAX: 203-354-7759

Wilkinson Arms, 26884 Pearl Rd., Parma, ID 83660/208-722-6771; FAX: 208-722-5197

Will-Burt Co., 169 S. Main, Orrville, OH 44667

William's Gun Shop, Ben, 1151 S. Cedar Ridge, Duncanville, TX 75137/214-780-1807

Williams Bullet Co., J.R., 2008 Tucker Rd., Perry, GA 31069/912-987-0274

Williams Gun Sight Co., 7389 Lapeer Rd., Box 329, Davison, MI 48423/810-653-2131, 800-530-9028; FAX: 810-658-2140

Williams Mfg. of Oregon, 110 East B St., Drain, OR 97435/541-836-7461; FAX: 541-836-7245

Williams Shootin' Iron Service, The Lynx-Line, 8857 Bennett Hill Rd., Central Lake, MI 49622/616-544-6615

Williamson Precision Gunsmithing, 117 W. Pipeline, Hurst, TX 76053/817-285-0064

Willig Custom Engraving, Claus, D-97422 Schweinfurt, Siedlerweg 17, GERMANY/01149-9721-41446; FAX: 01149-9721-44413

Willow Bend, P.O. Box 203, Chelmsford, MA 01824/508-256-8508; FAX: 508-256-8508

Willson Safety Prods. Div., P.O. Box 622, Reading, PA 19603-0622/610-376-6161; FAX: 610-371-7725

Wilson Case, Inc., P.O. Box 1106, Hastings, NE 68902-1106/800-322-5493; FAX: 402-463-5276
Wilson, Inc., L.E., Box 324, 404 Pioneer Ave., Cashmere, WA 98815/509-782-1328
Wilson Combat, Box 578, Rt. 3, Berryville, AR 72616/501-545-3618; FAX: 501-545-3310
Wilson's Gun Shop (See Wilson Combat)
Winchester Div., Olin Corp., 427 N. Shamrock, E. Alton, IL 62024/618-258-3566; FAX: 618-258-3599
Winchester Sutler, Inc., The, 270 Shadow Brook Lane, Winchester, VA 22603/540-888-3595; FAX: 540-888-4632
Winkle Bullets, R.R. 1 Box 316, Heyworth, IL 61745
Winter, Robert M., P.O. Box 484, Menno, SD 57045/605-387-5322
Wise Guns, Dale, 333 W. Olmos Dr., San Antonio, TX 78212/210-828-3388
Wolf's Western Traders, 40 E. Works, No. 3F, Sheridan, WY 82801/307-674-5352
Wolff Co., W.C., P.O. Box 458, Newtown Square, PA 19073/610-359-9600, 800-545-0077
Wood, Frank (See Classic Guns, Inc.)
Wood, Mel, P.O. Box 1255, Sierra Vista, AZ 85636/602-455-5541
Woodstream, P.O. Box 327, Lititz, PA 17543/717-626-2125; FAX: 717-626-1912
Woodworker's Supply, 1108 North Glenn Rd., Casper, WY 82601/307-237-5354
World of Targets (See Birchwood Casey)
World Trek, Inc., 7170 Turkey Creek Rd., Pueblo, CO 81007-1046/719-546-2121; FAX: 719-543-6886
Worthy Products, Inc., RR 1, P.O. Box 213, Martville, NY 13111/315-324-5298
Wyant Bullets, Gen. Del., Swan Lake, MT 59911
Wyoming Custom Bullets, 1626 21st St., Cody, WY 82414

X, Y

X-Spand Target Systems, 26-10th St. SE, Medicine Hat, AB T1A 1P7 CANADA/403-526-7997; FAX: 403-528-2362
Yankee Gunsmith, 2901 Deer Flat Dr., Copperas Cove, TX 76522/817-547-8433
Yavapai Firearms Academy Ltd., P.O. Box 27290, Prescott Valley, AZ 86312/520-772-8262
Yearout, Lewis E. (See Montana Outfitters)
Yesteryear Armory & Supply, P.O. Box 408, Carthage, TN 37030
Young Country Arms, P.O. Box 3615, Simi Valley, CA 93093
Yukon Arms Classic Ammunition, 1916 Brooks, P.O. Box 223, Missoula, MT 59801/406-543-9614

Z

Z's Metal Targets & Frames, P.O. Box 78, South Newbury, NH 03255/603-938-2826
Zanotti Armor, Inc., 123 W. Lone Tree Rd., Cedar Falls, IA 50613/319-232-9650
Z-Coat Industrial Coatings, Inc., 3375 U.S. Hwy. 98 S. No. A, Lakeland, FL 33803-8365/813-665-1734
Zeiss Optical, Carl, 1015 Commerce St., Petersburg, VA 23803/804-861-0033, 800-388-2984; FAX: 804-733-4024
Zero Ammunition Co., Inc., 1601 22nd St. SE, P.O. Box 1188, Cullman, AL 35056-1188/800-545-9376; FAX: 205-739-4683
Zonie Bullets, 790 N. Lake Havasu Ave., Suite 26, Lake Havasu City, AZ 86403/520-680-6303; FAX: 520-680-6201
Zriny's Metal Targets (See Z's Metal Targets & Frames)
Zufall, Joseph F., P.O. Box 304, Golden, CO 80402-0304

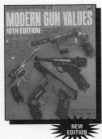
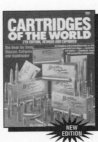